3rd EDITION

WARWICKSHIRE
STREET MAPS

A Comprehensive Guide to
Finding Your Way Around the County

s devised and used by the Warwickshire Fire and Rescue Service

Mary Ann Miller

1996

WARWICKSHIRE BOOKS

First published in 1990 by Warwickshire Books
Third Edition 1995

Copyright © 1990/1995 Warwickshire County Council Fire and
Rescue Service

ISBN 1 871942-11X

Maps provided by kind permission of the County Fire Officer,
Warwickshire Fire and Rescue Service. It is intended that this book
shall be regularly updated.

Printed and bound in Great Britain by
The Cromwell Press, Melksham, Wilts

WARWICKSHIRE BOOKS
An imprint of **Warwickshire County Council**

Sales
Distributed by Mr M. Lapworth
11 Melmerby, Wilnecote
Tapworth, Staffordshire B77 4LP
Tel: 01827 897461

COMPREHENSIVE MAP GUIDE
TO WARWICKSHIRE

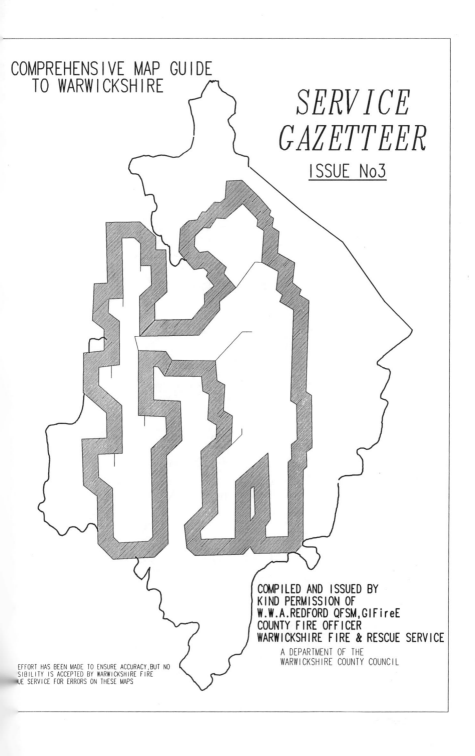

SERVICE
GAZETTEER
ISSUE No3

COMPILED AND ISSUED BY
KIND PERMISSION OF
W.W.A.REDFORD QFSM,GIFireE
COUNTY FIRE OFFICER
WARWICKSHIRE FIRE & RESCUE SERVICE

A DEPARTMENT OF THE
WARWICKSHIRE COUNTY COUNCIL

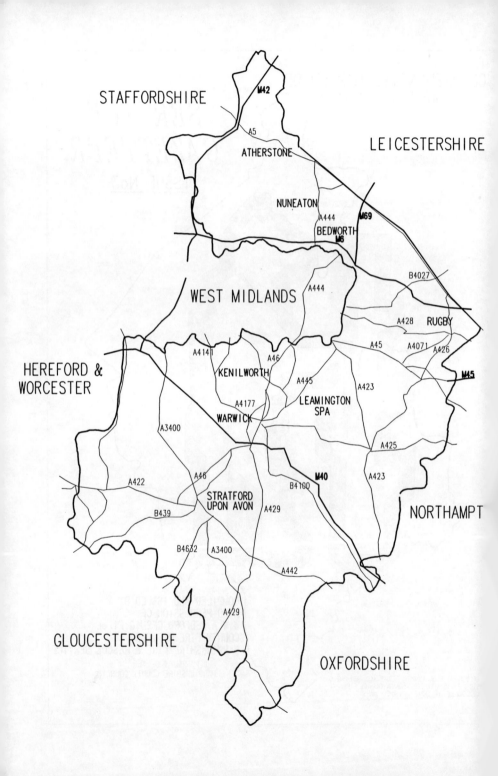

KEY

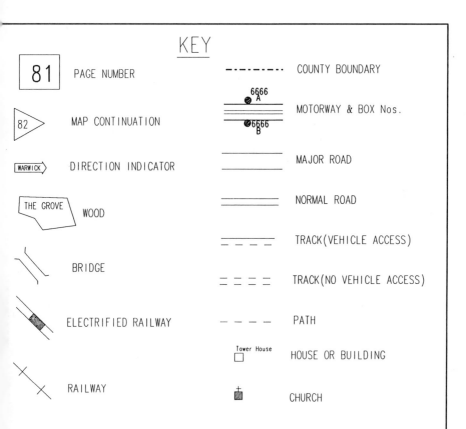

| 81 | PAGE NUMBER | — - — - — - — | COUNTY BOUNDARY |

81   PAGE NUMBER

82   MAP CONTINUATION

WARWICK   DIRECTION INDICATOR

THE GROVE   WOOD

BRIDGE

ELECTRIFIED RAILWAY

RAILWAY

— · — · — · —   COUNTY BOUNDARY

6666
A   MOTORWAY & BOX Nos.
6666
B

MAJOR ROAD

NORMAL ROAD

— — — —   TRACK(VEHICLE ACCESS)

= = = =   TRACK(NO VEHICLE ACCESS)

— — — —   PATH

Tower House   HOUSE OR BUILDING

✝   CHURCH

INTERPRETATION OF MAP

The map book consists of 196 pages,covering
the County of Warwickshire
Each page is divided into 12 Kilometre squares,
and takes the form of three columns:A,B and C,
and four rows:1,2,3 and 4.
Each Kilometre square is then divded into four
squares(not shown on the map),numbered 1,2,3 and 4

The street in the example opposite,Elm Tree Road,
would have a map reference of 41B24

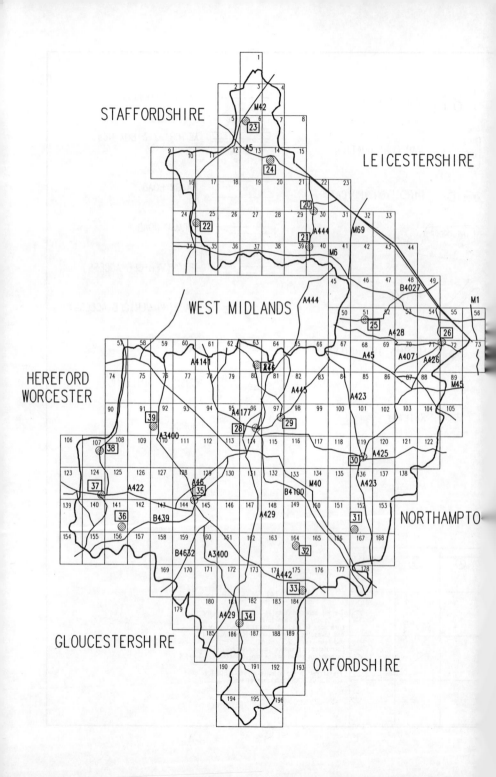

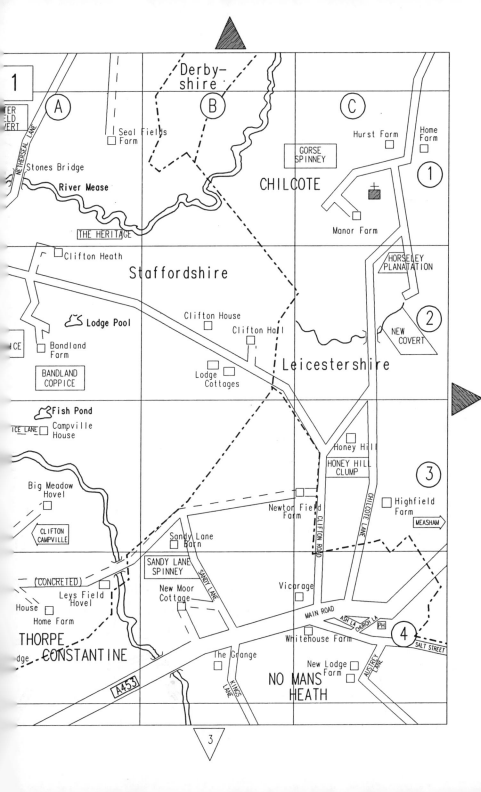

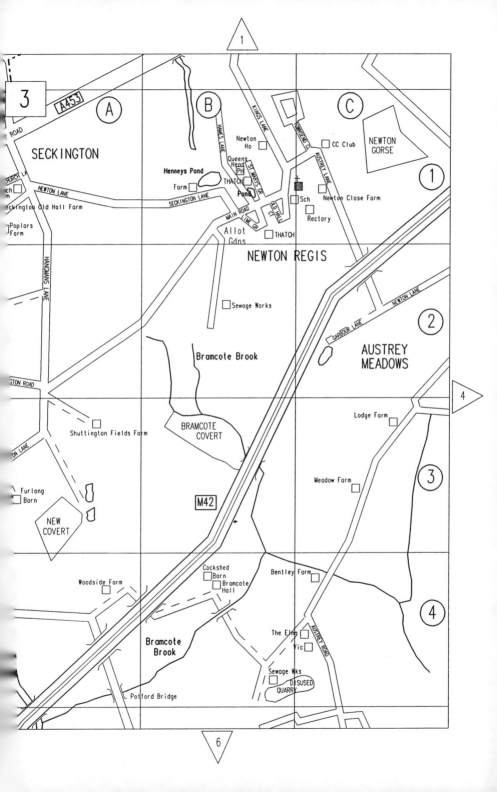

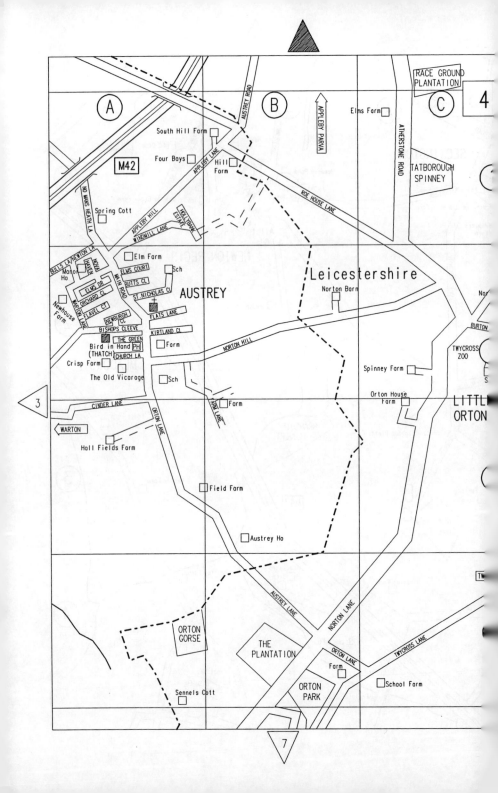

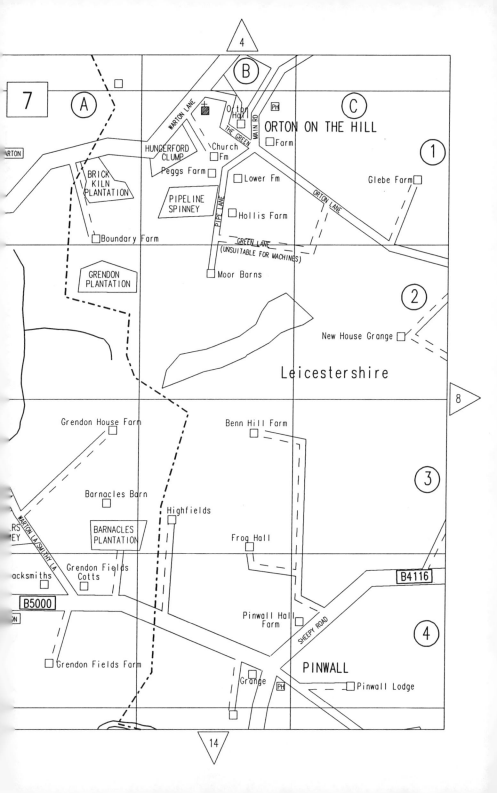

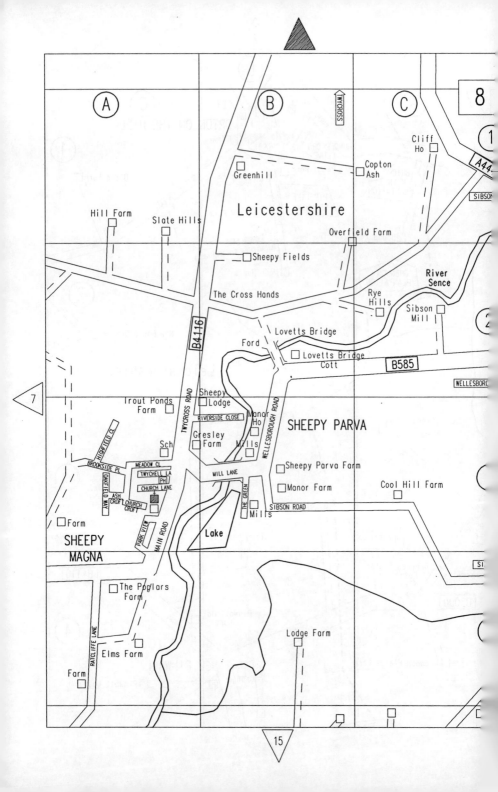

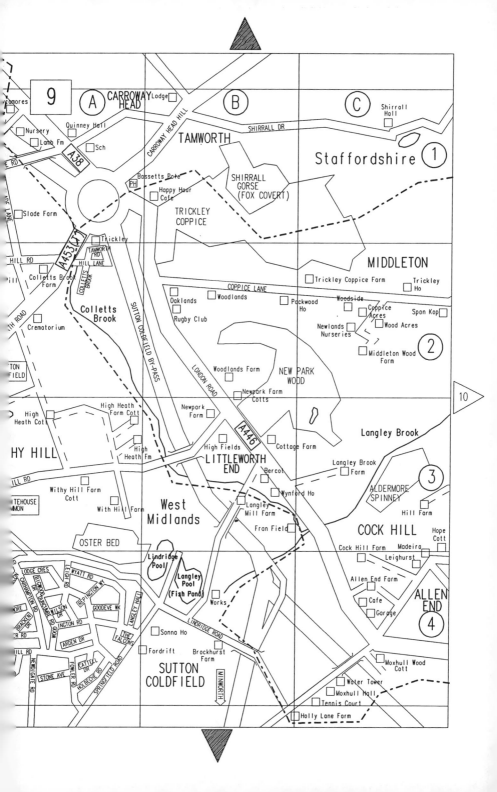

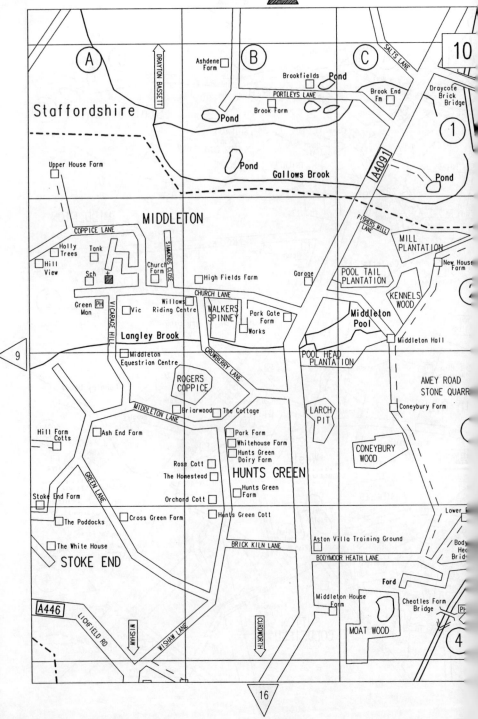

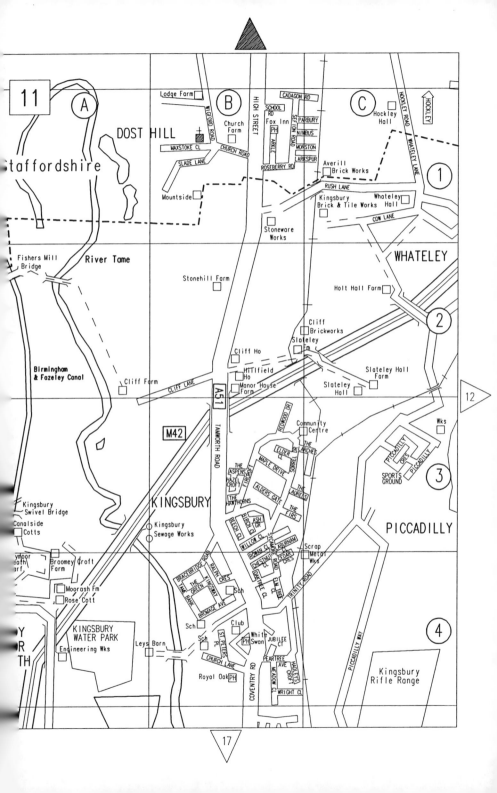

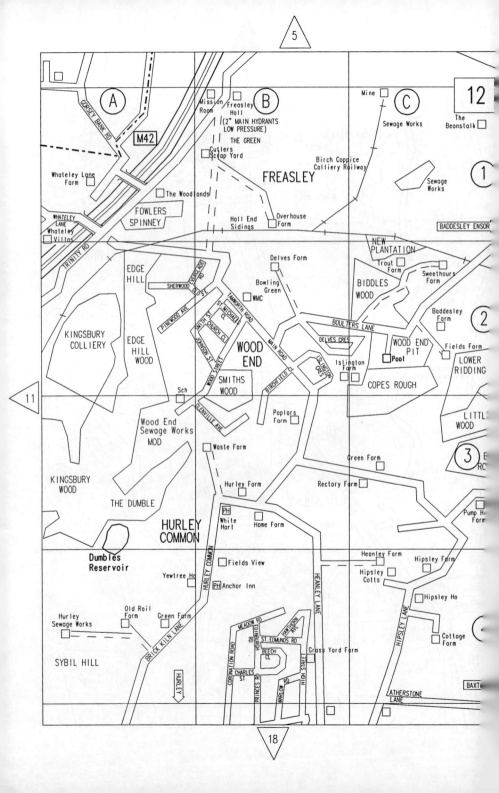

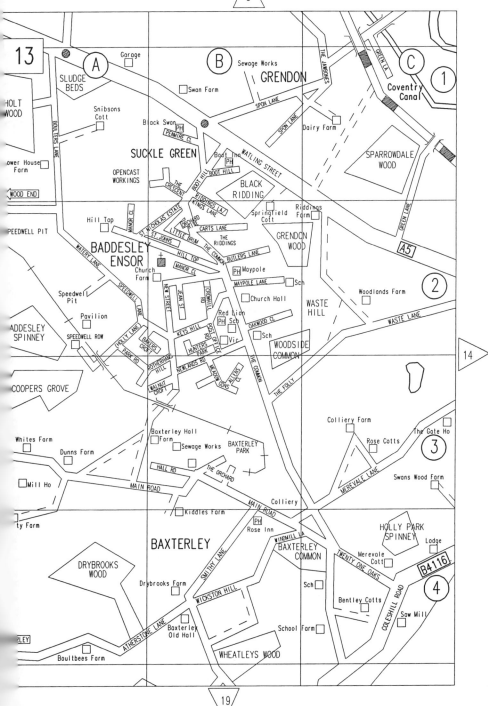

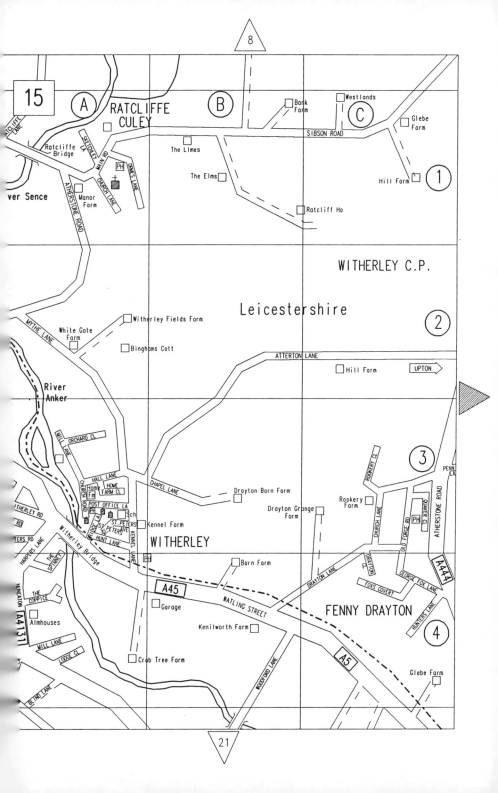

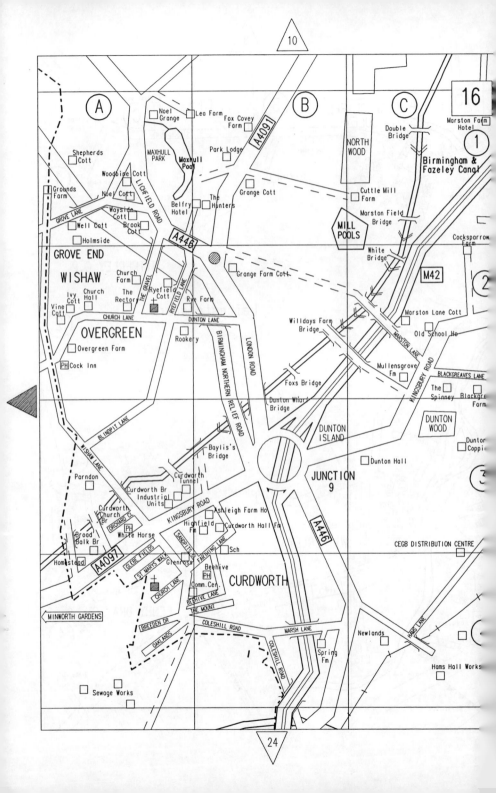

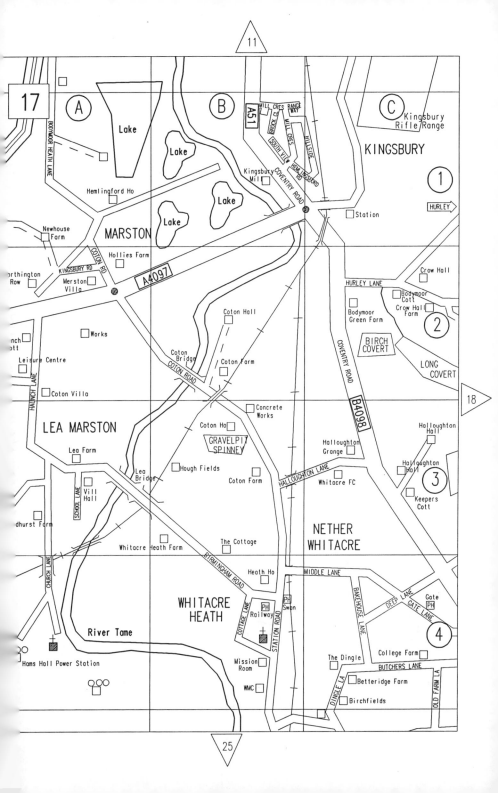

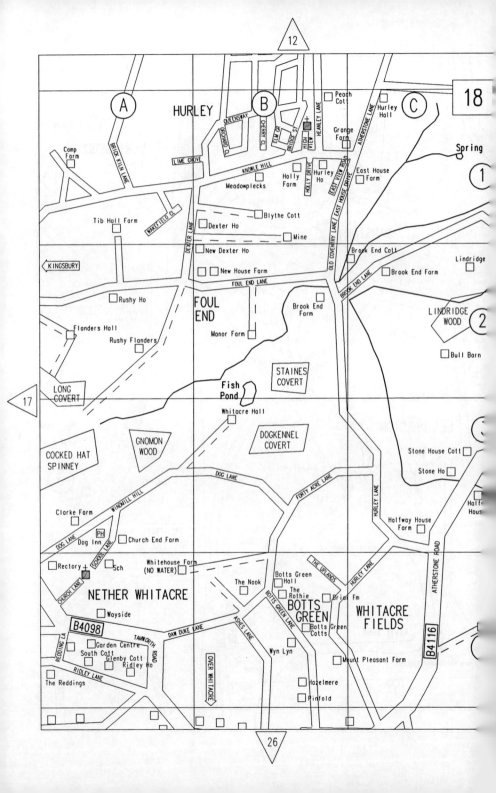

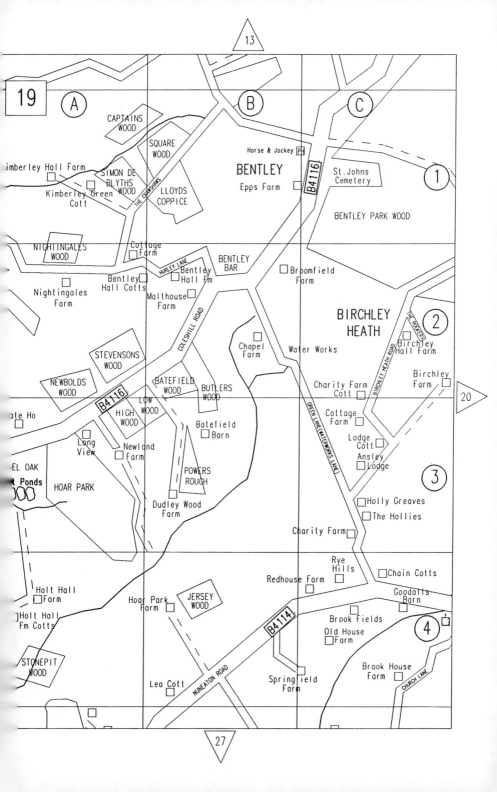

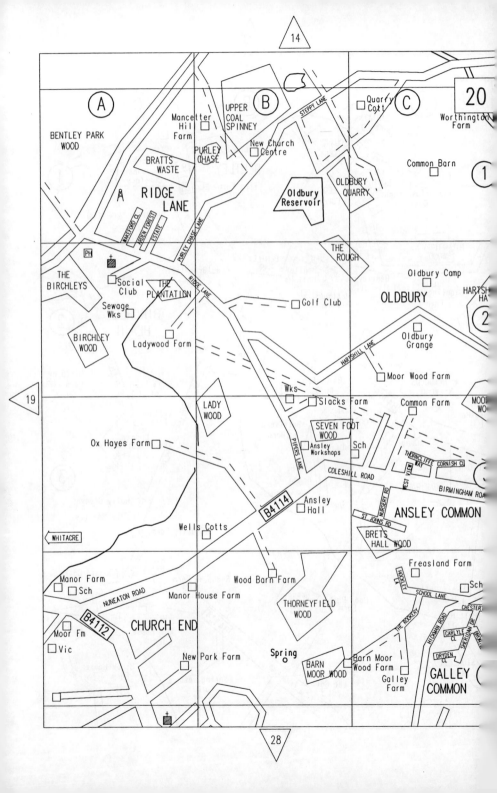

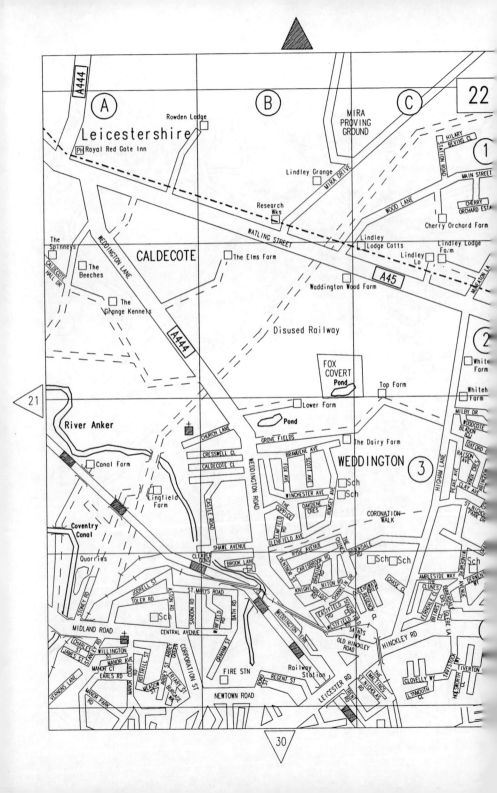

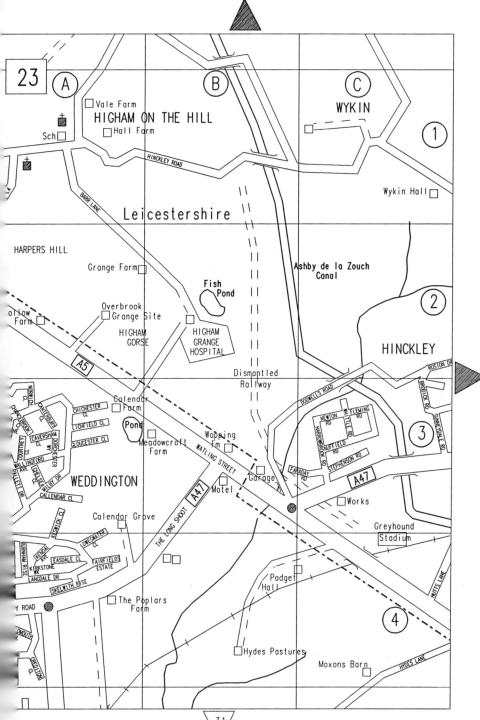

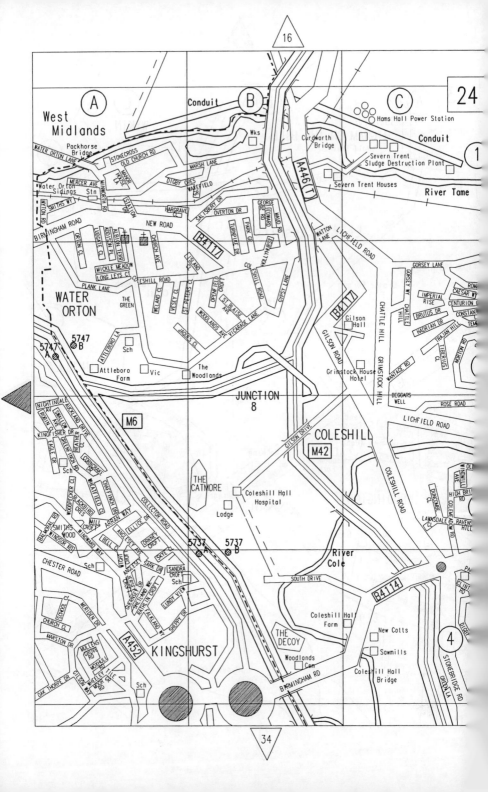

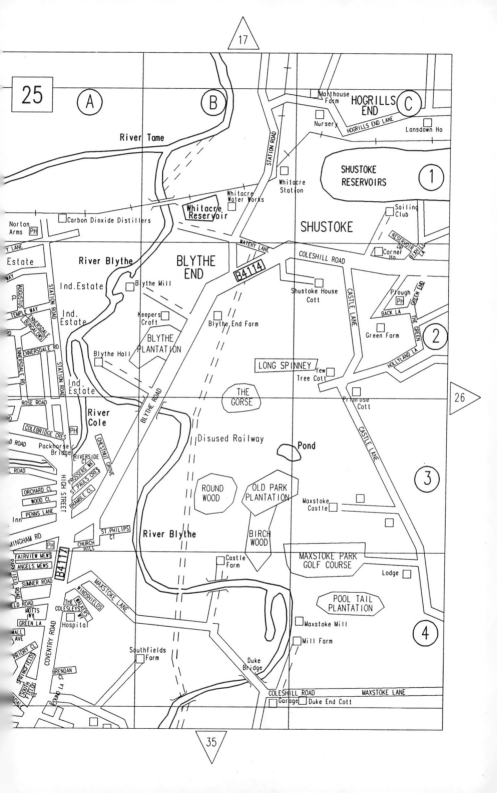

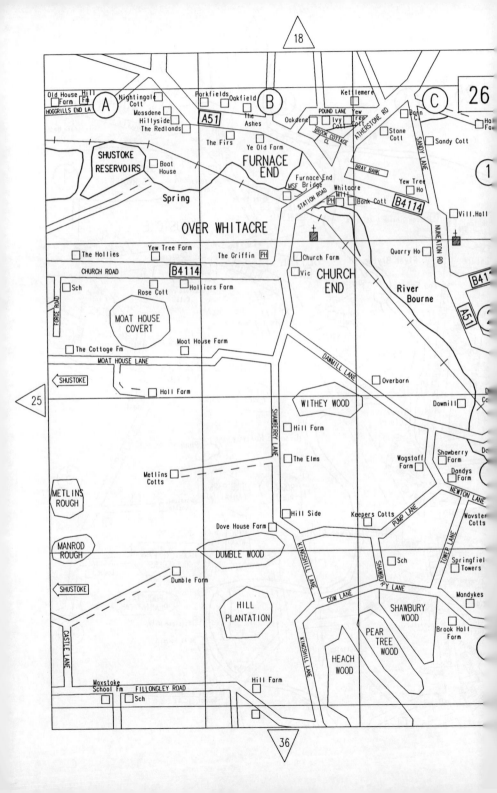

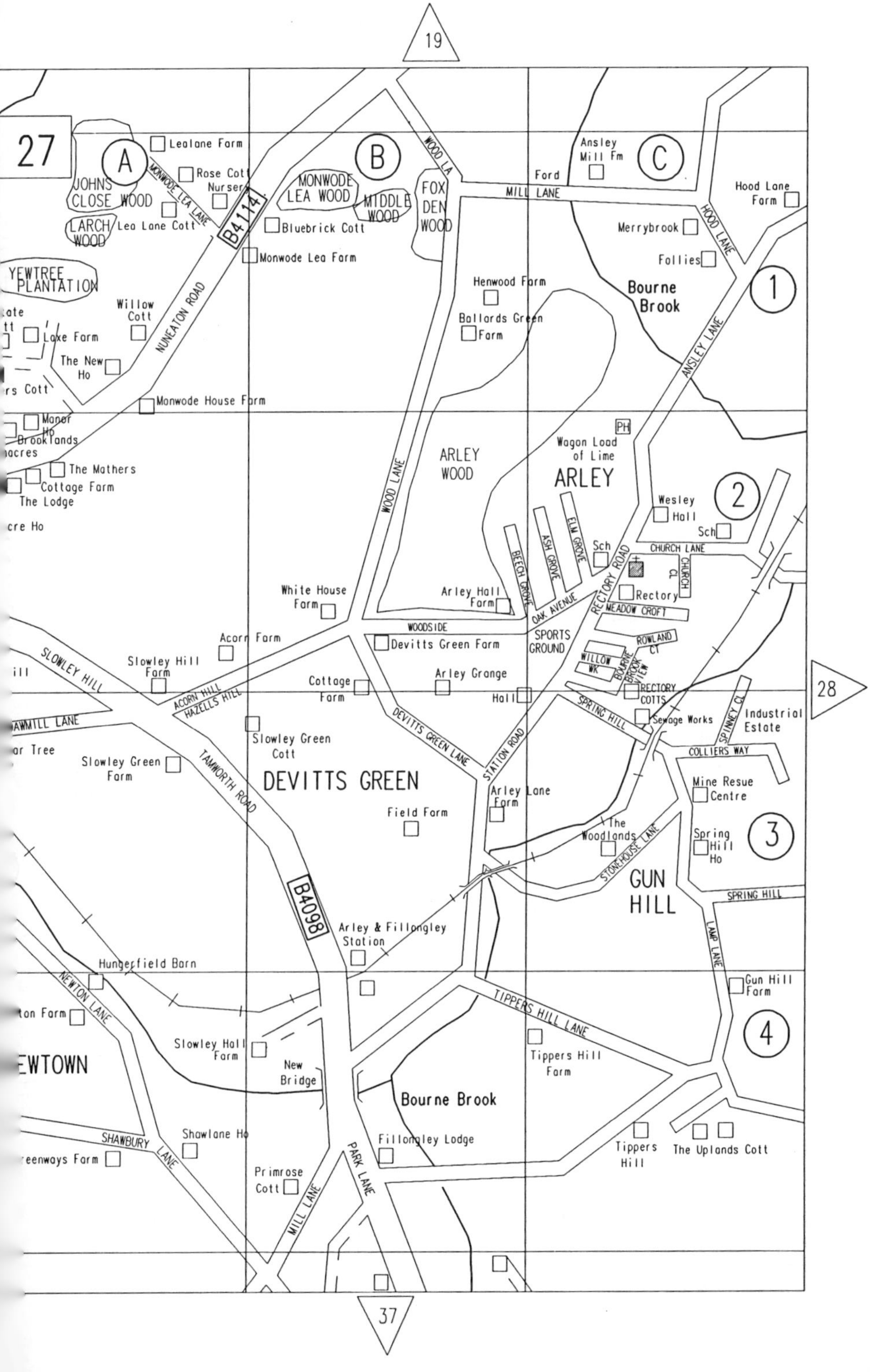

27

A

JOHNS
CLOSE WOOD

LARCH
WOOD

YEWTREE
PLANTATION

Lealane Farm

Rose Cott
Nursery

Lea Lane Cott

Bluebrick Cott

Monwode Lea Farm

Willow
Cott

Lake Farm

The New
Ho

Maner
Ho
Brooklands

acres

The Mathers

Cottage
Farm

The Lodge

cre Ho

B4114

MONWOOL LEA LANE

NUNEATON ROAD

Monwode House Farm

B

MONWODE
LEA WOOD

MIDDLE
WOOD

WOOD LA

FOX
DEN
WOOD

Henwood Farm

Ballards Green
Farm

WOOD LANE

ARLEY
WOOD

Ansley
Mill Fm

Ford

MILL LANE

Merrybrook

C

Hood Lane
Farm

Follies

Bourne
Brook

ANSLEY LANE

HOOD LANE

1

Wagon Load
of Lime

PH

ARLEY

Wesley
Hall

Sch

CHURCH LANE

Sch

2

White House
Farm

Acorn Farm

WOODSIDE

Devitts Green Farm

Arley Hall
Farm

BEECH GROVE

ASH GROVE

ELM GROVE

OAK AVENUE

RECTORY ROAD

MEADOW CROFT

Rectory

CHURCH

CL

SLOWLEY HILL

ll

Slowley Hill
Farm

ACORN HILL

HAZELLS HILL

Cottage
Farm

SPORTS
GROUND

Arley Grange

Hall

WILLOW
WK

BOURNE BROOK

ROWLAND
CT

RECTORY
COTTS

SPRING HILL

Sewage Works

28

SPINNEY CL

Industrial
Estate

AWMILL LANE

ar Tree

Slowley Green
Farm

TAMWORTH ROAD

Slowley Green
Cott

DEVITTS GREEN

Field Farm

DEVITTS GREEN LANE

STATION ROAD

Arley Lane
Farm

COLLIERS WAY

Mine Resue
Centre

Spring
Hill
Ho

GUN
HILL

SPRING HILL

3

The
Woodlands

STORHOUSE LANE

B4098

Arley & Fillongley
Station

Hungerfield Barn

NEWTON LANE

on Farm

Slowley Hall
Farm

New
Bridge

NEWTOWN

SHAWBURY LANE

Shawlane Ho

Greenways Farm

Primrose
Cott

MILL LANE

PARK LANE

Fillongley Lodge

Bourne Brook

TIPPERS HILL LANE

Tippers Hill
Farm

LANE LANE

Gun Hill
Farm

4

Tippers
Hill

The Uplands Cott

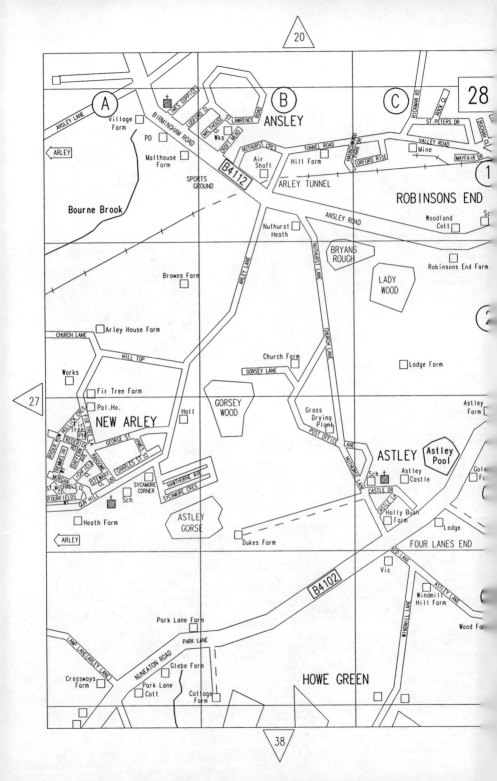

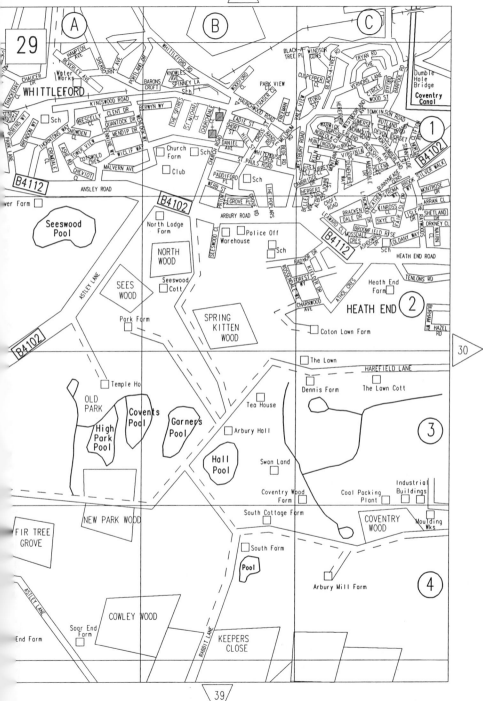

A   B   C

29

WHITTLEFORD

Water
Works

Hampton Ave
BEVERLEY AVE
CHAUCER DR
TENNYSON WY
SHERBOURN AVE
PORTLAND DR
WHITTLEFORD RD
BLACK-A-
TREE PL
WINDSOR
GDNS
WINDSOR ST
TRYAN RD
THE
BARPOOL RD
Dumble
Hole
Bridge

Coventry
Canal

BARONS
CROFT
KNOWLES AVE
SPINNEY LA
MOORFORD
PARK VIEW
CL (2)
CLAPEPPER
CL
CL
VERNONS LANE
TRICEL
FORD
HEREFORD LA
BLACK-A-TREE RD
BARPOOL RD

KINGSWOOD ROAD
Sch
BERWYN WY
ST. MICHAEL
THE SPIRES
CHURCHDALE
FRASER CL
PARK VIEW
VICE VIEW
TOMKINSON ROAD
RUTLAND
DEVON
DORSET
SURREY
CL
SILVER WALK

1

B4102

PRESCELLY
CL
CLENT DR
QUANTOCK DR
MENDIP DR
PENNINE WY
WICLIF WA
COTSWOLD CRES
CHURCH RD
LADIE ST
SHORT
ST
HILL ST
CROSS RD
BETHE RD
WESTBURY ROAD
NORFOLK
HUNTINGDON
SURREY
HELENA
VIRGINIA
MARTIN WK
SUNTINE
MONTROSE
ARRAN CL

THORNTONS WAY
SNOWDEN CL
CLENT DR
ASH RD
CRADALE
CHEVIOT
MALVERN AVE
Church
Farm
Sch
ST PAULS ROAD
WHIT
CREB
Sch
BRANYWAY RD
SKYE CL
ISLE
FAIR ISLE
ARRAN CL
RAYWOODS

B4112

Club

ANSLEY ROAD
PADDIFORD
PL
WEBB ST
GROVE PL
ARBURY ROAD
THE POPLARS
Sch
HERBERT
ALBERT JOHN
CROFT
ROAD
BRACKEN
DALE DR
KINROSS
CL
SKYE CL
OLDANY WALK
ORKNEY CL
NA TRN

er Farm

B4102

Seeswood
Pool

North Lodge
Farm
Warehouse
Police Off
Sch
RADFOR DR
K-ISLE DR
B4112
BROOMFIELD RISE
MOSSDALE
CRES
Sch
OLDANY WAY
HEATH END ROAD

NORTH
WOOD
SEESWOOD
COTT
SEESWOOD CL
ROSSENDALE
FOREST
WY
ATJOL CRES
HEATH END ROAD
TENLONS RD

SEES
WOOD
Park Farm
SPRING
KITTEN
WOOD
CHARNWOOD
AVE
Heath End
Farm

HEATH END

2

BURHAM AV
HAZEL
RD

ASTLEY LANE
B4102
Coton Lawn Farm

30

The Lawn
HAREFIELD LANE

Temple Ho
Dennis Farm
The Lawn Cott

OLD
PARK
Covents
Pool
High
Park
Pool
Garner's
Pool
Tea House
Arbury Hall
Hall
Pool
Swan Land

3

Coventry Wood
Farm
Coal Packing
Plant
Industrial
Buildings

NEW PARK WOOD
South Cottage Farm
COVENTRY
WOOD
Moulding
Wks

FIR TREE
GROVE
South Farm
Pool
Arbury Mill Farm

4

ASTLEY LANE
Soar End
Farm
COWLEY WOOD
RABBIT LANE
KEEPERS
CLOSE

End Farm

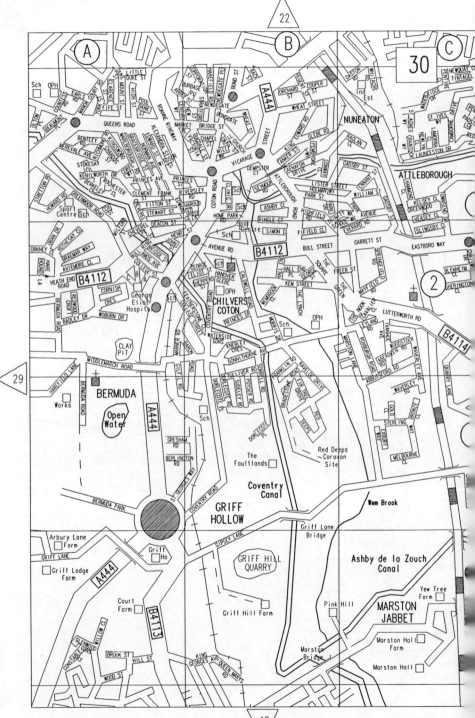

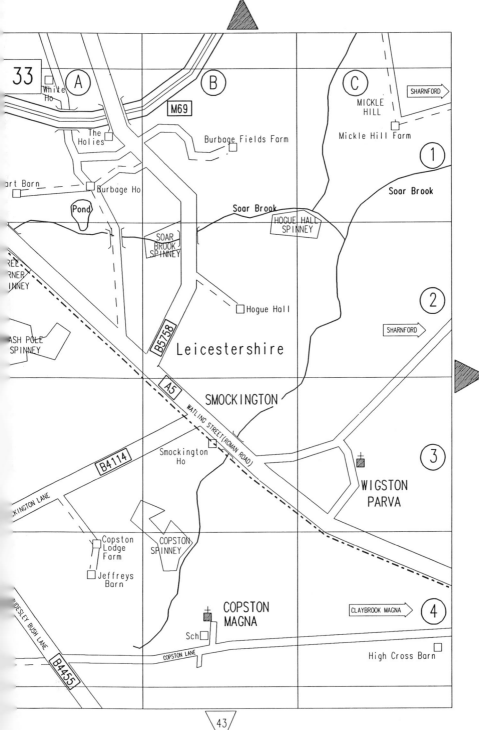

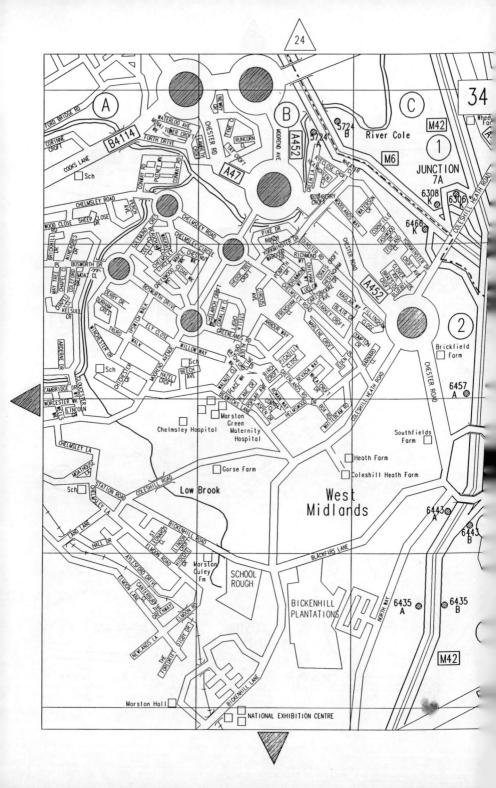

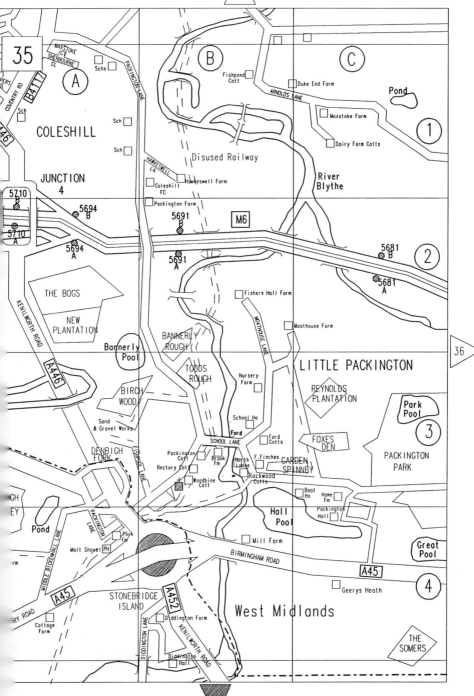

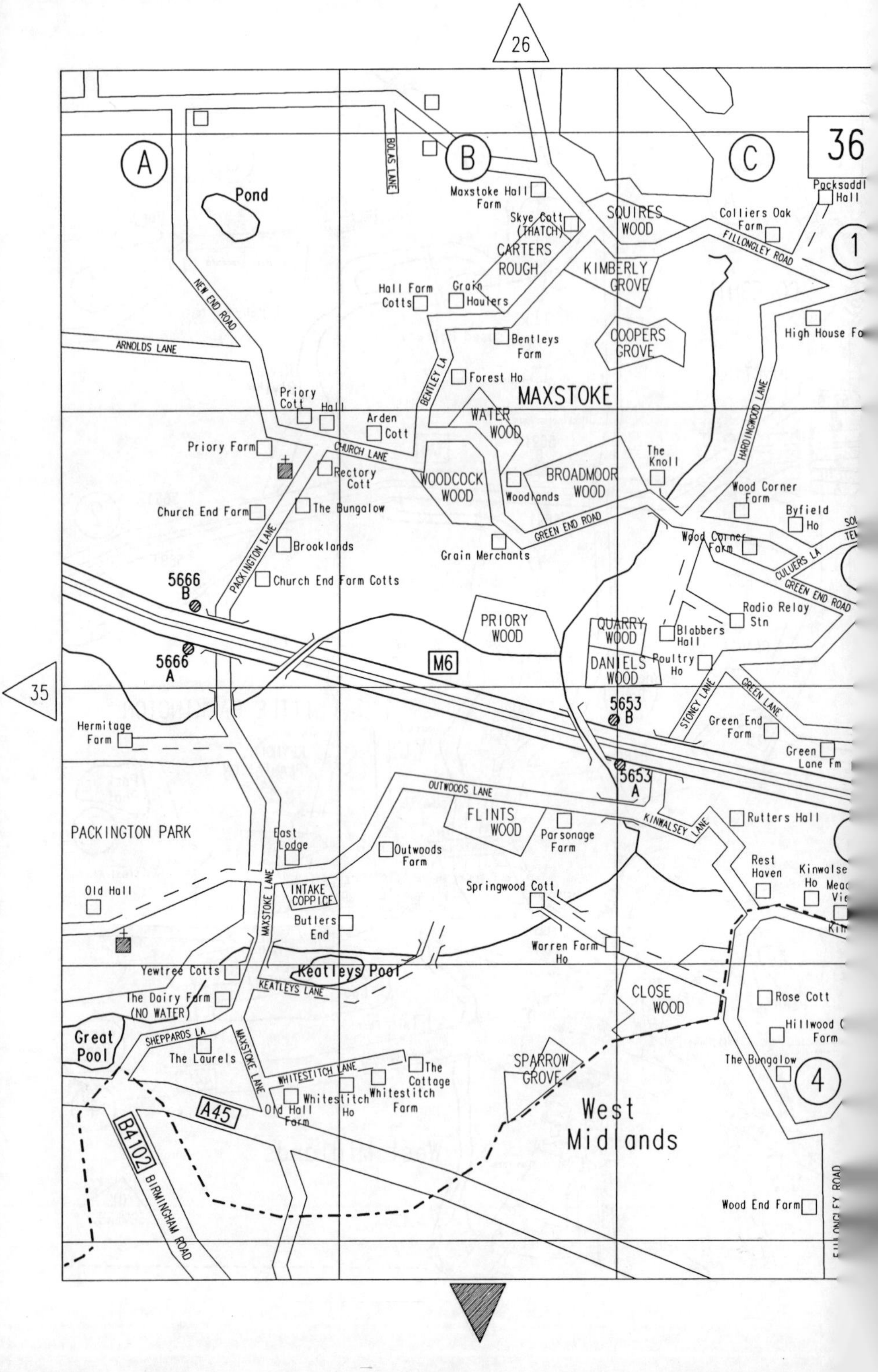

26

A

B

C

36

1

Pond

Maxstoke Hall Farm

Skye Cott (THATCH)

SQUIRES WOOD

Colliers Oak Farm

Packsaddl Hall

BOLAS LANE

CARTERS ROUGH

KIMBERLY GROVE

FILLONGLEY ROAD

NEW END ROAD

ARNOLDS LANE

Hall Farm Cotts

Grain Hauliers

Bentleys Farm

Forest Ho

COOPERS GROVE

High House Fa

MAXSTOKE

BENTLEY LA

Priory Cott

Hall

Arden Cott

WATER WOOD

HARDINGWOOD LANE

Priory Farm

CHURCH LANE

Rectory Cott

WOODCOCK WOOD

BROADMOOR WOOD

The Knoll

Church End Farm

The Bungalow

Woodlands

Wood Corner Farm

Byfield Ho

SOU TE

Brooklands

Grain Merchants

GREEN END ROAD

Wood Corner Farm

PACKINGTON LANE

Church End Farm Cotts

CULVERS LA

GREEN END ROAD

5666 B

PRIORY WOOD

QUARRY WOOD

Radio Relay Stn

5666 A

M6

Blabbers Hall

35

DANIELS WOOD

Poultry Ho

STONEY LANE

GREEN LANE

Hermitage Farm

5653 B

Green End Farm

Green Lane Fm

5653 A

KINWALSEY LANE

Rutters Hall

OUTWOODS LANE

FLINTS WOOD

Parsonage Farm

PACKINGTON PARK

East Lodge

Outwoods Farm

Rest Haven

Kinwalse Ho

Meac Vie

MAXSTOKE LANE

Old Hall

INTAKE COPPICE

Springwood Cott

Kin

Butlers End

Warren Farm Ho

Yewtree Cotts

KEATLEYS LANE

Keatleys Pool

CLOSE WOOD

Rose Cott

The Dairy Farm (NO WATER)

SHEPPARDS LA

Hillwood Farm

Great Pool

The Laurels

WHITESTITCH LANE

The Cottage

SPARROW GROVE

The Bungalow

4

B4102

A45

Whitestitch Ho

Whitestitch Farm

West Midlands

Old Hall Farm

BIRMINGHAM ROAD

FILLONGLEY ROAD

Wood End Farm

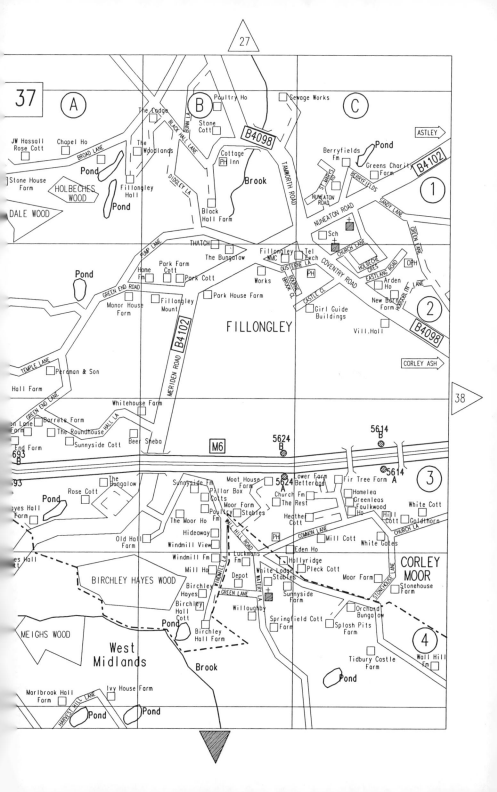

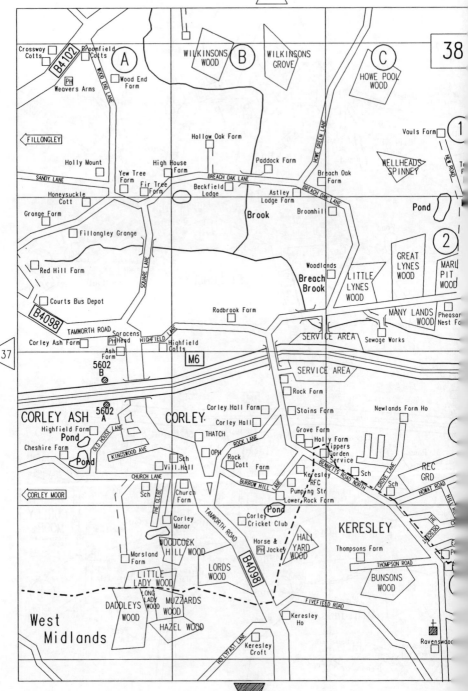

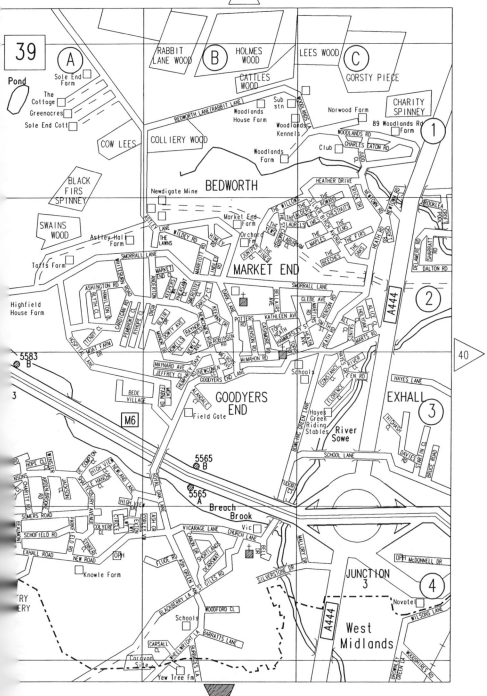

A   B   C

40
1

39

RETFORD DRR
COZENS
STUBBS
TURNER CL
SUTHERLAND ROAD
POLMAN
CURTOP
SANDBY
CHALFONT
DEMPSTER RD
NEWDEGATE
DERONDA
LILFORD CL
LOVELL
SEALAND DR
ASHFORD CL
MOUNT DR
MARGARET AVE
JOSEPH
RICHARDS
LUCKMAN RD
YORK KNIGHT
NUNEATON RD
ORCHARD ST
JUBILEE TERR
NEWMAN
KNIGHTSBRIDGE RD
COXLEY CL
MARSTON LANE
BEECHWOOD RD
MURDIN
GORDON CL
KIMBERLEY CL
DOWNING CRES
BANBURY
REGENT STREET
CONIFER
OPH
PINE TREE RD
FURNACE RD
CHESTNUT
BIRCH CL
CHARITY DOCKS
SEWAGE WORKS

LEICESTER ST
CHAMBERLAINE RD
RYE PIECE
LINDEN
RINGWAY
ALEXANDRA ST
EVANS CL
WILLS RD
NORTH CRES
HAZEL CL
WESTON STREET

WEM BROOK
WESTON WOOD FARM
WESTON WOOD BUNGALOW

NEWTOWN ROAD
MILL STREET
OLD MEETING
WYATTS
CHAPEL ST
CADMAN
LEICESTER ST
ALL SAINTS SQUARE
JOHNSON ROAD
LEWESBURY DR
KING GDNS
TINTERN
RAILWAY TERR
NEW ST
WILLIAM ST

BULKINGTON BRIDGE
B4029

THOMAS ST
GALLACHERS
HARRISON CRES
KIRKSTONE RD
TARN CL
DERWENT RD
RODAWAY RD
CHURCH WALK
PARK ROAD
SIMCOE CL
LINDALE
CHURCH WALK
KING ST
CROMWELL
QUEEN STREET
BULKINGTON ROAD
THE PRIORS
EAST AVE
NORTH AVE
YORK AVE
POPLAR RD
COLUMBIA GDNS
SHAKESPEARE AVE
WESTON LAWN FARM
CAMP FARM

DELAMERE RD
ELKSMERE RD
DALTON RD
OPH
TOWER RD
THIRLMERE RD
LAKESIDE
ULLSWATER RD
BRIARDENE AVE
SAUNDERS AVE
FIRE STN
BEDWORTH HIGH ST
SPITTAL FIELDS
RYE PIECE RINGWAY
SPRINGFIELD CRES
GIBSON CRES
LADY WARWICK AVE
BYRON AVE
GEORGE ELIOT AVE
DRAYTON RD
SHELLEY
HOSLEY RD

COALPIT FIELD

EDWARD TYLER RD
DIDSBURY
BENTLEY CL
JONES RD
DAFFERN RD
MARSHALL RD
HAYES LANE
RECTORY DRIVE
RECTORY
OPH
COVENTRY ROAD
DISUSED RAILWAY
THE OVAL Football/Cricket Ground
SPEEDWELL LANE
BLACK BANK
BUTLER
MANSE CL
POND BLACK BANK
COLLIERY LANE
COLLIERY LANE NORTH
WALTER SCOTT RD
WORDSWORTH RD
BURNS WALK

BEDWORTH

LAWRENCE RD
ARMSON RD
FIELD VIEW
MELVILLE
EXHALL
LOVELL
THE COPSE
MAWNAN
KENWYN
CEDARS RD
MAPLE AVE
THE LARCHES
TRELAWNEY
TRESILLIAN RD
TREGULLAN RD
IRENEERE RD
ROSEMULLION CL
DEVORAN
PARASON WAY
MARTINDALE RD
BATTON RD
TELFORD RD
BAYTON WAY
HOLLYHURST FARM
WESTON HAYES FARM
BEDWORTH HILL
POND
POND
HAWKESBURY HALL FARM

ROBERT DAVID RD
PARK VIEW
HENRY
HECKLEY CL
LONGFORD ROAD
COVENTRY ROAD
TREGLISSE
CARRICK
TREVITHIC
BRUNTON CL
CRINNAL
BRYANT RD
BAYTON ROAD
STEPHENSON
POND
HAWKESBURY COLLIERY FARM
COVENTRY CANAL
TOLDISH HALL
MILE TREE LANE
MILE TREE FARM
B4109

OPH
SCHOOL
B4113
EXHALL
BLACKHORSE ROAD
WHITEMORE
SANDERS RD
HAWKESBURY
OXFORD CANAL
POND
HAWKESBURY HALL
GERMANY FARM
HAWKESBURY LANE

BEDWORTH ROAD
5543 B
M6
5543 A
West Midlands
GRANGE RD
SUTTON STOP
SUTTON STOP
GRANGE FM
PARROTTS GROVE
ELMURE FARM
TROSSACKS Country Far Dairy
LENTONS LANE
5530 B
5530 A

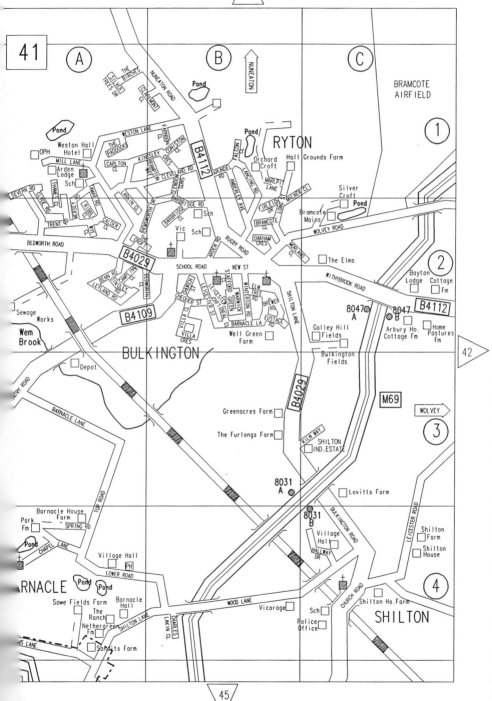

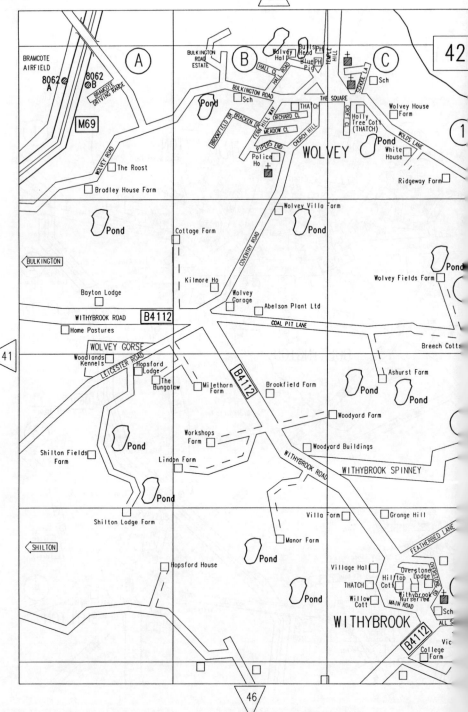

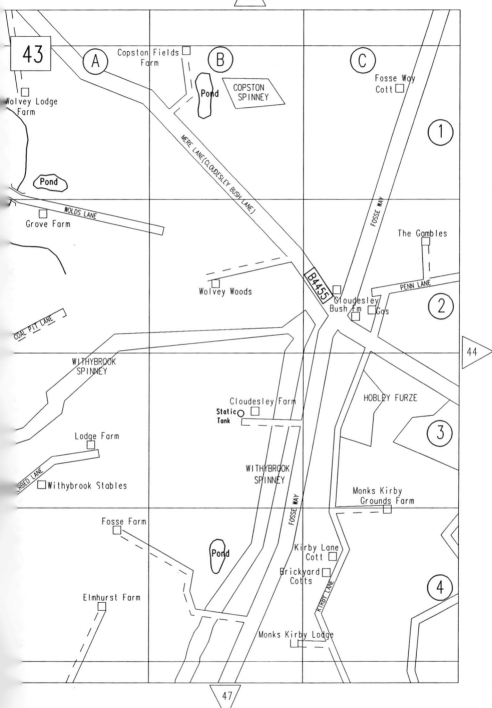

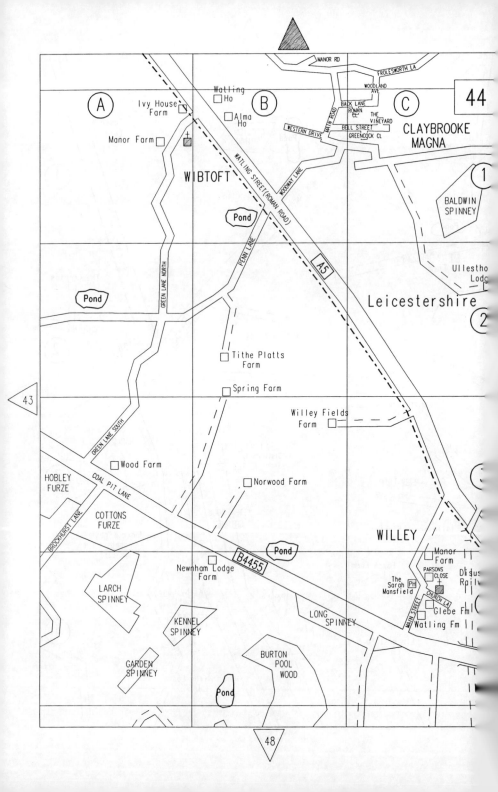

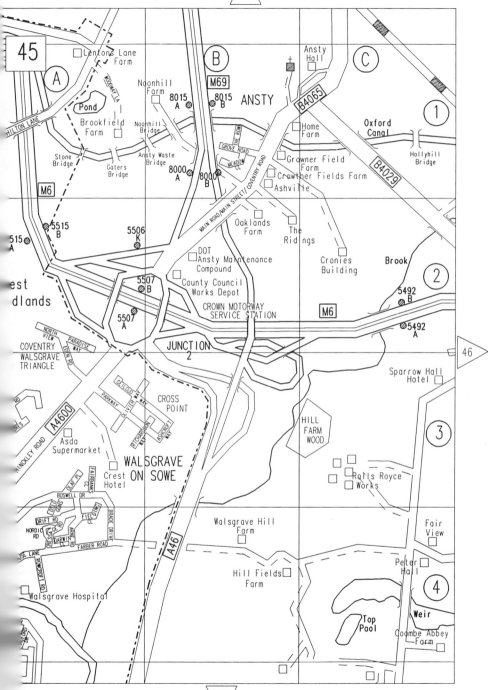

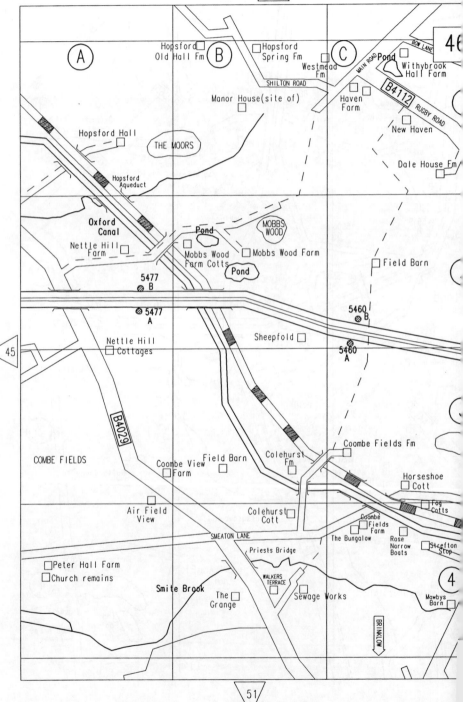

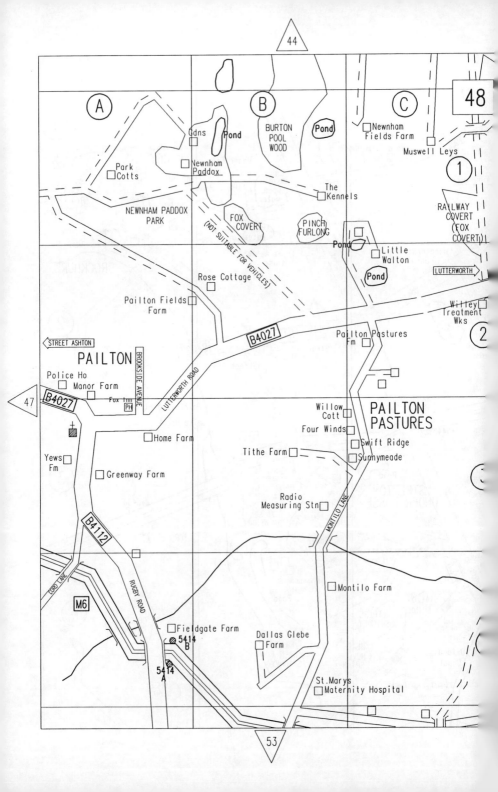

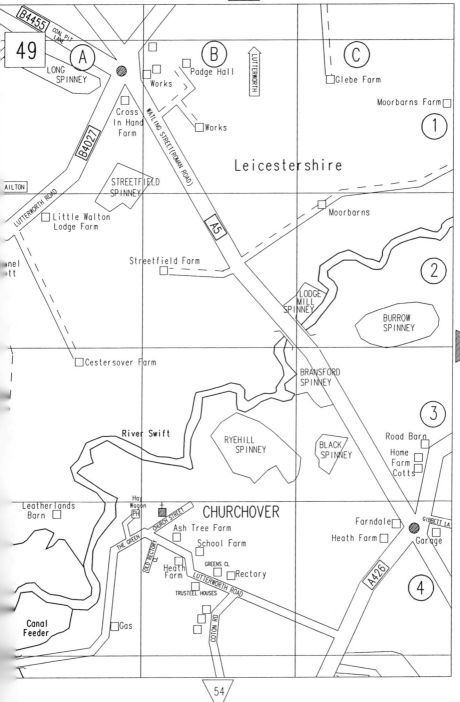

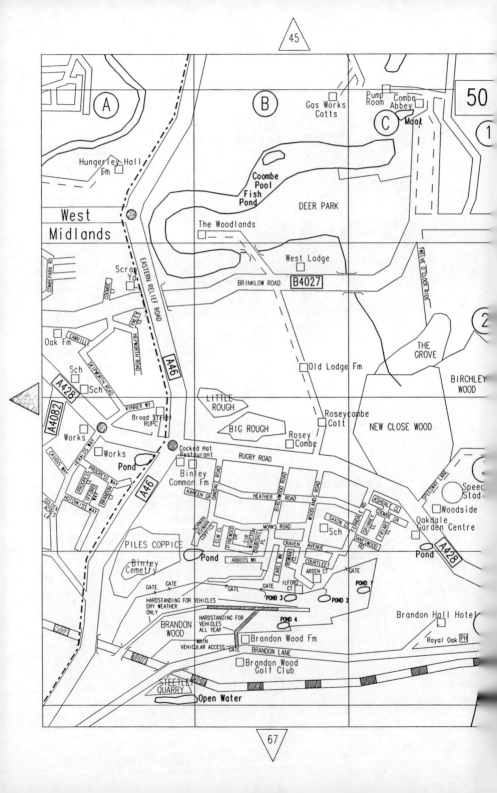

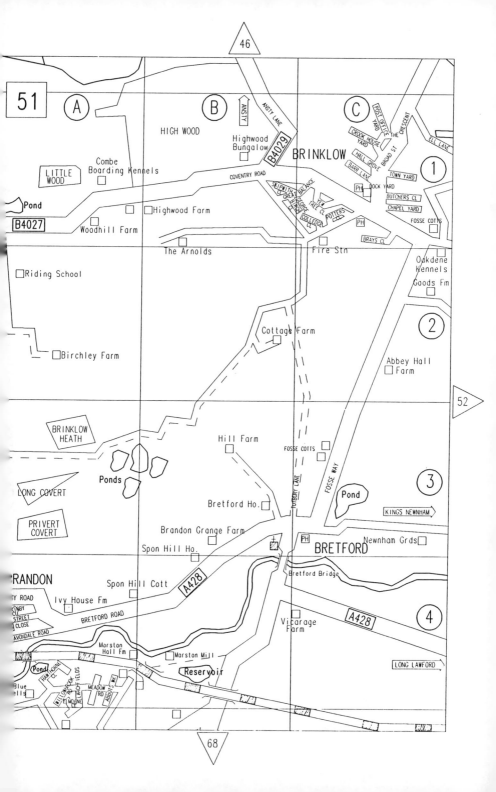

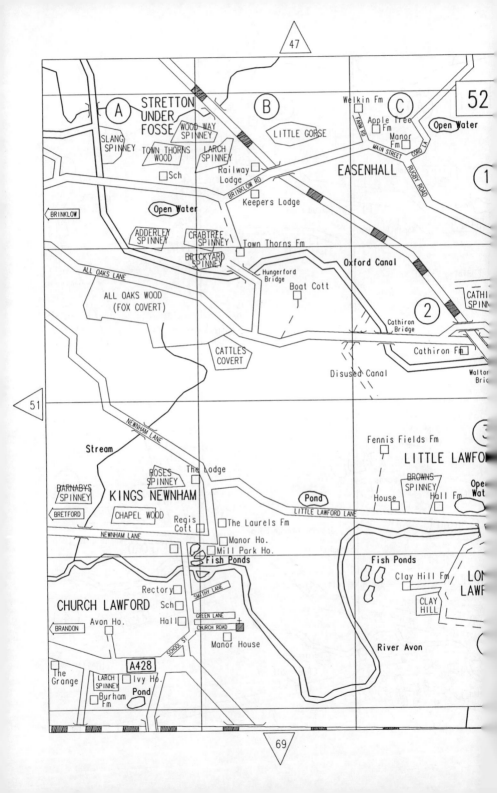

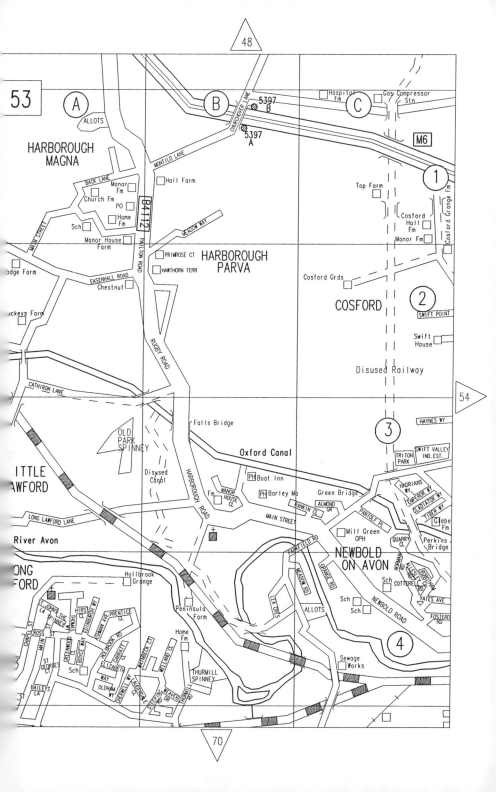

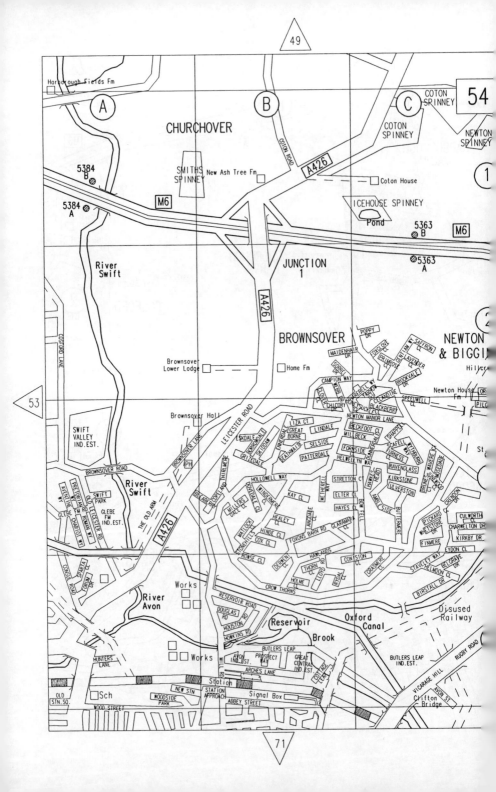

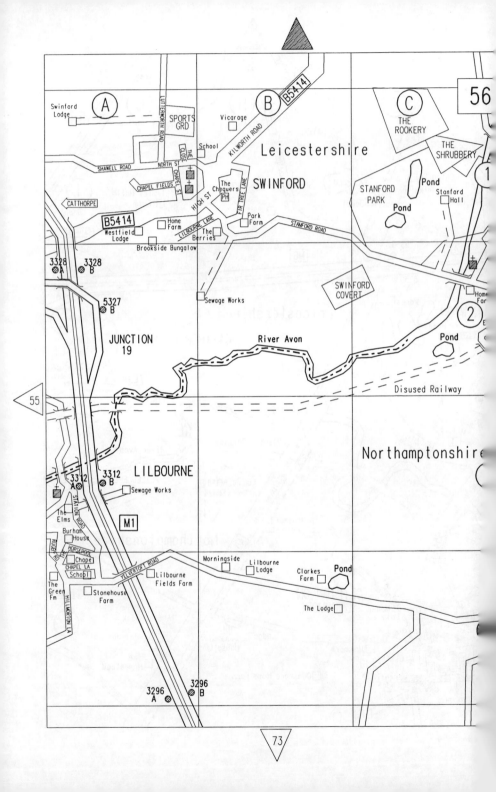

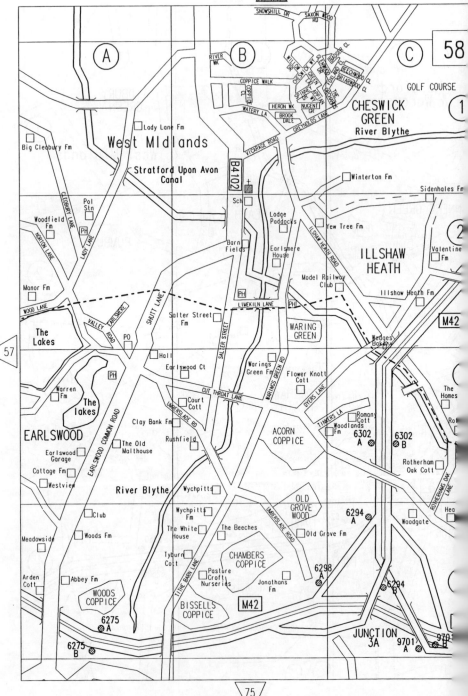

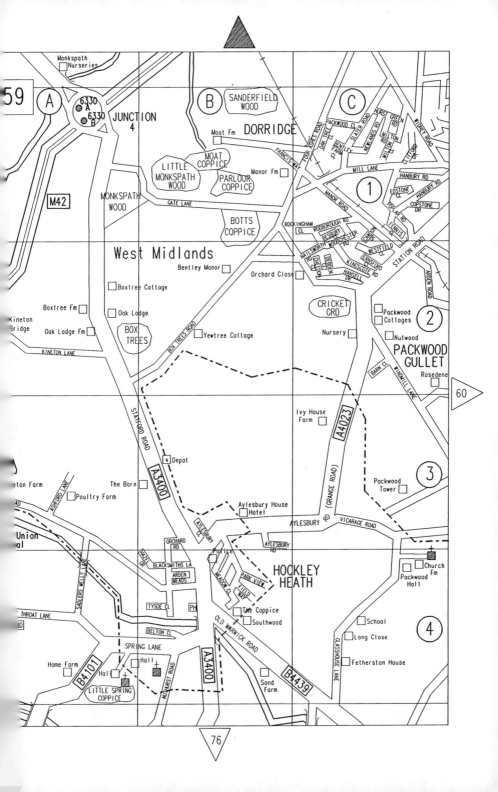

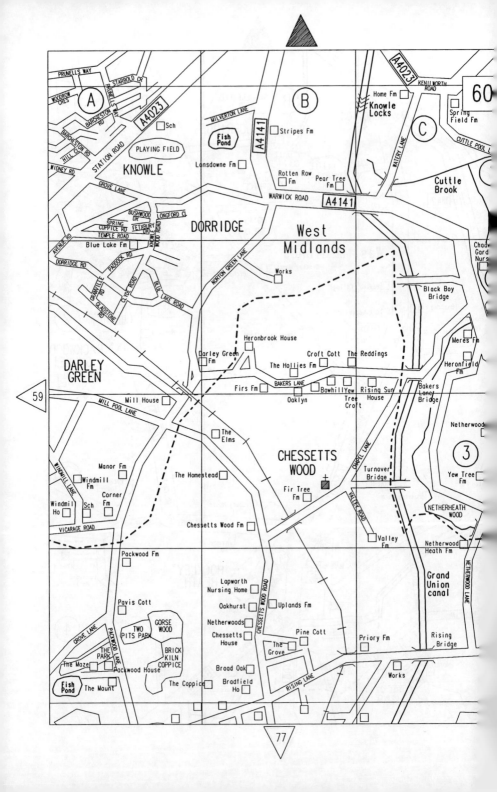

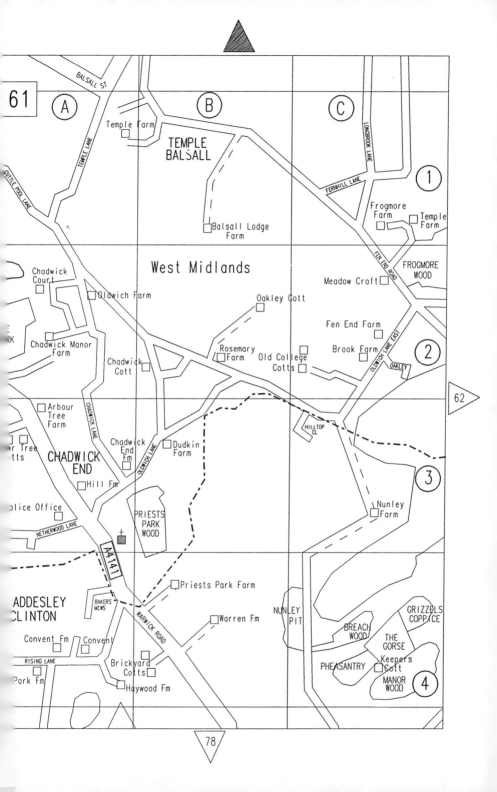

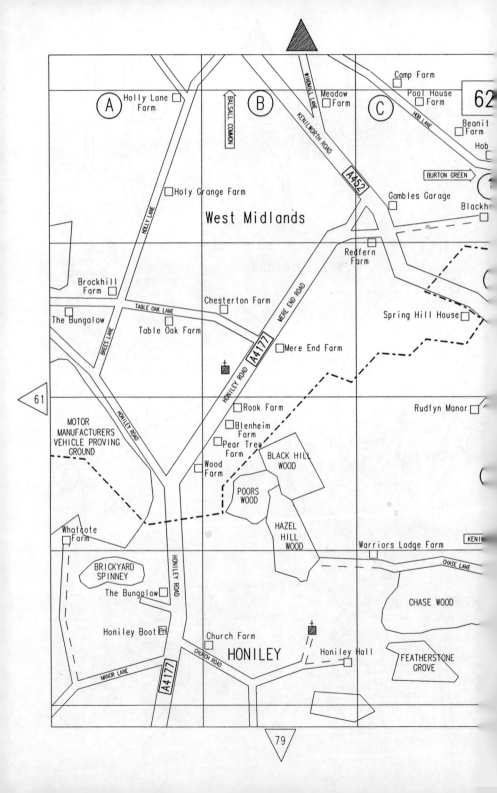

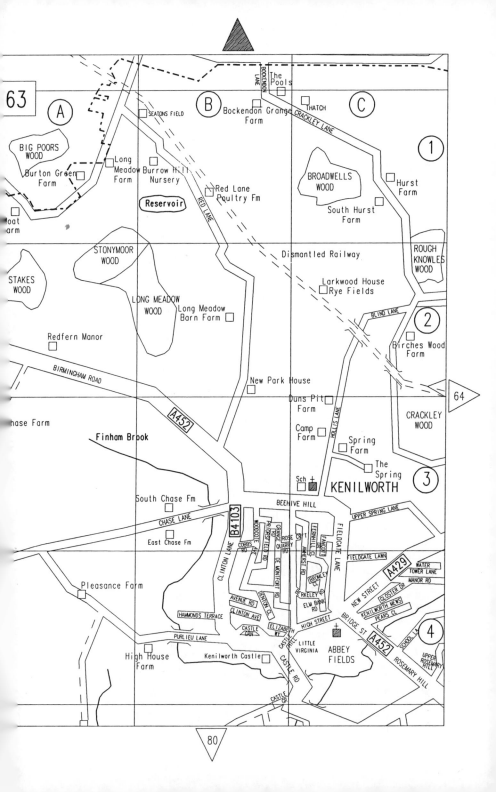

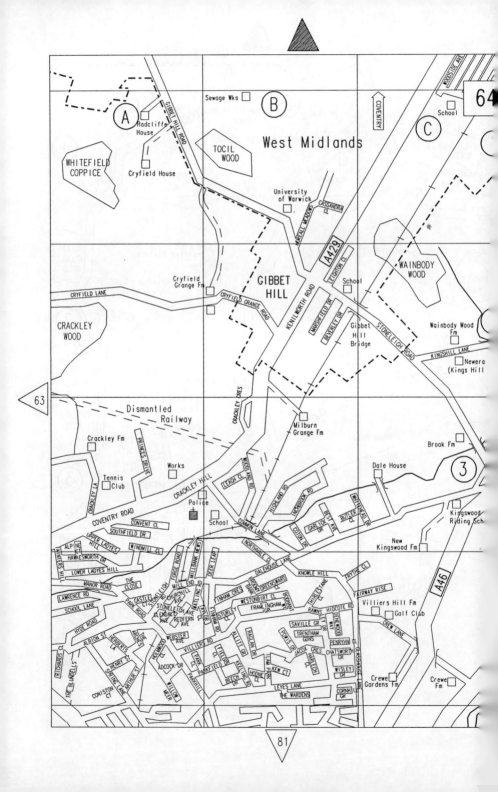

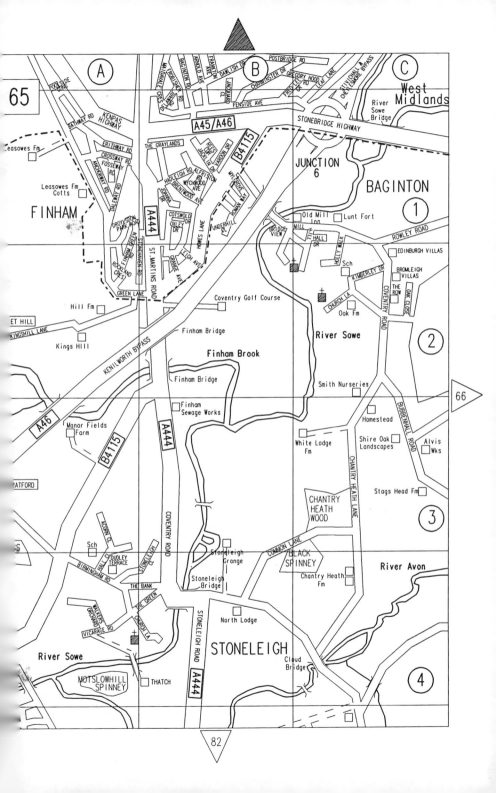

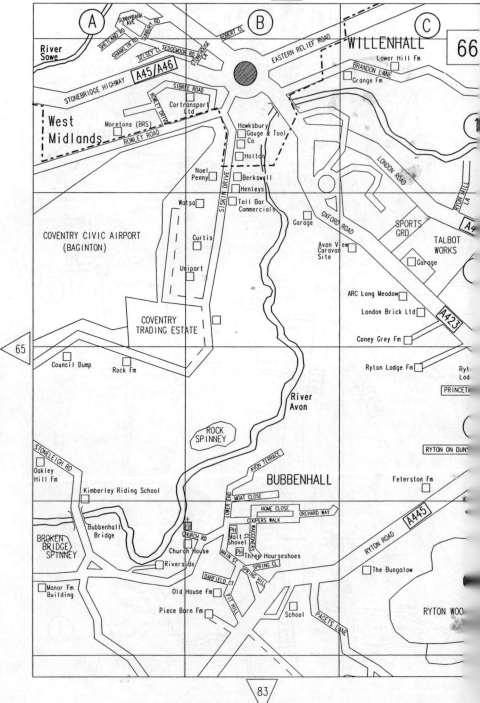

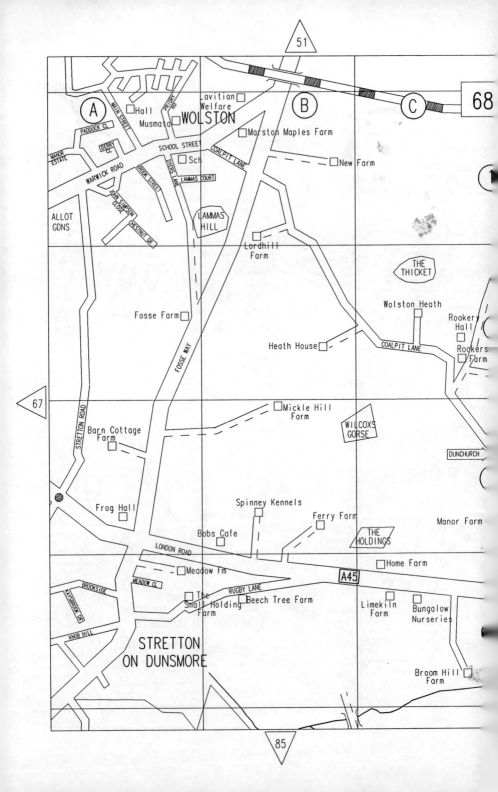

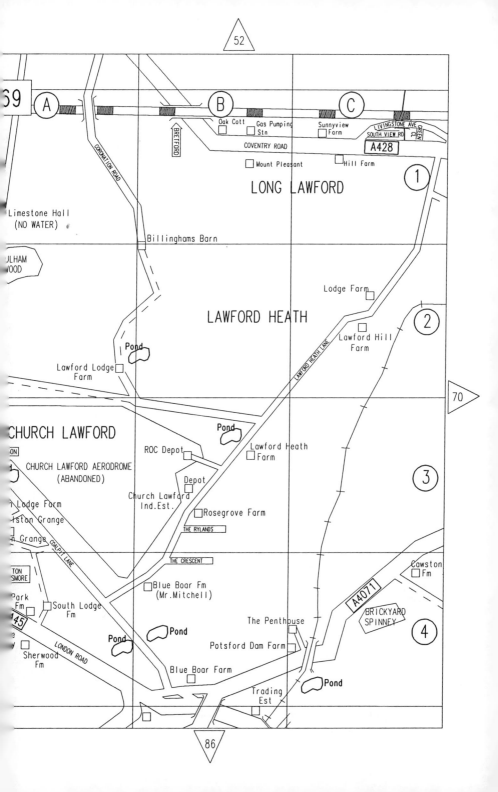

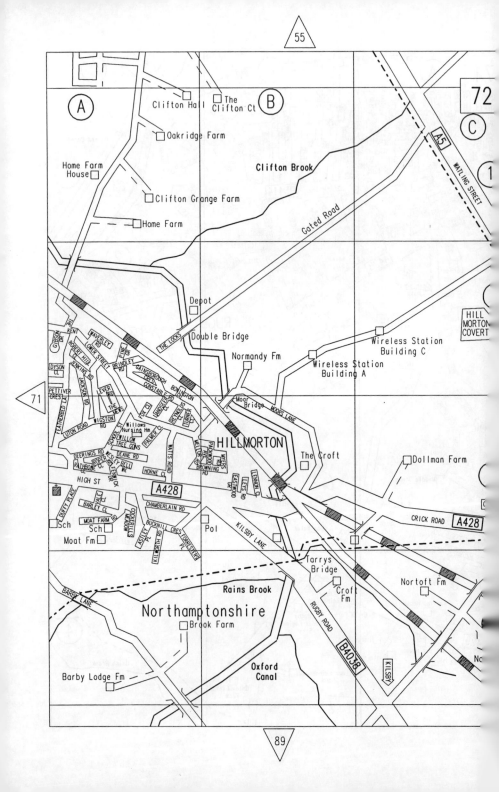

72

C

1

A

B

Clifton Hall
The Clifton Ct

Oakridge Farm

Clifton Brook

Home Farm House

A5

WATLING STREET

Clifton Grange Farm

Home Farm

Gated Road

Depot

Double Bridge

THE LOCKS

Normandy Fm

Wireless Station Building C

Wireless Station Building A

HILL MORTON COVERT

KENT

GIBSON CL

WAVERLEY RD

ROBERT FITH

OKER STREET

JENKINS RD

JACKSON RD

BRINDLEY RD

PINE CL

DYSON CL

PETTIVER CRES

LEVER RD

CAINSBOROUGH CRES

CONSTABLE

BONINGTON

THE LOCKS

LINKS

THE NENS

LUTON ROAD

WIGSTON RD

FEATHERBED LA

UNNS

SCHOOL

PALMER CL

TURNER

DIX CL

LANDSEER CL

REYNOLDS

MILTON

KEATS

BROWNING

WATTS ROAD

Willows Nursing Hm

WILLOW TREE GDNS

HILLMORTON

DEERINGS RD

RATHBONE CL

WESLEY RD

DEANE RD

PIPER CL

FENWICK

HORNE CL

EASTWOOD

YATES

LUCAS CL

LENNON CL

The Croft

Dollman Farm

HIGH ST

INKEY PLACE

BARLEY CL

LILES

MOAT FARM RD

Sch

Sch

COCKERILLS

BUCKNILL CRES

KILWORTH RD

KEITLEY

CHAMBERLAIN RD

A428

FORRESTERS PL

Pol

CRICK ROAD

A428

Moat Fm

KILSBY LANE

Tarrys Bridge

BARBY LANE

Rains Brook

Croft Fm

Nortoft Fm

Northamptonshire

Brook Farm

RUGBY ROAD

B4038

KILSBY

No

Barby Lodge Fm

Oxford Canal

71

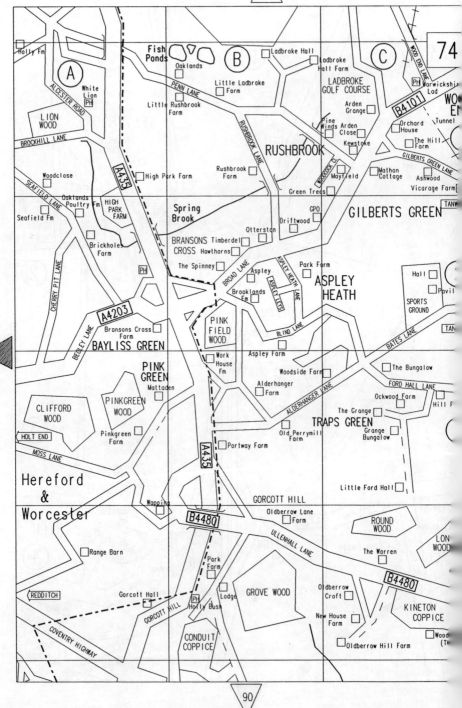

Holly Fm

Ⓐ

ALCESTER ROAD

White
Lion
PH

LION
WOOD

BROCKHILL LANE

Ⓑ

Fish
Ponds

Oaklands

PENN LANE

Little Rushbrook
Farm

Little Ladbroke
Farm

Ladbroke Hall

Ladbroke
Hall Farm

LADBROKE
GOLF COURSE

Arden
Grange

Pine
Winds

Arden
Close

Kewstoke

WOOD END LANE

PH

Warwickshire
Lad

B4101

Orchard
House

The Hill
Farm

WO
EN

Tunnel

RUSHBROOK

GILBERTS GREEN LANE

RUSHBROOK LANE

Woodclose

SEAFIELD LANE

A435

High Park Farm

Rushbrook
Farm

Mayfield

Green Trees

Mathan
Cottage

Ashwood

Vicarage Farm

Oaklands
Poultry Fm

HIGH
PARK
FARM

Spring
Brook

GPO

Driftwood

GILBERTS GREEN

TANW

Seafield Fm

CHERRY PIT LANE

Brickholes
Farm

PH

BRANSONS
CROSS

Timberdell

Hawthorns

The Spinney

Otterston

BROAD LANE

Aspley

Brooklands
Em

ASPLEY HEATH LANE

ASPLEY LEYS

Park Farm

ASPLEY
HEATH

Hall

Pavil

SPORTS
GROUND

BEDLEY LANE

A4203

Bransons Cross
Farm

BAYLISS GREEN

PINK
GREEN

Mattaden

PINK
FIELD
WOOD

Work
House
Fm

Aspley Farm

BLIND LANE

BATES LANE

TAN

CLIFFORD
WOOD

PINKGREEN
WOOD

HOLT END

Pinkgreen
Farm

MOSS LANE

Portway Farm

A435

Woodside Farm

Alderhanger
Farm

ALDERHANGER LANE

Old Perrymill
Farm

TRAPS GREEN

The Grange

Grange
Bungalow

The Bungalow

FORD HALL LANE

Ockwood Farm

Hill F

Hereford
&
Worcester

Wapping

REDDITCH

Range Barn

B4480

Gorcott Hall

GORCOTT HILL

COVENTRY HIGHWAY

GORCOTT HILL

Oldberrow Lane
Farm

ULLENHALL LANE

Park
Farm

PH
Holly Bush

Lodge

GROVE WOOD

CONDUIT
COPPICE

Little Ford Hall

ROUND
WOOD

The Warren

B4480

Oldberrow
Croft

New House
Farm

Oldberrow Hill Farm

LON
WOOD

KINETON
COPPICE

Wood
(T

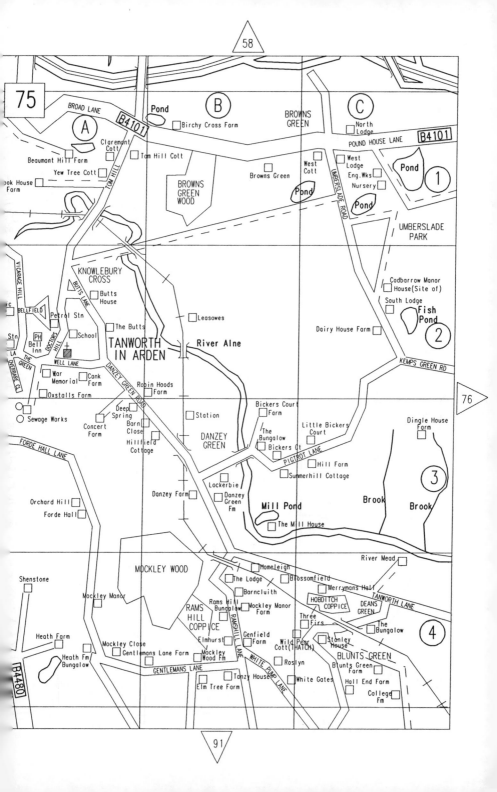

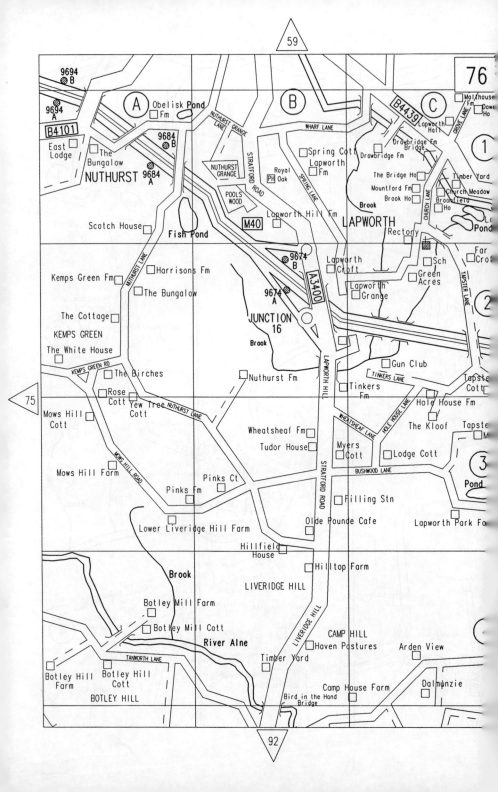

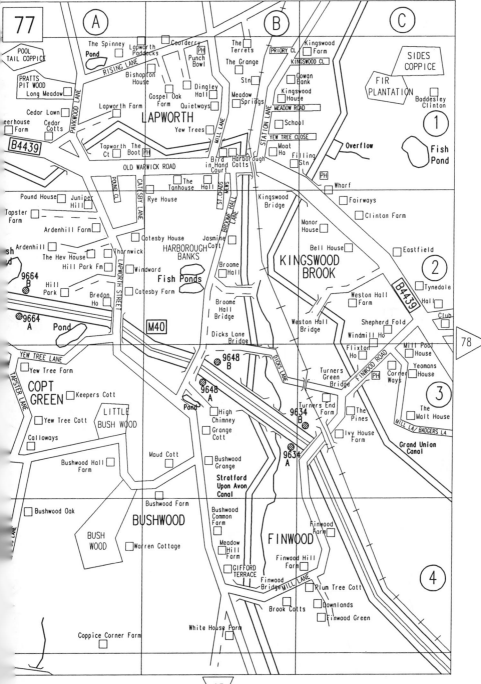

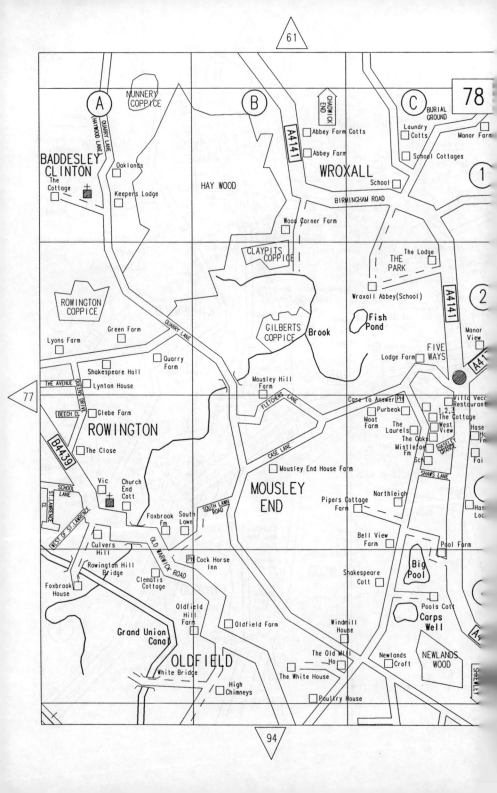

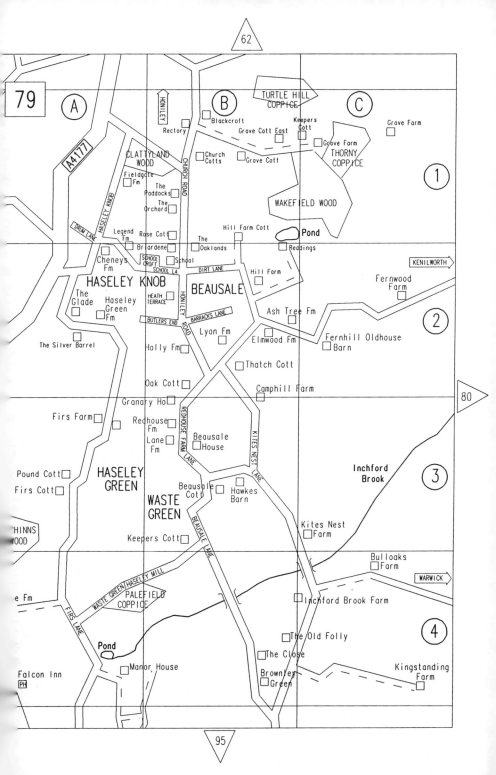

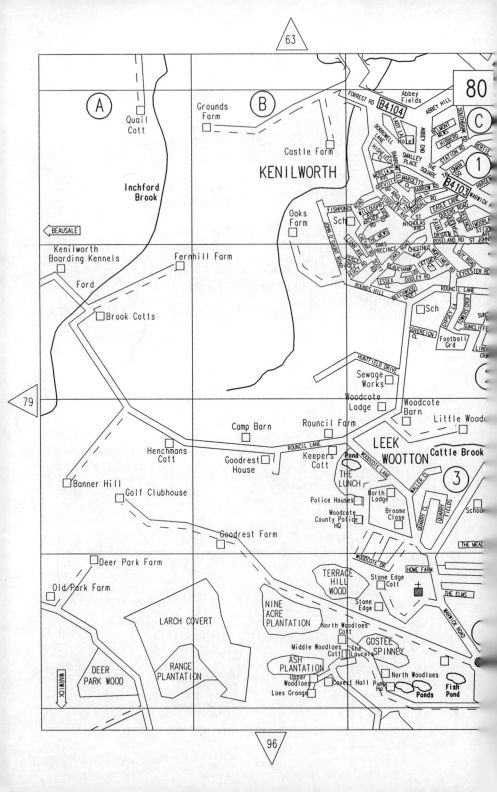

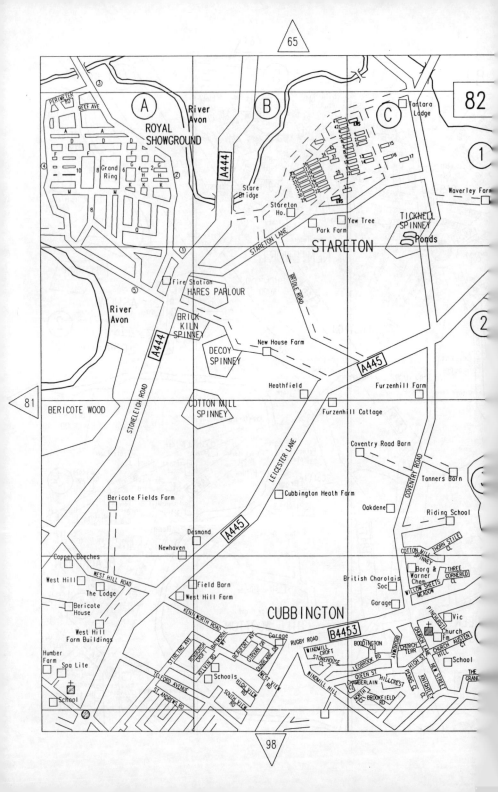

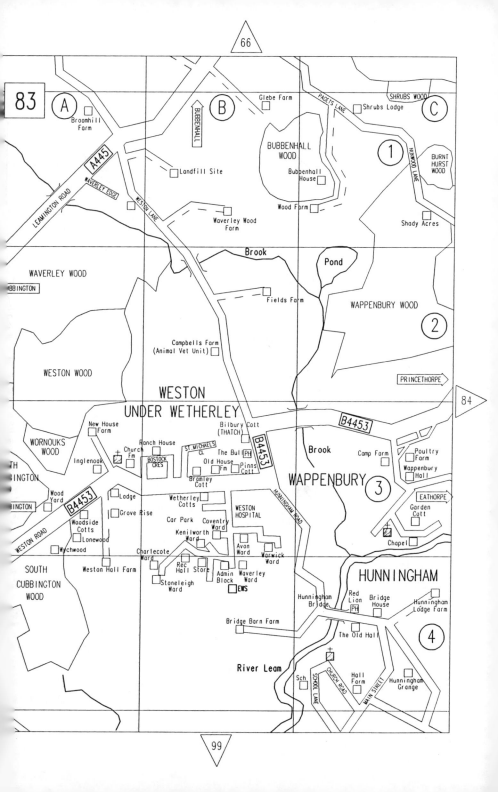

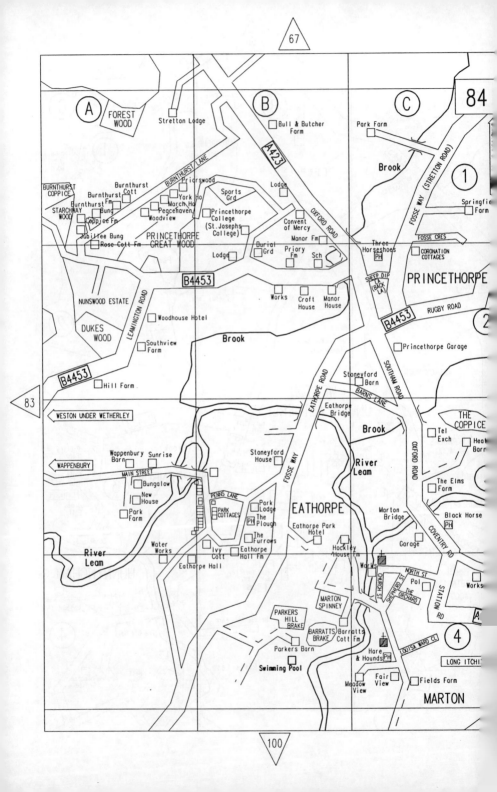

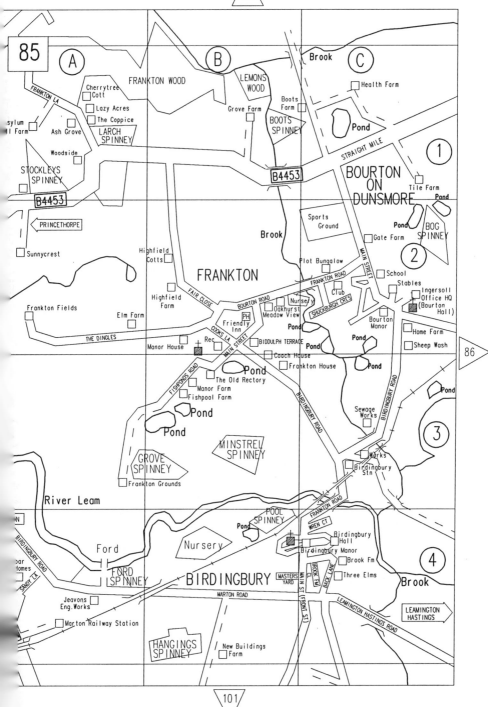

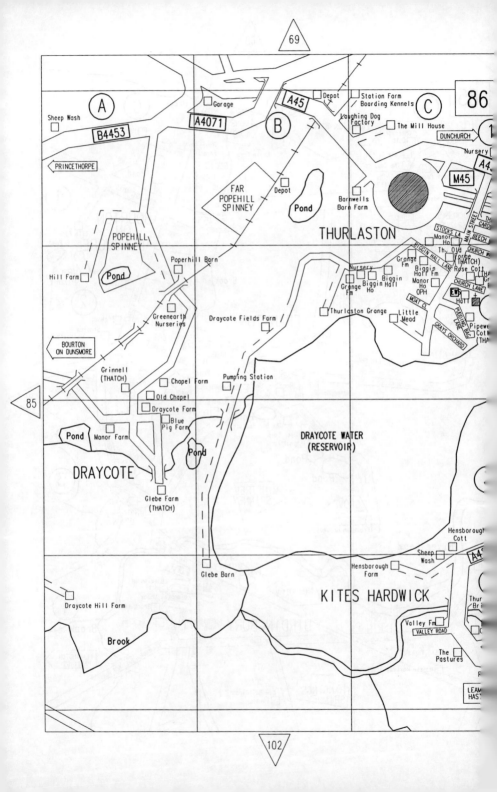

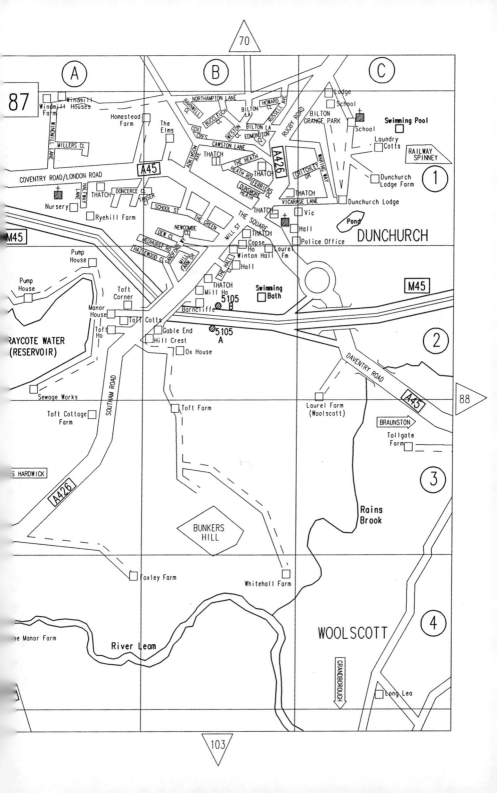

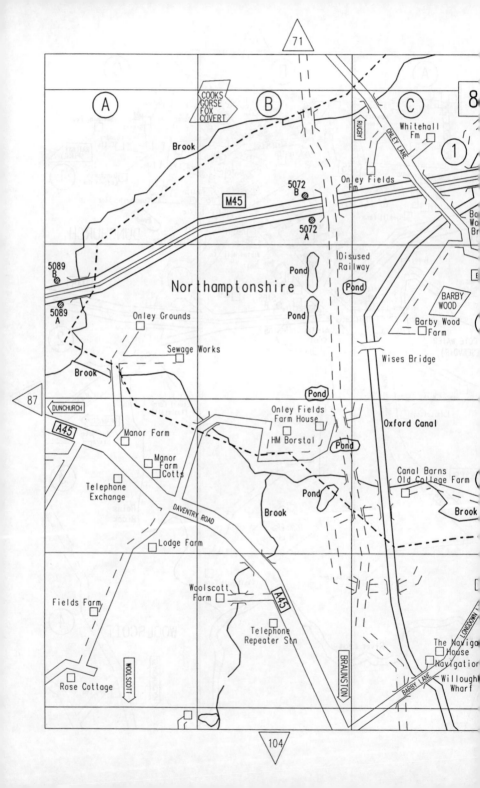

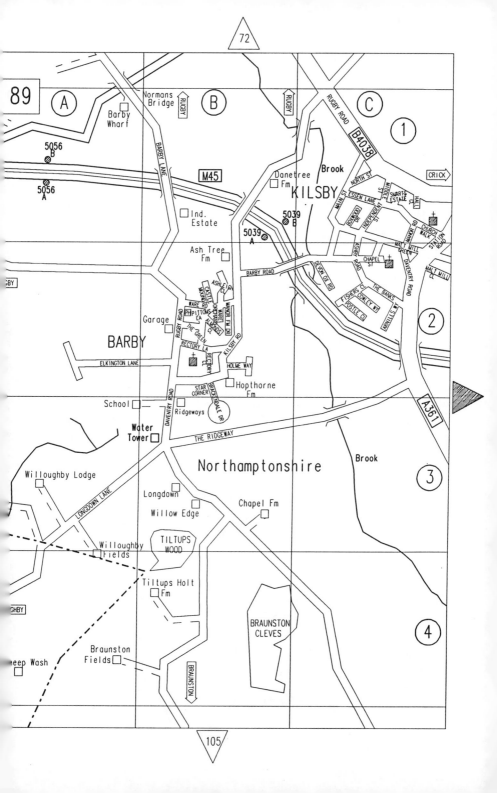

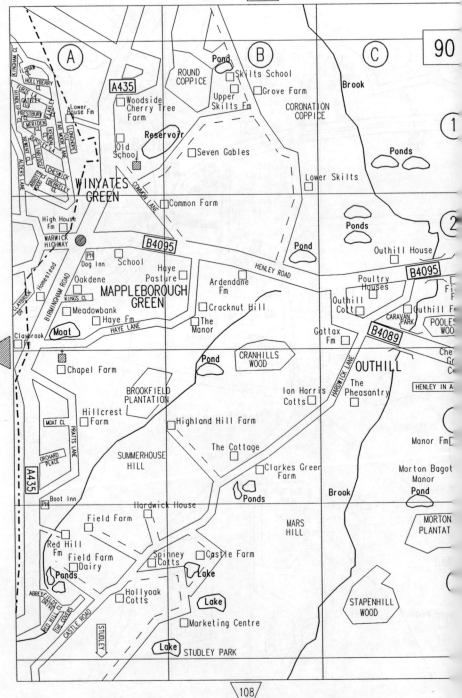

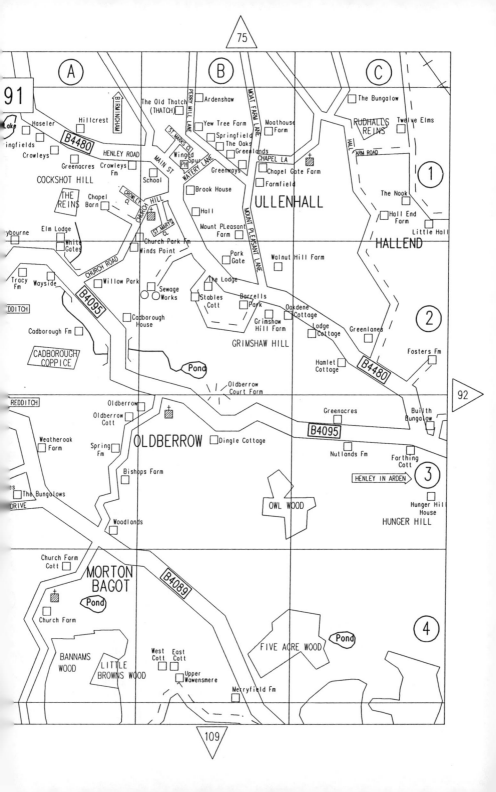

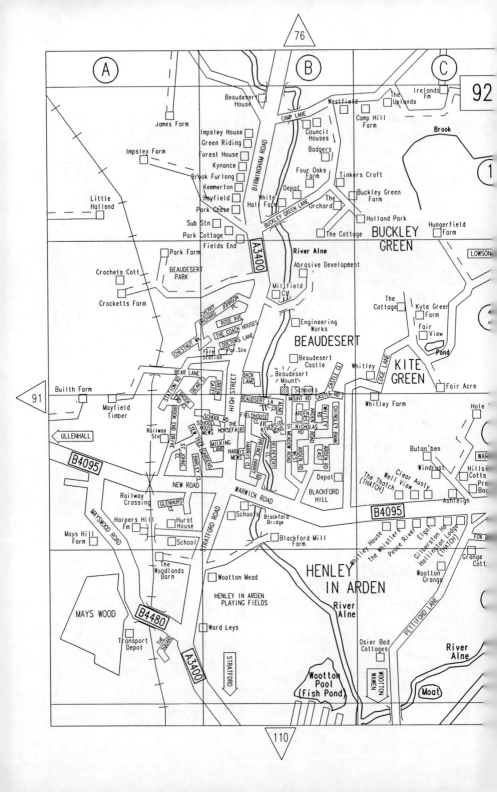

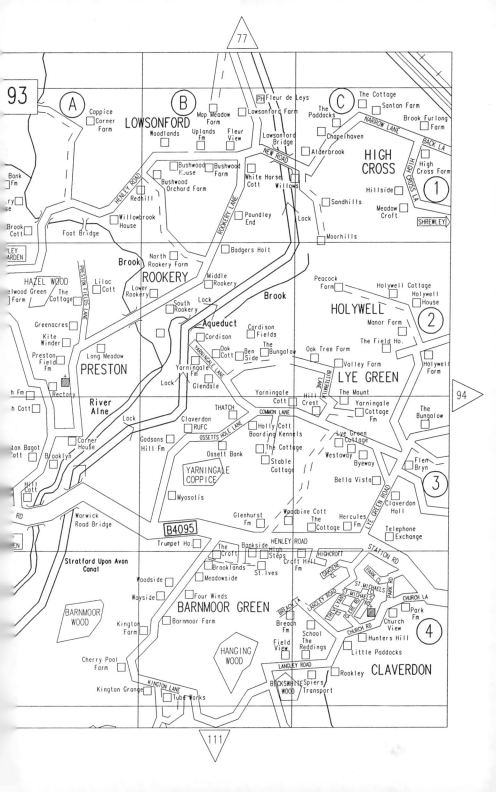

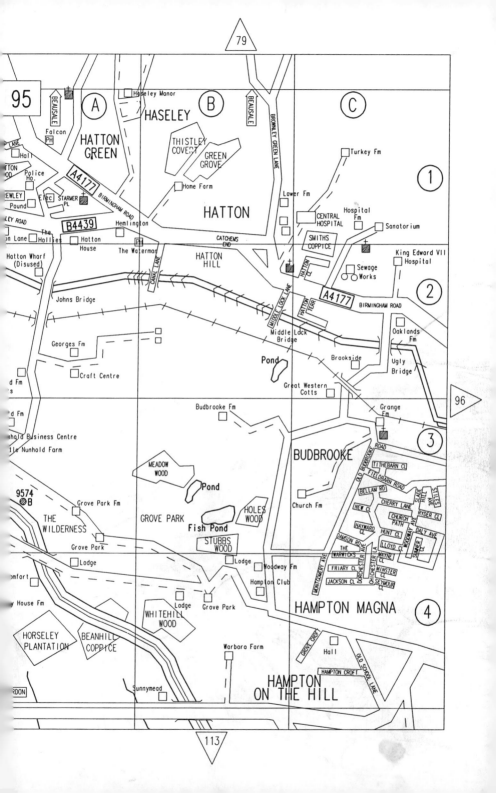

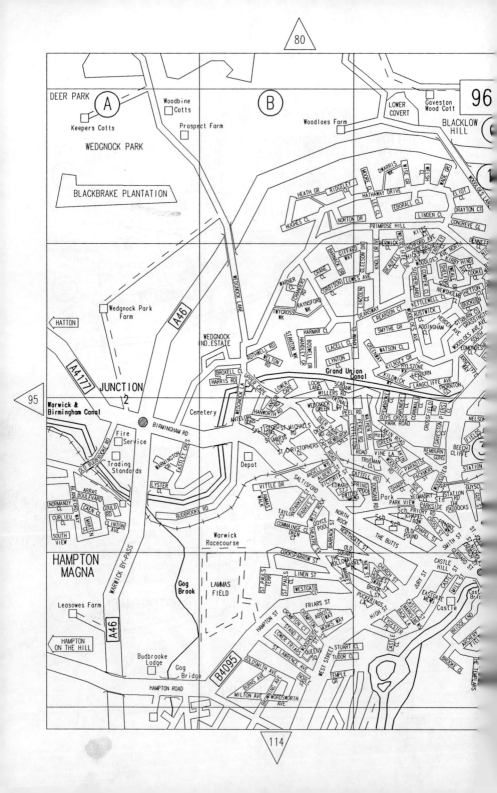

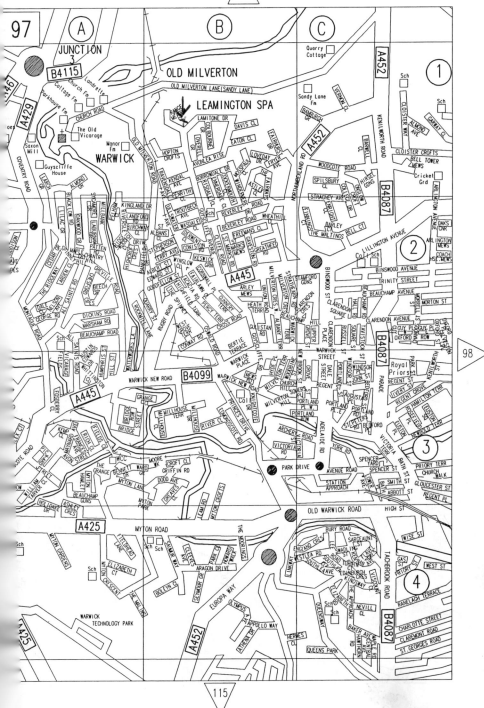

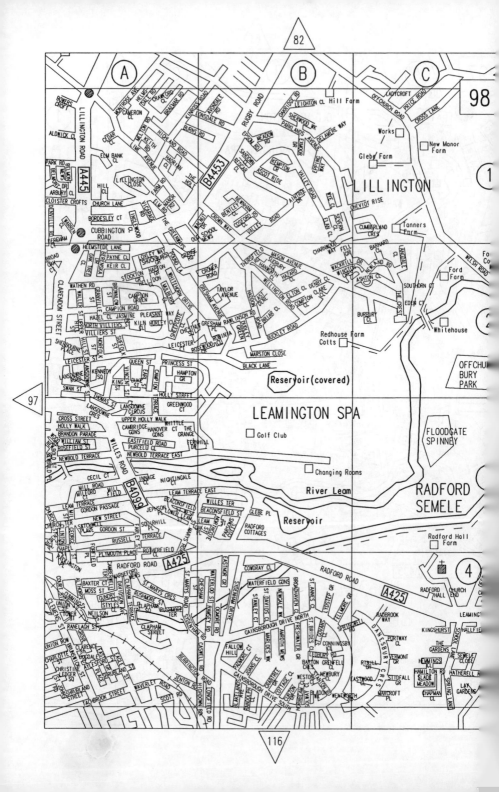

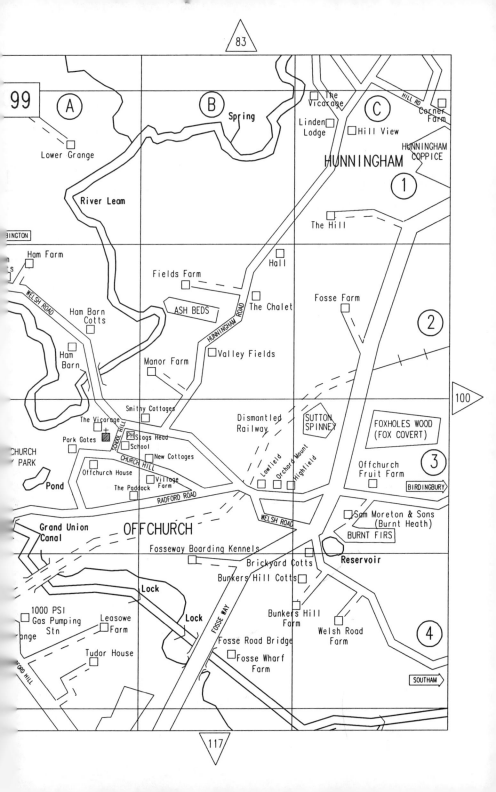

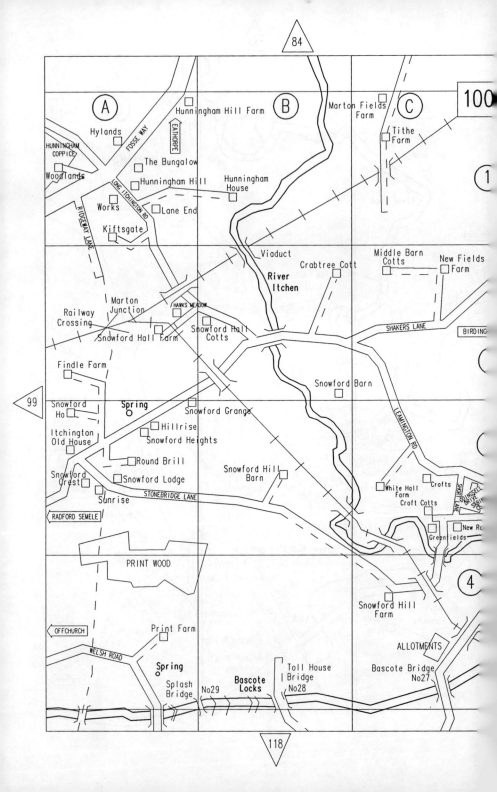

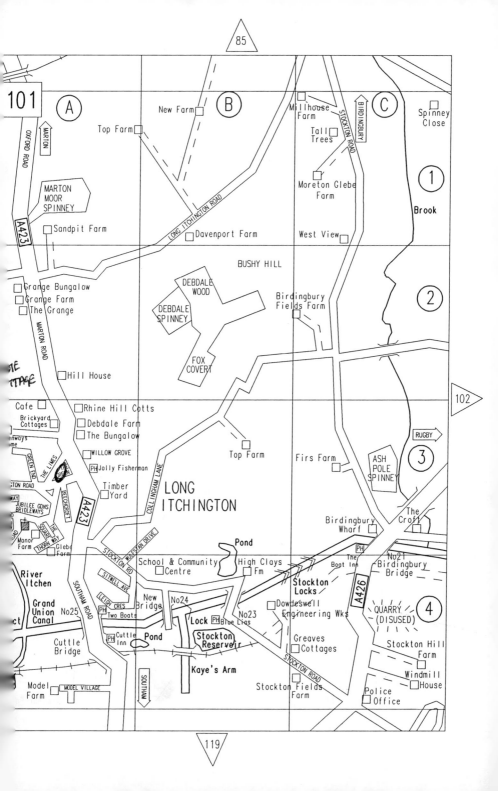

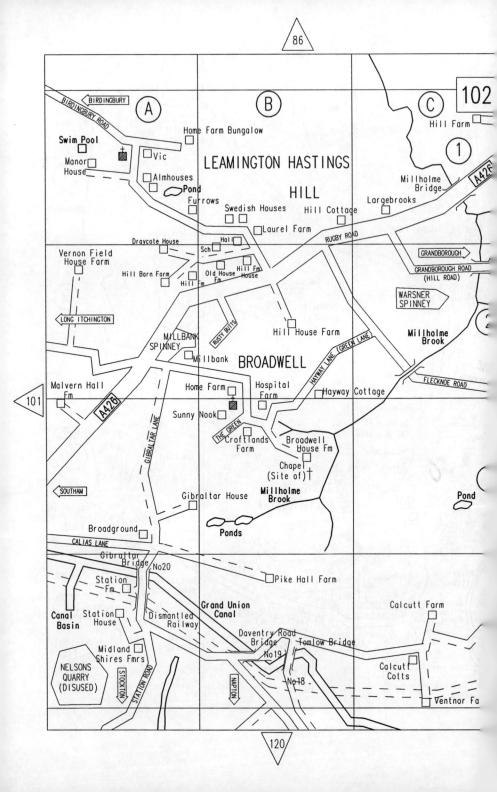

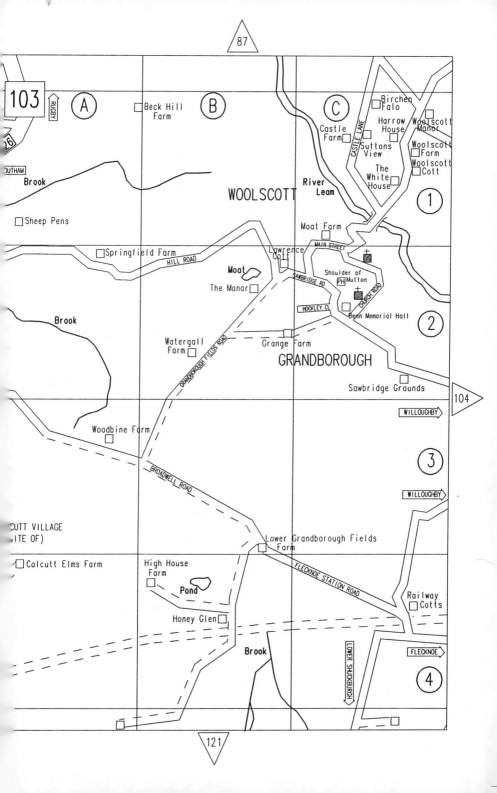

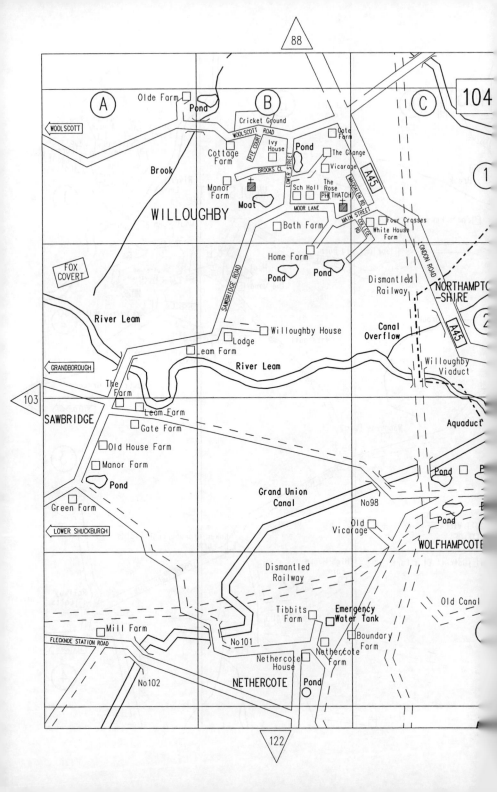

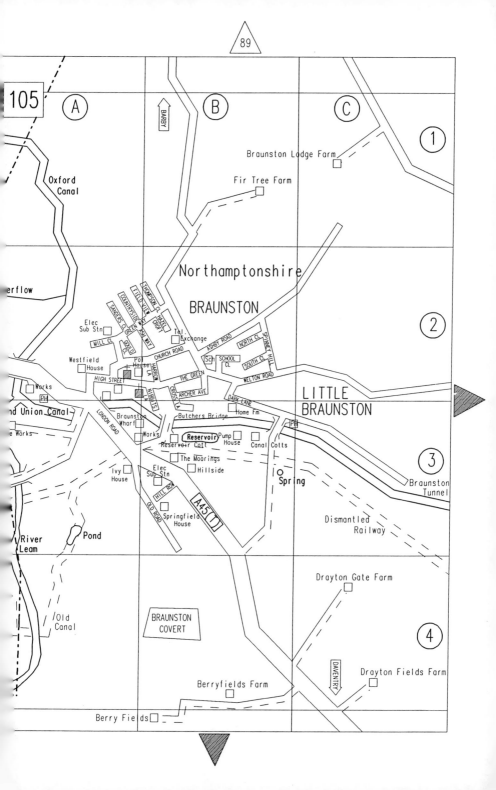

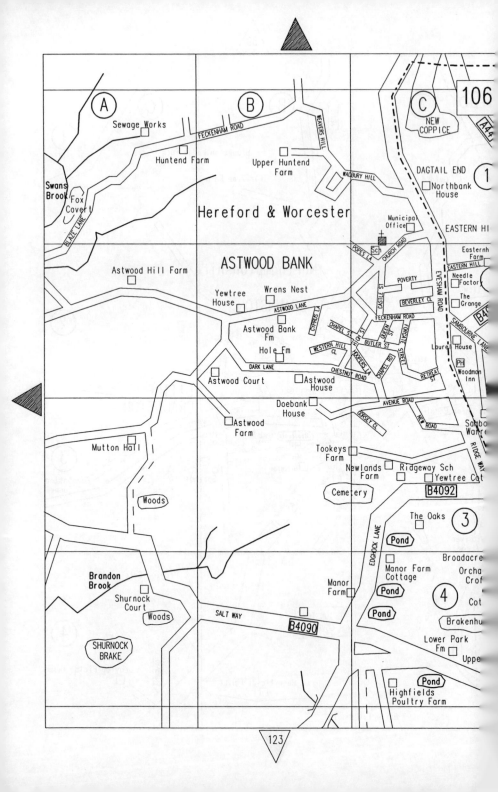

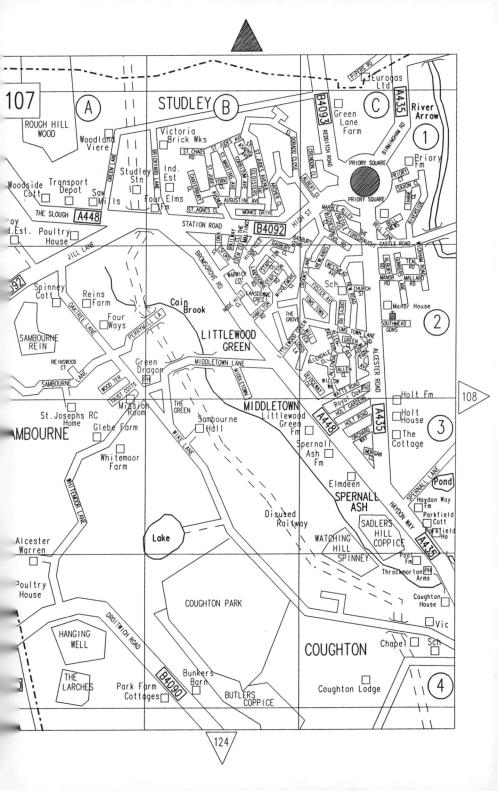

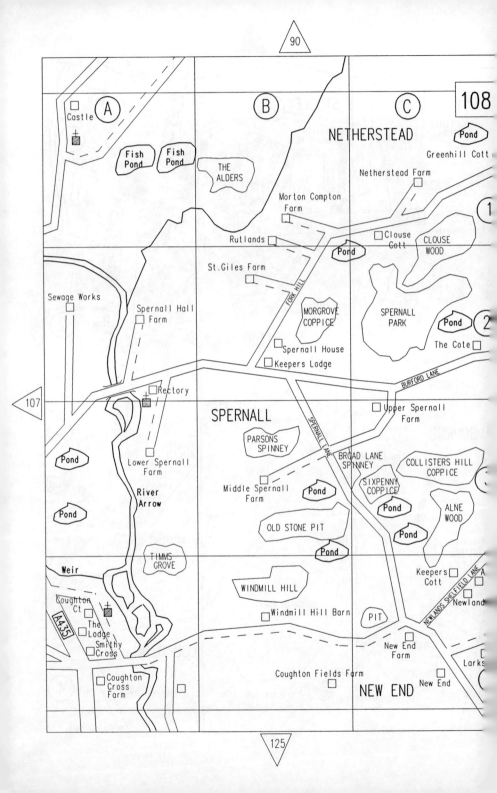

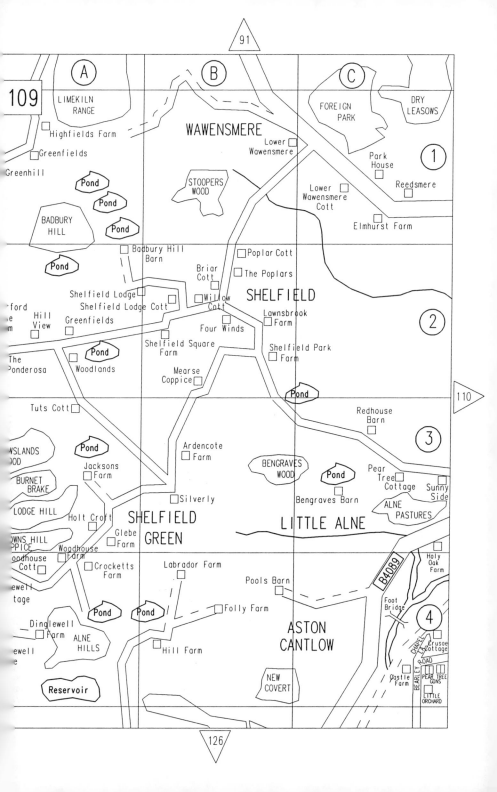

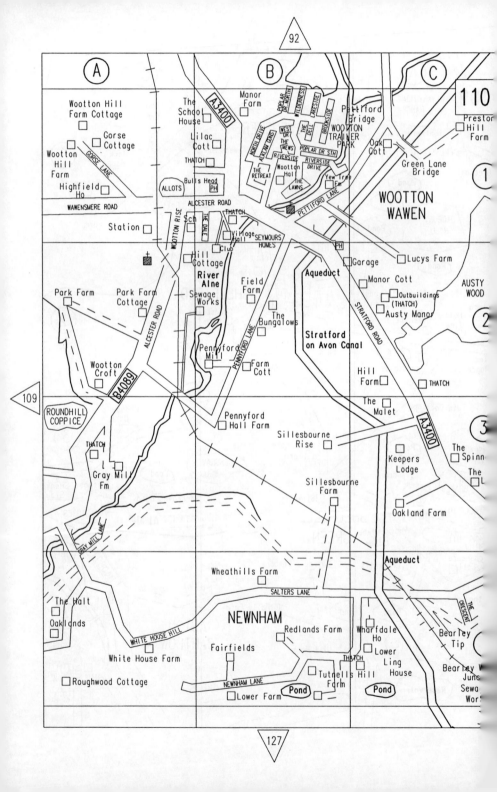

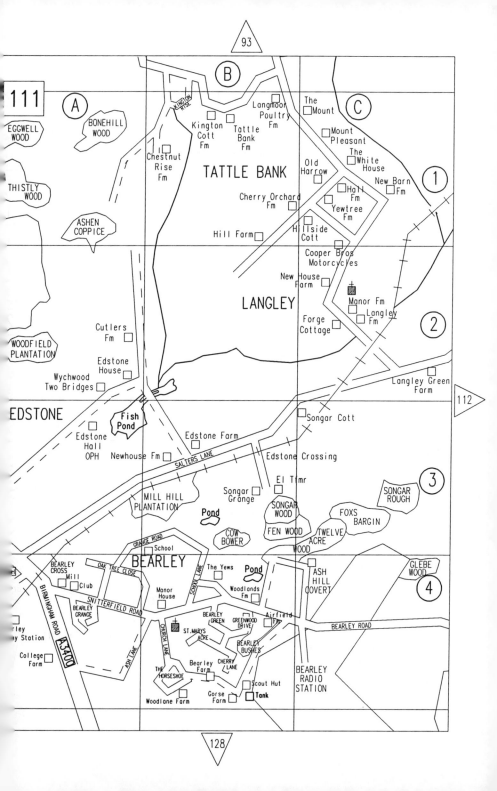

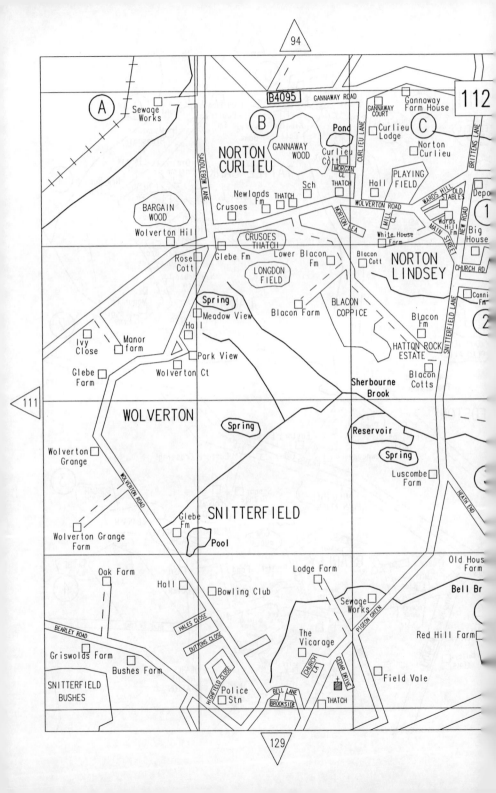

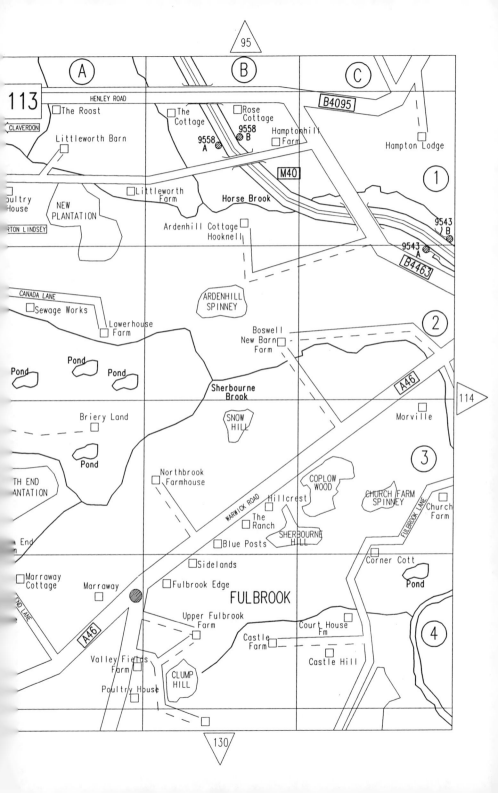

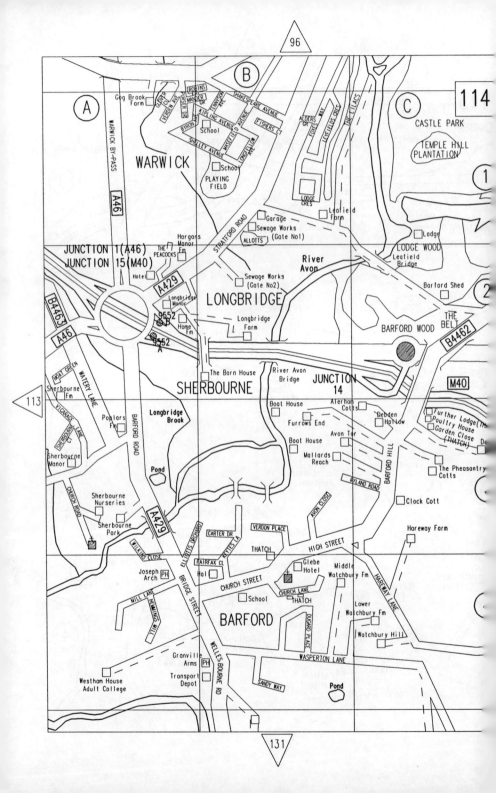

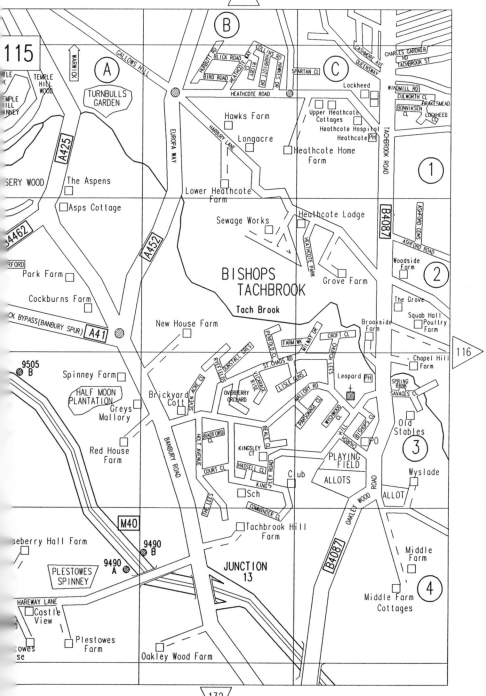

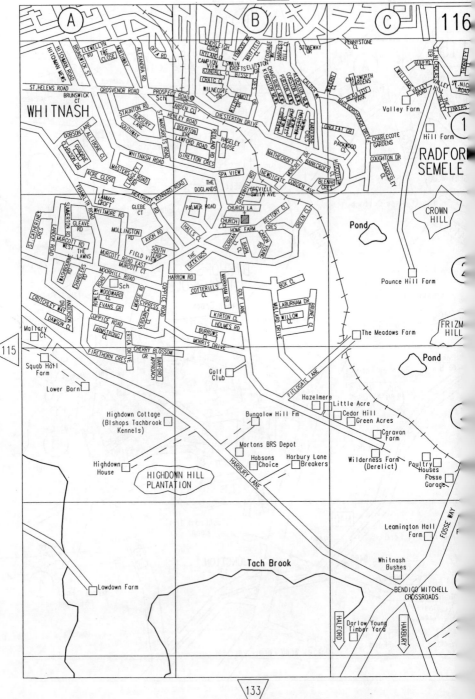

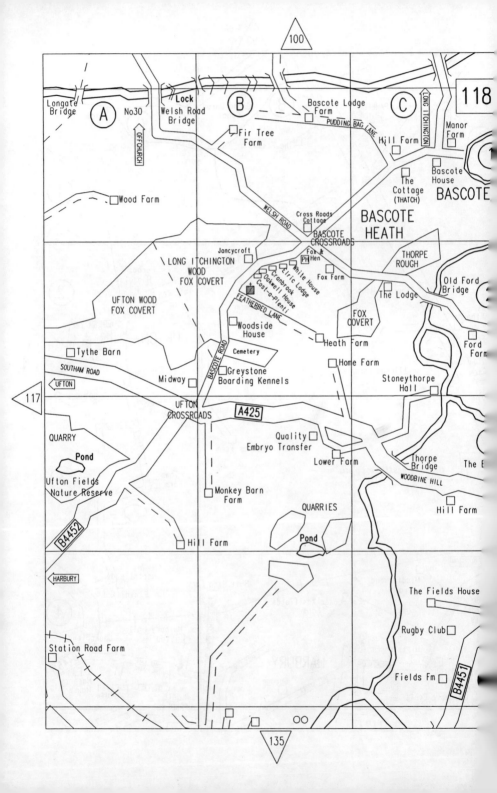

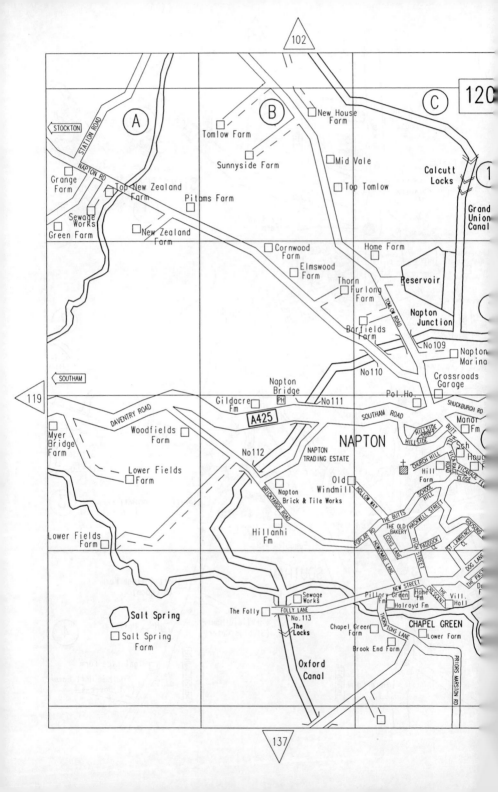

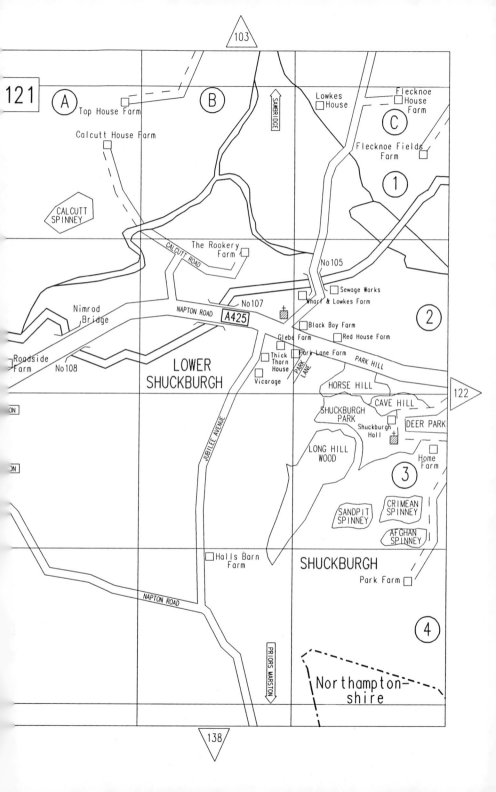

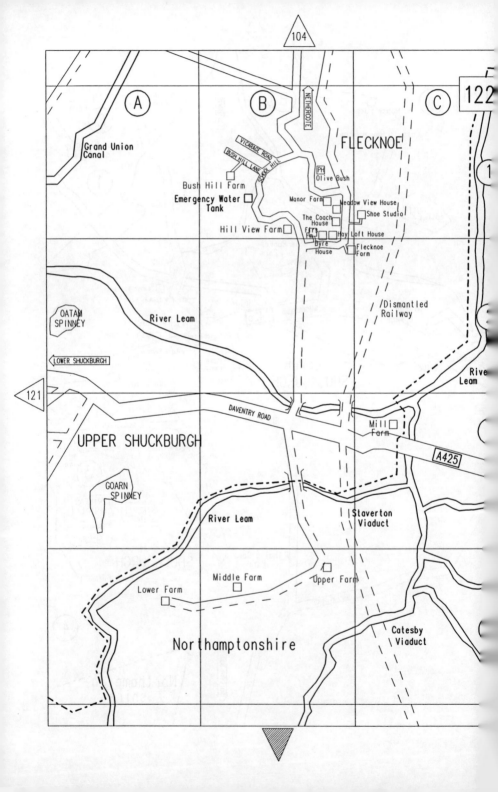

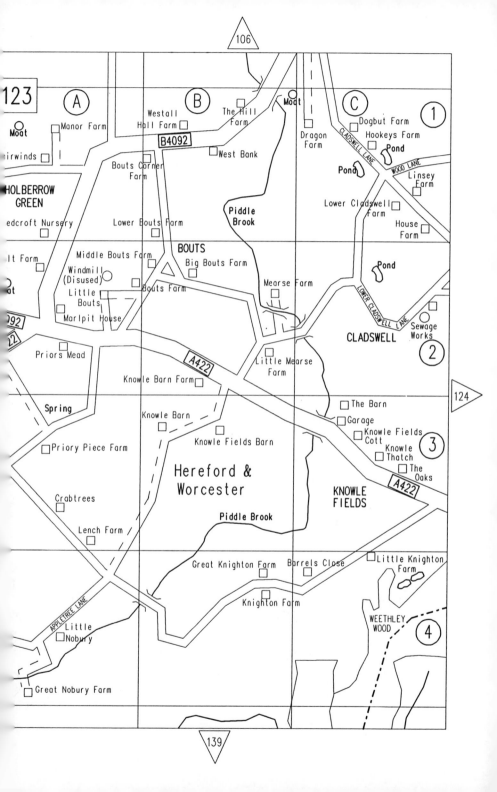

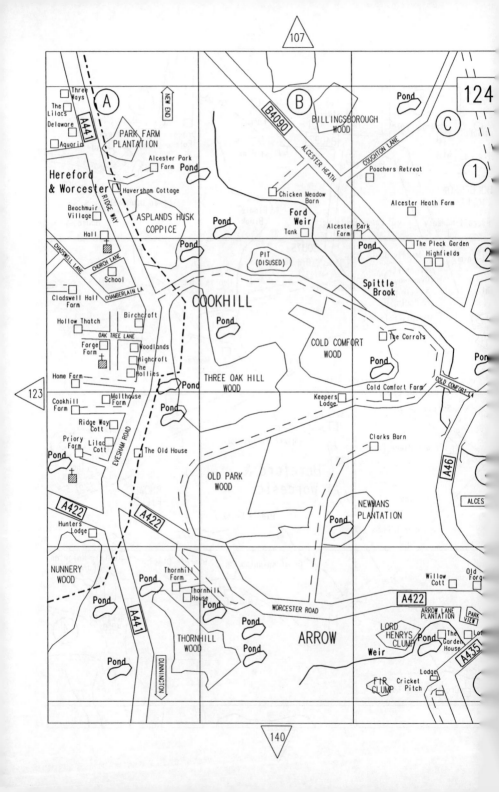

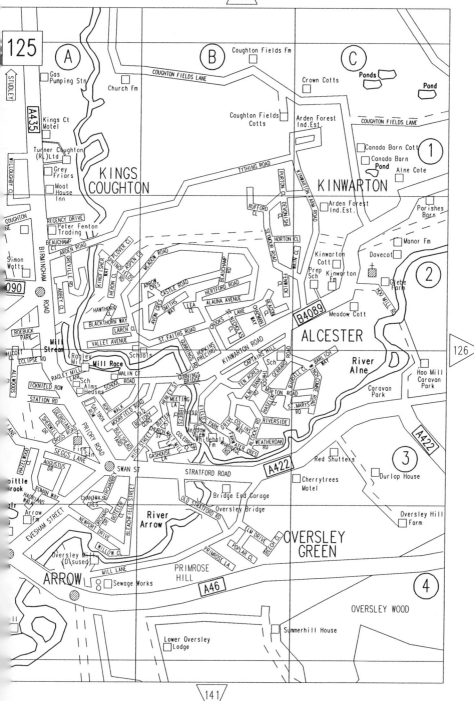

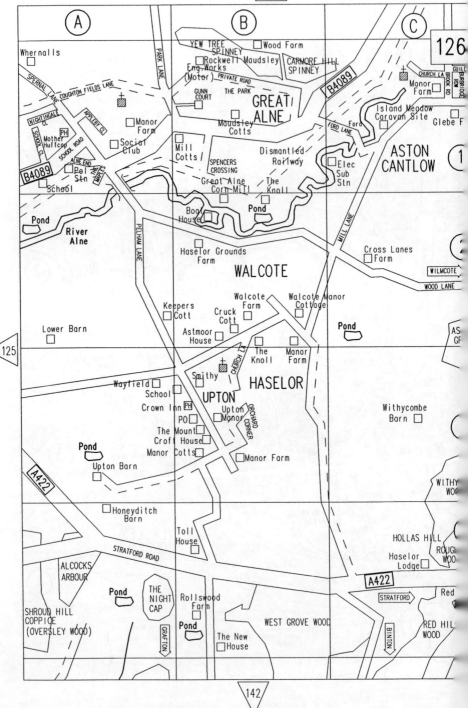

A

B

C

Whernalls

Wood Farm

YEW TREE SPINNEY

Rockwell Maudsley Eng.Works (Motor)

CARMORE HILL SPINNEY

B4089

CHURCH LA

BURBRIDGE

GUILL

BROOK RD

ROW

Manor Farm

PRIVATE ROAD

PARK LANE

SPERNAL LANE

COUGHTON FIELDS LANE

GUNN COURT

THE PARK

Island Meadow Caravan Site

Glebe F

ASTON CANTLOW

NIGHTINGALE CL

Mother Hufcap

PH

SCHOOL CL

SCHOOL ROAD

APPLEBY CL

Manor Farm

Social Club

Maudsley Cotts

GREAT ALNE

Dismantled Railway

FORD LANE

Ford

1

ALNE END

Pel Stn

B4089

HARTS

Mill Cotts

SPENCERS CROSSING

Great Alne Corn Mill

Elec Sub Stn

School

Boat House

The Knoll

Pond

MILL LANE

Pond

River Alne

PELHAM LANE

Haselor Grounds Farm

Cross Lanes Farm

WALCOTE

WILMCOTE

WOOD LANE

2

Keepers Cott

Walcote Farm

Walcote Manor Cottage

Lower Barn

Cruck Cott

Pond

AS GF

125

Astmoor House

The Knoll

Manor Farm

Wayfield

School

Smithy

HASELOR

CHURCH LA

Withycombe Barn

Crown Inn

PH

UPTON

Upton Manor

ORCHARD CORNER

PO

The Mount

Croft House

Manor Cotts

Manor Farm

Pond

A422

Upton Barn

Honeyditch Barn

Toll House

HOLLAS HILL

WITHY WOO

Haselor Lodge

ROUGH WOO

STRATFORD ROAD

A422

STRATFORD

Red

ALCOCKS ARBOUR

THE NIGHT CAP

Rollswood Farm

RED HILL WOOD

SHROUD HILL COPPICE (OVERSLEY WOOD)

Pond

GRAFTON

Pond

WEST GROVE WOOD

BINTON

The New House

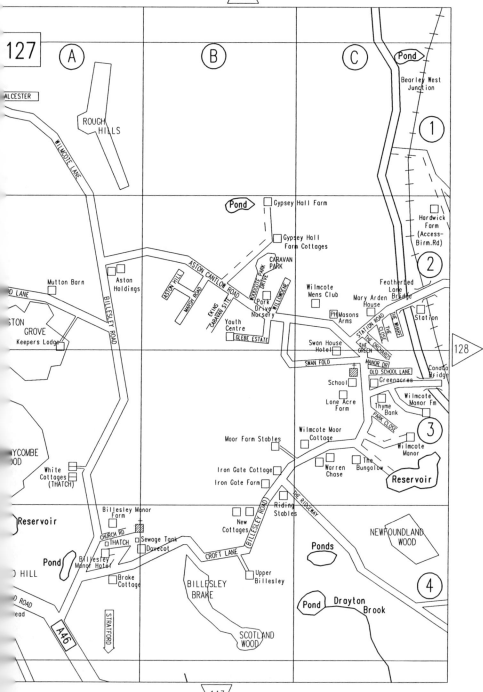

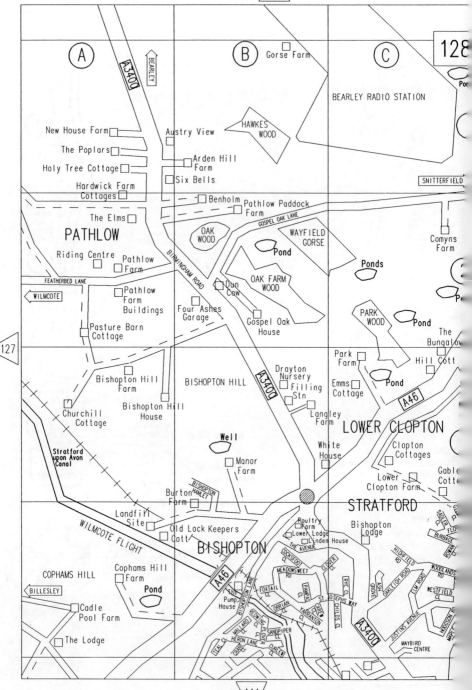

Ⓐ   Ⓑ   Ⓒ

129

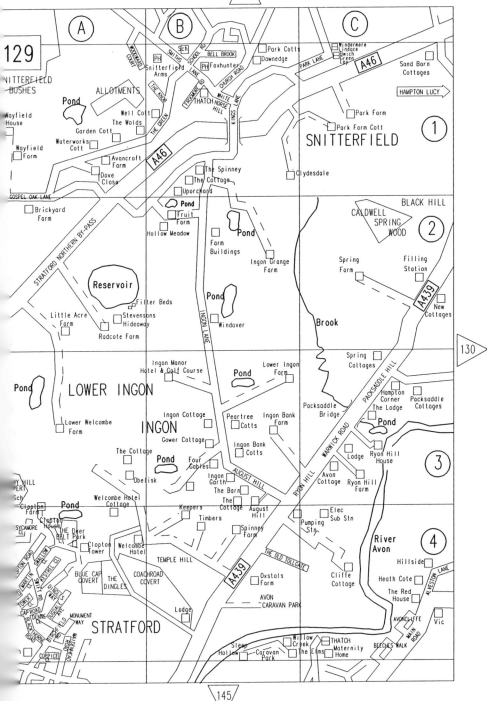

SNITTERFIELD
BUSHES

WOODLAND COURT
SMITHS RD
SCHOOL LANE
Sch
BELL BROOK
Park Cotts
Dawnedge
Windermere
Lindace
Beech
Green
PH   Snitterfield
         Arms
PH   Foxhunters
CHURCH ROAD
PARK LANE
A46
Sand Barn
Cottages

THE MOOR

ALLOTMENTS

IT BROOK

HAMPTON LUCY

Pond

WHITE HORSE HILL

THATCH

KINGS LANE

Park Farm

Wayfield
House

Well Cott

The Wolds

Park Farm Cott

THE GREEN

Garden Cott

SNITTERFIELD   ⓵

Waterworks
Cott

A46

Wayfield
Farm

Avoncroft
Farm

Clydesdale

Dove
Close

The Spinney

The Cottage

GOSPEL OAK LANE

Uporchard

BLACK HILL

Brickyard
Farm

Pond

CALDWELL
SPRING
WOOD

⓶

Fruit
Farm

STRATFORD NORTHERN BY-PASS

Hollow Meadow

Pond

Spring
Farm

Filling
Station

Farm
Buildings

Reservoir

Ingon Grange
Farm

A439

Filter Beds

Brook

New
Cottages

Little Acre
Farm

Stevensons
Hideaway

Pond

INGON LANE

Windover

Spring
Cottages

Ⓟ
130

Radcote Farm

Pond

LOWER INGON

Ingon Manor
Hotel & Golf Course

Lower Ingon
Farm

Pond

Packsaddle
Bridge

PACKSADDLE HILL

Hampton
Corner
The Lodge

Packsaddle
Cottages

Pond

INGON

Ingon Cottage

Peartree
Cotts

Ingon Bank
Farm

WARWICK ROAD

Pond

Lower Welcombe
Farm

Gower Cottage

Lodge

Ryon Hill
House

The Cottage

Ingon Bank
Cotts

RYON HILL

Pond

Four
Gables

AUGUST HILL

Avon
Cottage

Ryon Hill
Farm

⓷

Obelisk

Ingon
Garth

NY HILL
VERT
Sch

Welcombe Hotel
Cottage

The Barn
The
Cottage

Elec
Sub Stn

Pond

Clopton
Farm

Keepers

August
Hill

River
Avon

⓸

SYCAMORE
CL

THE DEER
BELT PARK

Clopton
House

Timbers

Spinney
Farm

Pumping
Stn

Hillside

MARTIN
CL

KESTREL CL

Clopton
Tower

Welcombe
Hotel

TEMPLE HILL

THE OLD TOLLGATE

Heath Cote

ALVESTON LANE

BLUE CAP
COVERT

THE
DINGLES

COACHROAD
COVERT

A439

Oxstals
Farm

Cliffe
Cottage

The Red
House

MONUMENT
WAY

Lodge

AVON
CARAVAN PARK

AVONCLIFFE

MAIN ROAD

Vic

STRATFORD

Sleep
Hollow

Caravan
Park

Willow
Creek
the Elms

THATCH
Maternity
Home

BEECHES WALK

COPPICE

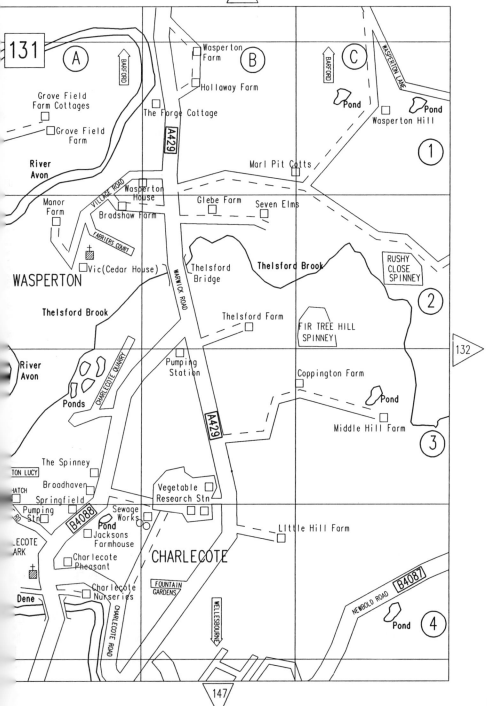

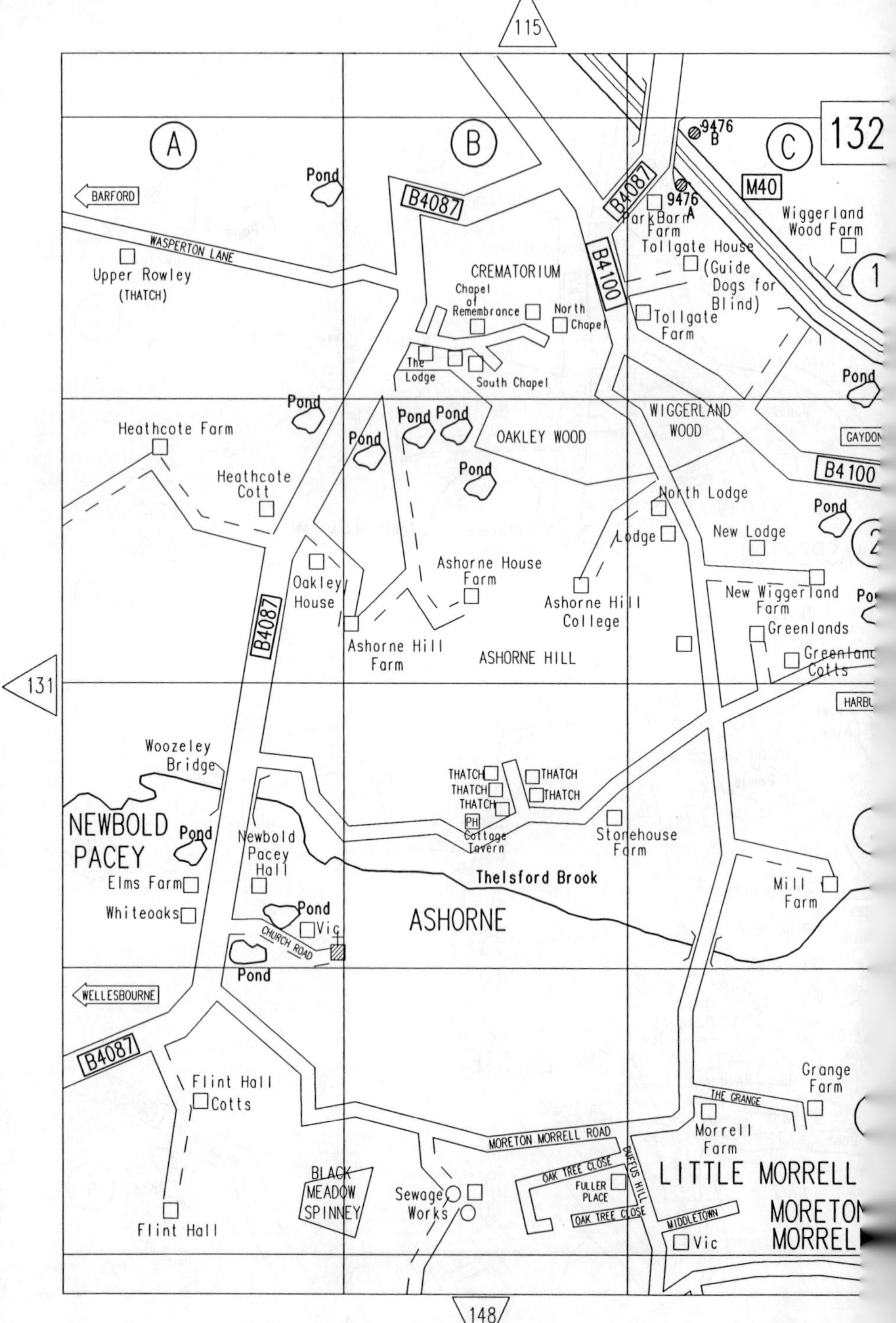
115
132
A
B
C
9476 B
9476 A
M40
BARFORD
WASPERTON LANE
Upper Rowley
(THATCH)
Pond
B4087
B4087
Park Barn Farm
Wiggerland Wood Farm
CREMATORIUM
B4100
Tollgate House (Guide Dogs for Blind)
Chapel of Remembrance
North Chapel
Tollgate Farm
The Lodge
South Chapel
Pond
Heathcote Farm
Pond
Pond
Pond
OAKLEY WOOD
WIGGERLAND WOOD
GAYDON
B4100
Pond
Heathcote Cott
North Lodge
Pond
Lodge
New Lodge
Oakley House
Ashorne House Farm
Ashorne Hill College
New Wiggerland Farm
B4087
Greenlands
Ashorne Hill Farm
ASHORNE HILL
Greenland Cotts
131
HARBU
Woozeley Bridge
THATCH
THATCH
THATCH
THATCH
THATCH
PH
Cottage Tavern
Stonehouse Farm
NEWBOLD PACEY
Pond
Newbold Pacey Hall
Thelsford Brook
Mill Farm
Elms Farm
Whiteoaks
Pond
Vic
ASHORNE
CHURCH ROAD
Pond
WELLESBOURNE
B4087
Grange Farm
Flint Hall Cotts
THE GRANGE
Morrell Farm
MORETON MORRELL ROAD
DUFFUS HILL
OAK TREE CLOSE
BLACK MEADOW SPINNEY
Sewage Works
FULLER PLACE
LITTLE MORRELL
OAK TREE CLOSE
MIDDLETOWN
MORETON MORREL
Flint Hall
Vic
148

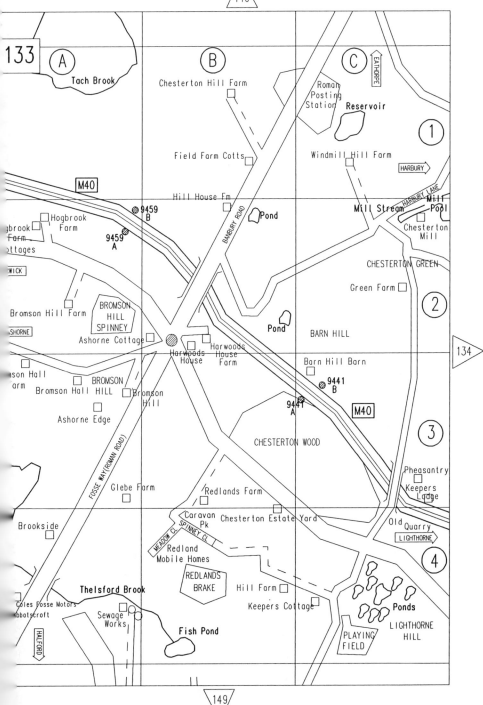

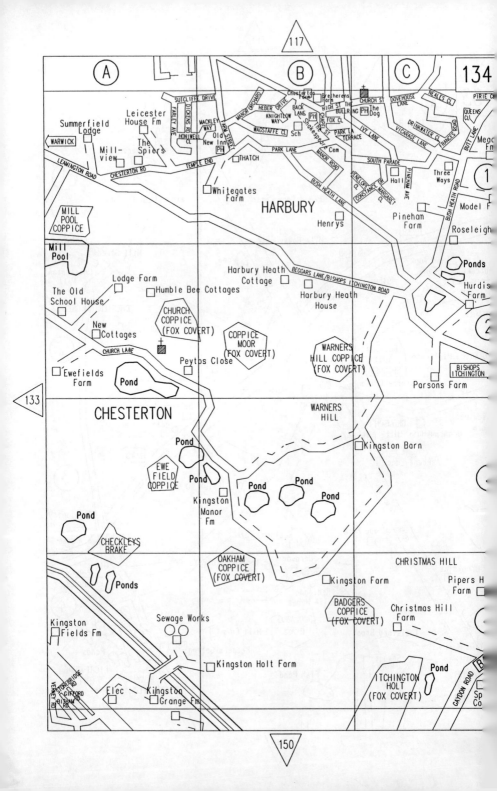

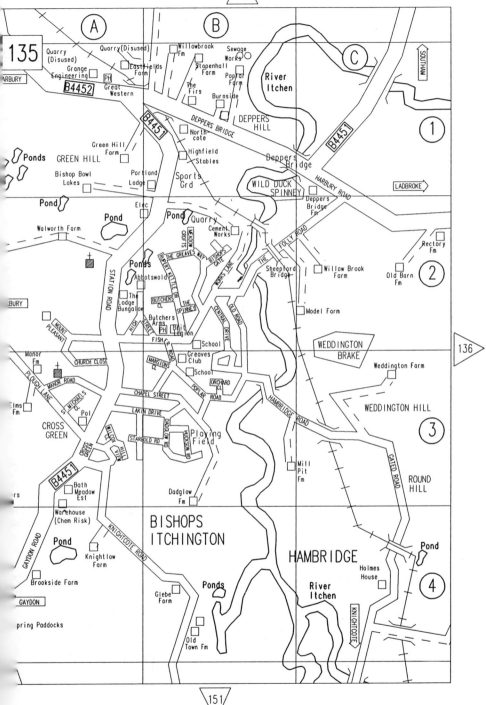

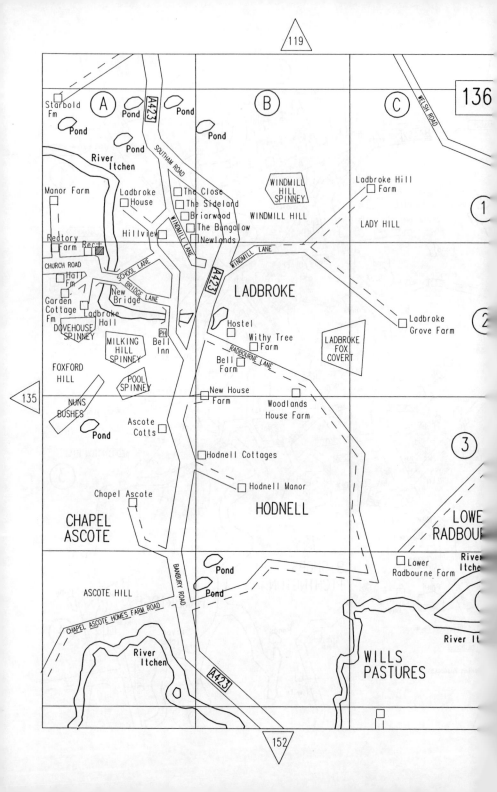

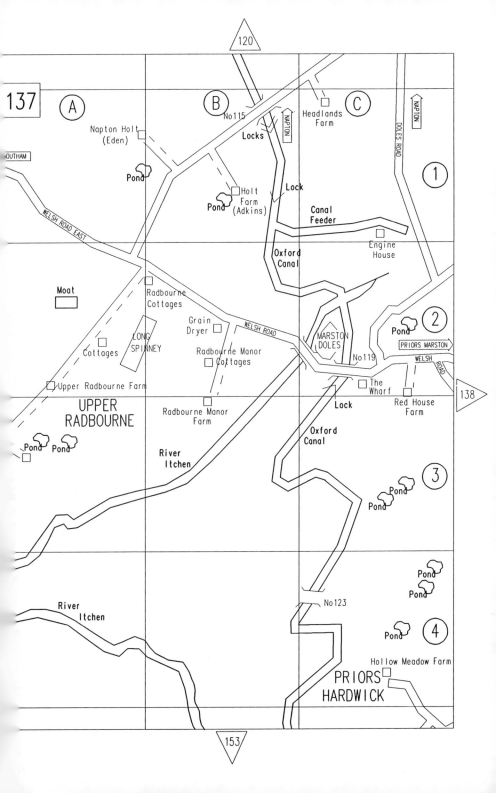

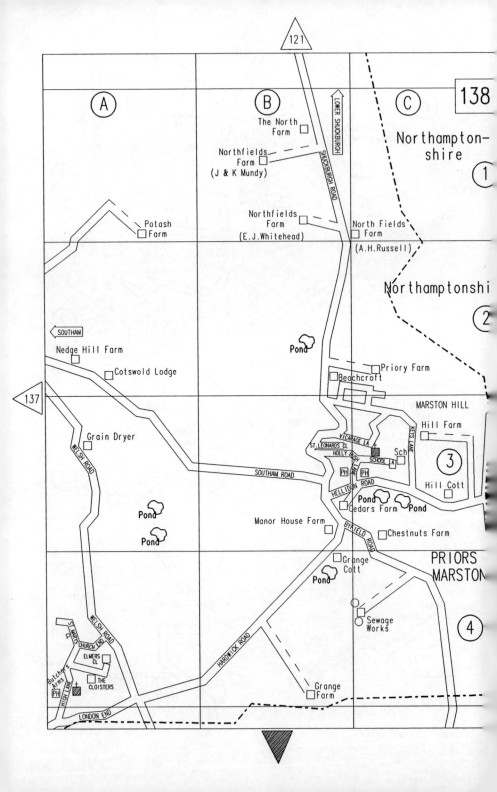

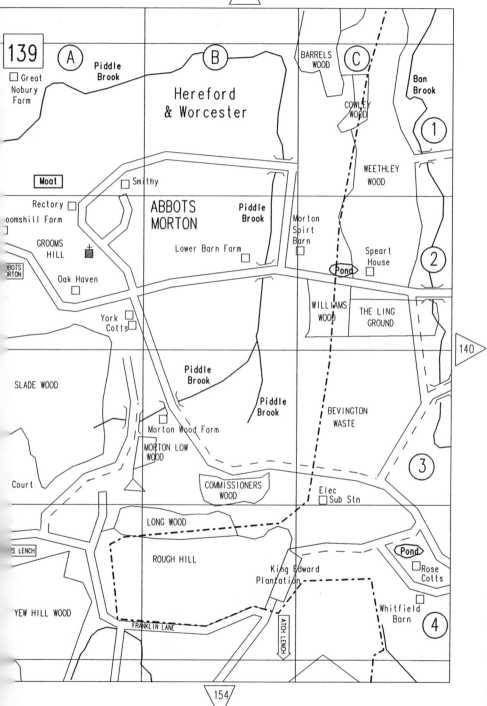

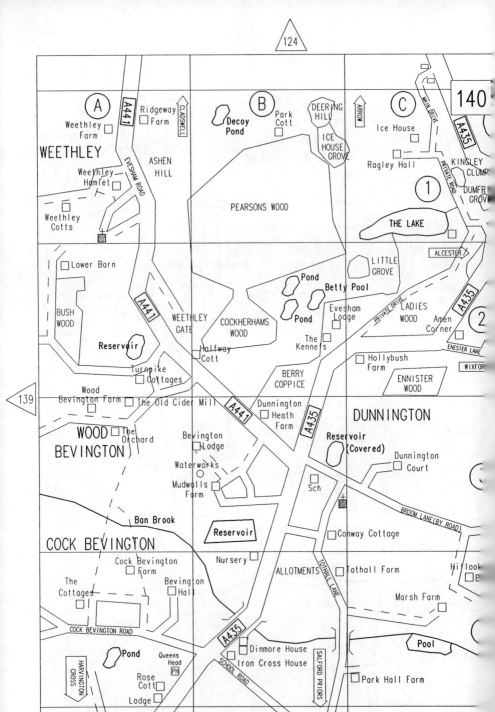

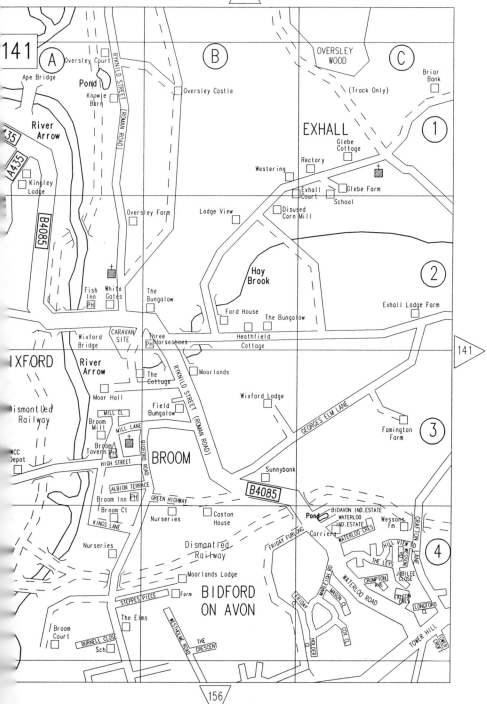

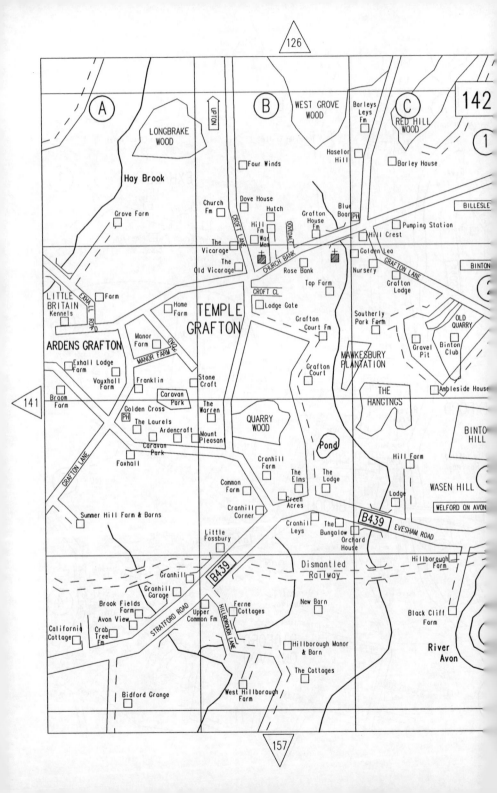

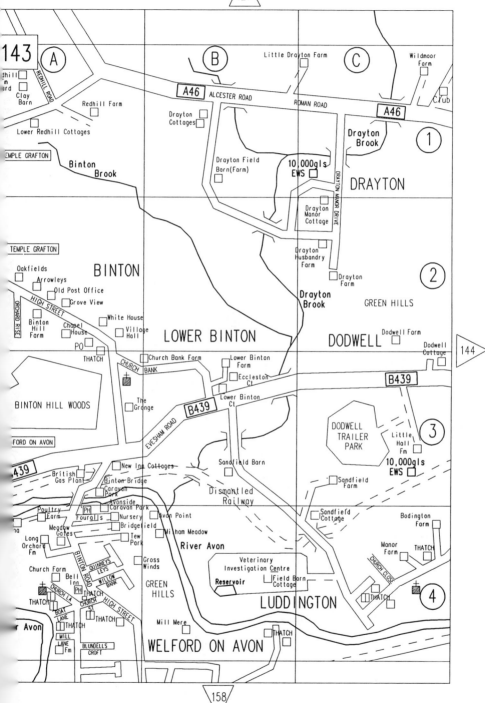

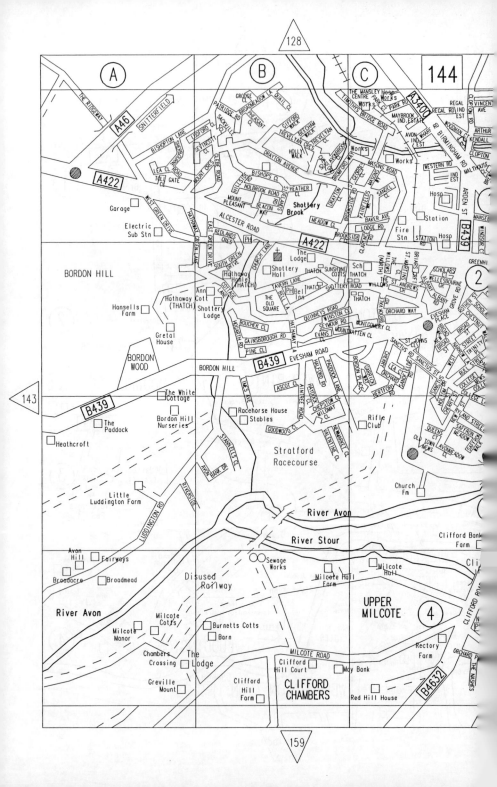

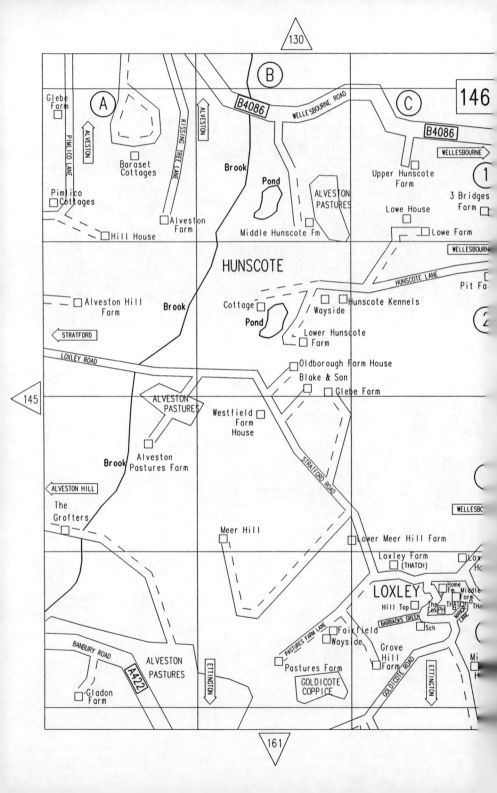

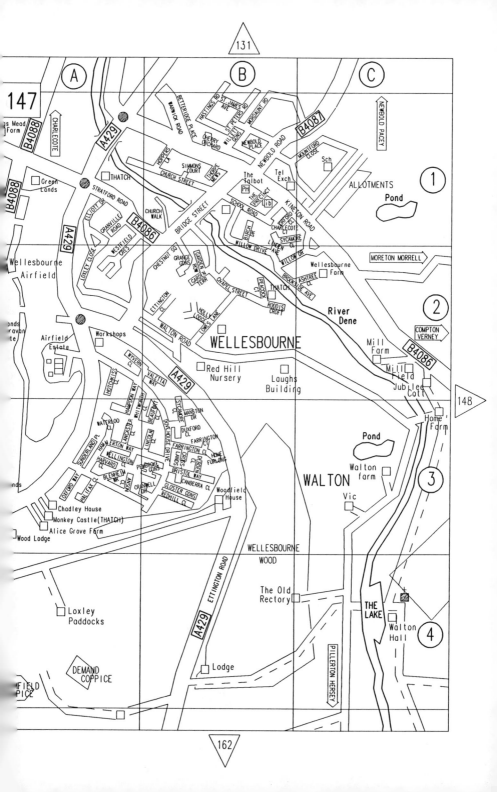

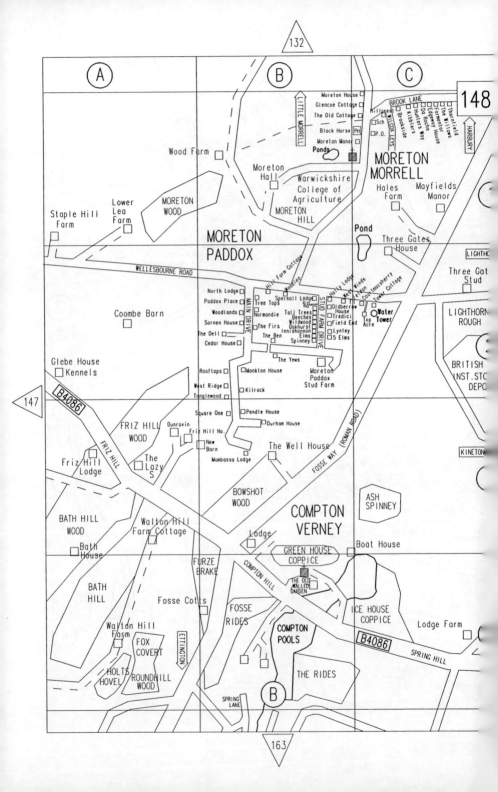

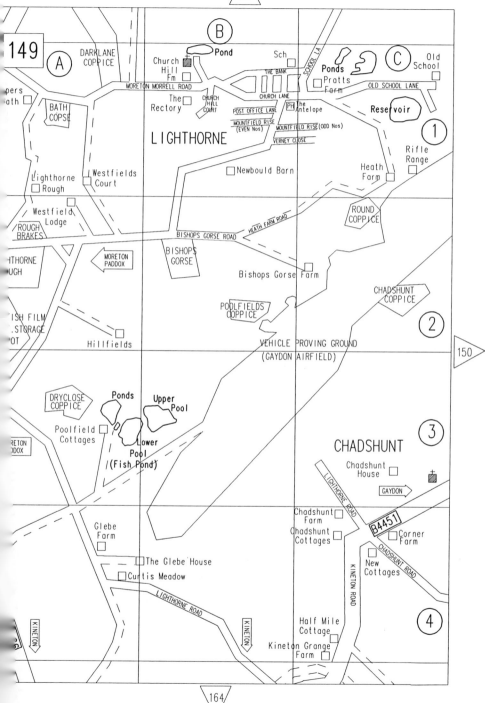

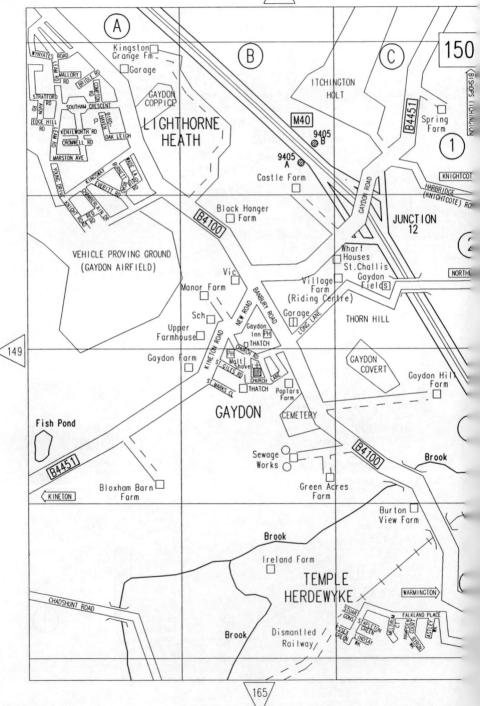

A

B

C

1

149

165

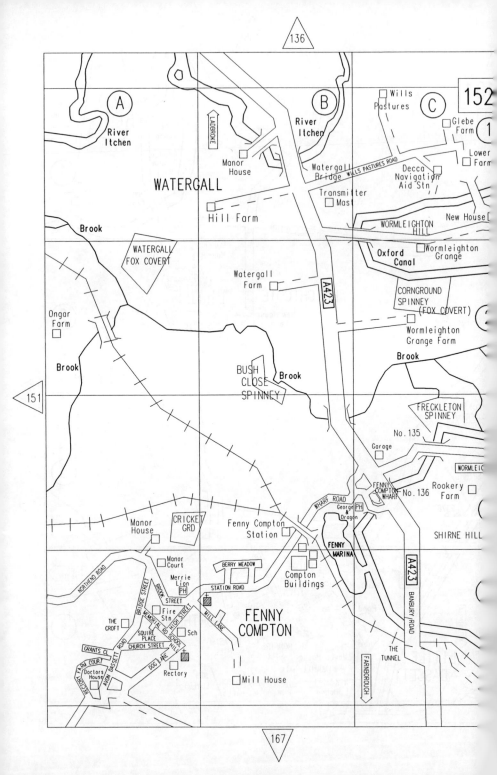

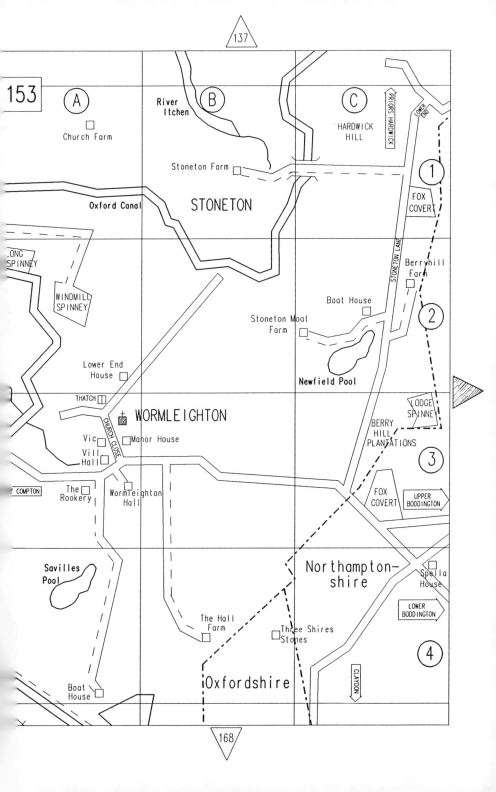

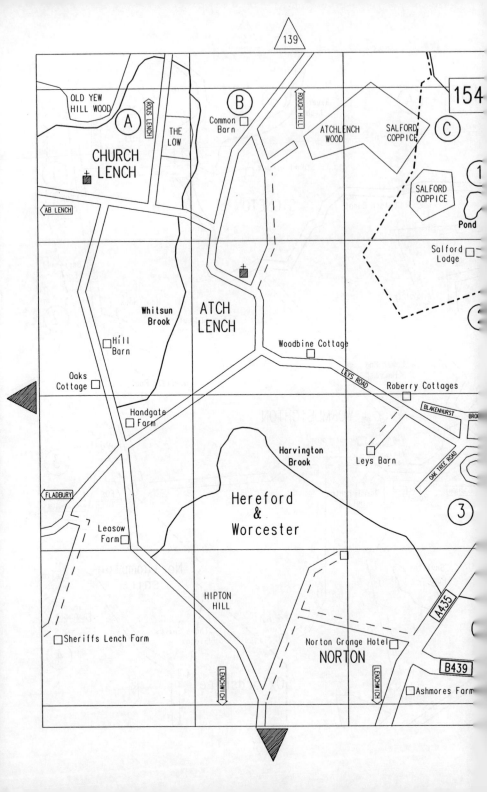

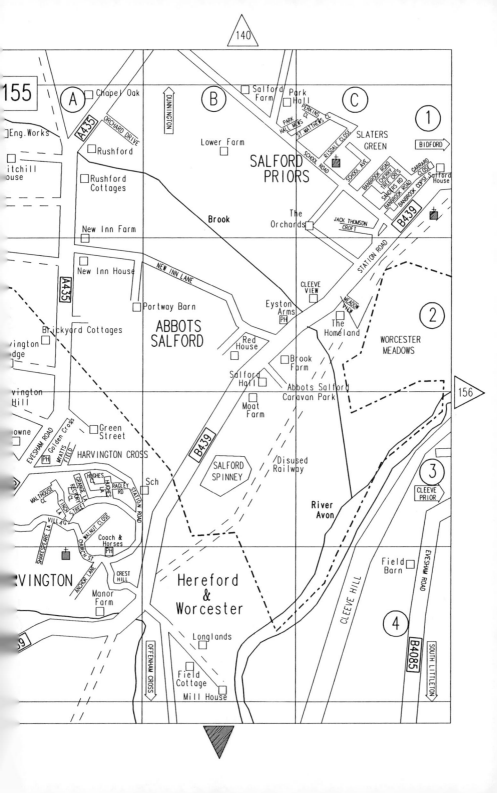

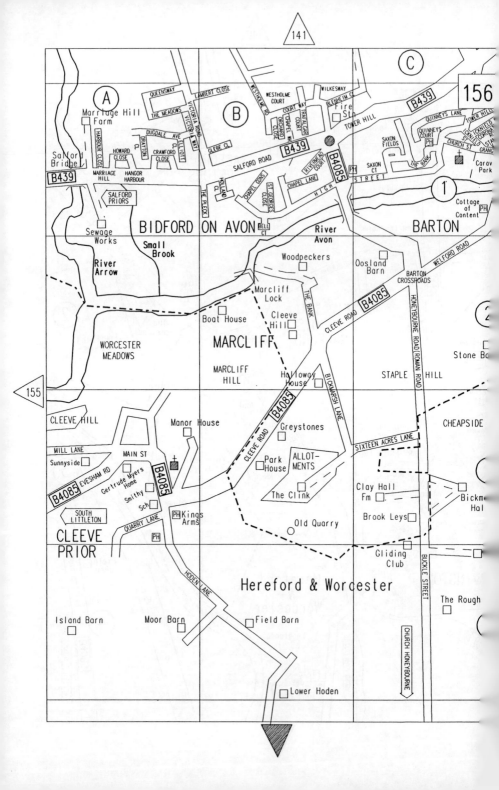

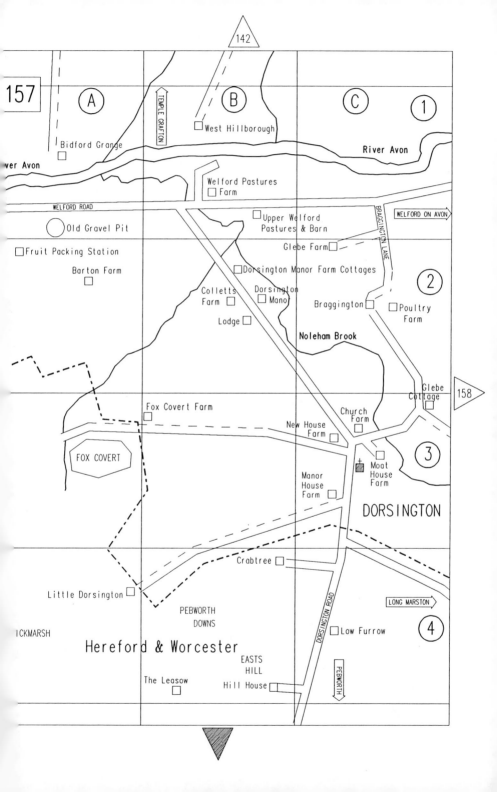

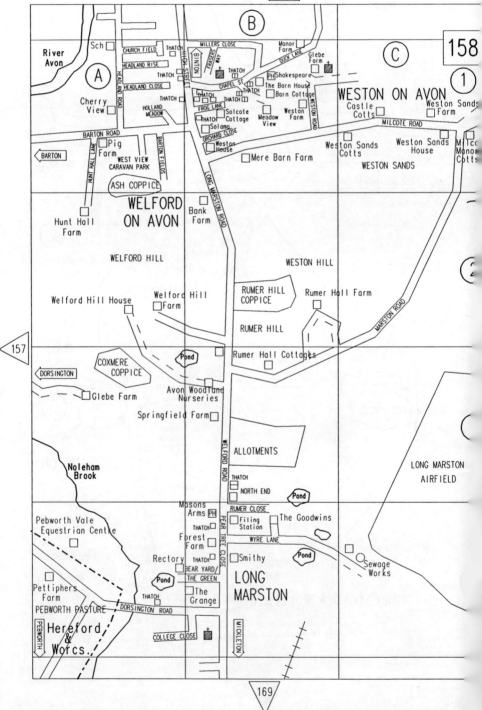

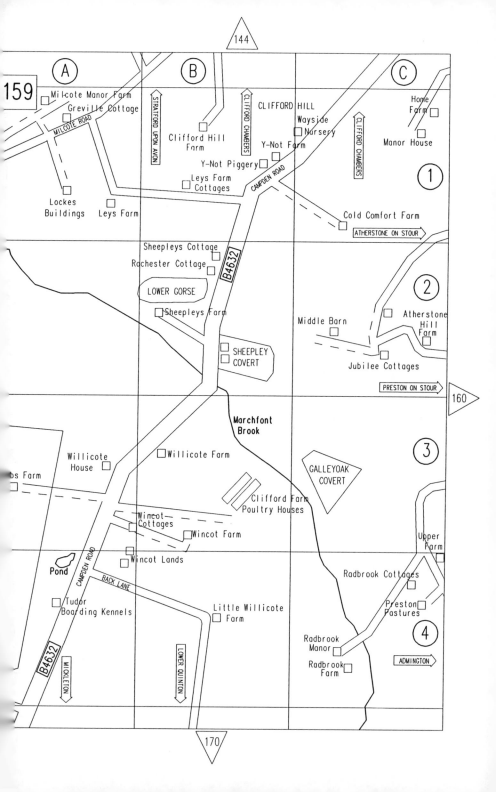

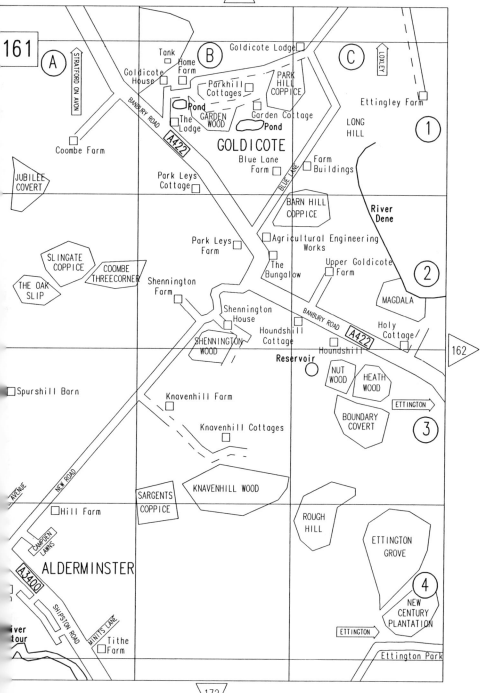

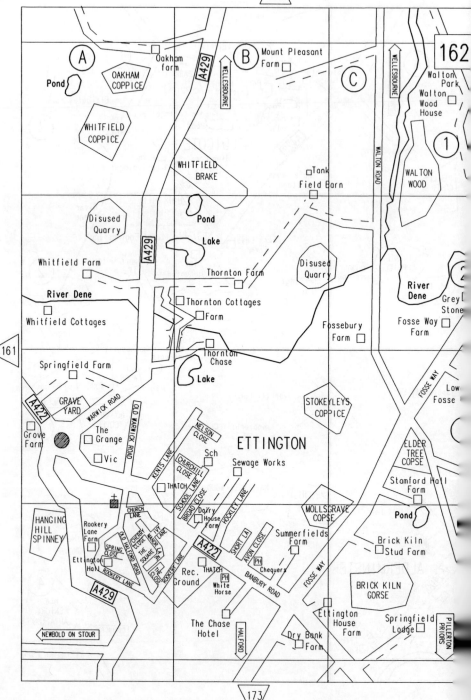

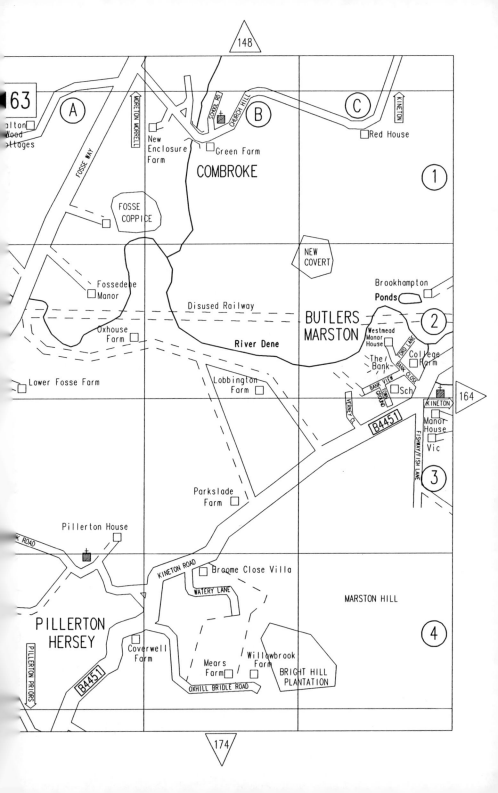

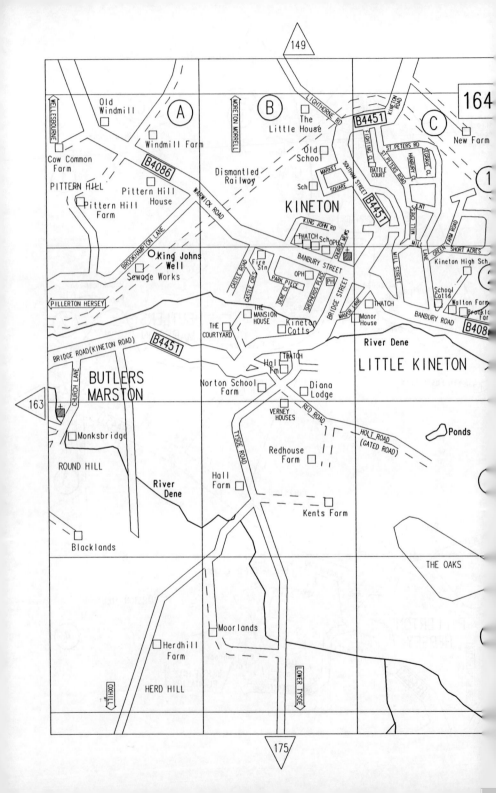

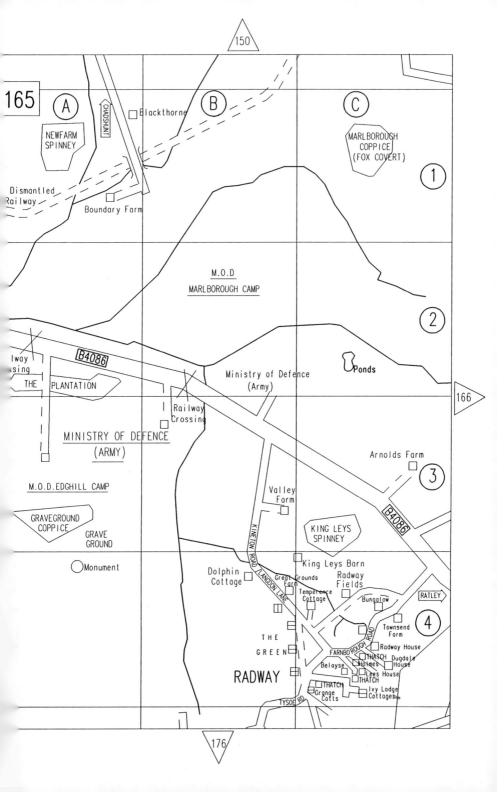

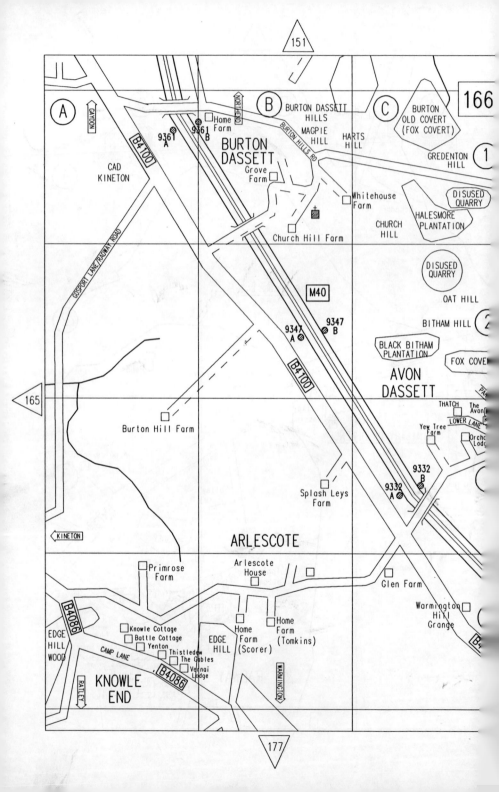

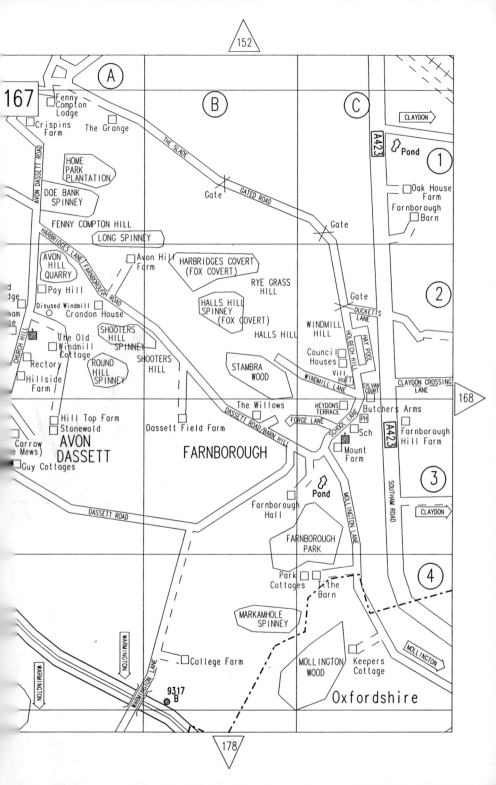

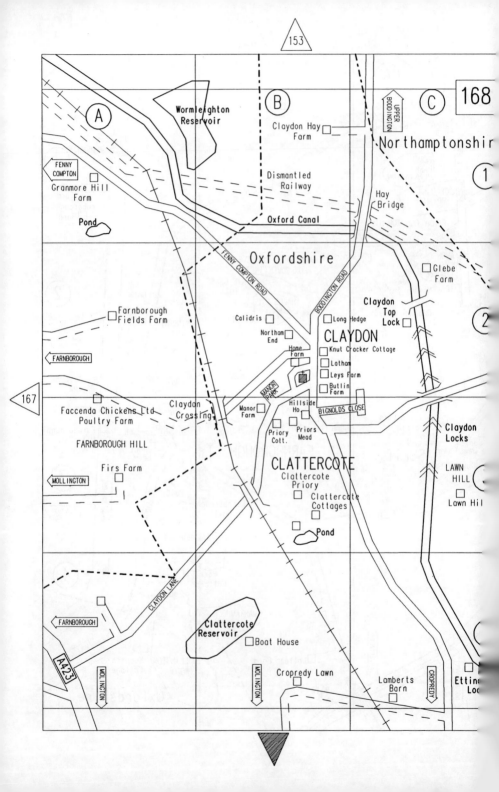

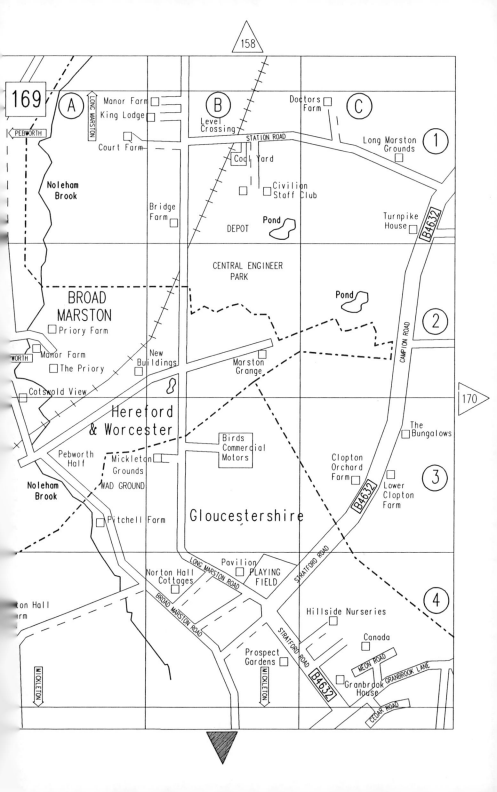

A   B   WARDS HILL   C

ETTINGTON

Rowan Cottage

ALDERMINSTER

Barton Farm

WARDS HILL COPPICE

Birchfurlong Cottages

Hill View

Eversfield

ETTINGTON ROAD

Reservoir

ETTINGTON PARK

STRATFORD ROAD

A3400

River Stour

Lower Andrews Farm

Lodge

The Elms

Upthorpe Farm

Ettington Park Hotel

1

Manor Fm

TALTON ROAD

Talton House

Talton Mill Farm

Browetts

Crimscote Hill

CRIMSCOTE

OULSTONS COPPICE

MILL LANE

Newbold Wharf Cottages

NEWBOLD ON STOUR

BROAD LESSOR COPPICE

Talton Farm

Park Edge

ALLOTMENTS

Lodge

A3400

CHAPEL LA

PH

HANDS PADDOCK

River Stour

MIDDLEFIELD LANE

War Memorial

ROOKERY LA

PARK VIEW

Rectory

BROOK LANE

Newbold Ho.

Newbold Corn Mill (Disused)

2

Talton Cottages

MOSS LANE

Sc

PH

Bird in the Hand

MAIN ROAD

CHURCH LANE

Church Farm

The Barn

Green Acres

MILL LANE

Pump House

HALFORD

Halford Cottage

THATCH

RINNELL CLOSE

CHURCH ROAD

Middlefield

Mansell Farm

SHIPSTON ROAD

The Mill House

ROMAN WAY

MILL LANE

The Bel PH

Moore Buildings

Stepstones Farm

A3400

Halford Bridge

A4

ARMSCOTE ROAD

R.B.Webb & Sons

A429

Armscote Manor House

Wagon Wheel

Manor Farm

PH

THATCH

HALFORD ROAD

Farm Buildings

Arms Fie Far

Crabtree Farm

THATCH

MIDDLE STREET

THATCH

ARMSCOTE

THATCH

The Channings

Little Chef

ILMINGTON ROAD

Berryfield

Whitegate Farm

Armscote Farm

Armscote Manor (THATCH)

TREDINGTON ROUNDABOUT

THATCH

Police Stn

Garage

A3400

Arms Fie Far

BLACKWELL

BLACKWELL

ARMSCOTE ROAD

TREDINGTON

A429

Orchard House

Fosse Way

Rive Sto

River Stour

171

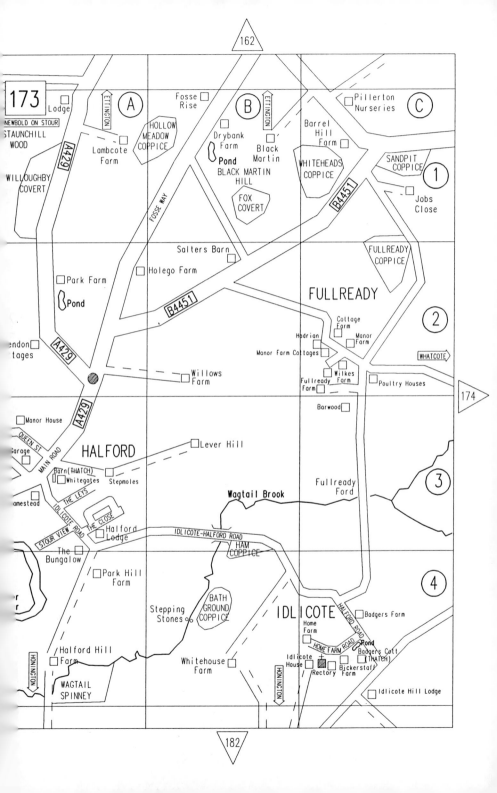

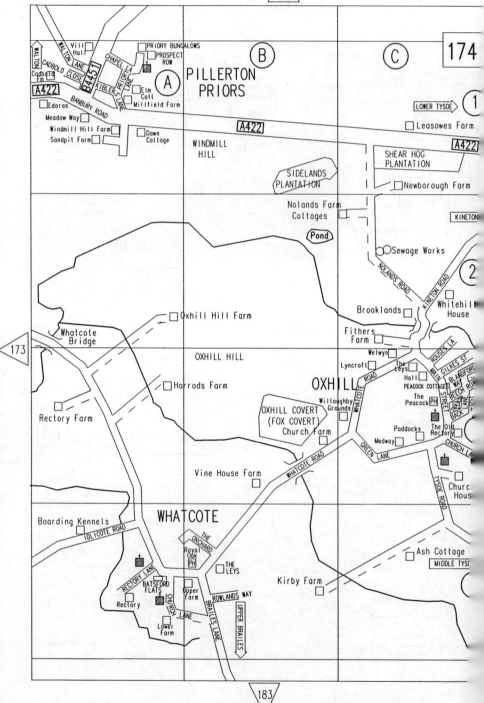

174

B   C

PILLERTON
PRIORS

A

LOWER TYSOE   1

Vill Hall

PRIORY BUNGALOWS
PROSPECT ROW

WALTON
WALTON LANE
CADBOLD CLOSE
Cadbold Fm
A422

CHAPEL LA
KIBLER'S LANE
PRIORY LANE

Elm Cott
Millfield Farm

Edoras
Meadow Way
Windmill Hill Farm
Sandpit Farm
BANBURY ROAD

Dawn Cottage

A422

Leasowes Farm

WINDMILL
HILL

A422

SHEAR HOG
PLANTATION

Newborough Farm

SIDELANDS
PLANTATION

Nolands Farm
Cottages

KINETON

Pond

Sewage Works

NOLANDS ROAD

2

Oxhill Hill Farm

Brooklands

KINETON ROAD

Whitehill
House

Watcote
Bridge

Fithers
Farm

Welwyn

ROUSES LA

173

OXHILL HILL

Lyncroft

The Leys
Hall
PEACOCK COTTAGE

GILKES ST
MAIN STREET
BEECH RO
BLANDFORD WAY
BACK LANE

Harrods Farm

OXHILL

The
Peacock PH

WHATCOTE ROAD

Rectory Farm

OXHILL COVERT
(FOX COVERT)
Church Farm

Willoughby
Grounds

Paddocks
Medway

The Old
Rectory

CHURCH LA

Vine House Farm

GREEN LANE

WHATCOTE ROAD

Churc
Hous

TYSOE ROAD

Boarding Kennels

WHATCOTE

IDLICOTE ROAD

THE ORCHARD

Royal Oak PH

THE LEYS

Kirby Farm

Ash Cottage
MIDDLE TYSO

RECTORY LANE

BATSFORD FLATS

Upper Farm

CHURCH LANE

Rectory

Lower Farm

ROWLANDS WAY

BRAILES LANE

UPPER BRAILES

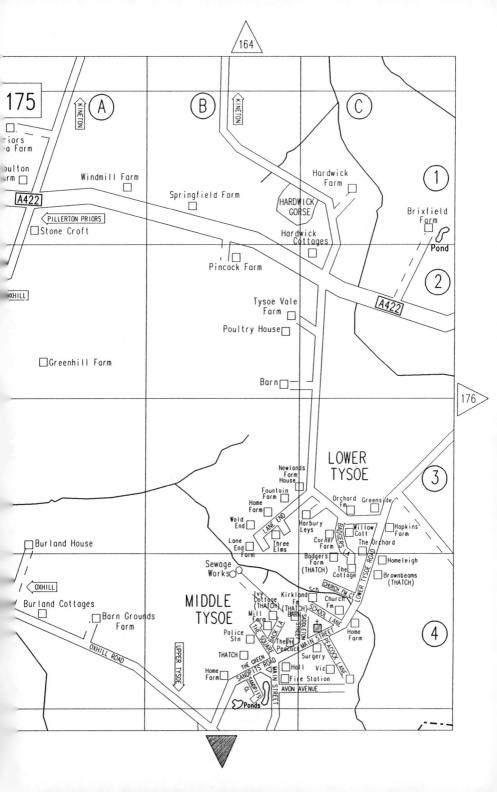

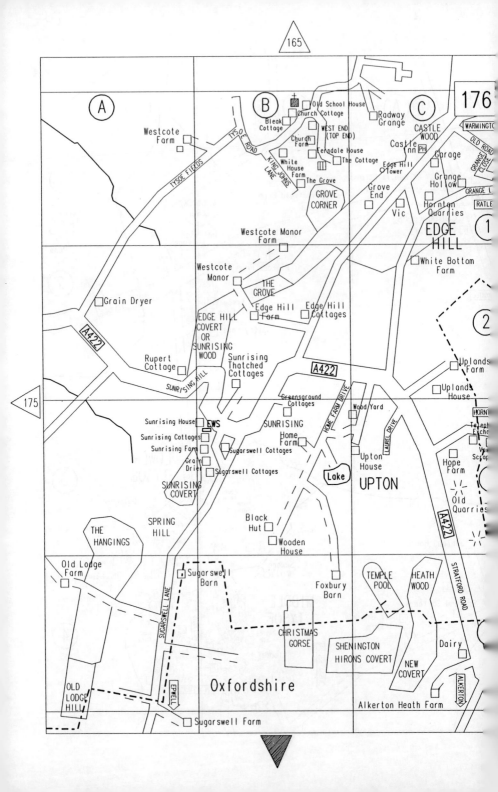

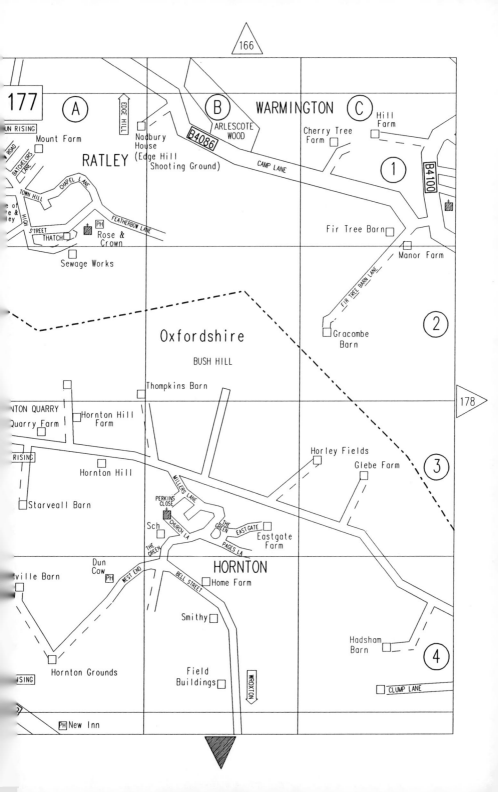

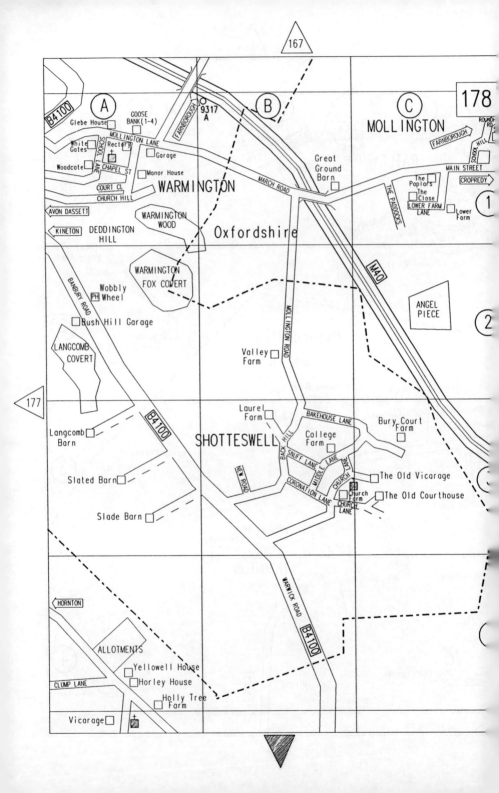

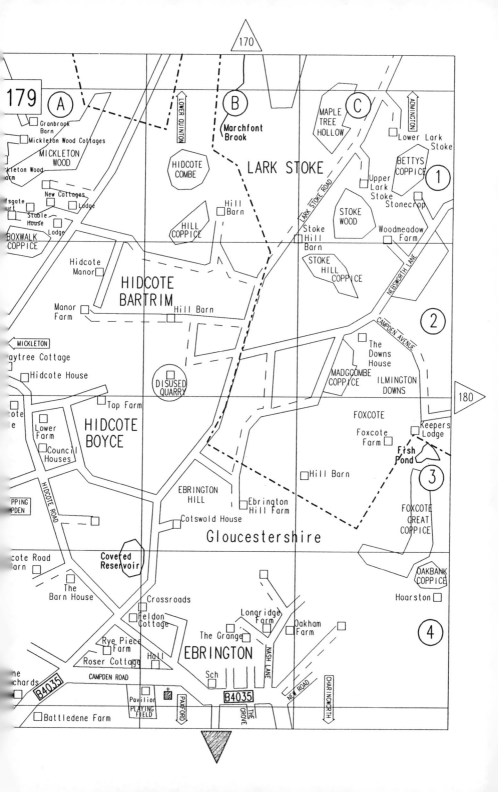

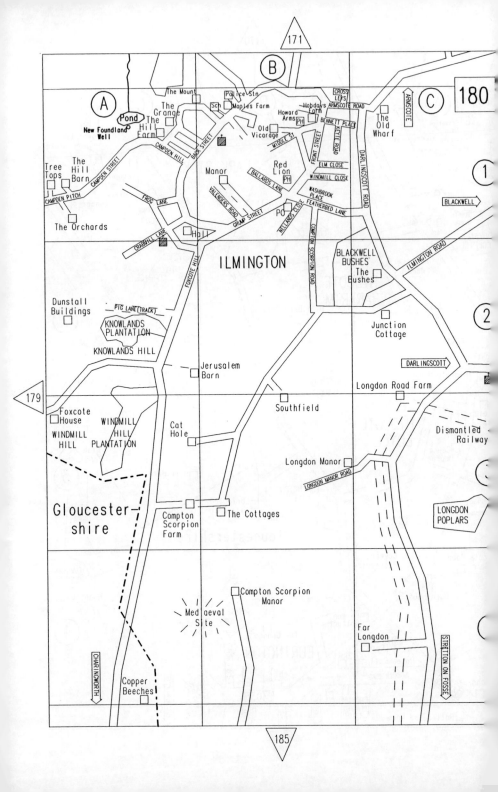

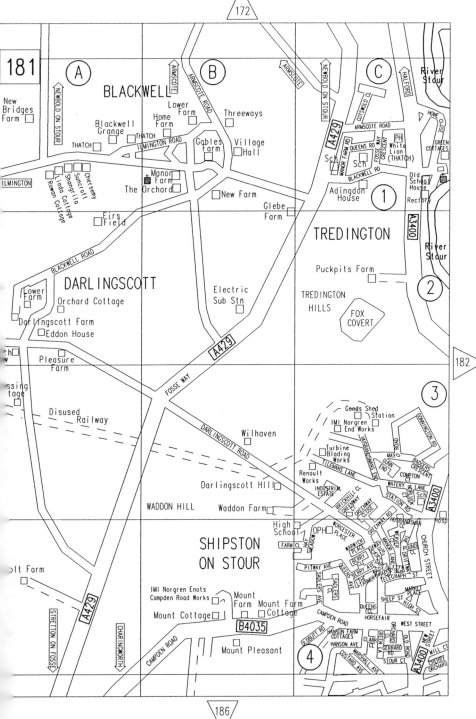

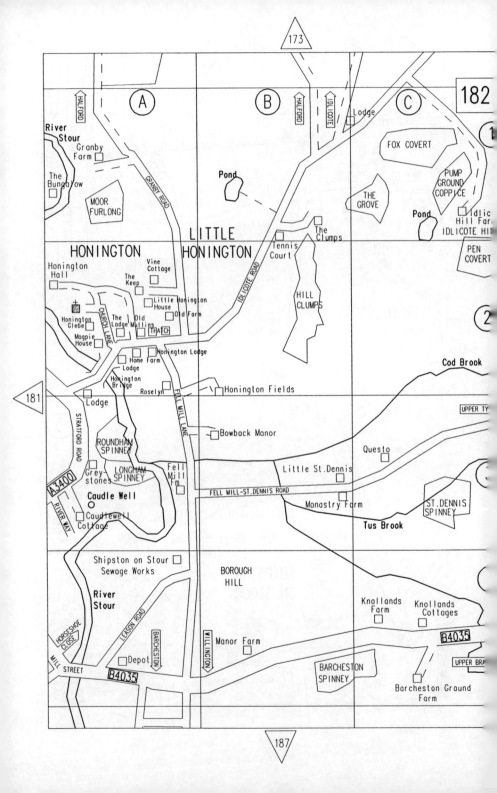

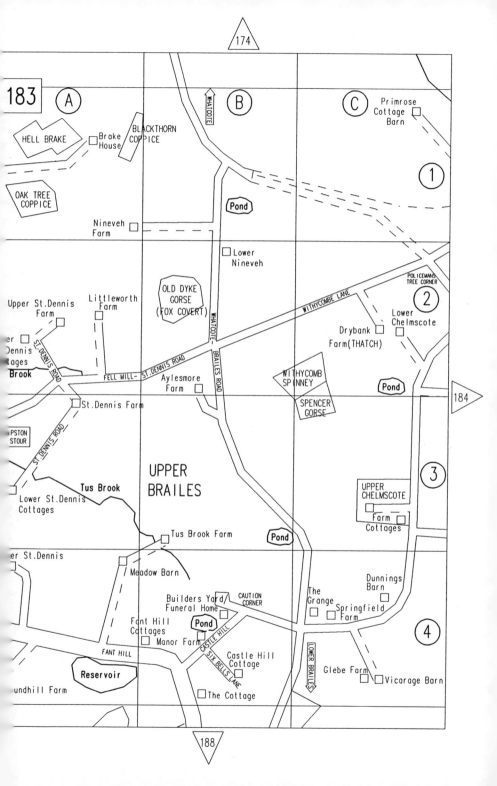

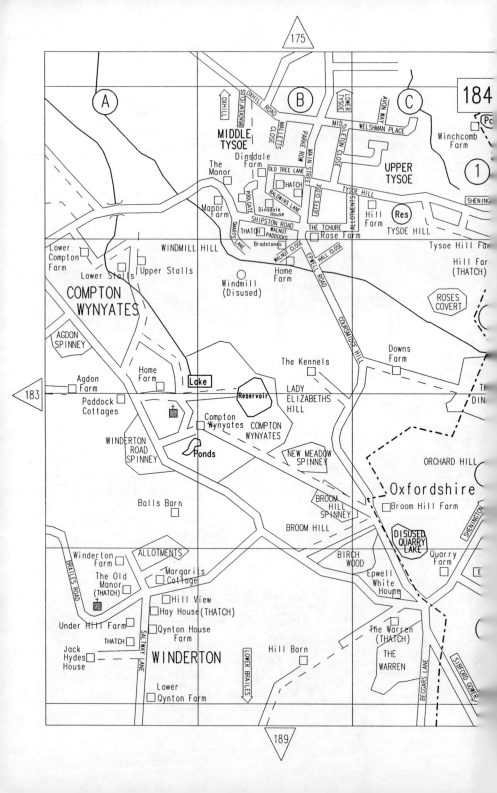

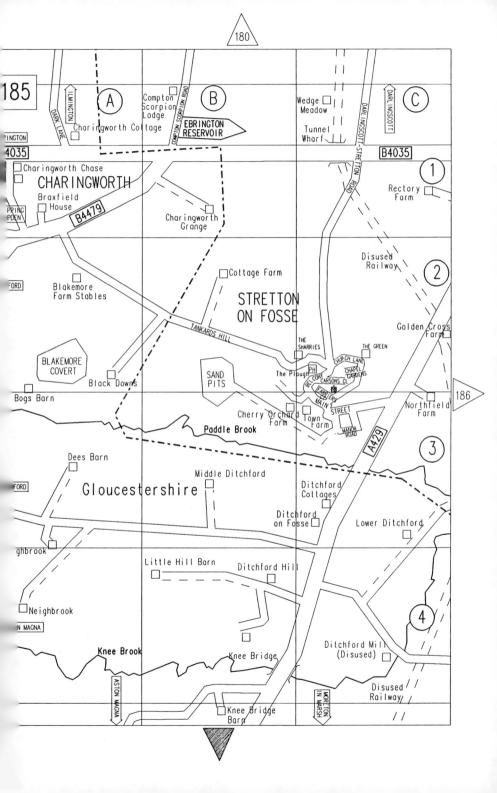

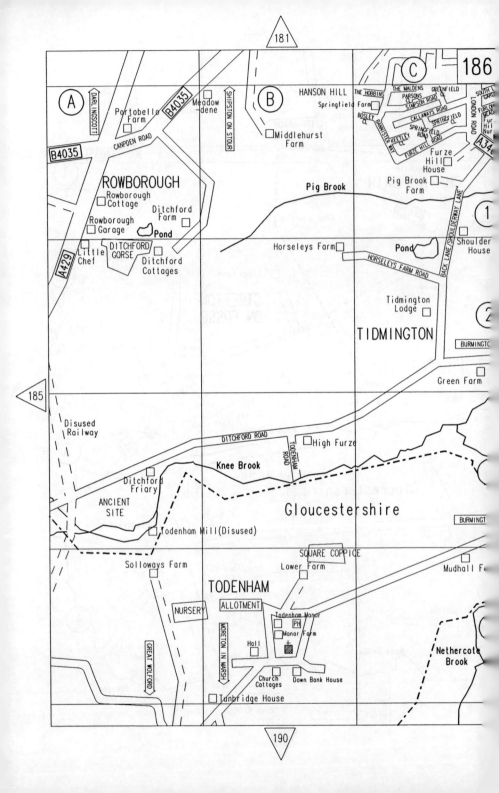

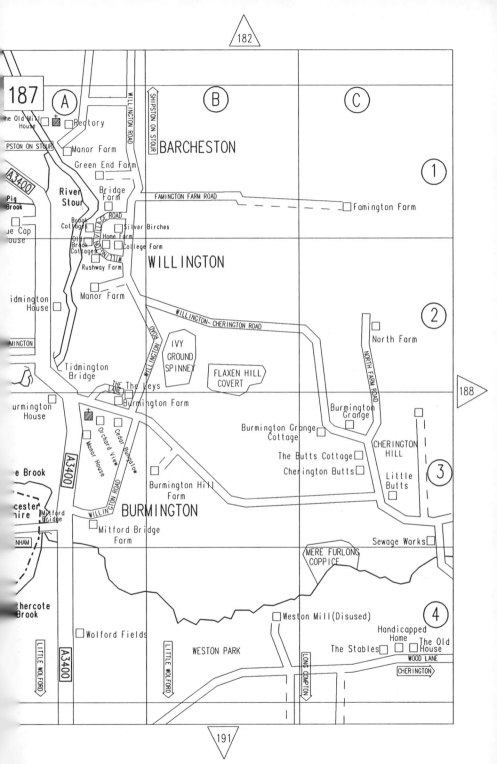

187

(A)   (B)   (C)

The Old Mill House

☩ Rectory

PSTON ON STOUR

Manor Farm

Green End Farm

River Stour

Pig Brook

Bridge Farm

WILLINGTON ROAD

SHIPSTON ON STOUR

BARCHESTON

FAMINGTON FARM ROAD

Famington Farm   (1)

A3400

ue Cap ouse

Brook Cottages

ROAD

Silver Birches

Old Brook Cottages

Home Farm

College Farm

WILLINGTON

Rushway Farm

idmington House

Manor Farm

WILLINGTON~CHERINGTON ROAD

North Farm   (2)

FAMINGTON

WILLINGTON ROAD

IVY GROUND SPINNEY

FLAXEN HILL COVERT

NORTH FARM ROAD

Tidmington Bridge

THE LEYS LANE

The Leys

Burmington Farm

Burmington Grange

188

urmington House

Orchard View

Cedar Bungalow

Manor House

Burmington Grange Cottage

The Butts Cottage

Cherington Butts

CHERINGTON HILL

Little Butts   (3)

e Brook

A3400

WILLINGTON ROAD

Burmington Hill Farm

cester hire

Mitford Bridge

BURMINGTON

Mitford Bridge Farm

NHAM

Sewage Works

thercote Brook

Wolford Fields

LITTLE WOLFORD

A3400

LITTLE WOLFORD

WESTON PARK

MERE FURLONG COPPICE

Weston Mill (Disused)

LONG COMPTON

Handicapped Home

The Stables

The Old House

WOOD LANE

CHERINGTON   (4)

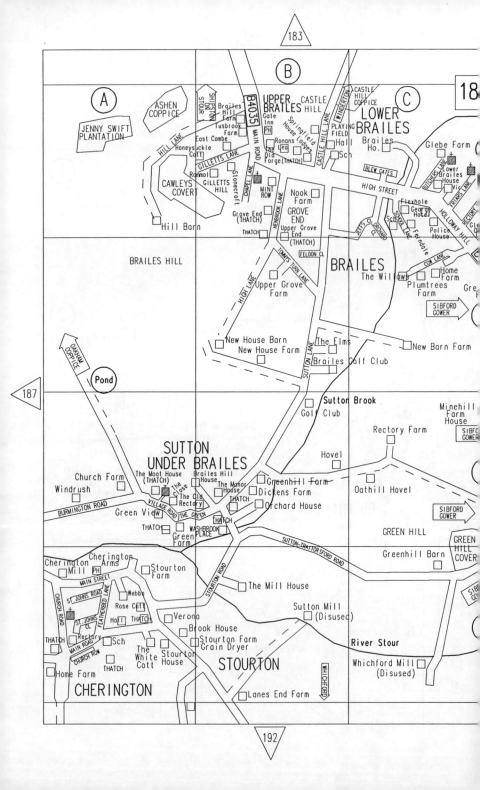

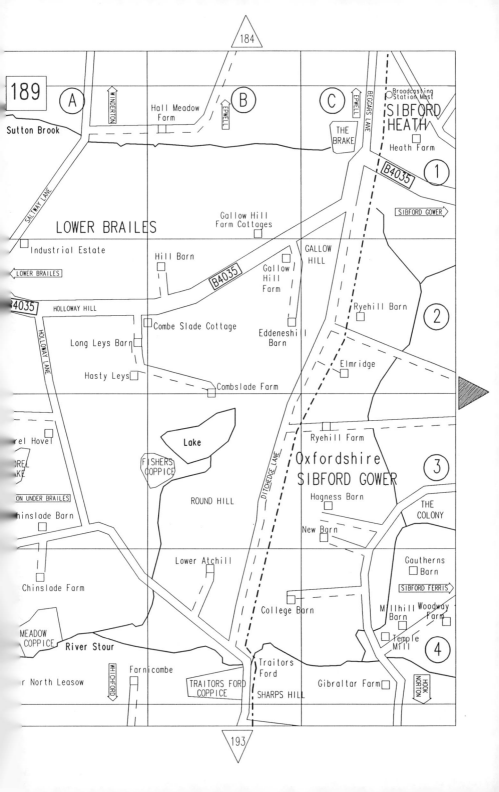

190

A

B

C

1

STRETTON ON FOSSE

BURMINGTON

Rectory

Dunsden Farm

Phillips Farm

Parsonage Barn

Red Barn

Red Mill

TODENHAM

Nethercote Brook

TODENHAM ROAD

Gloucestershire

GREAT WOLFORD

Mount Sorrell

THATCH

Manor Farm

Earthwork

Nethercote Bridge

MORETON IN MARSH

Lower Woodhills

THE GREEN

Sch

Nethercote Cottages

2

Ash House Farm

Moat House Nursery

Nethercote

LEMINGTON COPPICE

The Leys

Vic

Hillside Farm

PH
Fox & Hounds

COOPERS COPPICE

OAK COPPICE

INGRAM CLOSE

Rectory Farm

BARTON HEATH ROAD

WOLFORD WOOD

OLD COVERT

Hill Barn

HOPYARD COPPICE

Stanford Bridge

BARTON ON THE HEATH

Walford Lodge

Flat Heath Barn

Gravels Barn

Leys Farm

Home Farm

WOLFORD HEATH

FURZE BANK COPPICE

Stanford Brook

Lodge

Leyside Cott

Rose Cott

BAKERS FM. ROAD

Rainbow Ho

MORETON IN MARSH

FLAT HEATH

Barton Ho

Church Cott

CAMDEN CL

Four Shire House

GRAVELS COPPICE

Rectory Farm

New Barn

Rectory

LONG COMPTON

North Four Shire Farm

Four Shire Stone

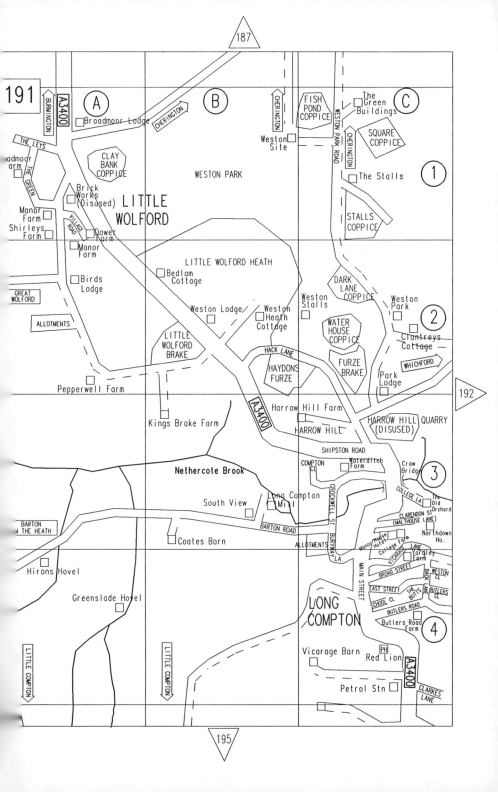

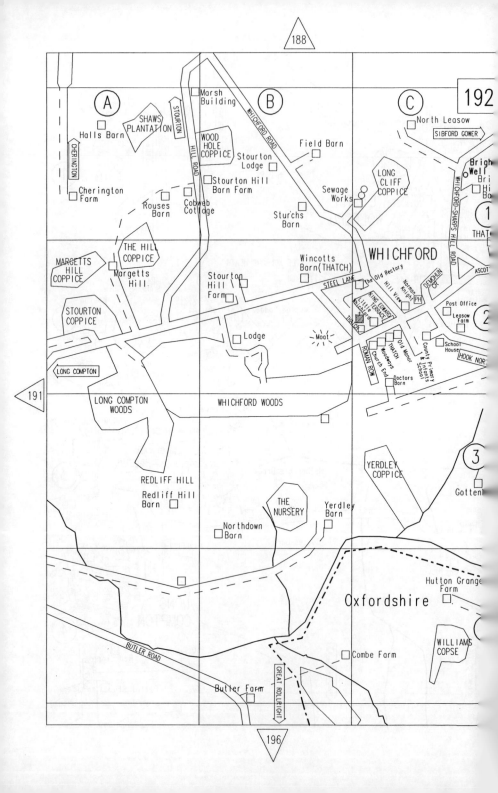

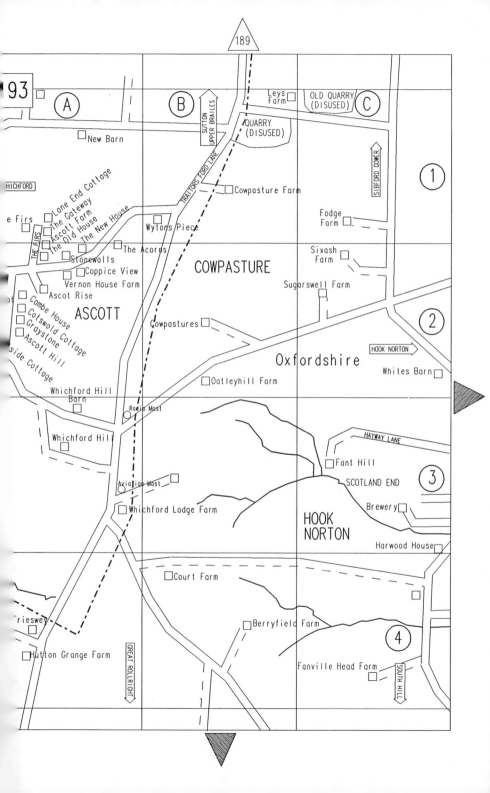

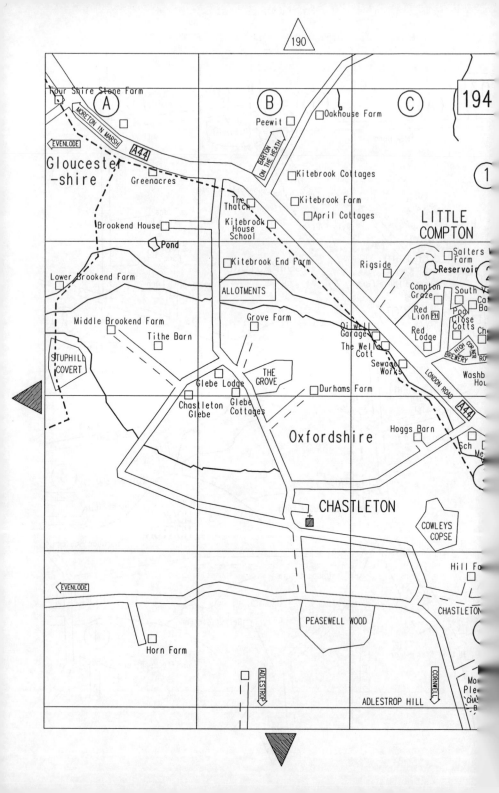

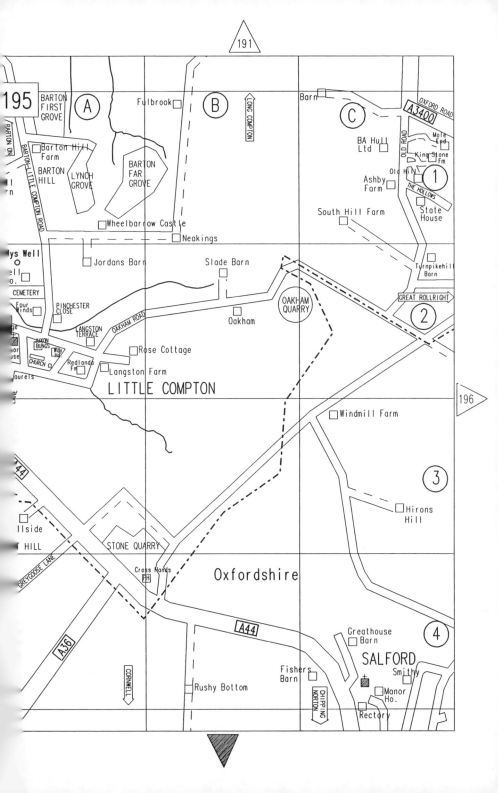

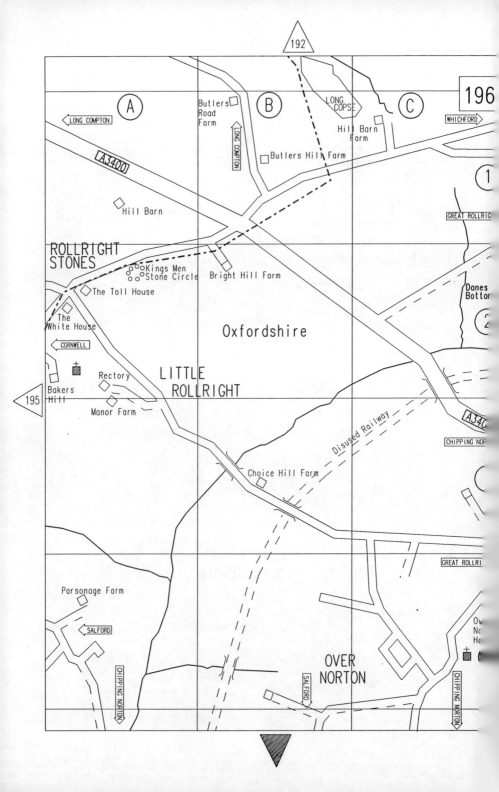

ref	Address	Map ref	Address
14	A34, Atherstone on Stour	133C41	A41, Lighthorne
21	A34, Beaudesert	150A14	A41, Lighthorne Heath, Gaydon
43	A34, Cheswick Green	166A11	A41, Little Dassett, Burton Dassett
43	A34, Hockley Heath, Dorridge	133B33	A41, Redlands Brake, Chesterton
14	A34, Newbold on Stour, Ettington	178A23	A41, Shotteswell
23	A34, Pathlow, Aston Cantlow	177C14	A41, Warmington
21	A3400 Alscot Park, Preston on Stour	114A22	A41, Warwick
41	A3400 Armscote, Tredington	114B24	A41, Warwick by pass
23	A3400 Burmington	78B12	A41, Wroxhall
32	A3400 Clifford Chambers	119A34	A4122, Southam
34	A3400 Drayton	21B11	A4131, Hartshill
14	A3400 Ettington Park, Alderminster	61A42	A4141 Baddesley Clinton
3	A3400 Henley-in-Arden	60B13	A4141 Dorridge
4	A3400 Lapworth	78A11	A4141, Baddesley Clinton
41	A3400 Little Wolford	61A34	A4141, Chadwick End
24	A3400 Long Compton	78C24	A4141, Five Ways
23	A3400 Over Norton	59A12	A4141, Monkspath
43	A3400 Rollright	78C13	A4141, Wroxhall
34	A3400 Shipston on Stour	96A31	A4177 Budbrooke
42	A3400 Stratford upon Avon	95A14	A4177 Haseley
13	A3400 Tidmington	95A11	A4177 Hatton
42	A3400 Wimpstone	95A14	A4177 Hatton Green
3	A3400 Wootton Wawen	96A32	A4177 Junction, Warwick by pass
3	A3400 Bearley	95B41	A4177, Budbrooke
41	A3400 Bearley Cross	78C24	A4177, Five Ways
	A3400 Beaudesert	78C24	A4177, Five Ways, Shrewley
2	A3400, Bishopton	62A34	A4177, Frogmore
	A3400 Buckley Green	79A31	A4177, Haseley
	A3400 Henley in Arden	79A21	A4177, Haseley Knob
	A3400 Hockley Heath	95A22	A4177, Hatton
	A3400 Lapworth	62A44	A4177, Honiley
	A3400 Liveridge Hill	62B23	A4177, Mere End
	A3400 Monkspath	96C42	A4177, Warwick
	A3400 Nuthurst	125B33	A422, Alcester
1	A3400 Pathlow	124A42	A422, Arrow
4	A3400 Wootton Wawen	127A43	A422, Billesley
	A38, Bassetts Pole	124A33	A422, Cook Hill, Inkberrow
	A38, Hints	143A12	A422, Drayton
	A4023, Aspley Heath, Tanworth in Arden	161C32	A422, Ettington
	A4023, Dorridge	161A12	A422, Goldicote, Alderminster
	A4023, Gilberts Green, Tanworth in Arden	125C32	A422, Haselor
	A4023, Hockley Heath, Cheswick Green	175C21	A422, Lower Tysoe, Tysoe
	A4023, Wood End, Tanworth in Arden	175A14	A422, Oxhill
	A4071, Dunchurch	173C11	A422, Pillerton Priors
	A4071, Rugby	176C42	A422, Ratley And Upton
	A4071, Thurlaston	143A12	A422, Red Hill
	A4082, Binley	176C44	A422, Shennington
	A4091, Bodymoor Heath, Middleton	144B14	A422, Stratford upon Avon
	A4091, Drayton Bassett	176A21	A422, Sunrising Hill, Tysoe
	A4091, Moxhull, Wishaw	150C14	A423, Burton Dassett
	A4097, Dunton, Curdworth	136A32	A423, Chapel Ascote
	A4097, Kingsbury	168A43	A423, Claydon
	A4097, Lea Marston	167C12	A423, Farnborough
	A41, Avon Dassett	152C43	A423, Fenny Compton
	A41, Hanwell	84C31	A423, Frankton
	A41, Harwoods House	150C13	A423, Gaydon
	A41, Kineton	136A12	A423, Ladbroke
		101A34	A423, Long Itchington
		84C34	A423, Marton

Map ref	Address
84C21	A423, Princethorpe
66B14	A423, Ryton on Dunsmore
119A33	A423, Southam
84B12	A423, Stretton on Dunsmore
66B22	A423, Toll Bar End
152B12	A423, Watergall
152C33	A423, Wormleighton
62C22	A425, Burton Green, Kenilworth
62C21	A425, Frogmore
97C41	A425, Leamington Spa
121A24	A425, Lower Shuckburgh
62C21	A425, Mere End
97A42	A425, Myton, Leamington Spa
120B32	A425, Napton on The Hill
98C41	A425, Radford Semele
119B24	A425, Southam
122C31	A425, Staverton
118B32	A425, Stoneythorpe, Long Itchington
115A13	A425, The Asps, Bishops Tachbrook
117B13	A425, Ufton
96B32	A425, Warwick
31A13	A4254, Nuneaton
101C34	A426, Birdingbury Wharf, Birdingbury
102A23	A426, Broadwell
54A43	A426, Brownsover, Rugby
49C43	A426, Churchover
49C42	A426, Cotesbach
86C44	A426, Kites Hardwick
101C32	A426, Leamington Hastings
119A22	A426, Southam
87A34	A426, Thurlaston
87B12	A426, Toft, Dunchurch
97A11	A426, Warwick
50A21	A427, Binley
50A22	A427, Binley Woods
46C44	A427, Brinklow
51A14	A427, Coombe Fields
54B12	A427, Gibbet Hill, Rugby
48B24	A427, Little Walton, Pailton
49A12	A427, Lutterworth
47B24	A427, Monks Kirby
47A34	A427, Newbold Revel
47A33	A427, Street Ashton, Stretton Under Fosse
50A31	A428, Binley
51B34	A428, Bretford
52A43	A428, Church Lawford
73B42	A428, Crick
72A31	A428, Hillmorton, Rugby
73A34	A428, Kilsby
69C12	A428, Long Lawford
71A14	A428, Rugby
51B42	A428, Wolston
172C42	A429, Armscote
114A33	A429, Barford
64C13	A429, Canley, Coventry
181B31	A429, Darlingscott, Tredington
185C33	A429, Ditchford
162A44	A429, Ettington

Map ref	Address
64B23	A429, Gibbet Hill, Coventry
97A13	A429, Guys Cliffe
173A31	A429, Halford
63C42	A429, Kenilworth
114B21	A429, Longbridge
147B31	A429, Loxley
185B44	A429, Moreton in The Marsh
147A22	A429, Mountford, Wellesbourne
186A11	A429, Rowborough, Stretton on Fo
114A24	A429, Sherbourne
131B23	A429, Thelsford, Charlecote
96C32	A429, Warwick
131B14	A429, Wasperton
152B12	A432, Watergall
74B23	A435, Bransons Cross, Beoley
107C42	A435, Coughton
140B32	A435, Dunnington, Salford Priors
57A33	A435, Forshaw Heath, Tanworth i Arden
90A12	A435, Gorcott, Studley
155A23	A435, Harvington
140B43	A435, Iron Cross
125A21	A435, Kings Coughton, Alcester
141A13	A435, Kingsley Corner, Arrow
90B23	A435, Mappleborough Green
154C42	A435, Norton
74B33	A435, Pink Green
155A11	A435, Pitchill
57A43	A435, Portway
107C34	A435, Spernall, Sambourne
195A34	A436, Chastleton
195B32	A436, Little Compton
195C24	A436, Little Rollright, Long Comp
195C23	A436, Salford
155C21	A439, Abbotts Salford, Salford P
141C43	A439, Bidford
130A13	A439, Blackhill
143C32	A439, Dodwell, Luddington
155A43	A439, Harvington
129B31	A439, Ingon
143B31	A439, Lower Binton, Binton
113A44	A439, Marraway Turn
155A42	A439, Norton
144C22	A439, Stratford upon Avon
142A42	A439, Temple Grafton
194A12	A44, Kitebrook, Little Compton
195B41	A44, Salford
124A41	A441, Arrow
124A22	A441, Cook Hill, Inkberrow
140B32	A441, Dunnington
40B32	A441, Salford Priors
140A24	A441, Weethley, Alcester
126B41	A442, Haselor
82A33	A444, Bericote, Ashow
30A32	A444, Bermuda
81C42	A444, Blackdown
22A22	A444, Caldecote
30B21	A444, Coten
39C33	A444, Exhall, Bedworth

Map ref	Address	Map ref	Address
32	A444, Fenny Drayton	63B31	A452, Burton Green
21	A444, Finham	34B11	A452, Chelmsley Wood
42	A444, Griff, Nuneaton	81B31	A452, Chesford, Leek Wootton
22	A444, Heath End	115A24	A452, Heathcote, Leamington Spa
11	A444, Higham, Higham on The Hill	81A22	A452, Kenilworth
31	A444, Kings Hill, Stoneleigh	24A42	A452, Kingshurst
42	A444, Neals Green	61B14	A452, Mere End
11	A444, Redgate	81C44	A452, Milverton
4	A444, Sheepy	115B11	A452, Whitnash
43	A444, Sutton Stop, Coventry	9A14	A453, Hints
1	A444, Weddington	1B42	A453, No Mans Heath, Newton Regis
42	A445, Cubbington		
32	A445, Emscote, Warwick	3A11	A453, Seckington
21	A445, Leamington Spa	9A22	A453, Sutton Coldfield
33	A445, Ryton on Dunsmore	2A21	A453, Thorpe Constantine
4	A445, Stoneleigh	45A43	A46 Coventry Eastern by pass, Binley, Coventry
3	A445, Waverley Woods, Bubbenhall		
1	A4455, Milverton, Leamington	45A24	A46, Anstey
2	A446 T, Curdworth	66A12	A46, Binley
4	A446 T, Jack O Watton, Water Orton	45A32	A46, Binley Woods
	A446, Allen End	129C24	A46, Blackhill, Hampton Lucy
	A446, Bassetts Pole	144A12	A46, Drayton, Stratford upon Avon
1	A446, Coleshill Pool	112B44	A46, Hampton Lucy
	A446, Dunton, Curdworth	159A42	A46, High Cross, Claybrook
	A446, Jack O Watton, Water Orton	64C34	A46, Kenilworth
	A446, Lea Marston, Coleshill	80C41	A46, Leek Wootton
1	A446, Little Packington	169C14	A46, Long Marston
	A446, Middleton	114A21	A46, Longbridge
	A446, Moxhull, Wishaw	170A11	A46, Lower Quinton, Quinton
	A446, Wishaw	113B41	A46, Marraway Turn, Fulbrook
	A447, Wolvey	113A44	A46, Marraway Turn, Norton Lindsey
4	A448, Sambourne	169C33	A46, Mickleton
4	A448, Spernall, Studley	113C31	A46, Sherbourne
	A45 Island, Warwick by pass	113B34	A46, Sherbourne Hill
	A45 Junction, Warwick by pass	129B14	A46, Snitterfield
	A45, Baginton	65A32	A46, Stoneleigh
	A45, Bickenhill	66A12	A46, Toll Bar End
	A45, Blue Boar Corner	114A22	A46, Warwick
2	A45, Braunston	66A12	A46, Willenhall Binley
	A45, Coventry	65B12	A46, Willenhall Binley, Coventry
	A45, Dordon	129B13	A46, Wilmcote
	A45, Dunchurch	45A23	A4600, Anstey
	A45, Grandborough	45A33	A4600, Walsgrave on Sowe
	A45, Great Packington	81A24	A462, Leek Wootton
	A45, Hall End, Dordon	19C41	A47, Ansley
	A45, Ryton on Dunsmore	21B34	A47, Camphill
	A45, Stonebridge	34B11	A47, Chelmsley Wood
	A45, Stretton on Dunsmore	23B34	A47, Hinckley
	A45, Thurlaston	23B33	A47, Long Shoot, Nuneaton
	A45, Toll Bar End	25A34	A47, Shustoke, Coleshill
	A45, Willenhall Binley	23A41	A47, Weddington
	A45, Willoughby	14C32	A5, Atherstone
	A452 Ashorne	22A13	A5, Caldecote
	A452 Bishops Tachbrook	49C34	A5, Churchover
	A452 Greys Mallory	44C34	A5, Claybrook Parva
	A452 Oakley Wood	55C43	A5, Clifton upon Dunsmore
	A452, Balsall Common	73B33	A5, Crick
	A452, Bickenhill	49A12	A5, Cross in Hand, Monks Kirby
	A452, Blackdown	49C42	A5, Gibbet Hill, Rugby

Map ref	Address
5B42	A5, Hall End, Dordon
15B44	A5, Hartshill
22C21	A5, Higham on The Hill
73A13	A5, Hillmorton
14B23	A5, Innage Park Estate, Grendon
73A33	A5, Kilsby
72C11	A5, Lilbourne
15B41	A5, Mancetter
14B23	A5, Merevale
55B31	A5, Newton And Biggin
22A11	A5, Redgate, Nuneaton
33B31	A5, Smockington, Hinckley
5B42	A5, Stoneydelph, Tamworth
44B13	A5, Wibtoft
44C34	A5, Willey
5A42	A5, Winecote
32C13	A5, Wolvey
73B33	A5, Yelvertoft
11B31	A51, Cliff, Kingsbury
26A14	A51, Furnace End, Over Whitacre
400B43	A600, Southern District
5B23	Abberly, Stoneydelph, Tamworth
125A23	Abbey Close, Alcester
119A32	Abbey Close, Southam
6A22	Abbey Croft, Polesworth
80C12	Abbey End, Kenilworth
78B12	Abbey Farm Cottage, Wroxhall
81C21	Abbey Farm, Ashow
58A43	Abbey Farm, Tanworth in Arden
32C32	Abbey Farm, Wolvey
78B12	Abbey Farm, Wroxhall
90A43	Abbeyfields Drive, Studley
6A31	Abbey Green Court, Polesworth
22A44	Abbey Green, Nuneaton
51C24	Abbey Hall Farm, Kings Newnham
63C44	Abbey Hill, Kenilworth
119A32	Abbey Lane, Southam
22A44	Abbey Street, Nuneaton
54B43	Abbey Street, Rugby
6A32	Abbey View, St Helena, Polesworth
90A43	Abbeyfields Drive, Studley
50B41	Abbots Walk, Binley Woods
51A44	Abbots Walk, Wolston
96B42	Abbots Way, Forbes Estate, Warwick
90A13	Abbots Wood Close, Redditch
30C31	Abbotsford Road, Nuneaton
97C34	Abbott Street, Leamington Spa
71C22	Abbotts Way, Rugby
14B21	Abeles Way, Innage Park Estate, Grendon
14B21	Abelesway, Atherstone
5A13	Abelia, Amington Ind.Est., Tamworth
30C23	Aberdeen Road, Nuneaton
22C32	Abingdon Way, Saint Nicholas Park, Nuneaton
40B14	Acacia Crescent, Bedworth
71A11	Acacia Grove, Rugby
21C44	Acacia Road, Camphill, Nuneaton

Map ref	Address
97B23	Acacia Road, Milverton, Leamington Spa
110B11	Acklam Gardens, Wootton Wawen
65A34	Acorn Close, Stoneleigh
98A21	Acorn Court, Lillington, Leamington Spa
70B31	Acorn Drive, Bilton
70A21	Acorn Drive, Long Lawford
27A24	Acorn Farm, Devitts Green, Arley
27B23	Acorn Hill, Devitts Green, Arley
116A13	Acre Close, Whitnash
70C13	Adams Street, New Bilton, Rugby
64A43	Adcock Drive, Kenilworth
39A41	Addenbrook Road, Keresley Newland Keresley
96C24	Addingham Close, Woodloes, War
21A43	Addison Close, Galley Common, Nuneaton
21A43	Addison Close, Robinsons End, Nuneaton
24A14	Addison Place, Water Orton
70C13	Addison Road, New Bilton, Rugby
39C22	Adelaide Court, Bedworth
97C31	Adelaide Road, Leamington Spa
87B11	Adkinson Avenue, Dunchurch
170C41	Admington Lane Farm, Admington
170C41	Admington Lane, Admington
170B41	Admington Lane, Colemans Hill, Quinton
170C41	Admington Road, Admington
170A14	Admington Road, Lower Quinton Stratford upon Avon
170C14	Admington Road, Preston on Stow
166A11	Administration Block, Marlborough Site, Kineton
70B23	Admirals Court, Rugby
97C33	Adrians Court, Leamington Spa
145A11	Adrians Court, Stratford upon A
184A23	Agdon Farm, Winderton, Brailes
148B13	Agricultural College, Moreton M
107B14	Agustine Avenue, Studley Comn Studley
160B14	Ailstone Farm Old Airfield, Ailst Atherstone on Stour
160B14	Ailstone Farm, Ailstone, Atherst Stour
40A12	Aintree Close, Collycroft, Nunea
144B24	Aintree Close, Stratford upon A
98B13	Aintree Drive, Lillington, Leami Spa
144B24	Aintree Road, Stratford upon A
147A23	Airfield Estate, Mountford, Wellesbourne
111B42	Airfield Farm, Bearley
55A43	Alan Close, Clifton upon Dunsr
55A43	Alan Lane, Clifton upon Dunsr
39B31	Alandale Court, Goodyears End Bedworth
125B23	Alauna Avenue, Alcester

Map ref	Address	Map ref	Address
B23	Alauna Avenue, Kinwarton	71A14	Alexandra Walk, Rugby
B32	Albany Court, Alcester	65B13	Alfirston Road, Finham
C22	Albany Place, Stratford upon Avon	165C43	Alford House, Radway
C22	Albany Road, Stratford upon Avon	71A21	Alfred Green Close, Rugby
24	Albany Terrace, Leamington Spa	70C14	Alfred Street, Rugby
C13	Albert Close, Studley	39C23	Alice Close, Exhall, Bedworth
14	Albert Square, Rugby	147A33	Alice Grove Farm, Mountford,
23	Albert Street, Milverton, Leamington		Wellesbourne
	Spa	176C44	Alkerton Heath Farm, Shennington
14	Albert Street, Rugby	31A13	Alliance Close, Nuneaton
21	Albert Street, Stockingford, Nuneaton	52A21	All Oaks Lane, Cathiron, Brinklow
34	Albert Street, Warwick	42C44	All Saints Close, Withybrook
A13	Albert Terrace, Stratford upon Avon	39C23	All Saints Road, Exhall, Bedworth
13	Albion Cottage, Water Orton	97A23	All Saints Road, Percy Estate, Warwick
43	Albion Street, Kenilworth	40B21	All Saints Square, Bedworth
33	Albion Terrace, Broom, Bidford	125B32	Allcocks Road, Alcester
14	Albion Terrace, Water Orton	107C23	Allen Close, Studley
22	Albury Road, Studley	107C23	Allen Dale Avenue, Tomstown,
13	Alcester Heath Farm, Alcester		Studley
13	Alcester Heath, Alcester	107C23	Allen Dale Crescent, Studley
24	Alcester Hospital, Kinwarton, Alcester	9C42	Allen End Farm, Allen End, Middleton
14	Alcester Park Farm, Alcester	107B24	Allendale Court, Studley
13	Alcester Park Farm, Coughton	13B32	Allens Close, Baddesley Ensor
32	Alcester Road, Dunnington	53C42	Allesley Road, Newbold on Avon,
31	Alcester Road, Little Alne, Aston		Rugby
	Cantlow	31A13	Alliance Close, Nuneaton
3	Alcester Road, Portway, Tanworth in	116A13	Allibone Close, Whitnash, Leamington
	Arden		Spa
11	Alcester Road, Red Hill	64A44	Allitt Grove, Kenilworth
14	Alcester Road, Stratford upon Avon	125C31	Allwoods Close, Alcester
13	Alcester Road, Studley	44B11	Alma House, Wibtoft
22	Alcester Road, Wootton Wawen	65B41	Almhouses, Stoneleigh
3	Alder Court, Atherstone	21B41	Almond Avenue, Camphill, Nuneaton
	Alder Drive, Chelmsley Wood	97C14	Almond Avenue, Leamington Spa
3	Alderbrook Drive, Attleborough,	53C33	Almond Grove, Newbold on Avon,
	Nuneaton		Rugby
	Alderhanger Farm, Pink Green, Beoley	97A21	Almond Grove, Percy Estate, Warwick
	Alderhanger Lane, Pink Green, Beoley	89B23	Almonds Close, Barby
	Alderhanger Lane, Tanworth in Arden	125B32	Alne Bank Road, Kinwarton
	Alderman Mcdonnell House, Exhall,	92B31	Alne Close, Henley in Arden
	Bedworth	64A41	Alpine Court, Kenilworth
4	Alderminster Farm, Alderminster	160A24	Alscot Park, Atherstone on Stour,
	Alders Gate, Kingsbury		Stratford upon Avon
2	Alders Grove, Lodge Wood Est,	98A41	Althorpe Street, Leamington Spa
	Warwick	2B44	Alvecote Lane, Alvecote, Polesworth
	Alders Lane, Chapel End, Nuneaton	97C13	Alverne Lodge, Leamington Spa
	Alders Lane, Redditch	146A14	Alveston Farm, Stratford upon Avon
	Alders Lane, Wynyates Green	130A33	Alveston Ford Road, Hampton Lucy
2	Alderton Mews, Sydenham Farm	145C24	Alveston Hill Farm, Stratford upon
	Estate, Leamington Spa		Avon
	Aldridge Close, Birchmoor, Polesworth	130A41	Alveston House, Alveston
	Aldwick Close, Leamington Spa	129C42	Alveston Lane, Alveston, Stratford
	Alexander Road, Bedworth		upon Avon
	Alexandra Court, Atherstone	146A32	Alveston Pastures Farm, Stratford
	Alexandra Court, Leamington Spa		upon Avon
	Alexandra Court, Rugby	97C24	Alveston Place, Leamington Spa
2	Alexandra Road, Leamington Spa	65C31	Alvis Test Sheds, Baginton
	Alexandra Road, Rugby	70B33	Alwyn Road, Bilton, Rugby
	Alexandra Street, Nuneaton	97C14	Ambassador Court, Leamington Spa

Map ref	Address
41B22	Amberley Avenue, Ryton, Bedworth
14B41	Ambien Road, Atherstone
40A13	Ambleside Road, Bedworth
22C41	Ambleside Way, Saint Nicholas Par, Nuneaton
54B34	Ambleside, Brownsover, Rugby
97A43	Ambulance Station, Warwick
63C41	Amherst Road, Kenilworth
5B23	Amicombe, Stoneydelph, Tamworth
30A22	Amos Avenue, Coten, Nuneaton
40A11	Amos Jaques Road, Collycroft, Bedworth
98B41	Amroth Mews, Sydenham Farm Estate, Leamington
155A42	Anchor Lane, Harvington
65A12	Anchorway Road, Finham
71A31	Anderson Avenue, Kingsway, Rugby
116A23	Anderson Drive, Whitnash
39B21	Anderton Road, Goodyears End, Bedworth
71A31	Andrews Crescent, Kingsway, Rugby
82A44	Andrews Road, Leamington Spa
98A34	Anfield Court, Leamington Spa
25A41	Angels Mews, Coleshill
24A42	Anglesey Avenue, Kingshurst
80C13	Angless Way, Kenilworth
30B14	Anker Street, Nuneaton
6A31	Anker View, Polesworth
6A21	Ankerside, Polesworth
94C31	Anley Hill Farm, Claverdon
144B21	Ann Hathaways Cottage, Shottery, Stratford upon Avon
47B33	Anns Lane, Stretton Under Fosse
96B32	Ansell Way, Warwick
20C34	Ansley Common, Ansley Common, Ansley
20C34	Ansley Common, Chapel End
20A44	Ansley Lane, Ansley
27C13	Ansley Lane, Arley
27C11	Ansley Mill Farm, Ansley
28C14	Ansley Road, Robinsons End
29A14	Ansley Road, Stockingford, Nuneaton
70B21	Anson Close, Bilton, Rugby
147A32	Anson Close, Mountford, Wellesbourne
46A23	Anstey Aerodrome, Anstey
51B12	Ansty Lane, Brinklow
45A32	Ansty Road, Walsgrave on Sowe
96B31	Antelope Gardens, Packmores, Warwick
144C12	Anthony House, Stratford upon Avon
94C24	Antrobus Close, Hatton Station, Hatton
97B44	Apollo Way, Leamington Spa
58B12	Appian Way, Cheswick Green
70A22	Apple Grove, Long Lawford
52C11	Apple Tree Farm, Easenhall
126A13	Appleby Close, Great Alne
4A21	Appleby Hill, Austrey
4A14	Appleby Lane, Austrey
21A14	Applepie Lane, Hartshill

Map ref	Address
123A42	Appletree Lane, inkberrow
97B41	Aragon Court, Leamington Spa
97B41	Aragon Drive, Myton, Warwick
70C33	Arbour Close, Shakespeare Gardens, Rugby
81B13	Arbour Close, Windy Arbour, Kenilworth
61A31	Arbour Tree Farm, Chadwick End
60C34	Arbour Tree Lane, Chadwick End
34B23	Arbour Way, Chelmsley Wood
40A13	Arbury Avenue, Bedworth
98A13	Arbury Close, Leamington Spa
29B32	Arbury Hall, Arbury
29B22	Arbury Hall, Nuneaton
41C24	Arbury House Cottage Farm, Wol▪
41C23	Arbury House Farm, Wolvey
29C41	Arbury Mill Farm, Arbury, Nunea▪
29B22	Arbury Road, Arbury, Nuneaton
105B23	Archer Avenue, Braunston
107B14	Archer Close, Studley
80C13	Archer Road, Kenilworth
96C44	Archery Field, Bridge End, Warwi▪
97C33	Archery Road, Leamington Spa
54B43	Arches Lane, Butlers Leap Estate,
14C33	Arden Avenue, Atherstone
92B32	Arden Close, Beaudesert, Henley Arden
97A23	Arden Close, Percy Estate, Warwi▪
116A12	Arden Close, Whitnash
70C41	Arden Close, Woodlands, Rugby
24C24	Arden Croft, Coleshill
60A24	Arden Drive, Darley Green
60A21	Arden Drive, Dorridge
9A44	Arden Drive, Sutton Coldfield
20A22	Arden Forest Estate, Mancetter
145C23	Arden Heath Farm, Stratford up▪ Avon
128A14	Arden Hill Farm, Pathlow, Aston Cantlow
14C33	Arden Hill, Atherstone
77A22	Arden Hill, Lapworth
59B41	Arden Meads, Hockley Heath, Cheswick Green
92B32	Arden Road E, Henley in Arden
92B34	Arden Road W, Henley in Arde▪
125A21	Arden Road, Alcester
92B32	Arden Road, Beaudesert
41B21	Arden Road, Bulkington, Bedwo▪
59C22	Arden Road, Dorridge
92B34	Arden Road, Henley in Arden
31A31	Arden Road, Whitestone, Nune▪
81A14	Arden Road, Windy Arbour, Kenilworth
14C33	Arden Street, Atherstone
144C22	Arden Street, Stratford upon A▪
109B31	Ardencote Farm, Aston Cantlo▪
90B21	Ardendane Farm, Studley
77A22	Ardenhill Farm, Lapworth
34A23	Arderne Drive, Chelmsley Woo▪

Map ref	Address
13	Argyle Street, Rugby
C31	Argyle Way, Bishops Tachbrook
42	Ariel Way, Woodlands, Rugby
14	Arkle, Dosthill, Tamworth
B42	Arlescote Road, Arlescote, Warmington
24	Arley Hall Farm, Arley Wood, Arley
23	Arley House Farm, Hilltop, Arley
32	Arley Lane Farm, Arley
43	Arley Lane, Fillongley
13	Arley Lane, Nuneaton
24	Arley Mews, Milverton, Leamington Spa
12	Arlidge Crescent, Kenilworth
22	Arlington Avenue, Lillington, Leamington Spa
14	Arlington Court, Leamington Spa
22	Arlington Mews, Leamington Spa
22	Arlington Way, Attleborough, Nuneaton
14	Arlon Avenue, Camphill, Nuneaton
41	Armscote Farm, Armscote, Tredington
42	Armscote Fields Farm, Armscote, Tredington
11	Armscote Road, Ilmington
32	Armscote Road, Newbold on Stour, Tredington
1	Armson Road, Exhall, Bedworth
3	Armstrong Close, Rugby
24	Armstrong Close, Whitnash
2	Arncliffe Close, Nuneaton
4	Arncliffe Way, Woodloes, Warwick
2	Arne Road, Walsgrave on Sowe
2	Arnhills Way, Kilsby
2	Arnold Street, Rugby
4	Arnold Villas, Rugby
12	Arnolds Farm, Radway
	Arnolds Lane, Duke End, Maxstoke
	Arran Close, Heath End, Nuneaton
	Arran Way, Kingshurst
	Arras Boulevard, Hampton Magna, Budbrooke
3	Arrow Crescent, Alcester
1	Arrow Farm, Arrow
1	Arrow Grange, Alcester
2	Arthur Road, Stratford upon Avon
	Arthur Street, Kenilworth
	Arundel Close, Guys Cross Park, Warwick
	Arundel Road, Ryton, Bedworth
	Ascot Close, Collycroft, Bedworth
	Ascot Close, Stratford upon Avon
	Ascote Way, Southam
1	Ascott Farm, Ascott, Whichford
	Ascott Road, Ascott, Whichford
	Ash Close, Hatton Station, Hatton
	Ash Court, Shakespeare Gardens, Rugby
	Ash Drive, Windy Arbour, Kenilworth
	Ash End Farm, Hunts Green, Middleton
	Ash End, Hunts Green, Middleton
	Ash Farm, Corley Ash, Corley

Map ref	Address
39B43	Ash Green Lane, Ash Green, Bedworth
27C23	Ash Grove, Arley
39B41	Ash Gove, Bedworth
39A42	Ash Grove, Exhall, Bedworth
11B34	Ash Grove, Kingsbury
119B21	Ash Grove, Southam
128C43	Ash Grove, Stratford upon Avon
190B24	Ash House Farm, Great Wolford
111A44	Ash Lane, Bearley
1C41	Ash Lane, No Mans Heath, Newton Regis
5C44	Ashlea, Dordon
89B21	Ash Tree Farm, Barby
79B22	Ash Tree Farm, Beausale
49B41	Ash Tree Farm, Churchover
105B21	Ash Way, Braunston
21A21	Ashbrook Rise, Hartshill
30B14	Ashby Court, Attleborough, Nuneaton
195C14	Ashby Farm, Long Compton
105B23	Ashby Road, Braunston
89C21	Ashby Road, Kilsby
3A11	Ashby Road, Seckington
2A21	Ashby Road, Thorpe Constantine
8A33	Ashcroft, Sheepy Magna, Sheepy
50C33	Ashdale Close, Binley Woods
10B11	Ashdene Farm, Drayton Bassett
81A12	Ashdene Gardens, Kenilworth
29C21	Ashdown Drive, Heath End, Nuneaton
29A14	Ashe Road, Stockingford, Nuneaton
26B11	Ashes Lane, Botts Green, Over Whitacre
18B41	Ashes Lane, Nether Whitacre
81A12	Ashfield Road, Windy Arbour, Kenilworth
40A13	Ashford Drive, Bedworth
115C22	Ashford Gardens, Whitnash
59A43	Ashford Lane, Cheswick Green, Hockley Heath
115C22	Ashford Road, Whitnash, Leamington Spa
39A24	Ashington Road, Goodyears End, Bedworth
98A41	Ashlawn House, Leamington Spa
71C32	Ashlawn Road, Dunchurch
71C32	Ashlawn Road, Hillmorton, Rugby
71C33	Ashlawn School, The Paddox, Rugby
107C34	Ashlea Court, Studley
89B21	Ashleigh Close, Barby
31A22	Ashleigh Drive, Nuneaton
97A42	Ashley Crescent, Myton, Leamington Spa
53A44	Ashman Avenue, Long Lawford
154C43	Ashmores Farm, Norton
132B22	Ashorne Hill College, Ashorne Hill, Ashorne
132B21	Ashorne Hill Farm, Ashorne, Newbold Pacey
132B23	Ashorne House Farm, Ashorne, Newbold Pacey

Map ref	Address	Map ref	Address
81B11	Ashow Close, Windy Arbour, Kenilworth	4C11	Atherstone Road, Appleby Magna
81B22	Ashow Road, Ashow	15C32	Atherstone Road, Fenny Drayton
98C21	Ashton Court, Lillington, Leamington Spa	26B14	Atherstone Road, Furnace End, Ove Whitacre
147C22	Ashtree Close, Wellesbourne Hastings, Wellesbourne	21A14	Atherstone Road, Hartshill
42C31	Ashurst Farm, Wolvey	18C11	Atherstone Road, Hurley, Kingsbur
73C21	Ashwells Lane, Yelvertoft	7B44	Atherstone Road, Pinwall, Sheepy
34C13	Ashwood Drive, Chelmsley Wood	15A13	Atherstone Road, Ratcliffe Culey, Witherley
21C41	Ashwood Road, Camphill, Nuneaton	4C21	Atherstone Road, Twycross
125A24	Aspen Close, Alcester	29C21	Athol Crescent, Arbury, Nuneaton
34B23	Aspen Drive, Chelmsley Wood	6A32	Atkins Walk, St Helena, Poleswort
81B12	Asplen Court, Kenilworth	24A24	Attelborough Lane, Water Orton
74B24	Aspley Farm, Aspley Heath, Tanworth in Arden	15C23	Atterton Lane, Atterton, Witherley
74B24	Aspley Heath Lane, Aspley Heath, Tanworth in Arden	15B31	Atterton Lane, Witherley
		24A24	Attleborough Farm, Woodlands, Coleshill
74B24	Aspley Leys, Aspley Heath, Tanworth in Arden	30B14	Attleborough Grange, Attleboroug Nuneaton
70B31	Assheton Close, Bilton, Rugby	24B24	Attleborough Lane, Water Orton, Coleshill
31A21	Aster Close, Attleborough, Nuneaton	30B14	Attleborough Road, Attleborough, Nuneaton
97B22	Astley Close, Leamington Spa		
39A22	Astley Hall Farm, Market End, Bedworth	30B14	Attleborough Road, B4114, Attleborough, Nuneaton
28C32	Astley Lane Farm, Nuneaton	24A31	Auckland Drive, Kingshurst
28C34	Astley Lane, Astley	28C12	Auden Close, Galley Common, Nuneaton
39B21	Astley Lane, Market End, Bedworth	97C31	Augusta Place, Leamington Spa
29B21	Astley Lane, Robinsons End, Nuneaton	107B14	Augustine Avenue, Studley Com Studley
38B14	Astley Lodge Farm, Astley	25A21	Augustus Close, Coleshill
38B14	Astley Lodge Farm, Corley	125A33	Augustus Drive, Arrow
72A34	Astley Place, Hillmorton, Rugby	14B42	Austin Close, Atherstone
150C44	Astley Walk, Temple Herdewyke, Burton Dassett	20C44	Austen Close, Galley Common, Nuneaton
145B23	Aston Cantlow Road, Stratford upon Avon	82C44	Austen Court, Cubbington
		21A43	Austin Close, Robinsons End, Nu
127B21	Aston Cantlow Road, Wilmcote, Aston Cantlow	97A32	Austin Edwards Drive, All Saints Warwick
27A41	Aston Farm, Fillongley	4B41	Austrey Lane, Austrey
127B23	Aston Hill, Wilmcote, Aston Cantlow	1C44	Austrey Lane, No Mans Heath, Regis
22A42	Aston Road, Nuneaton	4B44	Austrey Lane, Twycross
106B22	Astwood Bank Farm, Astwood Bank	4B11	Austrey Road, Appleby Magna
106B31	Astwood Farm, Astwood Bank	3C33	Austrey Road, Austrey
106A22	Astwood Hill Farm, Astwood Bank	6C11	Austrey Road, Warton, Poleswor
106B22	Astwood Lane, Astwood Bank	96C24	Austwick Close, Woodloes, War
31A22	Asygarth Close, Nuneaton	30C24	Avebury Close, Attleborough, N
97B44	Athena Drive, Leamington Spa	54A33	Aventine Way, Glebe Farm Esta Rugby
107C13	Atcheson Close, Studley		
13B43	Atherston Lane, Baxterley	128C433	Avenue Farm, Stratford upon A
14C32	Atherstone by pass, Atherstone	106C23	Avenue Road, Astwood Bank
14B23	Atherstone by pass, Innage Park Estate, Grendon	30B21	Avenue Road, Coten, Nuneaton
		60A21	Avenue Road, Dorridge
14B23	Atherstone by pass, Merevale	63B42	Avenue Road, Kenilworth
160A22	Atherstone Farm, Atherstone on Stour	97C33	Avenue Road, Leamington Spa
159C24	Atherstone Hill Farm, Atherstone on Stour	70C11	Avenue Road, New Bilton, Rug
160A14	Atherstone House Farm, Atherstone on Stour	145A11	Avenue Road, Stratford upon A
12C43	Atherstone Lane, Hurley, Kingsbury		

ρ ref	Address	Map ref	Address
33	Avenue Station Approach, Leamington Spa	183A24	Aylesmore Farm, Upper Brailes, Brailes
42	Avery Court, Warwick	170A14	Aylestone Close, Lower Quinton, Quinton
21	Aviemore Close, Heath End, Nuneaton	31A22	Aysgarth Close, Nuneaton
B44	Avon Avenue, Middle Tysoe, Tysoe	38A24	B4008, Corley
A31	Avon Carrow The Mews, Avon Dassett	50B32	B4027, Binley Woods
A31	Avon Carrow, Avon Dassett	51B14	B4027, Brinklow
334	Avon Close, Barford	49A12	B4027, Cross in Hand
341	Avon Close, Ettington	48C21	B4027, Little Walton
44	Avon Close, Marston Jabbett, Bedworth	48A32	B4027, Pailton
44	Avon Court, Kenilworth	47B23	B4027, Street Ashton
43	Avon Court, Rugby	47A34	B4027, Stretton Under Fosse
21	Avon Court, Warwick	45C11	B4029, Anstey
23	Avon Crescent, Alcester	41B32	B4029, Bedworth
22	Avon Crescent, Stratford upon Avon	51B32	B4029, Bretford
14	Avon Croft Farm, Snitterfield	46B41	B4029, Brinklow
43	Avon Dassett Road, Fenny Compton	40C21	B4029, Bulkington
22	Avon Hill Farm, Fenny Compton	46A21	B4029, Coombe Fields
4	Avon Industrial Estate, Butlers Leap Estate, Rugby	41B34	B4029, Shilton
		40C21	B4029, Weston in Arden
11	Avon Industrial Estate, Stratford upon Avon	51B42	B4029, Wolston
		182A43	B4035, Barcheston
13	Avon Mill, Stratford upon Avon	179B42	B4035, Ebrington
3	Avon Road, Kenilworth	182C42	B4035, Honington
11	Avon Road, Lighthorne Heath, Lighthorne	186A12	B4035, Rowborough, Stretton on Fosse
		181C44	B4035, Shipston on Stour
22	Avon Road, Whitnash	189C11	B4035, Sibford Gower
3	Avon Street, Emscote, Warwick	183B43	B4035, Upper Brailes, Brailes
3	Avon Street, Rugby	89C11	B4038, Crick
	Avon Terrace, Bubbenhall	72B42	B4038, Kilsby
	Avon View Caravan Site, Ryton on Dunsmore	45C11	B4065, Anstey
		148B41	B408, Compton Verney
1	Avon Way, Middle Tysoe, Tysoe	156C13	B4085, Barton, Bidford
1	Avonbank Drive, Stratford upon Avon	141C43	B4085, Bidford
2	Avonbrook Close, Stratford upon Avon	156A31	B4085, Cleeve Prior
4	Avoncliffe, Tiddington, Stratford upon Avon	156C21	B4085, Harcliff, Bidford
		141A13	B4085, Kingsley Corner, Arrow
	Avondale Road, Brandon	141A24	B4085, Wixford
	Avondale Road, Lillington, Leamington Spa	146B11	B4086, Charlecote
		164A11	B4086, Combrook
4	Avonfields Close, Alveston, Stratford upon Avon	148C44	B4086, Compton Verney
		164C24	B4086, Kineton
1	Avonhurst, Tiddington	166A43	B4086, Knowle End, Warmington
	Avonlea Rise, Leamington Spa	165B23	B4086, Radway
2	Avonmeadow Close, Stratford upon Avon	145B13	B4086, Tiddington, Stratford upon Avon
		147B14	B4086, Wellesbourne Hasting, Wellesbourne
4	Avonside, Stratford upon Avon		
	Axminster Close, Nuneaton	115C12	B4087, Heathcote, Whitnash
	Aylesbury Close, Hockley Heath, Cheswick Green	132A33	B4087, Newbold Pacey
		132B12	B4087, Oakley Wood, Bishops Tachbrook
	Aylesbury Road, Dorridge		
	Aylesbury Road, Hockley Heath	131B23	B4088, Thelsford, Charlecote
	Aylesbury Road, Lapworth	125B31	B4089, Alcester
	Aylesbury Road, Tanworth in Arden	109C34	B4089, Aston Cantlow
	Aylesford Court, Leamington Spa	91A31	B4089, Chesters Green, Morton Bagot
	Aylesford Drive, Chelmsley Wood	109C43	B4089, Great Alne
	Aylesford Street, Leamington Spa	125B24	B4089, Kinwarton

Map ref	Address
91A34	B4089, Morton Bagot
92C23	B4089, Outhill, Studley
91B34	B4089, Wootton Wawen
107A44	B4090, Alcester
106C43	B4090, Feckenham
106C44	B4090, Great Barr
106C34	B4092, Astwood Bank
123A21	B4092, Inkberrow
107B13	B4092, Node Hill, Sambourne
107B14	B4092, Studley
107C13	B4093, Studley
96A31	B4095, Budbrooke
93C33	B4095, Claverdon
94C43	B4095, Gannaway
92B33	B4095, Henley in Arden
90C21	B4095, Mappleborough Green
91B32	B4095, Oldberrow
90C21	B4095, Outhill, Studley
93A13	B4095, Preston Bagot
94C43	B4095, Shrewley
91A24	B4095, Ullenhall
96A44	B4095, Warwick
92A31	B4095, Wootton Wawen
27A32	B4098, Arley
38A23	B4098, Corley Ash, Corley
37C13	B4098, Fillongley
17C34	B4098, Halloughton, Kingsbury
17C42	B4098, Nether Whitacre
97B32	B4099, Milverton, Leamington Spa
36A43	B410, Meriden
166B24	B4100 Avon Dassett
133B23	B4100 Harwoods House
166C24	B4100 Kineton
133C41	B4100 Lighthorne
150A14	B4100 Lighthorne Heath, Gaydon
166A11	B4100 Little Dassett, Burton Dassett
74A33	B4101, Beoley
74B23	B4101, Bransons Cross
74C13	B4101, Gilberts Green
59B43	B4101, Hockley Heath
76B11	B4101, Nuthurst
75C11	B4101, Umberslade
74C11	B4101, Wood End
29B22	B4102, Arbury
28C34	B4102, Astley
37B33	B4102, Chapel Green, Fillongley
58B21	B4102, Cheswick Green
29C14	B4102, Heath End
37A33	B4102, Meriden
29B21	B4102, Robinsons End, Nuneaton
75A11	B4102, Tanworth in Arden
63B44	B4103, Kenilworth
41B22	B4109, Bulkington, Bedworth
32C11	B4109, Hinckley
32C14	B4109, Wolvey
41B22	B4112, Bulkington, Bedworth
20A41	B4112, Church End, Ansley
30A22	B4112, Coten

Map ref	Address
53B31	B4112, Harborough Parva, Harborou Magna
30A22	B4112, Heath End, Nuneaton
47A22	B4112, Monks Kirby
53C33	B4112, Newbold on Avon, Rugby
48A31	B4112, Pailton
29B21	B4112, Robinsons End
47B23	B4112, Street Ashton, Monks Kirby
46C11	B4112, Withybrook
41C23	B4112, Wolvey
40A33	B4113, Exhall, Bedworth
30A42	B4113, Griff, Nuneaton
30B14	B4114, Attleborough
24B43	B4114, Bacons End, Kingshurst
34A11	B4114, Chelmsley Wood
26B12	B4114, Church End, Shustoke
24C41	B4114, Coleshill
26B14	B4114, Furnace End, Over Whitacr
24A44	B4114, Kingshurst
27B11	B4114, Monwode Lea, Ansley
32B42	B4114, Shelford, Burton Hastings
33B31	B4114, Smockington, Hinckley
31A31	B4114, Whitestone, Nuneaton
32C41	B4114, Wolvey
81B23	B4115, Ashow
81B31	B4115, Chesford, Kenilworth
65B21	B4115, Finham
81B31	B4115, Leek Wootton
65A34	B4115, Stoneleigh
97A11	B4115, Warwick
14B32	B4116, Atherstone
13C44	B4116, Bentley Common, Bentley
26B14	B4116, Furnace End, Over Whitac
7B44	B4116, Pinwall
8A34	B4116, Sheepy Magna, Sheepy
35A11	B4117, Coleshill
24C31	B4117, Gilson, Coleshill
24B21	B4117, Water Orton
24B12	B4118, Water Orton
70C44	B4429, Dunchurch
71C32	B4429, The Paddox, Rugby
94C13	B4431, Shrewley
95A13	B4439, Hatton
59B41	B4439, Hockley Heath, Cheswick
77C21	B4439, Kingswood, Rowington
76C12	B4439, Lapworth
77C24	B4439, Rowington
164B23	B4451, Butlers Marston
149C42	B4451, Chadshunt
135A32	B4451, Cross Green, Bishops Itch
135B11	B4451, Deppers Bridge, Harbury
173B21	B4451, Ettington
150A32	B4451, Gaydon
173A22	B4451, Halford
135A12	B4451, Harbury
164A24	B4451, Kineton Road, Butlers M
164B24	B4451, Little Kineton, Kineton
163B41	B4451, Pillerton Hersey
163A44	B4451, Pillerton Priors

p ref	Address
A33	B4451, Southam
44	B4452, Cubbington
A12	B4452, Deppers Bridge, Harbury
B44	B4452, Harbury
B43	B4452, Ufton
11	B4453, Bourton on Dunsmore
14	B4453, Frankton
13	B4453, Lillington, Leamington Spa
13	B4453, Oxley
23	B4453, Princethorpe
31	B4453, Wappenbury
33	B4453, Weston Under Wetherl
11	B4455, Copston Magna
12	B4455, Cross in Hand, Monks Kirby
44	B4455, Willey
42	B4455, Wolvey Heath, Wolvey
33	B4462, Barford
21	B4453, Draycote
12	B4453, Marlborough Site
21	B4463, Sherbourne
13	B4479, Ebrington
2	B4480, Barrells Park, Ullenhall
3	B4480, Beoley
3	B4480, Mays Wood, Wootton Wawen
3	B453, Carroway Head
33	B4632, Clifford Chambers
13	B4632, Long Marston
34	B4632, Lower Clopton
23	B4632, Lower Quinton
43	B4632, Mickleton
	B5000, Grendon
	B5000, Pinwall
	B5000, Saint Helena, Polesworth
	B5000, Sheepy
	B5000, Stoneydelph, Tamworth
	B5414, Catthorpe
	B5414, Newton And Biggin
	B5414, Rugby
	B5414, Swinford
	B5758, Hinckley
	B585, Sheepy Parva, Sheepy
	Bachelors Bench, Atherstone
2	Back Hill, Warmington
	Back Lane, Birdingbury
	Back Lane, Harborough Magna
	Back Lane, Harbury
	Back Lane, Henley in Arden
	Back Lane, High Cross Claybrook
	Back Lane, Long Compton
	Back Lane, Long Lawford
	Back Lane, Lower Quinton, Quinton
	Back Lane, Middle Tysoe, Tysoe
	Back Lane, Oxhill
	Back Lane, Princethorpe
	Back Lane, Shipston on Stour
	Back Lane, Shustoke
	Back Lane, Sibson, Rowington
	Back Lane, Tidmington
	Back Lane, Ullenhall

Map ref	Address
96C41	Back Lane, Warwick
180B12	Back Street, Ilmington
22B43	Back Street, Nuneaton
107B22	Badbury Close, Studley
107B22	Badbury Gardens, Studley
71A33	Badby Leys, Hillside, Rugby
60C24	Baddesley Clinton Hall, Lapworth
116C13	Baddesley Close, Leamington Spa
13B34	Baddesley Colliery, Baddesley Ensor
12C24	Baddesley Farm, Baddesley Ensor
13C33	Baddesley Mine, Baddesley Ensor
13B34	Baddessley Colliery, Baxterley
58B12	Badger Close, Cheswick Green
181C34	Badgers Crescent, Shipston on Stour
173C43	Badgers Farm, Idlicote
175C41	Badgers Farm, Lower Tysoe, Tysoe
175C33	Badgers Lane, Lower Tysoe, Tysoe
77C32	Badgers Lane, Turners Green, Rowington
70C23	Baffin Close, Rugby
67A24	Bagshaw Close, Ryton on Dunsmore
53A43	Baileys Lane, Long Lawford
17C43	Bakehouse Lane, Nether Whitacre
70C14	Bakehouse Lane, New Bilton, Rugby
178B32	Bakehouse Lane, Shotteswell
97C44	Baker Avenue, Leamington Spa
144C13	Baker Avenue, Stratford upon Avon
40A42	Baker Street, Exhall, Bedworth
13A24	Bakers Croft, Baddesley Ensor
190C42	Bakers Farm Road, Barton on The Heath
60A24	Bakers Lane, Darley Green
60A24	Bakers Lane, Dorridge
60B23	Bakers Lane, Lapworth
61A42	Berks Mews, Baddesley Clinton
71B32	Balcombe Road, Ashlawn Estate, Rugby
184B13	Baldwins Lane, Upper Tysoe, Tysoe
27B14	Ballards Green Farm, Arley
27B12	Ballards Green Lane, Ansley
27B23	Ballards Green Lane, Arley
180B14	Ballards Lane, Ilmington
21C44	Balmoral Court, Camphill, Nuneaton
24A33	Balmoral Road, Kingshurst
82B43	Balmoral Way, Cubbington
61B13	Balsall Lodge Farm, Frogmore
155C14	Banbrook Copse, Salford Priors
155C14	Ban Brook Road, Salford Priors
164C22	Banbury Road Farm, Kineton
115B33	Banbury Road, Bishops Tachbrook
96C34	Banbury Road, Bridge End, Warwick
136A32	Banbury Road, Chapel Ascote
161C32	Banbury Road, Ettington
162B43	Banbury Road, Ettington
150B23	Banbury Road, Gaydon
161A12	Banbury Road, Goldicote, Alderminster
115A32	Banbury Road, Greys Mallory
133B23	Banbury Road, Harwoods House, Chesterton
164C24	Banbury Road, Kineton

Map ref	Address
136B22	Banbury Road, Ladbroke
133C42	Banbury Road, Lighthorne
150A14	Banbury Road, Lighthorne Heath, Gaydon
115B44	Banbury Road, Oakley Wood
174C13	Banbury Road, Pillerton Priors
178A23	Banbury Road, Shotteswell
119A32	Banbury Road, Southam
145B24	Banbury Road, Stratford upon Avon
152C41	Banbury Road, The Tunnel, Fenny Compton
114B24	Banbury Spur, Longbridge, Warwick
164B13	Banbury Street, Kineton
145A21	Bancroft Gardens, Stratford upon Avon
145A22	Bancroft Place, Stratford upon Avon
1A23	Bandland Farm, Clifton Campville
186C11	Banister Way, Shipston on Stour
155C16	Bankbrook Copse, Salford Priors
163C24	Bank Close, Butlers Marston
158B21	Bank Farm, Welford on Avon
15B12	Bank Farm, Witherley
14C31	Bank Road, Atherstone
98B42	Bank Side, Leamington spa
71A14	Bank Street, Rugby
163C24	Bank View, Butlers Marston
116B14	Bankcroft, Sydenham Farm Estate, Leamington Spa
97A22	Bankfield Drive, Milverton, Leamington Spa
80A31	Bannerhill Farm, Beausale
130A44	Baraset Farm, Alveston, Stratford upon Avon
67C23	Barbellows Farm, Ryton on Dunsmore
73C23	Barberry Farm, Yelvertoft
18C43	Barbers Farm, Over Whitacre
41B21	Barbridge Close, Bulkington
41A14	Barbridge Road, Bulkington, Bedworth
72A41	Barby Lane, Barby
71C32	Barby Lane, Hillmorton, Rugby
88C43	Barby Lane, Willoughby
72A44	Barby Lodge Farm, Barby
89B21	Barby Road, Barby
89B22	Barby Road, Kilsby
71A13	Barby Road, Rugby
88C23	Barby Wood Farm, Barby
182C43	Barcheston Ground Farm, Barcheston
60A11	Barcheston Road, Dorridge
6A31	Bardon View Road, Dordon, Polesworth
145A13	Bards Walk, Stratford upon Avon
120C23	Barfields Farm, Napton on The Hill
116A32	Barford Approach, Whitnash
114C31	Barford Hill, Barford
81B13	Barford Mews, Kenilworth
114A34	Barford Road, Sherbourne
81B13	Barford Road, Windy Arbour, Kenilworth
39A34	Barkers Farm, Ash Green, Bedworth
57A21	Barkers Lane, Tanners Green, Wythall
119B32	Barkus Close, Southam

Map ref	Address
92B31	Barley Close, Henley in Arden
72A34	Barley Close, Hillmorton, Rugby
112B44	Barley Close, Snitterfield
97C21	Barley Court, Lillington, Leamington Spa
142C11	Barleys Leys Farm, Temple Grafton
125C31	Barlich Way, Kinwarton
144C44	Barn Close Private Road, Clifford Chambers
144C44	Barn Close, Clifford Chambers
5C42	Barn Close, Dordon
59C24	Barn Close, Dorridge
116B21	Barn Close, Whitnash
68A31	Barn Cottage Farm, Wolston
6C13	Barn End Road, Little Warton, Polesworth
15C11	Barn Farm, Witherley
175A42	Barn Grounds Farm, Middle Tysoe, Tysoe
167B23	Barn Hill, Avon Dassett
167B32	Barn Hill, Farnborough
20B44	Barn Moor Wood Farm, Galley Common, Nuneaton
96C21	Barnack Drive, Woodloes, Warwick
41A42	Barnacle House Farm, Barnacle, Sh
41A31	Barnacle Lane, Barnacle, Shilton
41B24	Barnacle Lane, Bulkington, Bedwo
34C23	Barnard Close, Chelmsley Wood
98C21	Barnard Close, Lillington, Leaming Spa
97C13	Barnburgh Grove, Leamington Sp
31A34	Barne Close, Whitestone, Nuneato
93B41	Barnmoor Farm, Claverdon
84B24	Barns Lane, Princethorpe
14B42	Barnsley Close, Atherstone
87B11	Barnwell Close, Dunchurch
86C13	Barnwells Barn Farm, Thurlaston
173C31	Barnwood, Fulready
29B11	Barons Croft, Whittleford, Nunea
29C14	Barpool Road, Stockingford, Nun
51C13	Barr Lane, Brinklow
23A13	Barr Lane, Higham, Higham on Hill
96C33	Barrack Street, Warwick
146C41	Barracks Green, Loxley
79B21	Barracks Lane, Beausale
36C32	Barrats Farm, Green End, Fillong
84C43	Barratts Cottage Farm, Eathorpe
39B43	Barratts Lane, Ash Green, Bedwo
173C11	Barrel Hill Farm, Pillerton Priors
37A31	Barrets Farm, Newhall Green, Fi
70B21	Barrington Road, Bilton, Rugby
80C14	Barrow Road, Kenilworth
80C13	Barrowfield Court, Kenilworth
80C11	Barrowfield Lane, Kenilworth
14C31	Barsby Close, Atherstone
96C34	Bartlett Close, Coten End, Warw
98B44	Barton Court, Leamington Spa

p ref	Address
44	Barton Crescent, Sydenham Farm Estate, Leamington Spa
C21	Barton Crossroads, Barton on The Heath, Bidford
B11	Barton Farm, Alderminster
A22	Barton Farm, Barton on The Heath, Bidford
A14	Barton Fields, Welford on Avon
B22	Barton on Heath Road, Barton on The Heath
C43	Barton Road, Barton on The Heath
12	Barton Road, Bedworth
33	Barton Road, Bilton, Rugby
23	Barton Road, Hilltop, Nuneaton
A23	Barton Road, Little Compton
C33	Barton Road, Long Compton
A14	Barton Road, Welford on Avon
13	Barwell Close, Leamington Spa
14	Bascote Crossroads, Bascote, Long Itchington
12	Bascote Lodge Farm, Bascote, Long Itchington
A23	Bascote Rise, Southam
23	Bascote Road, Bascote
23	Bascote Road, Bascote Heath
33	Bascote Road, Long Itchington
24	Bascote Road, Ufton
13	Bastion Avenue, Lower Quinton, Quinton
2	Batchelors Bench, Atherstone
11	Batchelors Lane, Ratley, Ratley And Upton
3	Bateman Road, Coleshill
3	Bates Lane, Tanworth in Arden
4	Bath Farm, Willoughby
24	Bath Meadow, Bishops Itchington
4	Bath Place, Leamington Spa
3	Bath Road, Mancetter
	Bath Road, Nuneaton
	Bath Street, Leamington Spa
	Bath Street, Rugby
	Bathurst Close, Rugby
	Bathway Road, Coventry
1	Battle Court, Kineton
2	Batsford Flats, Whatcote
	Bawnmore Court, Bilton, Rugby
	Bawnmore Park, Shakespeare Gardens, Rugby
	Bawnmore Road, Bilton, Rugby
	Baxter Court, Leamington Spa
	Baxterley Hall Farm, Baxterley
	Bayton Road, Exhall, Bedworth
	Bayton Way, Exhall, Bedworth
	Bazzard Road, Bramcote
	Beacon Close, Alcester
	Beaconsfield Avenue, Rugby
	Beaconsfield Street, Leamington Spa
	Beale Close, Bishops Tachbrook
	Beanit Farm, Balsall Common

Map ref	Address
92B23	Bear Close, Henley in Arden
6A21	Bear Lane Close, Polesworth
92A24	Bear Lane, Henley in Arden
158B43	Bear Yard, Long Marston
77A13	Bearhouse Farm, Lapworth
111B44	Bearley Farm, Bearley
111A42	Bearley Grange, Bearley
111B41	Bearley Green, Bearley
111A41	Bearley Mill, Bearley
109C44	Bearley Road, Aston Cantlow
111B41	Bearley Road, Bearley
111C41	Bearley Road, Snitterfield
70B22	Beatty Drive, Bilton, Rugby
97C23	Beauchamp Avenue, Leamington Spa
34A14	Beauchamp Close, Chelmsley Wood
80C21	Beauchamp Court, Kenilworth
125A21	Beauchamp Court, Kings Coughton
97C23	Beauchamp Court, Leamington Spa
97A34	Beauchamp Gardens, Warwick
97C23	Beauchamp Hill, Milverton, Leamington Spa
97A24	Beauchamp Road, All Saints, Warwick
80C21	Beauchamp Road, Bulkington Estate, Kenilworth
125B23	Beauchamp Road, Kinwarton
97C23	Beauchamp Road, Leamington Spa
92B31	Beaudesert Lane, Henley in Arden
96C21	Beaufell Close, Woodloes, Warwick
82B43	Beaufort Avenue, Cubbington
147C31	Beaufort Close, Mountford, Wellesbourne
97C23	Beaufort House, Leamington Spa
116C11	Beaulieu Park, Radford Semele
116C11	Beaulieul Way, Sydenham Farm Estate, Leamington Spa
98A43	Beaumont Court, Leamington Spa
75A12	Beaumont Hill Farm, Tanworth in Arden
39A41	Beaumont Road, Keresley Newlands, Keresley
30A11	Beaumont Road, Nuneaton
79B34	Beausale Lane, Beausale
95B14	Beausale Lane, Hatton
103A12	Beck Hill Farm, Leamington Hastings
54C31	Beckfoot, Brownsover, Rugby
119C14	Becks Close, Stockton
119C12	Becks Lane, Stockton
40A11	Bede Road, Bedworth
29B14	Bede Road, Stockingford, Nuneaton
39A32	Bede Village, Goodyears End, Bedworth
97C33	Bedford Place, Leamington Spa
97C31	Bedford Street, Leamington Spa
39C33	Bedworth by passage, Exhall, Bedworth
40B21	Bedworth Civic Hall, Bedworth
41A22	Bedworth Close, Bulkington, Bedworth
40A22	Bedworth High Street, Bedworth
39B12	Bedworth Lane, Bedworth Woodlands, Bedworth
40A24	Bedworth Leisure Centre, Bedworth

Map ref	Address
41A21	Bedworth Road, Bulkington, Bedworth
40A41	Bedworth Road, Exhall, Bedworth
40A43	Bedworth Road, Sutton Stop, Coventry
39C24	Bedworth Rugby Football Club, Bedworth
40B21	Bedworth Youth Centre, Bedworth
34A24	Beech Avenue, Chelmsley Wood
96C32	Beech Cliffe, Warwick
12B43	Beech Close, Hurley, Kingsbury
125B42	Beech Close, Oversley Green, Alcester
78A31	Beech Close, Rowington
119A31	Beech Close, Southam
145B21	Beech Close, Stratford upon Avon
101A33	Beech Croft, Long Itchington
71C32	Beech Croft, Rugby
70B32	Beech Drive, Bilton, Rugby
64A44	Beech Drive, Kenilworth
86C14	Beech Drive, Thurlaston
27B24	Beech Grove, Arley
97A24	Beech Grove, Percy Estate, Warwick
174C32	Beech Road, Oxhill
68B41	Beech Tree Farm, Stretton on Dunsmore
58C11	Beech Wood Close, Cheswick Green
160C24	Beecham Farm Old Airfield, Ailstone, Preston on Stour
160C24	Beecham Farm, Ailstone, Preston on Stour
144B12	Beecham Walk, Stratford upon Avon
129C44	Beeches Walk, Tiddington, Stratford upon Avon
32B12	Beechwood Avenue, Hinckley
80C21	Beechwood Croft, Bulkington Estate, Kenilworth
40B12	Beechwood Road, Bedworth
21B42	Beechwood Road, Camphill, Nuneaton
51A41	Beechvers Keep, Brandon
63C34	Beehive Hill, Kenilworth
16B41	Beehive Lane, Curdworth
134C21	Beggars Lane, Harbury
189C11	Beggars Lane, Lower Brailes, Brailes
184C41	Beggars Lane, Winderton
165C43	Belayse, Radway
185C23	Belcony, Stretton on Fosse
92B31	Beldesert Close, Henley in Arden
16B21	Belfry Hotel, Wishaw
54C34	Belgrade Drive, Brownsover, Rugby
129B11	Bell Brook, Smithfield
24A42	Bell Close, Kingshurst
59B44	Bell Cottage, Lapworth
145A21	Bell Court Shopping Centre, Stratford upon Avon
156B14	Bell Court, Bidford
97C21	Bell Court, Lillington, Leamington Spa
145A21	Bell Court, Stratford upon Avon
39B42	Bell Drive, Ash Green, Bedworth
136B23	Bell Farm, Ladbroke
47C21	Bell Lane, Monks Kirby
47C21	Bell Lane, Pailton
144B22	Bell Lane, Shottery, Stratford upon Avon
129B12	Bell Lane, Snitterfield
107C13	Bell Lane, Studley
107C14	Bell Mews, Studley
177B41	Bell Street, Hornton
97C14	Bell Tower Mews, Leamington Spa
78C33	Bell View Farm, Shrewley
72A32	Bell Walk, Hillmorton, Rugby
97B22	Bell Yard, Milverton, Leamington S
39B24	Bellairs Drive, Goodyears End, Bedworth
95C34	Bellam Road, Hampton Magna, Budbrooke
29C21	Bellevue, Stockingford, Nuneaton
75A21	Bellfield, Tanworth in Arden
98A13	Belmont Court, Leamington Spa
98A13	Belmont Drive, Leamington Spa
80C12	Belmont Mews, Kenilworth
98A13	Belmont Mews, Leamington Spa
71A31	Belmont Road, Kingsway, Rugby
59B43	Belton Close, Hockley Heath, Che Green
71A11	Ben Hall, Rugby
116C43	Bendigo Mitchell Cross Roads, Chesterton, Harbury
116C43	Bendigo Mitchell Cross Roads, Leamington Spa
116C43	Bendigo Mitchell, Chesterton, Ha
14B34	Benedicts Close, Atherstone
7B32	Benn Hill Farm, Sheepy
41A22	Benn Road, Bulkington, Bedwort
71B21	Benn Street, Rugby
67C14	Bennett Court, Wolston
97A42	Bennett Drive, Myton, Leamingto
180B12	Bennett Place, Ilmington
70C14	Bennett Street, Rugby
38B24	Bennetts Road N, Corley
38C33	Bennetts Road N, Keresley, Cove
71A13	Bennfield Road, Rugby
145A11	Benson Road, Stratford upon Av
98B13	Bentley Close, Lillington, Leamir Spa
3C41	Bentley Farm, Polesworth
19B21	Bentley Hall Farm, Bentley
13C44	Bentley House Nursing Home,
36B13	Bentley Lane, Maxstoke
40A23	Bentley Road, Exhall, Bedworth
30A11	Bentley Road, Nuneaton
36B14	Bentleys Farm, Maxstoke
59C11	Bently Farm Close, Dorridge
74B23	Beoley Lane, Bransons Cross, Be
98A21	Berenska Drive, Leamington Spa
81C31	Bericote Farm, Ashow
82A33	Bericote Fields Farm, Cubbingto
81C34	Bericote Road, Bericote, Blackdo
82A42	Bericote Road, Cubbington
30A13	Berkeley Close, Nuneaton
90A13	Berkeley Close, Redditch

Map ref	Address	Map ref	Address
?41	Berkeley Road, Kenilworth	112C22	Big House Farm, Norton Lindsey
?13	Berkshire Close, Stockingford, Nuneaton	86C21	Biggin Hall Farm, Thurlaston
?34	Berlington Road, Griff, Nuneaton	86C22	Biggin Hall Lane, Thurlaston
?34	Bermuda Industrial Estate, Bermuda, Nuneaton	168B32	Bignolds Close, Claydon
		9A41	Bigwood Drive, Sutton Coldfield
?34	Bermuda Park, Nuneaton	127A42	Billesley Manor Farm, Billesley
?21	Bermuda Road, Bermuda, Nuneaton	127A42	Billesley Manor Hotel, Billesley, Alcester
?21	Bermuda Road, Heath End		
?34	Bermuda Trading Estate, Bermuda, Nuneaton	127A42	Billesley Manor, Billesley, Alcester
		127A22	Billesley Road, Aston Cantlow
?42	Beron Close, Woodlands, Rugby	127A32	Billesley Road, Billesley
?32	Berrington Road, Camphill, Nuneaton	70C44	Bilton Fields Farm, Dunchurch
?3	Berrington Road, Sydenham Farm Estate, Leamington Spa	87B12	Bilton Lane, Dunchurch
		70A23	Bilton Lane, Long Lawford
?41	Berry Avenue, Shipston on Stour	70C21	Bilton Road, Bilton, Rugby
?22	Berry Close, Little Compton	50A32	Binley Common Farm, Binley Woods
?41	Berry Close, Shipston on Stour	97C22	Binswood Avenue, Leamington Spa
?31	Berry Fields Farm, Ilmington	117A44	Binswood End, Harbury
?1	Berry Football Club, Rugby	97C22	Binswood Mansions, Leamington Spa
?41	Berry Meadow, Fenny Compton	97C23	Binswood Street, Leamington Spa
?42	Berryfield Farm, Hook Norton	143A23	Binton Hill Farm, Binton
?44	Berryfields Farm, Braunston	143A34	Binton Road, Binton
?1	Berryfields Farm, Fillongley	143A41	Binton Road, Welford on Avon
?23	Berryfields Road, Honington	125A34	Birch Abbey, Alcester
?3	Berryfields, Fillongley	40B12	Birch Close, Bedworth
?22	Berryhill Farm, Stoneton	11B34	Birch Close, Kingsbury
?2	Bertie Road, Kenilworth	5B42	Birch Coppice Colliery, Dordon
?4	Bertie Terrace, Milverton, Leamington Spa	34B24	Birch Croft, Chelmsley Wood
		70A22	Birch Drive, Long Lawford
?5	Berwick Close, Woodloes, Warwick	5B34	Birch Grove, Birchmoor, Polesworth
?4	Berwicks Lane, Chelmsley Wood	147C21	Birch Grove, Wellesbourne Hasting, Wellesbourne
?2	Berwyn Way, Stockingford, Nuneaton		
	Best Avenue, Kenilworth	21B41	Birch Tree Road, Camphill, Nuneaton
	Beswick Gardens, Bilton, Rugby	81A14	Birches Lane, Windy Arbour, Kenilworth
	Betteridge Farm, Nether Whitacre		
?1	Betteridge Place, Charlecote	63C24	Birches Wood Farm, Crackley
	Bettina Close, Whittleford, Nuneaton	63C24	Birches Wood Farm, Crackley, Kenilworth
	Beverley Avenue, Whittleford, Nuneaton		
		63C24	Birches Wood Farm, Stoneleigh
	Beverley Road, Leamington Spa	12B24	Birchfield Close, Wood End, Kingsbury
	Beverly Drive, Gibbet Hill, Coventry	129A43	Birchfield Road, Stratford upon Avon
	Beyer Close, Amington Ind.est., Tamworth	19C24	Birchley Farm, Birchley Heath, Ansley
		51A23	Birchley Farm, Brinklow
	Biart Place, Rugby	19C24	Birchley Hall Farm, Birchley Heath, Mancetter
	Bickenhill Lane, Chelmsley Wood		
	Bickenhill Road, Chelmsley Wood	37B41	Birchley Hall Farm, Chapel Green, Fillongley
	Bickers Court Farm, Danzey Green, Tanworth in Arden	19C22	Birchley Heath Road, Birchley Heath, Ansley
	Bickerstaff Farm, Idlicote		
	Bickmarsh Hall Farm, Honeybourne, Bidford	5C34	Birchmoor Avenue, Dordon
		5C33	Birchmoor Farm, Birchmoor, Polesworth
	Bickmarsh Hall, Bickmarsh, Bidford	5C32	Birchmoor Road, Birchmoor, Polesworth
	Bickmarsh Lane, Marcliff, Bidford	97A22	Birchway Close, Milverton, Leamington Spa
	Bidavon Industrial Estate, Bidford		
	Biddulph Terrace, Frankton	5C34	Birchwood Avenue, Dordon
	Bidford Road, Broom, Bidford	50B32	Birchwood Road, Binley Woods
	Bidford Road, Wixford	75B11	Birchy Cross Farm, Tanworth in Arden
	Big Bouts Farm, Inkberrow	92B21	Bird in Hand Cottage, Henley in Arden
	Big Cleobury Farm, Cheswick Green	115B11	Bird Road, Heathcote, Whitnash

Map ref	Address
150A14	Bird Road, Lighthorne Heath, Lighthorne
150A14	Birdhaven Close, Lighthorne Heath
101C21	Birdingbury Fields Farm, Birdingbury
85C24	Birdingbury Road, Bourton And Draycote
85C33	Birdingbury Road, Frankton
102A11	Birdingbury Road, Leamington Hastings
84C42	Birdingbury Road, Marton
85C24	Birdingbury Road, Oxley
169B24	Birds Commercial Metals, Long Marston
169B24	Birds Commercial Motors, Long Marston
31A24	Birkdale Close, Whitestone, Nuneaton
28B13	Birmingham Road, Ansley
20C34	Birmingham Road, Ansley Common
24B43	Birmingham Road, Bacons End, Kingshurst
111A41	Birmingham Road, Bearley Cross, Bearley
111A41	Birmingham Road, Bearley Cross, Bearley
92B21	Birmingham Road, Beaudesert
35B41	Birmingham Road, Bickenhill
128C41	Birmingham Road, Bishopton, Stratford upon Avon
96C31	Birmingham Road, Budbrooke
63B31	Birmingham Road, Burton Green, Kenilworth
24C41	Birmingham Road, Coleshill
78B12	Birmingham Road, Five Ways, Shrewley
35B41	Birmingham Road, Great Packington
95A14	Birmingham Road, Hatton Green, Hatton
92B21	Birmingham Road, Henley in Arden
125A21	Birmingham Road, Kings Coughton, Alcester
24A21	Birmingham Road, Kingshurst
17A34	Birmingham Road, Lea Marston
90A22	Birmingham Road, Mappleborough Green
36A43	Birmingham Road, Meriden
128B23	Birmingham Road, Pathlow, Aston Cantlow
67A33	Birmingham Road, Ryton on Dunsmore
78C24	Birmingham Road, Shrewley
65A34	Birmingham Road, Stoneleigh
107C12	Birmingham Road, Studley
96B32	Birmingham Road, Warwick
24A13	Birmingham Road, Water Orton
17B42	Birmingham Road, Whitacre Heath, Nether Whitacre
16A14	Birmingham Road, Wishaw
92A42	Birmingham Road, Wootton Wawen
78B12	Birmingham Road, Wroxhall
54C42	Birstall Drive, Rugby
4A23	Bishops Cleeve, Austrey
115C32	Bishops Close, Bishops Tachbrook
144B14	Bishops Close, Stratford upon Avon
91A34	Bishops Farm, Oldberrow
135B21	Bishops Gate, Bishops Itchington
149C21	Bishops Gorse Farm, Lighthorne
149B21	Bishops Gorse Road, Lighthorne
149A21	Bishops Gorse Road, Lighthorne Rough, Compton Verney
134C21	Bishops Itchington Road, Harbury
128C43	Bishopton Fields, Stratford upon A
128B33	Bishopton Hamlet, Bishopton, Dray
128A32	Bishopton Hill Farm, Stratford upo Avon
128B42	Bishopton Lane, Bishopton
144A14	Bishopton Lane, Drayton, Stratford upon Avon
116B12	Bisset Crescent, Sydenham Farm Estate, Leamington Spa
134C43	Bitham Road, Lighthorne Heath, Lighthorne
25C22	Bixhill Lane, Shustoke
108A41	Bl Cars, Studley
150A14	Bl Proving Ground, Lighthorne H Gaydon
90A44	Bl Staff College, Studley
40A24	Black Bank, Blackbank, Bedworth
121C21	Black Boy Farm, Lower Shuckbur
142C42	Black Cliff Farm, Temple Grafton
37B14	Black Hall Farm, Fillongley
37B12	Black Hall Lane, Fillongley
150B21	Black Hanger Farm, Gaydon
113C11	Black Lane, Budbrooke
98B23	Black Lane, Lillington, Leamingto
29C12	Blackatree Court, Stockingford, Nuneaton
29C11	Blackatree Place, Stockingford, Nuneaton
29C12	Blackatree Road, Stockingford, Nuneaton
54C31	Blackberry Close, Brownsover, R
39B43	Blackberry Lane, Ash Green, Be
39B43	Blackberry Lane, Ash Green, Be
24A33	Blackbird Crescent, Kingshurst
34A13	Blackcat Close, Chelmsley Woo
81C42	Blackdown Farm, Blackdown
81C41	Blackdown Hotel, Blackdown, Leamington Spa
81C33	Blackdown Mill, Blackdown, Leamington Spa
81C41	Blackdown Restaurant, Blackdo
5B23	Blackdown, Stoneydelph, Tamw
34C32	Blackfirs Lane, Chelmsley Woo
92B34	Blackford Hill, Henley in Arder
92B33	Blackford Mill Farm, Wootton
174C32	Blackford Way, Oxhill
16C24	Blackgreaves Farm, Lea Marsto
16C24	Blackgreaves Lane, Lea Marsto
70C12	Blackham Way, Rugby
62C14	Blackhales Farm, Balsall Comm

Map ref	Address
A14	Blackhill Farm, Blackhill, Snitterfield
A13	Blackhill, Stratford upon Avon
41	Blackhorse Road, Exhall, Coventry
A33	Blacklands Farm, Butlers Marston
21	Blacklow Road, Percy Estate, Warwick
11	Blacksmith Lane, Bentley
41	Blacksmiths Lane, Hockley Heath, Cheswick Green
341	Blacksmiths Lane, Northend
14	Blackthorn Road, Windy Arbour, Kenilworth
A24	Blackthorn Way, Alcester
22	Blackthorne Grove, Attleborough, Nuneaton
A43	Blackthorne Road, Stratford upon Avon
A21	Blackwell Road, Darlingscott
13	Blackwell Road, Tredington
2	Blackwood Avenue, Bilton, Rugby
21	Blacon Farm Barn, Norton Lindsey
22	Blacon Farm, Lower Norton
22	Blacon Farm, Norton Lindsey
13	Blacon Way, Stratford upon Avon
2	Bladon Close, Saint Nicholas Park, Nuneaton
4	Bladon Walk, Sydenham Farm Estate, Leamington
	Blair Drive, Goodyears End, Bedworth
	Blair Grove, Chelmsley Wood
	Blaise Avenue, Water Orton
	Blake Close, Bilton, Rugby
	Blake Close, Galley Common, Nuneaton
	Blake Close, Robinsons End, Nuneaton
	Blake Lands Avenue, Sydenham Farm Estate, Leamington
2	Blakenhurst, Harvington
	Blandford Drive, Walsgrave on Sowe
	Blandford Road, Milverton, Leamington Spa
	Blandford Way, Hampton Magna, Budbrooke
2	Blaze Lane, Hunt End
	Bleaberry, Brownsover, Rugby
4	Bleachfield Street, Alcester
	Bleak Cottage, Radway
	Blenheim Close, Bidford on Avon
	Blenheim Close, Attleborough, Nuneaton
	Blenheim Crescent, Sydenham Farm Estate, Leamington
	Blenheim Farm, Frogmore
	Blenheim Walk, Mountford, Wellesbourne
	Blew Grates, Brailes
	Blick Road, Heathcote Industrial, Whitnash
	Blind Lane, Kenilworth
	Blind Lane, Aspley Heath, Tanworth in Arden
16A31	Blind Pit Lane, Curdworth
16A24	Blind Pit Lane, Overgreen, Wishaw
40B11	Blockley Road, Bedworth
70C14	Bloxam Gardens, Rugby
150A34	Bloxham Barn Farm, Chadshunt
69B43	Blue Boar Farm, Blue Boar Corner, Long Lawford
86B11	Blue Boar Island To Junction 1 M45, Park Farm South
86B11	Blue Boar Island To Ryton Island, Park Farm South
86B11	Blue Boar Island To Thurlaston Island, Park Farm South
86B11	Blue Boar Island, Park Farm South
129A43	Blue Cap Road, Stratford upon Avon
60A14	Blue Lake Farm, Dorridge
60A22	Blue Lake Road, Dorridge
161B14	Blue Lane Farm, Goldicote, Alderminster
161C11	Blue Lane, Goldicote, Alderminster
36A32	Blue Pig Farm, Little Packington
34C21	Bluebell Drive, Chelmsley Wood
68A11	Bluemel Brothers, Wolston
75C44	Blunts Green Farm, Blunts Green, Ullenhall
75C44	Blunts Green, Ullenhall
39A24	Blyth Close, Goodyears End, Bedworth
25B31	Blythe Court, Shustoke
25B24	Blythe End Farm, Blythe End, Shustoke
25B23	Blythe Hall, Shustoke, Coleshill
25A22	Blythe Mill, Shustoke, Coleshill
25B31	Blythe Road, Shustoke, Coleshill
73C44	Boat House Lane, Crick
143A43	Boat Lane, Welford on Avon
68B33	Bobs Cafe, Stretton on Dunsmore
63B12	Bockendon Lane, Westwood Heath
82C43	Boddington Close, Cubbington
168C11	Boddington Road, Claydon
143C42	Bodington Farm, Welford on Avon
64B41	Bodnant Way, Kenilworth
17C21	Bodymoor Green Farm, Kingsbury
17A13	Bodymoor Heath Lane, Bodymoor Heath, Kingsbury
17A14	Bodymoor Heath Lane, Marston, Lea Marston
10B42	Bodymoor Heath Lane, Middleton
36B11	Bolas Lane, Maxstoke, Bolehall, Tamworth
97B41	Boleyn Close, Myton, Warwick
156A11	Bomford And Evershed, Salford Priors
42C44	Bon Lane, Withybrook
47C13	Bond End, Monks Kirby
70C14	Bond Street, New Bilton, Rugby
22B43	Bond Street, Nuneaton
22B43	Bondgate, Nuneaton
72A24	Bonington Close, Lower Hillmorton, Rugby
115C12	Bonniksen Close, Leamington Spa
13B13	Boot Hill, Grendon

Map ref	Address	Map ref	Address
85C11	Boots Farm, Bourton on Dunsmore	71C31	Bowen Road, Rugby
85C11	Boots Farm, Oxley	98A11	Bowers Croft, Leamington Spa
98A13	Bordesley Court, Lillington, Leamington Spa	39C31	Bowling Green Lane, Exhall, Bedwo◄
		96B42	Bowling Green Street, Warwick
144B23	Bordon Hill, Stratford upon Avon	116B24	Box Close, Whitnash
144C23	Bordon Place, Stratford upon Avon	34B32	Box Road, Chelmsley Wood
182B43	Borough Hill Farm, Barcheston	59A22	Box Tree Farm, Cheswick Green
97B21	Borrowdale Drive, Leamington Spa	59B14	Box Trees Road, Dorridge
54B31	Borrowdale, Brownsover, Rugby	73B41	Box 3264A, M1
80C11	Borrowell Lane, Kenilworth	73B42	Box 3264B, M1
80C11	Borrowell Terrace, Kenilworth	73B23	Box 3288A, M1
39B31	Boscastle House, Goodyears End, Bedworth	73B24	Box 3288B, M1
		56A44	Box 3296A, M1
186C11	Bosley Close, Shipston on Stour	56A44	Box 3296B, M1
83A32	Bostock Crescent, Weston Under Wetherley	56A33	Box 3312A, M1
		56A33	Box 3312B, M1
45A41	Boswell Drive, Walsgrave on Sowe	56C21	Box 3328A, M1
96C23	Boswell Green, Woodloes, Warwick	56A21	Box 3328B, M1
96B24	Boswell Grove, Woodloes, Warwick	88A21	Box 5089A, M45
70C34	Boswell Road, Shakespeare Gardens, Rugby	88A21	Box 5089B, M45
		56A11	Box 5323B, M6
34A21	Bosworth Drive, Chelmsley Wood	56A11	Box 5327B, M6
125A42	Boteler Close, Alcester	55C22	Box 5336A, M6
75C44	Botley Hill Farm, Ullenhall	55C22	Box 5336B, M6
76A42	Botley Mill Farm, Tanworth in Arden	55B22	Box 5350A, M6
151B41	Bottom Street, Northend, Burton Dassett	55A22	Box 5350B, M6
		54C21	Box 5363A, M6
22A44	Bottrill Street, Nuneaton	54C13	Box 5363B, M6
18B44	Botts Green Lane, Botts Green, Over Whitacre	54B13	Box 5384A, M6
		54B13	Box 5384B, M6
18B41	Botts Green Lane, Nether Whitacre	53C12	Box 5397A, M6
144B24	Boucher Close, Shottery, Stratford upon Avon	53C12	Box 5397B, M6
		48A44	Box 5414A, M6
54B41	Boughton Road, Brownsover, Rugby	48A44	Box 5414B, M6
13A44	Boultbees Farm, Baxterley	48A44	Box 5415A, M6
12C23	Boulters Lane, Baddesley Ensor	48144	Box 5415B, M6
13A11	Boulters Lane, Dordon	47C33	Box 5430A, M6
12B24	Boulters Lane, Wood End, Kingsbury	47C33	Box 5430B, M6
165A14	Boundary Farm, Chadshunt	47A32	Box 5445A, M6
7A14	Boundary Farm, Twycross	57B31	Box 5445B, M6
145C21	Boundary Lane, Stratford upon Avon	46C23	Box 5460A, M6
71B22	Boundary Road, Rugby	46C23	Box 5460B, M6
104C43	Boundry Farm, Nethercote, Wolfhamcote	46A23	Box 5477A, M6
		46A23	Box 5477B, M6
7A14	Boundry Farm, Twycross	45B23	Box 5492A, M6
144B23	Bourden Hill, Drayton	45B23	Box 5492B, M6
37B22	Bourne Brook Close, Fillongley	45A22	Box 5506K, M69
14C13	Bourne Close, Atherstone	45A23	Box 5515A, M6
119A33	Bourne End, Southam	45A23	Box 5515B, M6
27C23	Bournebrook View, Arley	40C43	Box 5530A, M6
116B11	Bourton Drive, Whitnash, Leamington Spa	40C43	Box 5530B, M6
		39C41	Box 5542B, M6
85C24	Bourton Hall, Bourton on Dunsmore	40A43	Box 5543A, M6
85C21	Bourton on Dunsmore, Rugby	40A44	Box 5543B, M6
85B24	Bourton Road, Frankton	39B33	Box 5565A, M6
123A12	Bouts Corner Farm, Inkberrow	39B33	Box 5565B, M6
123A22	Bouts Farm, Inkberrow	39A31	Box 5583A, M6
54B34	Bow Fell, Brownsover, Rugby	39A31	Box 5583B, M6
46C12	Bow Lane, Withybrook	38A32	Box 5602A, M6

ref	Address	Map ref	Address
32	Box 5602B, M6	58C44	Box 6307B, M42
32	Box 5614A, M6	34C13	Box 6308K, M42
32	Box 5614B, M6	59A21	Box 6317A, M42
32	Box 5624A, M6	59A21	Box 6317B, M42
32	Box 5624B, M6	59A12	Box 6330A, M42
32	Box 5639A, M6	59A12	Box 6330B, M42
32	Box 5639B, M6	34C32	Box 6457A, M42
32	Box 5653A, M6	34C12	Box 6465A, M42
2	Box 5653B, M6	34C13	Box 6465K, M42
2	Box 5654A, M6	34C13	Box 6466K, M42
2	Box 5654B, M6	34C13	Box 6468K, M42
4	Box 5666A, M6	34C12	Box 6475A, M42
4	Box 5666B, M6	34C12	Box 6484A, M42
4	Box 5677B, M6	24A34	Box 6484J, M42
2	Box 5681A, M6	24B33	Box 6485K, M42
2	Box 5681B, M6	24C33	Box 6486J, M42
1	Box 5691A, M6	24B34	Box 6490K, M42
1	Box 5691B, M6	34C12	Box 6492A, M42
3	Box 5693A, M6	34C12	Box 6495A, M42
1	Box 5693B, M6	24B34	Box 6495K, M42
2	Box 5694A, M6	24B34	Box 64951, M42
2	Box 5694B, M6	24B34	Box 6499K, M42
2	Box 5695A, M6	24B34	Box 6500J, M42
2	Box 5695B, M6	24C34	Box 6500L, M42
	Box 5703M, M6	24B32	Box 6503J, M42
	Box 5704A, M6	16B33	Box 6519A, M42
	Box 5704B, M6	16B32	Box 6588A, M42
	Box 5710A, M6	5C21	Box 6637A, M42
	Box 5710B, M6	5C21	Box 6637B, M42
	Box 5711L, M6	6A13	Box 6653A, M42
	Box 5724A, M6	6A12	Box 6653B, M42
	Box 5724B, M6	6A12	Box 6667A, M42
	Box 6238A, M42	6A12	Box 6667B, M42
	Box 6238B, M42	3B41	Box 6682A, M42
	Box 6247A, M42	3B41	Box 6682B, M42
	Box 6247B, M42	3C22	Box 6697A, M42
	Box 6260A, M42	3C22	Box 6697B, M42
	Box 6260B, M42	4A11	Box 6714A, M42
	Box 6275A, M42	4A11	Box 6714B, M42
	Box 6275B, M42	45A43	Box 7979A, Warwick by pass
	Box 6277A, M42	45A43	Box 7979B, Warwick by pass
	Box 6277B, M42	45B14	Box 8000B, M69
	Box 6282A, M42	45A22	Box 8015A, M69
	Box 6282B, M42	45B11	Box 8015B, M69
	Box 6286K, M42	41B34	Box 8031A, M69
	Box 6286L, M42	41C41	Box 8031B, M69
	Box 6288B, M42	41C23	Box 8047A, M69
	Box 6289A, M42	41C24	Box 8047B, M69
	Box 6289L, M42	42A11	Box 8062A, M69
	Box 6294A, M42	42A11	Box 8062B, M69
	Box 6294B, M42	32A34	Box 8077A, M69
	Box 6297B, M42	32A34	Box 8077B, M69
	Box 6297M, M42	32B23	Box 8087A, M69
	Box 6298A, M42	32B23	Box 8087B, M69
	Box 6299J, M42	178B11	Box 9317A, M40
	Box 6301B, M42	167B32	Box 9317B, M40
	Box 6302A, M42	166C33	Box 9332A, M40
	Box 6302B, M42	166C33	Box 9332B, M40
	Box 6306K, M42	166B22	Box 9347A, M40

Map ref	Address
166B22	Box 9347B, M40
166A12	Box 9361A, M40
166A12	Box 9361B, M40
151A33	Box 9376A, M40
151A33	Box 9376B, M40
150B14	Box 9405A, M40
150B14	Box 9405B, M40
134B43	Box 9423A, M40
134B43	Box 9423B, M40
133C31	Box 9441A, M40
133C31	Box 9441B, M40
133A22	Box 9459A, M40
133A22	Box 9459B, M40
115C43	Box 9476A, M40
115C43	Box 9476B, M40
115B41	Box 9490A, M40
115B41	Box 9490B, M40
115A31	Box 9505A, M40
115A31	Box 9505B, M40
114B23	Box 9521A, M40
114B23	Box 9521B, M40
114A21	Box 9532A, M40
114A21	Box 9532B, M40
114A22	Box 9532B, M40
113C13	Box 9543A, M40
113C13	Box 9543B, M40
113B11	Box 9558A, M40
113B11	Box 9558B, M40
95A33	Box 9574A, M40
95A33	Box 9574B, M40
94C31	Box 9588A, M40
94C23	Box 9588B, M40
94A14	Box 9602A, M40
94A14	Box 9602B, M40
94A11	Box 9618A, M40
94A11	Box 9618B, M40
77B34	Box 9634A, M40
77B34	Box 9634B, M40
77B31	Box 9648A, M40
77B31	Box 9648B, M40
77A23	Box 9664A, M40
77A23	Box 9664B, M40
76B12	Box 9674A, M40
76B12	Box 9674B, M40
58C44	Box 9681A, M40
76A12	Box 9684A, M40
76A12	Box 9684B, M40
58C44	Box 9689A, M40
76A11	Box 9694A, M40
76A11	Box 9694B, M40
58C44	Box 9697A, M40
58C44	Box 9697J, M40
58C42	Box 9700A, M42
58C44	Box 9700B, M42
58C44	Box 9700J, M40
58C44	Box 9700K, M42
58C44	Box 9700L, M42
58C44	Box 9700M, M42
58C34	Box 9705J, M40

Map ref	Address
58C44	Box 9705M, M42
58B44	Box 9706A, M42
53A44	Boyce Way, Long Lawford
14B34	Bracebridge Road, Atherstone
11B33	Bracebridge Road, Kingsbury
30A12	Bracebridge Street, Nuneaton
70C23	Bracken Close, Overslade, Rugby
34B14	Bracken Croft, Chelmsley Wood
42B14	Bracken Drive, Wolvey
89B31	Brackendale Drive, Barby
29C21	Brackendale Drive, Heath End, Nuneaton
45A42	Brade Drive, Walsgrave on Sowe
30B24	Bradestone Road, Caldwell, Nune
115B33	Bradford Close, Bishops Tachbroo
22B42	Brading Road, Weddington, Nune
42A21	Bradley House Farm, Wolvey
131A22	Bradshaw Farm, Wasperton
98A12	Braemar Road, Lillington, Leamin Spa
30A21	Braemar Way, Heath End, Nunea
34C21	Braeside Croft, Chelmsley Wood
71A33	Brafield Leys, Hillside, Rugby
157C14	Braggington Lane, Bragginton, Welford on Avon
188B11	Brailes Hill Farm, Upper Brailes, Brailes
174B43	Brailes Lane, Whatcote
183B23	Brailes Road, Idlicote
183B23	Brailes Road, Upper Brailes, Brai
183B21	Brailes Road, Whatcote
184A41	Brailes Road, Winderton
183B21	Brailles Road, Whatcote
5A23	Brain Street, Amington Ind.est., Tamworth
70C24	Braken Drive, Overslade, Rugby
9A43	Braken Drive, Sutton Coldfield
115C12	Brakesmead, Leamington Spa
31A14	Bramble Close, Attleborough, N
25A34	Bramble Close, Coleshill
5A33	Brambling, Stoneydelph, Tamw
31C42	Bramcote Barracks, Bramcote, B Hastings
31C33	Bramcote Childrens Hospital, B
41B22	Bramcote Close, Ryton, Bedwor
42A12	Bramcote Driving Range
31C33	Bramcote Hospital, Bramcote, N
22B31	Bramdene Avenue, Weddington Nuneaton
41A14	Brampton Way, Bulkington, Be
50A32	Brandon Court, Binley Woods
51B33	Brandon Grange Farm, Brando
67A11	Brandon Grounds Farm, Brand
50C44	Brandon Hall Hotel, Brandon
45A44	Brandon Lane, Binley Woods
50C44	Brandon Lane, Brandon, Wolst
50C44	Brandon Lane, Coten
66B12	Brandon Lane, Coventry
50A44	Brandon Lane, Willenhall, Binl

ref	Address	Map ref	Address
31	Brandon Parade, Leamington Spa	83B42	Bridge Barn Farm, Weston Under
31	Brandon Speedway, Brandon		Wetherley
31	Brandon Stadium, Brandon	119A34	Bridge Court, Southam
3	Brandon Wood Farm, Brandon	96C44	Bridge End, Bridge End, Warwick
3	Brandon Wood Farm, Brandon Woods	119B31	Bridge End, Southam
4	Bransons Cross Farm, Bransons Cross,	14C22	Bridge Farm, Atherstone
	Beoley	6C43	Bridge Farm, Dordon
11	Braunston Lodge Farm, Braunston	169B13	Bridge Farm, Long Marston
2	Braunston Place, Ashlawn Estate, Rugby	187A14	Bridge Farm, Willington, Barcheston
1	Brawning Close, Robinsons End,	98A33	Bridge House, Leamington Spa
	Nuneaton	136A22	Bridge Lane, Ladbroke
4	Bray Bank, Furnace End, Over Whitacre	15A34	Bridge Lane, Witherley
4	Brays Close, Brinklow	164A24	Bridge Road, Butlers Marston
1	Breach Farm, Claverdon	97A32	Bridge Row, Emscote, Warwick
1	Breach Lane, Claverdon	152A42	Bridge Street, Avon Dassett
	Breach Oak Farm, Astley	114A42	Bridge Street, Barford
	Breach Oak Farm, Corley	30A22	Bridge Street, Coten
	Breach Oak Lane, Astley	97A32	Bridge Street, Emscote, Warwick
	Breach Oak Lane, Corley	152A42	Bridge Street, Fenny Compton
	Breach Oak Lane, Fillongley	130C34	Bridge Street, Hampton Lucy
	Bread Lane	18B12	Bridge Street, Hurley, Kingsbury
	Breeden Drive, Curdworth	63C44	Bridge Street, Kenilworth
	Brees Lane, Frogmore	164B22	Bridge Street, Kineton
	Brendan Close, Coleshill	147B13	Bridge Street, Mountford, Wellesbourne
	Brendon Way, Stockingford, Nuneaton	30B11	Bridge Street, Nuneaton
	Brendon, Stoneydelph, Tamworth	6A23	Bridge Street, Polesworth
	Brentwood Avenue, Finham	71B12	Bridge Street, Rugby
	Brese Avenue, Woodloes, Warwick	145A21	Bridge Street, Stratford upon Avon
	Bretford Road, Brandon	65B14	Bridge View, Baginton
	Bretford Road, Wolston	145A22	Bridgefoot, Stratford upon Avon
	Brethrens Farm, Harbury	125A32	Bridgend, Alcester
	Bretts Hall Estate, Ansley Common,	70C12	Bridget Street, Rugby
	Ansley	145B31	Bridgetown Farm, Stratford upon Avon
	Brewer Road, Bulkington, Bedworth	145A24	Bridgetown Green, Stratford upon
	Brewery Lane, Little Compton		Avon
	Brewery Row, Little Compton	145A24	Bridgetown Road, Stratford upon
	Brewery Street, Stratford upon Avon		Avon
	Brewery Terrace, Leamington Spa	145A22	Bridgeway, Stratford upon Avon
	Briar Close, Lillington, Leamington Spa	70C11	Bridle Road, New Bilton, Rugby
	Briar Farm, Botts Green, Over Whitacre	150A11	Bridle Road, Lighthorne Heath
	Briar Wood Close, Cheswick Green	51C13	Brierleys Farm, Brinklow
	Briar, Amington Ind.est., Tamworth	97A23	Brigade Stores, Warwick
	Briardene Avenue, Bedworth	196B21	Bright Hill Farm, Rollright
	Briars Close, Long Lawford	14B21	Bridnley Close, Atherstone
	Briars Close, Nuneaton	40A34	Brindley Road, Exhall, Bedworth
	Briars Court, Stratford upon Avon	72A24	Brindley Road, Lower Hillmorton,
	Briars Croft, Stratford upon Avon		Rugby
	Brick Hill Drive, Chelmsley Wood	45C33	Brinklow Road, Anstey
	Brick Kiln Farm, Pillerton Priors	50A22	Brinklow Road, Binley
	Brick Kiln Lane, Hunts Green,	50A22	Brinklow Road, Binley Woods
	Middleton	45C33	Brinklow Road, Coombe Fields, Anstey
	Brick Kiln Lane, Hurley, Kingsbury	52A13	Brinklow Road, Easenhall
	Brickfield Farm, Coleshill	39C22	Brisbane Court, Bedworth
	Brickhill Close, Shipston on Stour	147A32	Bristol Way, Mountford, Wellesbourne
	Brickholes Farm, Bransons Cross, Beoley	14C23	British Home Stores, Atherstone
	Brickyard Farm, Snitterfield	150A14	British Leyland Proving Ground,
	Brickyard Lane, Haseley Knob, Haseley		Lighthorne Heath, Gaydon
	Brickyard Lane, Studley	90A44	British Leyland Staff College, Studley
	Brickyards Road, Napton on The Hill		

Map ref	Address
47A34	British Telecom Management College, Newbold Revel
31A33	Britten Close, Whitestone, Nuneaton
112C12	Brittens Lane, Lower Norton
112C12	Brittens Lane, Lower Norton, Wolverton
175C14	Brixfield Farm, Tysoe
23A43	Brixham Close, Nuneaton
162B41	Broad Close, Ettington
117C31	Broad Close, Ufton
74B23	Broad Lane, Bransons Cross, Beoley
37B11	Broad Lane, Fillongley
75A12	Broad Lane, Wood End, Tanworth in Arden
169B43	Broad Marston Road, Mickleton
98A21	Broad Oak Court, Leamington Spa
51C14	Broad Street, Brinklow
96C34	Broad Street, Coten End, Warwick
191C42	Broad Street, Long Compton
144C24	Broad Street, Stratford upon Avon
144C24	Broad Walk, Stratford upon Avon
98B42	Broadhaven Close, Sydenham Farm Estate, Leamington Spa
144B11	Broadmeadow Lane, Stratford upon Avon
191A11	Broadmoor Farm, Little Wolford
82C43	Broadway, Cubbington
102B33	Broadwell House Farm, Broadwell, Leamington Hastings
103B31	Broadwell Road, Grandborough
17B12	Brock Close, Kingsbury
63B12	Brockendon Grange Farm, Stoneleigh
62A21	Brockhill Farm, Frogmore
74A13	Brockhill Lane, Pink Green, Beoley
32B12	Brockhurst Avenue, Hinckley
47C14	Brockhurst Farm, Monks Kirby
9B43	Brockhurst Farm, Sutton Coldfield
44A33	Brockhurst Lane, Monks Kirby
47C1	Brockhurst Road, Monks Kirby
23C32	Brodick Road, Hinckley
29C14	Brodick Way, Heath End, Nuneaton
11B41	Bromage Avenue, Kingsbury
77B14	Brome Hall Lane, Lapworth
144B14	Bromford Way, Stratford upon Avon
63C41	Bromley Close, Kenilworth
107C34	Bromsgrove Road, Spernall, Studley
133B31	Bromson Hall Farm, Newbold Pacey
133A23	Bromson Hill Farm, Newbold Pacey
71C24	Bromwich Road, Hillmorton, Rugby
20C44	Bronte Close, Galley Common, Nuneaton
21A43	Bronte Close, Robinsons End, Nuneaton
71B14	Bronte Close, Rugby
30C31	Bronze Close, Nuneaton
5A33	Brook Avenue, Stoneydelph, Tamworth
96C44	Brook Close, Bridge End, Warwick
26B12	Brook Cottage Close, Furnace End, Over Whitacre
187B22	Brook Cottage, Willington

Map ref	Address
187A14	Brook Cottage, Willington, Barches
58B12	Brook Dale, Cheswick Green
92A32	Brook End Close, Henley in Arden
92A32	Brook End Drive, Henley in Arden
18B22	Brook End Farm, Brook End, King
120C43	Brook End Farm, Chapel Green, Napton on The Hill
10C11	Brook End Farm, Drayton Bassett
18B22	Brook End Lane, Brook End, King
85C43	Brook Farm Close, Birdingbury
155B24	Brook Farm, Abbotts Salford, Salf Priors
72A44	Brook Farm, Barby
85C43	Brook Farm, Birdingbury
10B12	Brook Farm, Drayton Bassett
61C23	Brook Farm, Frogmore
6C32	Brook Farm, Grendon
35B33	Brook Farm, Little Packington
64C32	Brook Farm, Stoneleigh
142A42	Brook Fields Farm, Bidford
93C12	Brook Furlong Farm, Sibson, Row
26C42	Brook Hall Farm, Shawbury, Fill
19C44	Brook House Farm, Ansley
76B24	Brook House Farm, Lapworth
75A14	Brook House Farm, Tanworth in
148C11	Brook Lane, Moreton Morrell
172B24	Brook Lane, Newbold on Stour, Tredington
22B41	Brook Lane, Weddington, Nunea
126C14	Brook Road, Aston Cantlow
30A44	Brook Street, Collycroft, Bedwor
152A42	Brook Street, Fenny Compton
96C41	Brook Street, Warwick
68A12	Brook Street, Wolston
172B24	Brook Terrace, Newbold on Sto
14C42	Brook Walk, Mancetter
22C33	Brookdale Road, Weddington, N
154C32	Brookdale, Harvington
81A12	Brooke Road, Windy Arbour, Kenilworth
42B11	Brookfield Drive, Wolvey
45A14	Brookfield Farm, Shilton
42B32	Brookfield Farm, Wolvey
82C43	Brookfield Road, Cubbington
164A14	Brookhampton Lane, Kineton
97B21	Brookhurst Court, Leamington
74B24	Brooklands Farm, Aspley Heat Tanworth in Arden
164B23	Brooklands Farm, Kineton
39C22	Brooklea, Bedworth
104B12	Brooks Close, Willoughby
80C11	Brookside Avenue, Kenilworth
48A32	Brookside Avenue, Pailton
147B22	Brookside Avenue, Wellesbour Hasting, Wellesbourne
71A21	Brookside Close, Rugby
144C13	Brookside Close, Stratford upo
73C13	Brookside Close, Yelvertoft
115C23	Brookside Farm, Bishops Tach

ref	Address	Map ref	Address
A41	Brookside Holding Mushroom Farm, Bishops Itchington	28C12	Buchan Close, Galley Common, Nuneaton
1	Brookside Place, Sheepy Magna, Sheepy	70C23	Buchanan Road, Overslade, Rugby
C13	Brookside Road, Stratford upon Avon		Buchhers Yard, Gatehouse Lane, Bedworth
343	Brookside, Snitterfield	96C24	Buckden Close, Woodloes, Warwick
41	Brookside, Stretton on Dunsmore	5B23	Buckden, Stoneydelph, Tamworth
12	Brookside, Wootton Wawen	156C31	Buckle Street, Bickmarsh
21	Brookvale Road, Stratford upon Avon	92B14	Buckley Green Farm, Buckley Green, Beaudesert
23	Brookville Drive, Brownsover, Rugby	92B13	Buckley Green Lane, Buckley Green, Beaudesert
3	Brookweed, Amington Ind.est., Tamworth	98B23	Buckley Road, Lillington, Leamington Spa
3	Broom Close, Overslade, Rugby	72A34	Bucknill Crescent, Hillmorton, Rugby
23	Broom Farm, Ardens Grafton, Bidford	73C41	Bucknills Lane, Crick
41	Broom Farm, Broom, Bidford	21A34	Bucks Hill Fields Farm, Bucks Hill, Nuneaton
33	Broom Hall Farm, Epwell	21B41	Buckshill, Bucks Hill, Nuneaton
2	Broom Hill Farm, Bubbenhall	55A44	Buckwell Lane, Clifton upon Dunsmore
4	Broom Hill Farm, Stretton on Dunsmore	95B32	Budbrooke Farm, Budbrooke
32	Broom Lane, Dunnington, Salford Priors	96B31	Budbrooke Road, Warwick
34	Broom Mill, Broom, Bidford	92A31	Builth Farm, Henley in Arden
3	Broome Close, Leek Wootton	31A32	Bulkington Lane, Whitestone, Nuneaton
3	Broomey Croft Farm, Kingsbury	41B21	Bulkington Recreation Ground, Bulkington
	Broomfield Farm, Bentley	42B11	Bulkington Road Estate, Wolvey
	Broomfield Rise, Heath End, Nuneaton	40B22	Bulkington Road, Bulkington, Bedworth
2	Broomy Bank, Kenilworth	41B34	Bulkington Road, Shilton
	Brosley Estate, Kingsbury	40C21	Bulkington Road, Weston in Arden
	Browning Avenue, Forbes Estate, Warwick	42A14	Bulkington Road, Wolvey
4	Browning Close, Galley Common, Nuneaton	55B11	Bull Acre Lane, Shawell
	Browning Road, Hillmorton, Rugby	84B12	Bull And Butcher Farm, Stretton on Dunsmore
	Brownley Green Lane, Bedworth	117B44	Bull Ring Farm Road, Harbury
	Brownley Green Lane, Beausale, Hatton	117B42	Bull Ring Farm, Harbury
	Brownlow Street, Leamington Spa	30B22	Bull Street, Attleborough, Nuneaton
4	Browns Bridge Road, Southam	119A24	Bull Street, Southam
	Browns Farm, Arley	144C24	Bull Street, Stratford upon Avon
	Browns Lane, Dordon	81A21	Bullimore Grove, Kenilworth
	Brownsover Hall, Brownsover, Rugby	81A24	Bullimore Lodge, Leek Wootton
	Brownsover Lane, Newton And Biggin	79C41	Bulloaks Farm, Beausale
	Brownsover Lane, Rugby	4A21	Bulls Lane, Austrey
	Brownsover Road, Brownsover, Rugby	16A23	Bulls Lane, Overgreen, Wishaw
	Brownsover Road, Glebe Farm Estate	125A34	Bullshead Yard, Alcester
	Brownsover Road, Newbold on Avon	37B11	Bun Lane, Fillongley
	Brownsover Road, Swift Valley Estate	15A43	Bund Lane, Mancetter
	Broxell Close, Wedgenock Industrial, Warwick	82B44	Bungalow Farm, Cubbington
	Bruce Road, Exhall, Bedworth	151B21	Bungalow Farm, Knightcote, Burton Dassett
	Brunel Close, Whitnash	119B33	Bungalow Farm, Southam
	Brunel Walk, Polesworth	116B34	Bungalow Hill Farm, Whitnash
	Brunes Court, Brownsover, Rugby	124B12	Bunkers Hill Farm, Alcester
	Brunswick Court, Leamington Spa	99C41	Bunkers Hill Farm, Offchurch
	Brunswick Street, Leamington Spa	128C42	Burbage Avenue, Stratford upon Avon
	Bruton Farm, Admington	33B14	Burbage Fields Farm, Hinckley
	Brutus Drive, Coleshill	39B43	Burbages Lane, Ash Green, Bedworth
	Bryant Road, Exhall, Bedworth	40B11	Burbury Close, Bedworth
	Bubbenhall Lane, Baginton	98C21	Burbury Close, Lillington, Leamington Spa
	Bubbenhall Road, Baginton		
	Buccleuch Close, Dunchurch		

Map ref	Address
109A23	Burford Lane Farm, Great Alne
109A23	Burford Lane, Aston Cantlow
108B24	Burford Lane, Morgrove Coppice, Spernall
116B14	Burford Mews, Sydenham Farm Estate, Leamington Spa
145B22	Burford Road, Stratford upon Avon
30B11	Burgage Place, Nuneaton
97A21	Burges Grove, Warwick
30C22	Burghley Close, Attleborough, Nuneaton
125B32	Burgundy Court, Alcester
29C24	Burmah Way, Heath End, Nuneaton
25A43	Burman Drive, Coleshill
187A32	Burmington Farm, Burmington
187B31	Burmington Hill Farm, Burmington
188A34	Burmington Road, Cherington
21A44	Burnaby Close, Whittleford, Nuneaton
141B43	Burnell Close, Bidford
150A14	Burnett Road, Lighthorne Heath, Lighthorne
52A44	Burnham Farm, Stretton Under Fosse
23A41	Burnham Rise, Saint Nicholas Park, Nuneaton
96B43	Burns Avenue, Forbes Estate, Warwick
98A12	Burns Road, Lillington, Leamington Spa
40B32	Burns Walk, Bedworth
70C22	Burnside, Rugby
99C33	Burnt Heath Farm, Offchurch
84A13	Burnthurst Farm, Stretton on Dunsmore
84A22	Burnthurst Lane, Princethorpe
67B43	Burnthurst Lane, Stretton on Dunsmore
38B34	Burrow Hill Lane, Corley
116B23	Burrows Close, Whitnash
166B13	Burton Dassett Road, Burton Dassett
128B41	Burton Farm, Bishopton, Drayton
63A14	Burton Green Farm, Burton Green, Kenilworth
166A32	Burton Hill Farm, Burton Dassett
166B12	Burton Hills Road, Burton Dassett Hills, Burton Dassett
31C34	Burton Lane, Burton Hastings
31C31	Burton Mill, Burton Hastings
4C24	Burton Road, Twycross
150C41	Burton View Farm, Burton Dassett
178C31	Bury Court Farm, Shotteswell
97C42	Bury Road, Leamington Spa
191C41	Buryway Lane, Long Compton
134B12	Bush Heath Lane, Harbury
134C11	Bush Heath Road, Harbury
122B13	Bush Hill Farm, Flecknoe, Wolfhamcote
122B11	Bush Hill Lane, Flecknoe, Wolfhamcote
34B14	Bushberry Croft, Chelmsley Wood
112A44	Bushes Farm, Snitterfield
77B41	Bushwood Common Farm, Lapworth
60A14	Bushwood Drive, Dorridge
77B41	Bushwood Farm, Bushwood
93B11	Bushwood Farm, Lowsonford, Rowington
77A34	Bushwood Hall Farm, Bushwood
77A34	Bushwood Lane, Bushwood
76B34	Bushwood Lane, Lapworth
93B11	Bushwood Orchard Farm, Lowsonf Rowington
135B23	Butchers Close, Bishops Itchington
51C14	Butchers Close, Brinklow
17C43	Butchers Lane, Nether Whitacre
64B41	Butler Close, Kenilworth
192B43	Butler Road Farm, Long Compton
106C23	Butler Street, Astwood Bank
191C42	Butlers Close, Long Compton
40A23	Butlers Crescent, Exhall, Bedworth
79B21	Butlers End, Haseley
196B11	Butlers Hill Farm, Long Compton
13B21	Butlers Lane, Grendon Common, Grendon
54B43	Butlers Leap, Butlers Leap Estate,
196B11	Butlers Road Farm, Long Compto
191C44	Butlers Road, Long Compton
168B24	Butlin Farm, Claydon
71C11	Butlin Road, Rugby
120C32	Butt Hill, Napton on The Hill
117C44	Butt Lane, Harbury
125B31	Butter Street, Alcester
23A41	Buttermere Avenue, Saint Nichola Park, Nuneaton
54B34	Buttermere, Brownsover, Rugby
93C31	Buttermilk Lane, Yarningale, Cla
4A22	Butts Close, Austrey
75A24	Butts Lane, Tanworth in Arden
39C24	by pass, Bedworth
155A42	by pass, Norton
71B12	Byart Place, Rugby
138B34	Byfield Road, Priors Marston
29C12	Byford Court, Nuneaton
29C12	Byford Street, Stockingford, Nun
40B24	Byron Avenue, Bedworth
114B11	Byron Avenue, Forbes Estate, W
145A24	Byron Road, Stratford upon Avo
11B12	Cadagon Road, Dosthill, Tamwo
174A11	Cadbold Close, Pillerton Priors
174A11	Cadbold Farm, Pillerton Priors
91A24	Cadborough Farm, Oldberrow
128A43	Cadie Pool Farm, Stratford upor
128A43	Cadle Pool Farm, The Ridgeway Stratford upon Avon
40B13	Cadman Close, Bedworth
96A33	Caen Close, Hampton Magna, Budbrooke
30B14	Caernafan Drive, Nuneaton
80C21	Caesar Road, Kenilworth
24C22	Caesar Way, Coleshill
103A41	Calcutt Elms Farm, Tomlow, Grandborough
102C43	Calcutt Farm, Tomlow, Grandb

ref	Address
A12	Calcutt House Farm, Calcutt, Grandborough
321	Calcutt Road, Lower Shuckburgh
11	Caldcote Park, Rugby
31	Caldecote Close, Weddington, Nuneaton
21	Caldecote Hall Drive, Caldecote
4	Caldecote Hall, Caldecote, Nuneaton
3	Caldecott Street, Rugby
22	Calder Close, Bulkington, Bedworth
12	Calder Walk, Sydenham Farm Estate, Leamington
	Calder, Stoneydelph, Tamworth
1	Caldwell Road, Caldwell, Nuneaton
4	Calendar Farm, Weddington, Nuneaton
33	Calias Lane, Birdingbury Wharf, Birdingbury
41	Calias Lane, Leamington Hastings
12	Callaways Road, Shipston on Stour
3	Callender Crescent, Saint Nicholas Park, Nuneaton
4	Callendar Crescent, Weddington, Nuneaton
	Camberwell Terrace, Leamington Spa
	Camborne Drive, Nuneaton
	Cambourne House, Goodyears End, Bedworth
	Cambray Cottage, Leamington Spa
	Cambridge Drive, Chelmsley Wood
	Cambridge Drive, Stockingford, Nuneaton
	Cambridge Gardens, Leamington Spa
	Cambridge Street, Rugby
4	Camden Close, Barton on The Heath
	Camelot Grove, Kenilworth
	Cameron Close, Lillington, Leamington Spa
	Camhouses, Stoneydelph, Tamworth
	Camp Farm, Hurley, Kingsbury
	Camp Farm, Kenilworth
	Camp Farm, Wappenbury
	Camp Farm, Weston in Arden, Bedworth
	Camp Hill Farm, Beaudesert
	Camp House Farm, Beaudesert
	Camp Lane, Beaudesert
	Camp Lane, Knowle End, Warmington
	Camp Lane, Lapworth
	Camp Lee Crescent, Chelmsley Wood
	Campbell Street, New Bilton, Rugby
	Campbells Farm, Weston Under Wetherley
	Campden Avenue, Ilmington
	Campden Hill, Ilmington
	Campden Lawns, Alderminster
	Campden Pitch, Ilmington
	Campden Road, Clifford Chambers
	Campden Road, Ebrington
	Campden Road, High Cross Claybrook
	Campden Road, Quinton

Map ref	Address
186A12	Campden Road, Rowborough, Stretton on Fosse
181C44	Campden Road, Shipston on Stour
180A13	Campden Street, Ilmington
21B34	Camphill Drive, Camphill, Nuneaton
79B24	Camphill Farm, Beausale
21B34	Camphill Road, Camphill, Nuneaton
98A22	Campion Green, Leamington Spa
98A21	Campion Road, Leamington Spa
169C24	Campion Road, Lower Clopton, Quinton
98A24	Campion Terrace, Leamington Spa
116B11	Campion View, Sydenham Farm Estate, Leamington Spa
54B24	Campion Way, Brownsover, Rugby
41A24	Campling Close, Bulkington, Bedworth
50B21	Camville, Binley Woods
113A21	Canada Lane, Norton Lindsey
145A21	Canal Basin, Stratford upon Avon
22A31	Canal Farm, Nuneaton
95B13	Canal Lane, Hatton
145A13	Canalside, Stratford upon Avon
147B31	Canberra Close, Mountford, Wellesbourne
39C22	Canberra Court, Bedworth
75A24	Cank Farm, Tanworth in Arden
112C22	Cannings Farm, Norton Lindsey
39B41	Canon Drive, Ash Green, Nuneaton
116B22	Canon Young Road, Whitnash
107B13	Canterbury Close, Studley Common, Studley
81B13	Canterbury Close, Windy Arbour, Kenilworth
34A42	Canterbury Drive, Chelmsley Wood
23A32	Canterbury Way, Saint Nicholas Park, Nuneaton
96B32	Cape Road, The Cape, Warwick
125B32	Captains Hill, Kinwarton, Alcester
70C41	Capulet Close, Woodlands, Rugby
116B32	Caravan Farm, Whitnash
94B32	Caravan Fields, Great Pinley
82B12	Caravan Parr, Stoneleigh
39A24	Cardigan Road, Goodyears End, Bedworth
128C43	Carew Close, Stratford upon Avon
70B23	Carew Walk, Bilton, Rugby
9A43	Carhampton Road, Sutton Coldfield
34B22	Carisbroke Avenue, Chelmsley Wood
22B42	Carisbrook Road, Weddington, Nuneaton
5A24	Carlcroft, Stoneydelph, Tamworth
41A14	Carlton Close, Bulkington, Bedworth
70B24	Carlton Road, Bilton, Rugby
20C44	Carlyle Close, Galley Common, Nuneaton
	Carlyle Close, Robinsons End, Nuneaton
14C23	Carlyon Road, Atherstone
31B23	Carnoiste Close, Whitestone, Nuneaton

Map ref	Address	Map ref	Address
31A33	Caroline Close, Nuneaton	71A14	Castle Street, Rugby
	Carolyn Lane Court, Blackham Way, Rugby	90A44	Castle Street, Studley
5A23	Carradoc, Stoneydelph, Tamworth	96C41	Castle Street, Warwick
9A14	Carroway Head Hill, Hints	21A24	Castle View, Hartshill
39B43	Carsall Close, Ash Green, Bedworth	98B43	Caswell Road, Sydenham Farm Es
185C23	Carson Close, Stretton on Fosse		Leamington
114B33	Carter Drive, Barford	95B14	Catchems End, Hatton
145C11	Carters Lane, Tiddington, Stratford	77A24	Catesby Farm, Lapworth
	upon Avon	77A22	Catesby Lane, Lapworth
13B21	Carts Lane, Grendon Common, Grendon	71B24	Catesby Road, Rugby
78B32	Case Lane, Mousley End, Rowington	2A41	Catherine Place, Amington, Tamw
78C23	Case Lane, Shrewley	52C24	Cathiron Farm, Cathiron, Harboro
115C12	Cashmore Avenue, Leamington Spa		Magna
39B24	Cashmore Road, Goodyears End,	52C23	Cathiron Lane, Easenhall
	Bedworth	53B23	Cathiron Lane, Harborough Magr
81B14	Cashmore Road, Kenilworth	52C22	Cathiron, Brinklow
81B11	Casita Grove, Windy Arbour,	9A44	Cattell Drive, Sutton Coldfield
	Kenilworth	96C33	Cattell Road, Warwick
64B14	Cassandra Close, Canley	55C23	Catthorpe Road, Catthorpe
92B32	Castle Close, Beaudesert	55A14	Catthorpe Road, Shawell
37C21	Castle Close, Fillongley	14B31	Cattle Arches, Merevale
96C41	Castle Close, Warwick	71B11	Cattle Market, Rugby
64A41	Castle Court, Kenilworth	183B42	Caution Corner, Upper Brailes
96C41	Castle Court, Warwick	30C23	Cavalier Close, Nuneaton
164B21	Castle Crescent, Kineton	50A31	Cavans Way, Binley Woods
28C33	Castle Drive, Astley	71B14	Cavell Court, Rugby
25A43	Castle Drive, Coleshill	31B32	Cavendish Walk, Nuneaton
109C44	Castle Farm, Aston Cantlow	23A31	Caversham Close, Saint Nicholas
113B44	Castle Farm, Fulbrook		Nuneaton
150B14	Castle Farm, Gaydon	59C14	Cawdon Grove, Dorridge
80B12	Castle Farm, Kenilworth	69C42	Cawston Farm, Cawston, Dunch
25B41	Castle Farm, Maxstoke	70A31	Cawston Grange Farm, Cawston
90B41	Castle Farm, Washford, Studley		Dunchurch
103C11	Castle Farm, Woolscott, Grandborough	70A33	Cawston House, Cawston, Dunc
98A11	Castle Froma, Lillington, Leamington	95C34	Cawston House, Hampton Magr
	Spa	70A33	Cawston Lane, Cawston, Dunch
96C41	Castle Gate Mews, Warwick	70A23	Cawston Old Farm, Dunchurch
63B44	Castle Green, Kenilworth	70B34	Cawston Way, Bilton, Rugby
63B44	Castle Grove, Kenilworth	80C21	Ceaser Road, Kenilworth
5A23	Castle Hall, Amington Ind.est.,	98A31	Cecil Court, Leamington Spa
	Tamworth	98A11	Cedar Close, Lillington, Leamin
63C43	Castle Hill, Kenilworth	145A12	Cedar Close, Stratford upon Av
183B42	Castle Hill, Upper Brailes, Brailes	59B44	Cedar Cottage, Lapworth
96C42	Castle Hill, Warwick	11B42	Cedar Crescent, Kingsbury
28C33	Castle Lane, Astley	112B44	Cedar Drive, Snitterfield
25C34	Castle Lane, Maxstoke	97A21	Cedar Grove, Percy Estate, War
25C21	Castle Lane, Shustoke	21C41	Cedar Road, Camphill, Nuneat
96C41	Castle Lane, Warwick	169C43	Cedar Road, Mickleton
103C13	Castle Lane, Woolscott, Grandborough	34A22	Cedar Walk, Chelmsley Wood
89B21	Castle Mound, Barby	138B34	Cedars Farm, Priors Marston
125A24	Castle Road, Alcester	40A32	Cedars Road, Exhall, Bedworth
92B32	Castle Road, Beaudesert, Henley in	32A31	Ceicy Lane, Burton Hastings
	Arden	54C31	Celandine, Brownsover, Rugby
21A24	Castle Road, Hartshill	21A24	Cemetery Lane, Hartshill
63C43	Castle Road, Kenilworth	97C43	Central Avenue, Leamington S
164B13	Castle Road, Kineton	22A44	Central Avenue, Nuneaton
90A43	Castle Road, Washford, Studley	145A21	Central Chambers, Stratford u
22B33	Castle Road, Weddington, Nuneaton		Avon
106C21	Castle Street, Astwood Bank	135B23	Central Drive, Bishops Itching

Map ref	Address	Map ref	Address
C14	Central Engineers Park, Long Marston	156B14	Chapel Lane, Bidford
13	Central Hospital, Hatton	60B33	Chapel Lane, Chessetts Wood, Lapworth
23	Centram Way, Brownsover, Rugby	55A43	Chapel Lane, Clifton upon Dunsmore
22	Centurion Close, Coleshill	73C44	Chapel Lane, Crick
14	Ceolmund Crescent, Chelmsley Wood	188B11	Chapel Lane, Grove End, Brailes
C14	Cep, Long Marston	56A41	Chapel Lane, Lilbourne
32	Cesterover Farm, Churchover	172B24	Chapel Lane, Newbold on Stour,
22	Chadbury Grove, Lillington,		Tredington
	Leamington Spa	174A12	Chapel Lane, Pillerton Priors
41	Chadshunt Farm, Chadshunt	177A13	Chapel Lane, Ratley, Ratley And
A44	Chadshunt Road, Burton Dassett		Upton
42	Chadshunt Road, Chadshunt	67A22	Chapel Lane, Ryton on Dunsmore
A21	Chadswell Lane, Cook Hill, Inkberrow	145A21	Chapel Lane, Stratford upon Avon
32	Chadwick End Farm, Chadwick End	91B12	Chapel Lane, Ullenhall
34	Chadwick Lane, Chadwick End	15A34	Chapel Lane, Witherley
24	Chadwick Manor Farm, Chadwick End	155A12	Chapel Oak Farm, Salford Priors
34	Chaffinch Drive, Kingshurst	106C23	Chapel Road, Astwood Bank
11	Chalfont Close, Collycroft, Bedworth	194C24	Chapel Row, Little Compton
43	Chamberlain Close, Cubbington	96C33	Chapel Row, Warwick
21	Chamberlain Drive, Lighthorne Heath,	106C21	Chapel Street, Astwood Bank
	Lighthorne	40B13	Chapel Street, Bedworth
22	Chamberlain Lane, Cook Hill,	135A32	Chapel Street, Bishops Itchington
	Inkberrow	134B12	Chapel Street, Harbury
4	Chamberlain Road, Hillmorton, Rugby	89C21	Chapel Street, Kilsby
3	Chamberlaine Street, Bedworth	98A33	Chapel Street, Leamington Spa
1	Chamberlains Walk, Coleshill	70A11	Chapel Street, Long Lawford
2	Chance Fields, Radford Semele	147B21	Chapel Street, Mountford,
4	Chancery Court, Chapel End, Nuneaton		Wellesbourne
4	Chancery Lane, Chapel End, Nuneaton	30B11	Chapel Street, Nuneaton
4	Chanders Road, Woodloes, Warwick	71A13	Chapel Street, Rugby
	Chandlers Drive, Amington, Tamworth	145A21	Chapel Street, Stratford upon Avon
21	Chandlers Road, Whitnash	56A14	Chapel Street, Swinford
4	Chandos Street, Leamington Spa	178A11	Chapel Street, Warmington
4	Chandos Street, Nuneaton	96C33	Chapel Street, Warwick
2	Changebrook Close, Saint Nicholas	158A12	Chapel Street, Welford on Avon
	Park, Nuneaton	156B12	Chapel Walk, Bidford
	Chantry Close, Wedgenock Industrial,	51C14	Chapel Yard, Brinklow
	Warwick	34A21	Chapelhouse Road, Chelmsley Wood
4	Chantry Crescent, Alcester	98C43	Chapman Close, Radford Semele
	Chantry Heath Lane, Baginton	97A32	Chapman Court, Warwick
	Chantry Heath Lane, Stoneleigh	125B24	Chapman Way, Alcester
4	Chapel Ascote Hill, Chapel Ascote	54A33	Chariot Way, Glebe Farm Estate, Rugby
2	Chapel Ascote Home Farm Road,	19C33	Charity Farm, Ansley
	Chapel Ascote	13A41	Charity Farm, Baxterley
	Chapel Close, Chelmsley Wood	21A24	Charity Farm, Hartshill
3	Chapel End, Radway	39A41	Charity Road, Keresley Newlands,
	Chapel Farm, Barby		Keresley
	Chapel Farm, Bentley	116B12	Charlbury Mews, Sydenham Farm
	Chapel Farm, Draycote		Estate, Leamington Spa
	Chapel Farm, Studley	145C13	Charlecote Close, Tiddington,
	Chapel Fields, Swinford		Stratford upon Avon
	Chapel Gardens, Bidford	147B14	Charlecote Court, Wellesbourne
	Chapel Gardens, Stretton on Fosse	116C13	Charlecote Gardens, Radford Semele
	Chapel Gate Farm, Ullenhall	131B23	Charlecote Park, Charlecote,
	Chapel Green Farm, Chapel Green,		Wellesbourne
	Napton on the Hill	131A32	Charlecote Quarry, Charlecote
	Chapel Hill Farm, Bishops Tachbrook	131A41	Charlecote Road, Charlecote
	Chapel Lane, Aston Cantlow	96C34	Charles Court, Coten End, Warwick
	Chapel Lane, Barnacle, Shilton		

Map ref	Address
39C14	Charles Eaton Road, Bedworth Woodlands, Bedworth
97C44	Charles Gardener Road, Leamington Spa
41B43	Charles Larrin Close, Barnacle, Shilton
14C34	Charles Road, Mancetter
97A31	Charles Street, All Saints, Warwick
12B43	Charles Street, Hurley, Kingsbury
28A32	Charles Street, New Arley, Arley
22A43	Charles Street, Nuneaton
70C14	Charles Street, Rugby
71A14	Charles Warren Close, Rugby
98A22	Charles Watson Court, Lillington, Leamington Spa
71A31	Charlesfield Road, Kingsway, Rugby
97C44	Charlotte Street, Leamington Spa
71A12	Charlotte Street, Rugby
29C23	Charnwood Avenue, Arbury, Nuneaton
21A21	Charnwood Drive, Hartshill
98B14	Charnwood Way, Lillington, Leamington Spa
71C31	Charter Road, Ashlawn Estate, Rugby
30C24	Chartwell Close, Attleborough, Nuneaton
54C34	Charwelton Drive, Brownsover, Rugby
71B23	Chas Watts, Rugby
22C41	Chase Close, Weddington, Nuneaton
63A31	Chase Farm, Burton Green, Kenilworth
63B34	Chase Lane, Burton Green, Kenilworth
6A31	Chator Road, Polesworth
30C22	Chatsworth Drive, Attleborough, Nuneaton
116C11	Chatsworth Gardens, Sydenham Farm Estate, Leamington Spa
64B43	Chatsworth Grove, Kenilworth
24C23	Chattle Hill, Coleshill
29A11	Chaucer Drive, Galley Common, Nuneaton
21A43	Chaucer Drive, Robinsons End, Nuneaton
70C42	Chaucer Road, Hillside, Rugby
59C21	Cheedon Close, Dorridge
59A33	Cheeton Farm, Cheswick Green
25A41	Chelmsley Avenue, Coleshill
34A14	Chelmsley Circle, Chelmsley Wood
34A31	Chelmsley Lane, Chelmsley Wood
34B13	Chelmsley Road, Chelmsley Wood
23A33	Chelsea Close, Saint Nicholas Park, Nuneaton
40A12	Cheltenham Close, Collycroft, Bedworth
79A22	Cheneys Farm, Haseley
145B32	Chepstow Close, Stratford upon Avon
	Cheque House, Chequer Street, Nuneaton
41B23	Chequer Street, Bulkington, Bedworth
192A13	Cherington Farm, Cherington
187C44	Cherington House, Cherington
187C23	Cherington Road, Burmington
187A22	Cherington Road, Willington, Barcheston

Map ref	Address
116A32	Cherry Blossom Grove, Whitnash
162A42	Cherry Close, Ettington
18B11	Cherry Close, Hurley, Kingsbury
70C31	Cherry Grove, Bilton, Rugby
111B43	Cherry Lane, Bearley
95C34	Cherry Lane, Hampton Magna, Budbrooke
22C14	Cherry Orchard Estate, Higham, Higham on The Hill
22C14	Cherry Orchard Farm, Higham, Higham on The Hill
111B14	Cherry Orchard Farm, Langley
185B32	Cherry Orchard Farm, Stretton on Fosse
111B12	Cherry Orchard House, Langley
92B23	Cherry Orchard, Henley in Arden
181C44	Cherry Orchard, Shipston on Stou
144C23	Cherry Orchard, Stratford upon A
147B11	Cherry Orchard, Wellesbourne
81A12	Cherry Orchard, Whitemore, Kenilworth
74A31	Cherry Pit Lane, Bransons Cross,
93A44	Cherry Pool Farm
96C34	Cherry Street, Coten End, Warwic
144C24	Cherry Street, Stratford upon Avo
21C41	Cherry Tree Avenue, Camphill, Nuneaton
155C14	Cherry Tree Crescent, Salford Pri
177C11	Cherry Tree Farm, Camp Lane, Warmington
119B21	Cherry Tree Walk, Southam
81A11	Cherry Way, Whitemore, Kenilwo
21A21	Cherryfield Close, Hartshill
21A13	Cherrytree Farm, Mancetter
53B43	Cherwell Way, Rugby
97A24	Chesford Crescent, Percy Estate, Warwick
81B31	Chesford Grange Hotel, Chesford Kenilworth
81B31	Chesford Grange, Chesford, Keni
144B12	Chesford Grove, Stratford upon
81A24	Chesford Island To Gaveston Isla Warwick by pass
81A24	Chesford Island To Leek Wootto Island, Warwick by pass
81A24	Chesford Island To Stoneleigh Is Warwick by pass
81A24	Chesford Island, Warwick by pa
98B41	Chesham Street, Leamington Sp
70B31	Cheshire Close, Bilton, Rugby
38A33	Cheshire Farm, Corley Ash, Cor
71A12	Chesnut Field, Rugby
98A24	Chesnut Square, Leamington Sp
138C33	Chesnuts Farm, Priors Marston
60B33	Chessetts Wood Farm, Chessetts Lapworth
60A32	Chessetts Wood Road, Chessetts Lapworth
35A33	Chester Road, Bickenhill

ɔ ref	Address	Map ref	Address
11	Chester Road, Chelmsley Wood	5B24	Chiltern Road, Stoneydelph, Tamworth
42	Chester Road, Kingshurst	92B34	Chingley Bank, Henley in Arden
12	Chester Street, Rugby	189A41	Chinslade Farm, Sutton Under Brailes
44	Chesterton Drive, Galley Common, Nuneaton	180A12	Chipping Campden Hill, Ilmington
43	Chesterton Drive, Robinsons End, Nuneaton	196B33	Choice Hill Farm, Over Norton
		98A21	Chorlton Court, Leamington Spa
311	Chesterton Drive, Sydenham Farm Estate, Leamington Spa	14B22	Choyce Close, Atherstone
		98A43	Christine Ledger Square, Leamington Spa
21	Chesterton Farm, Frogmore		
12	Chesterton Hill Farm, Chesterton	134C43	Christmas Hill Farm, Bishops Itchington
34	Chesterton Hill, Redlands Brake, Chesterton	96B32	Christopher Close, Packmores, Warwick
44	Chesterton House Farm, Harbury	24A14	Church Avenue, Water Orton
13	Chesterton Road, Harbury	143A24	Church Bank Farm, Lower Binton, Binton
4	Chestnut Avenue, Bulkington Estate, Kenilworth	143B32	Church Bank, Lower Binton, Binton
2	Chestnut Close, Kingsbury	142B21	Church Bank, Temple Grafton
43	Chestnut Cottage, Radway	27C22	Church Close, Arley
1	Chestnut Crescent, Camphill, Nuneaton	135A32	Church Close, Bishops Itchington
3	Chestnut Green, Wolston	21A32	Church Close, Hartshill
4	Chestnut Grove, Coleshill	24A41	Church Close, Kingshurst
22	Chestnut Place, Southam	195A24	Church Close, Little Compton
	Chestnut Rise Farm, Wootton Wawen	143C44	Church Close, Luddington
23	Chestnut Road, Astwood Bank	116B21	Church Close, Whitnash
2	Chestnut Road, Bedworth	12B23	Church Close, Wood End, Kingsbury
4	Chestnut Square, Leamington Spa	153A32	Church Close, Wormleighton
14	Chestnut Square, Mountford, Wellesbourne	176B12	Church Cottage, Radway
		155C21	Church Cottage, Salford Priors
2	Chestnut Walk, Chelmsley Wood	8A34	Church Croft, Sheepy Magna, Sheepy
	Chestnut Walk, Henley in Arden	36A22	Church End Farm, Maxstoke
2	Chestnut Walk, Stratford upon Avon	18A34	Church End Farm, Nether Whitacre
	Cheswick Close, Redditch	138A43	Church End, Priors Hardwick
	Cheswick Way, Cheswick Green	98C41	Church End, Radford Semele
	Chetwynd Avenue, Polesworth	28B23	Church Farm, Astley
	Chetwynd Drive, Whitestone, Nuneaton	13B23	Church Farm, Baddesley Ensor
	Cheveral Road, Bedworth	95C33	Church Farm, Budbrooke
	Cheverel Place, Coten, Nuneaton	188A34	Church Farm, Cherington
	Cheverel Street, Coten, Nuneaton	26B22	Church Farm, Church End, Shustoke
	Cheviot Close, Stockingford, Nuneaton	38B33	Church Farm, Corley
	Cheviot Rise, Lillington, Leamington Spa	125A12	Church Farm, Coughton
		82C44	Church Farm, Cubbington
	Cheviot, Stoneydelph, Tamworth	157C31	Church Farm, Dorsington
	Chichester Close, Saint Nicholas Park, Nuneaton	11B12	Church Farm, Dosthill, Tamworth
		37C33	Church Farm, Fillongley
	Chichester Grove, Chelmsley Wood	113C34	Church Farm, Fulbrook
	Chichester Lane, Hampton Magna, Budbrooke	39A24	Church Farm, Goodyears End, Bedworth
	Chickabiddy Lane, Southam	53A14	Church Farm, Harborough Magna
	Chicken Farm, Wolston	62B43	Church Farm, Honiley
	Chicory Close, Brownsover, Rugby	35B33	Church Farm, Little Packington
	Chilcote Lane, Appleby Magna	175C41	Church Farm, Middle Tysoe, Tysoe
	Chilcote Lane, Calcutt	10A24	Church Farm, Middleton
	Chilcote Lane, Chilcote	91A41	Church Farm, Morton Bagot
	Chilcote Lane, No Mans Heath, Newton Regis	172B24	Church Farm, Newbold on Stour, Tredington
	Chilcote Lane, Streetton En Le Fiel	16A22	Church Farm, Overgreen, Wishaw
	Childs Close, Stratford upon Avon	174C34	Church Farm, Oxhill
	Chilham Drive, Chelmsley Wood	59C42	Church Farm, Packwood, Lapworth
		93A23	Church Farm, Preston Bagot

Map ref	Address
160A23	Church Farm, Preston on Stour
176B12	Church Farm, Radway
177A14	Church Farm, Ratley, Ratley And Upton
67A22	Church Farm, Ryton on Dunsmore
3A13	Church Farm, Seckington
178B34	Church Farm, Shotteswell
2C34	Church Farm, Shuttington
29B13	Church Farm, Stockingford, Nuneaton
144C32	Church Farm, Stratford upon Avon
67C43	Church Farm, Stretton on Dunsmore
142B13	Church Farm, Temple Grafton
7B11	Church Farm, Twycross
143A43	Church Farm, Welford on Avon
83A32	Church Farm, Weston Under Wetherl
153A12	Church Farm, Wormleighton
158A12	Church Field, Welford on Avon
64A42	Church Hill Avenue, Kenilworth
149B11	Church Hill Court, Lighthorne
166B14	Church Hill Farm, Burton Dassett Hills, Burton Dasset
149B11	Church Hill Farm, Lighthorne
167A21	Church Hill, Avon Dassett
115C32	Church Hill, Bishops Tachbrook
25A34	Church Hill, Coleshill
163B12	Church Hill, Combrook
82C43	Church Hill, Cubbington
167A13	Church Hill, Fenny Compton
97C31	Church Hill, Milverton, Leamington Spa
120C32	Church Hill, Napton on The Hill
99A32	Church Hill, Offchurch
67C44	Church Hill, Stretton on Dunsmore
91B13	Church Hill, Ullenhall
178A13	Church Hill, Warmington
32B44	Church Hill, Wolvey
130A43	Church Lane, Alveston, Stratford upon Avon
39B41	Church Lane, Ash Green, Bedworth
126C12	Church Lane, Aston Cantlow
4A24	Church Lane, Austrey
65C21	Church Lane, Baginton
114B41	Church Lane, Barford
111B41	Church Lane, Bearley
164A23	Church Lane, Butlers Marston
134A24	Church Lane, Chesterton
20A41	Church Lane, Church End, Ansley
93C42	Church Lane, Claverdon
124A21	Church Lane, Cook Hill, Inkberrow
38A34	Church Lane, Corley Moor, Corley
82C43	Church Lane, Cubbington
16A42	Church Lane, Curdworth
6A43	Church Lane, Dordon
162A42	Church Lane, Ettington
15C34	Church Lane, Fenny Drayton, Witherley
37C13	Church Lane, Fillongley
150B31	Church Lane, Gaydon
134C21	Church Lane, Harbury
28A23	Church Lane, Hilltop, Arley
182A21	Church Lane, Honington

Map ref	Address
177B33	Church Lane, Hornton
11B44	Church Lane, Kingsbury
76C13	Church Lane, Lapworth
17A31	Church Lane, Lea Marston
149B12	Church Lane, Lighthorne
98A13	Church Lane, Lillington, Leamington Spa
36A22	Church Lane, Maxstoke
10B24	Church Lane, Middleton
18A41	Church Lane, Nether Whitacre
27C22	Church Lane, New Arley, Arley
172B24	Church Lane, Newbold on Stour, Tredington
1C41	Church Lane, No Mans Heath, Ne Regis
28B24	Church Lane, Nuneaton
16A24	Church Lane, Overgreen, Wishaw
174C34	Church Lane, Oxhill
15A14	Church Lane, Ratcliffe Culey, With
3A13	Church Lane, Seckington
8A34	Church Lane, Sheepy Magna, She
144B21	Church Lane, Shottery, Stratford t Avon
178B34	Church Lane, Shotteswell
2C31	Church Lane, Shuttington
112B44	Church Lane, Snitterfield
65B41	Church Lane, Stoneleigh
185C23	Church Lane, Stretton on Fosse
86C22	Church Lane, Thurlaston
126B23	Church Lane, Walcote, Haselor
22B31	Church Lane, Weddington, Nune
143A43	Church Lane, Welford on Avon
174A44	Church Lane, Whatcote
116B13	Church Lane, Whitnash
44C42	Church Lane, Willey
115C31	Church Lees, Bishops Tachbrook
164B22	Church Mews, Kineton
91A14	Church Parr Farm, Ullenhall
95C34	Church Path, Hampton Magna, Budbrooke
81C23	Church Road, Ashow
106C21	Church Road, Astwood Bank
127A42	Church Road, Billesley
105B23	Church Road, Braunston
66B41	Church Road, Bubbenhall
188A43	Church Road, Cherington
52A44	Church Road, Church Lawford
93C42	Church Road, Claverdon
6A43	Church Road, Dordon
11B12	Church Road, Dosthill, Tamwor
150B23	Church Road, Gaydon
103C21	Church Road, Grandborough
21A32	Church Road, Hartshill
79B13	Church Road, Haseley Knob, H
62A44	Church Road, Honiley
83C43	Church Road, Hunningham
136A21	Church Road, Ladbroke
101A33	Church Road, Long Itchington

ref	Address	Map ref	Address
B32	Church Road, Newbold on Stour, Tredington	162B33	Churchill Close, Ettington
		160C32	Churchill Farm, Alderminster
A34	Church Road, Newbold Pacey	98C31	Churchill House, Leamington Spa
C22	Church Road, Norton Lindsey	71A23	Churchill Road, Rugby
22	Church Road, Ryton on Dunsmore	9A44	Churchill Road, Sutton Coldfield
A33	Church Road, Sherbourne	117C42	Churchland Farm, Ufton
43	Church Road, Shilton	53B11	Churchover Lane, Harborough Parva, Harborough Magna
21	Church Road, Shustoke		
311	Church Road, Snitterfield	32A31	Cicey Lane, Burton Hastings
12	Church Road, Stockingford, Nuneaton	4A31	Cinder Lane, Austrey
22	Church Road, Ullenhall	34B21	Circus Avenue, Chelmsley Wood
4	Church Road, Warton, Polesworth	107C23	Cireus Road, Tomstown, Studley
C31	Church Road, Wilmcote	124A21	Cladswell Hall Farm, Cook Hill, Inkberrow
31	Church Road, Witherley		
21	Church Row, Baddesley Ensor	98A42	Clapham Square, Leamington Spa
A43	Church Row, Cherington	98A42	Clapham Street, Leamington Spa
333	Church Street, Alcester	98A42	Clapham Terrace, Leamington Spa
2	Church Street, Atherstone	98B22	Clare Close, Lillington, Leamington Spa
A42	Church Street, Barford	70C12	Clare Court, Rugby
C12	Church Street, Bidford	41B11	Claremont Close, Bulkington, Bedworth
3	Church Street, Bulkington, Bedworth	97C44	Claremont Road, Leamington Spa
13	Church Street, Charlecote	71B13	Claremont Road, Rugby
1	Church Street, Churchover	97C23	Clarence Mansions, Leamington Spa
3	Church Street, Clifton upon Dunsmor	70C14	Clarence Road, New Bilton, Rugby
2	Church Street, Crick	144C13	Clarence Road, Stratford upon Avon
44	Church Street, Fenny Compton	98A43	Clarence Street, Leamington Spa
34	Church Street, Hampton Lucy	30A11	Clarence Street, Nuneaton
11	Church Street, Harbury	97C31	Clarence Terrace, Leamington Spa
34	Church Street, Harvington	119A32	Clarence Terrace, Southam
3	Church Street, Leamington Spa	97C23	Clarendon Avenue, Leamington Spa
1	Church Street, Marton	97C23	Clarendon Crescent, Milverton, Leamington Spa
	Church Street, Nuneaton		
4	Church Street, Rugby	97C23	Clarendon Place, Leamington Spa
43	Church Street, Shipston on Stour	81A13	Clarendon Road, Whitemore, Kenilworth
4	Church Street, Stockton		
4	Church Street, Stratford upon Avon	97C23	Clarendon Square, Leamington Spa
1	Church Street, Studley	98A23	Clarendon Street, Leamington Spa
	Church Street, Warwick	191C34	Clarendon Street, Long Compton
44	Church Street, Welford on Avon	18A33	Clarke Farm, Nether Whitacre
3	Church Street, Wellesbourne	81A13	Clarkes Avenue, Whitemore, Kenilworth
	Church Terrace, Cubbington		
2	Church Terrace, Harbury	56B42	Clarkes Farm, Lilbourne
	Church Terrace, Leamington Spa	90B34	Clarkes Green Farm, Clarkes Green, Studley
	Church View, Warton, Polesworth		
	Church Walk, Atherstone	191C44	Clarkes Lane, Long Compton
	Church Walk, Barby	116A13	Clarkson Drive, Whitnash, Leamington Spa
	Church Walk, Bedworth		
	Church Walk, Bilton, Rugby	181C43	Clarr Close, Shipston on Stour
	Church Walk, Curdworth	94B42	Claverdon Lodge Farm, Claverdon
	Church Walk, Kilsby	22C34	Clay Avenue, Saint Nicholas Park, Nuneaton
	Church Walk, Leamington Spa		
	Church Walk, Mancetter	143A11	Clay Barn, Drayton
4	Church Walk, Mountford, Wellesbourne	58B33	Clay Bank Farm, Tanworth in Arden
		156C33	Clay Hall Farm, Bickmarsh
	Church Walk, Polesworth	52C41	Clay Hill Farm, Long Lawford
	Church Walk, Thurlaston	52C34	Clay Hill Lane, Little Lawford
	Church Way, Bedworth	52C42	Clay Hill Lane, Long Lawford
	Churchdale Close, Stockingford, Nuneaton	90A21	Claybrook Drive, Redditch

Map ref	Address	Map ref	Address
90A23	Claybrook Farm, Mappleborough Green, Studley	145A13	Clopton Court, Stratford upon Avo
167C24	Claydon Crossing Lane, Farnborough	34B11	Clopton Crescent, Chelmsley Wood
168B12	Claydon Hay Farm, Claydon	129A41	Clopton Farm, Stratford upon Avo
168A42	Claydon Lane, Farnborough	129A41	Clopton House, Stratford upon Ave
5B23	Cleasey, Stoneydelph, Tamworth	169C33	Clopton Orchard Farm, Quinton
22B33	Cleaver Gardens, Weddington, Nuneaton	144C12	Clopton Road, Stratford upon Avo
		43C23	Cloudesley Bush Farm, Monks Kirl
97B41	Cleaves Avenue, Leamington Spa	33A43	Cloudesley Bush Lane B4455, Woly
155C41	Cleeve Hill, North Littleton		Heath, Wolvey
156B22	Cleeve Road, Barton, Bidford	32C42	Cloudesley Bush Lane, Wolvey He
156C21	Cleeve Road, Marcliff, Bidford		Wolvey
155C21	Cleeve View, Salford Priors	43B32	Cloudesley Farm, Withybrook
97B41	Cleeves Avenue, Myton, Warwick	32C42	Cloudsley Bush Lane, Wolvey Hea
5A13	Clematis, Amington Ind.est., Tamworth	22C43	Clovelly Way, Nuneaton
98A41	Clemens Street, Leamington Spa	34C21	Clover Avenue, Chelmsley Wood
30A14	Clement Street, Nuneaton	54B32	Clover Close, Brownsover, Rugby
98A41	Clements Street, Leamington Spa	128C43	Clover Close, Stratford upon Avo
29A12	Clent Drive, Stockingford, Nuneaton	57C33	Cloweswood Farm, Tanworth in A
97C14	Cleveland Court, Leamington Spa	57C34	Cloweswood Lane, Clowes Wood, Tanworth in Arden
41B13	Cleveland Road, Bulkington, Bedworth		
21B34	Cleveley Drive, Camphill, Nuneaton	41A21	Clyde Road, Bulkington, Bedwortl
11A24	Cliff Farm, Cliff, Kingsbury	60A21	Clyde Road, Dorridge
96C32	Cliff Hill, Warwick	97C22	Coach House Mews, Leamington
11B23	Cliff Lane, Cliff, Kingsbury	49A12	Coal Pit Lane, Cross in Hand, Mo Kirby
96C32	Cliffe Court, Leamington Spa		
97B24	Cliffe Road, Milverton, Leamington Spa	44C44	Coal Pit Lane, Willey
97A31	Cliffe Way, Warwick	42B23	Coal Pit Lane, Wolvey
144C34	Clifford Bank Farm, Clifford Chambers	40B23	Coalpit Fields Road, Bedworth
145A33	Clifford Chambers, Clifford Chambers	69B43	Coalpit Lane, Church Lawford
145A43	Clifford Daireys, Clifford Chambers	68B11	Coalpit Lane, Wolston
59C12	Clifford Drive, Dorridge	63B34	Cobbs Road, Kenilworth
159B34	Clifford Farm, Clifford Chambers	116B14	Cobden Avenue, Sydenham Farm Estate, Leamington Spa
145A41	Clifford Forge Farm, Stratford upon Avon		
		140A42	Cock Bevington Farm, Cock Bevington, Salford Priors
159B11	Clifford Hill Farm, Clifford Chambers		
144C42	Clifford Lane, Clifford Chambers	140A44	Cock Bevington Road, Cock Bevington, Salford Priors
145A33	Clifford Road, Stratford upon Avon		
145A43	Clifford Trout Farm, Clifford Chambers	9C41	Cock Hill Farm, Allen End, Mide
		115A24	Cockburns Farm, Barford
98B33	Clifton Court, Leamington Spa	115A24	Cockburns Farm, Bishops Tachbr
72A14	Clifton Grange Farm, Clifton upon Dunsmor	72A34	Cockerills Meadow, Hillmorton,
		97B21	Cockermouth Close, Leamington
2A14	Clifton Lane, Thorpe Constantine	128B44	Cocksfoot Close, Stratford upon
1C33	Clifton Road, No Mans Heath, Appleby Magna	16C22	Cocksparrow Farm, Lea Marston
		96B42	Cocksparrow Street, Warwick
71B13	Clifton Road, Rugby	5C33	Cockspur Street, Birchmoor, Pole
29C14	Clifton Road, Stockingford, Nuneaton	90C11	Coffee Pot Lane, Little Shrewley
30B13	Clinic Drive, Nuneaton	70C43	Coin Farm, Dunchurch
96A33	Clinton Avenue, Hampton Magna, Budbrooke	97B13	Colbourne Grove, Leamington S
		159C13	Cold Comfort Farm, Clifford Ch
63B42	Clinton Avenue, Kenilworth	124C31	Coldcomfort Farm, Arrow
77C21	Clinton Farm, Rowington	71A31	Coldwell Court, Rugby
63B44	Clinton Lane, Kenilworth	71A13	Coldwells Court, Rugby
24C42	Clinton Road, Coleshill	34A22	Cole Court, Chelmsley Wood
98A33	Clinton Street, Leamington Spa	25A31	Colebridge Crescent, Coleshill
97C14	Cloister Crofts, Leamington Spa	125B33	Colebrook Close, Alcester
97C14	Cloister Way, Leamington Spa	34A21	Coleford Drive, Chelmsley Woo
145A22	Clopton Bridge, Stratford upon Avon	46B34	Colehurst Farm, Coombe Fields

p ref	Address
B41	Colemans Hill Farm, Colemans Hill, Quinton
:34	Colemeadow Road, Cole End, Coleshill
:34	Colemeadow Road, Kings Rise, Coleshill
:21	Coleshill Cold Store, Coleshill
:21	Coleshill Gas Plant, Coleshill
44	Coleshill Hall Farm, Coleshill
33	Coleshill Hall Hospital, Coleshill
32	Coleshill Heath Farm, Chelmsley Wood
14	Coleshill Heath Road, Chelmsley Wood
12	Coleshill Heath Road, Coleshill
21	Coleshill Pool, Coleshill
34	Coleshill Road, Ansley Common, Ansley
:2	Coleshill Road, Atherstone
44	Coleshill Road, Bentley Common, Bentley
34	Coleshill Road, Chapel End, Nuneaton
2	Coleshill Road, Chelmsley Wood
:1	Coleshill Road, Coleshill
4	Coleshill Road, Curdworth
4	Coleshill Road, Dure End, Maxstoke
2	Coleshill Road, Merevale
2	Coleshill Road, Shustoke
1	Coleshill Road, Water Orton
2	Coleshill Street, Atherstone
2	Collector Road, Chelmsley Wood
3	Colledge Close, Brinklow
24	Colledge Farm, Butlers Marston
34	Colledge Lane, Long Compton
44	College Close, Long Marston
4	College Drive, Leamington Spa
43	College Farm, Bearley
3	College Farm, Farnborough
34	College Farm, Long Compton
22	College Farm, Lower Quinton, Quinton
2	College Farm, Nether Whitacre
1	College Farm, Shotteswell
22	College Farm, Willington, Barcheston
	College Farm, Withybrook
4	College Lane, Stratford upon Avon
4	College Mews, Stratford upon Avon
2	College Of Agriculture, Moreton Morrell
	College Of Management, Dunchurch, Rugby
3	College Road, Willoughby
	College Street, Coten, Nuneaton
4	College Street, Stratford upon Avon
	Collets Brook Farm, Sutton Coldfield
	Collett, Amington Ind.est., Tamworth
	Colletts Brook, Middleton
	Colletts Farm, Dorsington
	Collier Grove, Leamington Spa
	Colliers Oak Farm, Fillongley
	Colliers Way, Gun Hill, Arley
	Colliery Farm, Merevale
	Colliery Lane, Blacrbank, Bedworth
	Colliery Lane, North, Bedworth

Map ref	Address
101A34	Collingham Lane, Long Itchington
70B22	Collingham Way, Bilton, Rugby
101B24	Collinghan Lane, Birdingbury
70B22	Collingwood Avenue, Bilton, Rugby
115B12	Collins Road, Heathcote Industrial, Whitnash
125B31	Collins Way, Alcester
40A12	Collycroft Park, Bedworth
9A41	Colmore Drive, Sutton Coldfield
32B12	Colts Close, Hinckley
40C21	Columbia Gardens, Bedworth
39A42	Colyere Close, Keresley Newlands, Keresley
50A21	Combeparr Road, Binley
189B23	Combslade Farm, Lower Braile, Brailes
96B34	Commaigne Drive, Warwick
96B34	Commainge Close, Warwick
115B34	Commander Close, Bishops Tachbrook
20C31	Common Farm, Hartshill
90A22	Common Farm, Mappleborough Green, Studley
142B33	Common Farm, Temple Grafton
37C34	Common Lane, Corley Moor, Corley
64A34	Common Lane, Crackley, Kenilworth
93C31	Common Lane, Lye Green, Claverdon
90B21	Common Lane, Mappleborough Green, Studley
6A31	Common Lane, Polesworth
65B42	Common Lane, Stoneleigh
93B32	Common Lane, Yarningale, Claverdon
11B34	Community Centre, Kingsbury
152B42	Compton Buildings, Fenny Compton
98B22	Compton Close, Lillington, Leamington Spa
191C33	Compton Court, Long Compton
34B24	Compton Crescent, Chelmsley Wood
148B41	Compton Hill, Compton Verney
150A11	Compton Road, Lighthorne Heath, Lighthorne
180A34	Compton Scorpion Farm, Ilmington
180C21	Compton Scorpion Road, Ilmington
148B42	Compton Verney Estate, Compton Verney
184A32	Compton Wynyates House, Compton Wynyates
98A24	Comyn Street, Leamington Spa
128C22	Comyns Farm, Snitterfield
75A32	Concert Farm, Tanworth in Arden
97C22	Concorde House, Leamington Spa
10C31	Coney Bury Farm, Bodymoor Heath, Middleton
66C23	Coney Grey Farm, Ryton on Dunsmore
96C14	Congreve Close, Woodloes, Warwick
40A22	Congreve Walk, Bedworth
40B12	Conifer Close, Bedworth
40B12	Conifer Court, Bedworth
98B44	Coningsby Close, Sydenham Farm Estate, Leamington Spa

Map ref	Address
54B34	Coniston Close, Brownsover, Rugby
41B13	Coniston Close, Bulkington, Bedworth
97B24	Coniston Court, Leamington Spa
81A11	Coniston Grange, Whitemore, Kenilworth
97B21	Coniston Road, Leamington Spa
22C34	Coniston Way, Saint Nicholas Park, Nuneaton
70C42	Conrad Close, Hillside, Rugby
30A43	Constable Close, Collycroft, Bedworth
72A24	Constable Road, Lower Hillmorton, Rugby
39C31	Constance Close, Exhall, Bedworth
134C11	Constance Drive, Harbury
24C22	Constantine Lane, Coleshill
54A41	Consul Road, Glebe Farm Estate, Rugby
14C33	Convent Close, Atherstone
64A33	Convent Close, Crackley, Kenilworth
61A43	Convent Farm, Baddesley Clinton
14C33	Convent Lane, Atherstone
60C43	Convent Of Poor Claires, Baddesley Clinton
30B14	Conway Close, Nuneaton
34A14	Conway Road, Chelmsley Wood
97B24	Conway Road, Milverton, Leamington Spa
14C31	Cook Close, Atherstone
54B33	Cook Close, Brownsover, Rugby
124A21	Cook Hill, Cook Hill, Alcester
96C22	Cooke Close, Woodloes, Warwick
124A31	Cookhill Farm, Cook Hill, Inkberrow
145A13	Cooks Ally, Stratford upon Avon
14C31	Cook Close, Atherstone
34A11	Cooks Lane, Chelmsley Wood
85B23	Cooks Lane, Frankton
8C33	Cool Hill Farm, Sheepy
45C44	Coombe Abbey Farm, Coombe Fields
45C43	Coombe Abbey, Coombe Fields, Brinklow
50B21	Coombe Court, Binley Woods
50A21	Coombe Court, Coombe Fields
50C33	Coombe Drive, Binley Woods
161A14	Coombe Farm, Goldicote, Alderminster
192B44	Coombe Farm, Great Rollright
46C41	Coombe Fields Farm, Coombe Fields
50C11	Coombe Park, Coombe Fields
46A34	Coombe View Farm, Coombe Fields
30B12	Cooper Street, Nuneaton
66B41	Coopers Walk, Bubbenhall
54B33	Copeland, Brownsover, Rugby
128A44	Cophams Hill Farm, Stratford upon Avon
94B43	Cophill Farm, Gannaway, Claverdon
2B21	Copnill Farm, Shuttington
58B11	Coppice Close, Cheswick Green
129A43	Coppice Close, Stratford upon Avon
93A12	Coppice Corner Farm, Bushwood
5C34	Coppice Drive, Dordon
84A13	Coppice Farm, Stretton on Dunsmore

Map ref	Address
10A24	Coppice Lane, Middleton
1A31	Coppice Lane, Thorpe Constantine
116A24	Coppice Road, Whitnash, Leamingto Spa
58B11	Coppice Walk, Cheswick Green
131B32	Coppington Farm, Charlecote
31A34	Copsewood Avenue, Whitestone, Nuneaton
43B11	Copston Fields Farm, Copston Mag
33A44	Copston Lane, Copston Magna
33A42	Copston Lodge Farm, Wolvey
59C14	Copstone Drive, Dorridge
34B23	Coralin Close, Chelmsley Wood
170A14	Corbett House, Lower Quinton, Stratford upon Avon
71B12	Corbett Street, Rugby
6A41	Corbin Road, Dordon
96B24	Corbison Close, Woodloes, Warwic
107B14	Corbizum Avenue, Studley
52C11	Cord Lane, Easenhall
48A33	Cord Lane, Pailton
70C41	Cordelia Way, Woodlands, Rugby
30A13	Corfe Way, Nuneaton
5B23	Coreen, Stoneydelph, Tamworth
34A11	Corinne Croft, Chelmsley Wood
38A23	Corley Ash Farm, Corley Ash, Cor
38B32	Corley Hall Farm, Corley
37C34	Corley Residential School, Corley Moor, Corley
38B34	Corley Rocks, Corley
38B32	Corley Services Northbound, M6
38B32	Corley Services Southbound, M6
39B41	Corley View, Keresley Newlands, Bedworth
24A33	Corncrake Drive, Kingshurst
34A11	Corne Croft, Chelmsley Wood
5A13	Cornel, Amington Ind.est., Tamw
34B31	Cornell Close, Chelmsley Wood
149C42	Corner Farm, Chadshunt
60A33	Corner Farm, Darley Green
60A33	Corner Farm, Dorridge
99C12	Corner Farm, Hunningham
175C33	Corner Farm, Lower Tysoe, Tyso
34C13	Cornfield Crescent, Chelmsley W
64B43	Cornhill Grove, Kenilworth
20C32	Cornish Close, Ansley Common
30A21	Cornish Crescent, Heath End, N
	Cornne Croft, Chelmsley Wood
96C32	Cornwall Close, Guys Cross Par Warwick
97B24	Cornwall Place, Milverton, Lean Spa
70B23	Cornwallis Road, Bilton, Rugby
120B21	Cornwood Farm, Napton on Th
6A22	Coronation Avenue, Polesworth
2C31	Coronation Crescent, Shuttingto
178B34	Coronation Lane, Shotteswell
52A44	Coronation Road, Church Lawfc
18B11	Coronation Road, Hurley, Kings

ref	Address	Map ref	Address
32	Coronation Road, Lawford Heath, Long Lawford	53C42	Cotterell Road, Newbold on Avon, Rugby
C12	Coronation Row, Bidford	116B23	Cotterills Close, Whitnash
44	Corporation Street, Nuneaton	64B41	Cotton Drive, Kenilworth
13	Corporation Street, Rugby	82C41	Cotton Mill Spinney, Cubbington
12	Corston Mews, Sydenham Farm Estate, Leamington Spa	108A41	Coughton Court, Coughton, Alcester
3	Cosford Close, Lillington, Leamington Spa	108A43	Coughton Cross Farm, Coughton
		116C13	Coughton Drive, Leamington Spa
4	Cosford Grange Farm, Cosford	125B12	Coughton Fields Farm, Coughton
4	Cosford Hall Farm, Cosford	125C11	Coughton Fields Lane, Coughton
23	Cosford Lane, Cosford	125C22	Coughton Fields Lane, Great Alne
31	Cosford Lane, Rugby	125C21	Coughton Fields Lane, Kinwarton
43	Costard Avenue, Shipston on Stour	108A43	Coughton Hill, Coughton
4	Coten End, Coten End, Warwick	124C13	Coughton Lane, Coughton
4	Coton Farm, Churchover	112A24	Council Houses, Wolverton
2	Coton Farm, Nether Whitacre	30A11	Countess Road, Nuneaton
3	Coton Farm, Newton And Biggin	105A22	Countryside, Braunston
3	Coton Farm, Whitacre Heath, Nether Whitacre	184C23	Coursmidge Hill, Compton Wynyates
		184B22	Coursmidge Hill, Upper Tysoe, Tysoe
1	Coton House, Rugby	115B34	Court Close, Bishops Tachbrook
3	Coton Lawn Farm, Arbury, Nuneaton	178A13	Court Close, Warmington
4	Coton Road, Churchover	30A44	Court Farm, Griff, Nuneaton
3	Coton Road, Hillmorton, Rugby	193B41	Court Farm, Hook Norton
2	Coton Road, Marston, Lea Marston	169A12	Court Farm, Long Marston
	Coton Road, Nuneaton	142B24	Court Farm, Temple Grafton
	Coton Road, Whitacre Heath, Nether Whitacre	156B12	Court Way, Bidford
		81B12	Courthouse Croft, Kenilworth
1	Cotswold Close, Tredington	50B34	Courtleet Road, Binley Woods
4	Cotswold Crescent, Stockingford, Nuneaton	50B34	Courtleet, Binley Woods
		23A33	Courtney Close, Saint Nicholas Park, Nuneaton
	Cotswold Drive, Finham	96C44	Courtyard, The, Warwick
	Cottage Close, Sydenham Farm Estate, Leamington	97C23	Covent Garden, Leamington Spa
	Cottage Farm, Astley	66B23	Coventry Airport, Baginton, Coventry
	Cottage Farm, Bentley	45A32	Coventry by passage, Coventry
	Cottage Farm, Bickenhill	66B23	Coventry Civic Airport, Baginton, Coventry
	Cottage Farm, Birchley Heath, Ansley	38C44	Coventry Colliery, Keresley
	Cottage Farm, Brinklow	45A43	Coventry Eastern by passage, Coventry
	Cottage Farm, Burton Hastings	74A43	Coventry Highway, Redditch
	Cottage Farm, Devitts Green, Arley	66B12	Coventry Island To Ryton Island, Park Farm South
	Cottage Farm, Earlswood, Tanworth in Arden	66B12	Coventry Island, Park Farm South
	Cottage Farm, Fulready, Ettington	45B14	Coventry Road, Anstey
	Cottage Farm, Hurley, Kingsbury	65C22	Coventry Road, Baginton
	Cottage Farm, Middleton	40A24	Coventry Road, Bedworth
	Cottage Farm, Over Whitacre	35B41	Coventry Road, Bickenhill
	Cottage Farm, Pinley Green, Rowington	50A31	Coventry Road, Binley
	Cottage Farm, Stretton on Fosse	51C13	Coventry Road, Brinklow
	Cottage Farm, Willoughby	41B21	Coventry Road, Bulkington
	Cottage Farm, Wolston	69C11	Coventry Road, Church Lawford
	Cottage Farm, Wolvey	25A44	Coventry Road, Coleshill
	Cottage Lane, Shottery, Stratford upon Avon	30B21	Coventry Road, Coten
	Cottage Lane, Whitacre Heath, Nether Whitacre	82C41	Coventry Road, Cubbington
		26C23	Coventry Road, Daw Mill, Shustoke
		87A12	Coventry Road, Dunchurch
	Cottage Leap, Butlers Leap Estate, Rugby	40A32	Coventry Road, Exhall
		37C24	Coventry Road, Fillongley
		30B33	Coventry Road, Griff, Nuneaton

Map ref	Address
97A13	Coventry Road, Guys Cliffe
17C34	Coventry Road, Halloughton, Kingsbury
30B23	Coventry Road, Hilltop
81A13	Coventry Road, Kenilworth
81A23	Coventry Road, Leek Wootton
119A12	Coventry Road, Long Itchington
69C12	Coventry Road, Long Lawford, Rugby
84C34	Coventry Road, Marton
17C42	Coventry Road, Nether Whitacre
47C23	Coventry Road, Pailton
119A14	Coventry Road, Southam
65B33	Coventry Road, Stoneleigh
86C11	Coventry Road, Thurlaston
96C32	Coventry Road, Warwick
42B23	Coventry Road, Wolvey
30B11	Coventry Street, Nuneaton
67A33	Coventry Street, Ryton on Dunsmore
119A24	Coventry Street, Southam
66B13	Coventry Trading Estate, Baginton
45A31	Coventry Walsgrave Triangle, Walsgrave
39B43	Coventry Welsh Rugby Football Club, Ash Green
29C33	Coventry Wood Farm, Arbury, Nuneaton
70C13	Coverley Place, New Bilton, Rugby
73B33	Covert Farm, Kilsby
90A43	Covers, The, Mappleborough Crescent
163A44	Coverwell Farm, Pillerton Hersey
164A11	Cow Common Farm, Combrook
188C22	Cow Lane, Brailes
26B42	Cow Lane, Shawbury, Fillongley
11C14	Cow Lane, Whately, Kingsbury
70A24	Cowan Close, Bilton, Rugby
98B41	Cowdray Close, Sydenham Farm Estate, Leamington Spa
89C21	Cowley Way, Kilsby
193B14	Cowpasture Farm, Hook Norton
96C22	Cowper Close, Woodloes, Warwick
141C43	Cox Close, Bidford
87B11	Cox Crescent, Dunchurch
30A14	Coxs Close, Nuneaton
120C33	Coxs Lane, Napton on The Hill
151C24	Crab Castle Farm, Knightcote, Burton Dassett
172A41	Crab Tree Farm, Armscote, Tredington
142A43	Crab Tree Farm, Bidford
15A44	Crab Tree Farm, Mancetter
180A14	Crabmill Lane, Ilmington
98B43	Crabtree Grove, Sydenham Farm Estate, Leamington Spa
81A13	Crackley Cottage, Kenilworth
64B31	Crackley Crescent, Crackley, Kenilworth
64A31	Crackley Farm, Crackley, Kenilworth
64A34	Crackley Hill, Crackley, Kenilworth
64A33	Crackley Lane, Crackley, Kenilworth
63C22	Crackley Lane, Stoneleigh
21B33	Craddock Drive, Camphill, Nuneaton

Map ref	Address
116B11	Craig Close, Sydenham Farm Estate, Leamington
34B22	Craig Croft, Chelmsley Wood
128B43	Crane Close, Stratford upon Avon
96B22	Crane Close, Woodloes, Warwick
142B33	Crane Hill, Bidford
97B24	Cranesthorpe Court, Leamington S
142B33	Cranhill Corner, Temple Grafton
142B33	Cranhill Farm, Temple Grafton
82C43	Cranleigh Court, Cubbington
30C12	Crantock Way, Nuneaton
147B33	Cranwell Drive, Mountford, Wellesbourne
50B34	Craven Avenue, Binley Woods
119A32	Craven Court, Southam
119A32	Craven End, Southam
119A32	Craven Lane, Southam
71A12	Craven Road, Rugby
5A23	Craven, Stoneydelph, Tamworth
156A12	Crawford Close, Bidford
98A12	Crawford Close, Leamington Spa
91A14	Crawleys Close, Ullenhall
23A43	Crediton Close, Nuneaton
107C11	Crendon Close, Studley
45A41	Cressage Road, Walsgrave on Sov
22B31	Cresswell Close, Weddington, Nu
155B33	Crest Hill, Harvington
45A32	Crest Hotel, Anstey
2A43	Crestwood, Amington, Tamworth
64C43	Crew Farm, Kenilworth
64B44	Crew Lane, Kenilworth
64C43	Crewe Gardens Farm, Kenilwortl
73A42	Crick Road, Crick
72B33	Crick Road, Hillmorton, Rugby
73A34	Crick Road, Kilsby
73C22	Crick Road, Yelvertoft
5B23	Crigdon, Stoneydelph, Tamwortl
171B23	Crimscote Downs Farm, Crimsco Downs, Whitchurch
171C22	Crimscote Fields Farm, Crimscot Downs, Whitchurch
4A23	Crisp Farm, Austrey
167A11	Crispins Farm, Fenny Compton
87B14	Critchley Drive, Dunchurch
109A42	Crocketts Farm, Alne Hills, Grea
92A21	Crocketts Farm, Beaudesert, He Arden
191C34	Crockwell Street, Long Comptor
93B42	Croft, The, Barnmoor Green
115C23	Croft Close, Bishops Tachbrook
97B33	Croft Close, Myton, Leamington
67C34	Croft Close, Stretton on Dunsm
142B21	Croft Close, Temple Grafton
42C11	Croft Close, Wolvey
72B42	Croft Farm, Kilsby
40A14	Croft Fields, Bedworth
93C41	Croft Hill Farm, Claverdon
127A42	Croft Lane, Billesley, Alcester
142B11	Croft Lane, Haselor

Map ref	Address
11	Croft Lane, Little Shrewley
B21	Croft Lane, Temple Grafton
11	Croft Mead, Ansley
14	Croft Pool, Bedworth Woodlands, Bedworth
24	Croft Road, Atherstone
22	Croft Road, Bedworth Woodlands, Bedworth
14	Croft Road, Heath End, Nuneaton
33	Croft Road, Leek Wootton
331	Croftlands Farm, Broadwell, Leamington Hastings
13	Cromdale Close, Stockingford, Nuneaton
22	Cromer Road, Lillington, Leamington Spa
43	Crompton Avenue, Bidford
2	Crompton Court, Forbes Estate, Warwick
34	Crompton Court, Shipston on Stour
4	Crompton Street, Forbes Estate, Warwick
3	Cromwell Lane, Burton Green, Kenilworth
13	Cromwell Place, Lighthorne Heath, Lighthorne
3	Cromwell Road, Hillmorton, Rugby
4	Crondal Road, Exhall, Bedworth
1	Crook House Yard, Brinklow
23	Crooks Lane, Alcester
23	Crooks Lane, Kinwarton
4	Crooks Lane, Littlewood Green, Studley
34	Cross Green Farm, Cross Green, Bishops Itchington
2	Cross Green Farm, Hunts Green, Middleton
4	Cross Green, Bishops Itchington
	Cross Green, Hunts Green, Middleton
	Cross in Hand Farm, Monks Kirby
3	Cross Lane, Braunston
	Cross Lane, Cubbington
1	Cross Lanes Farm, Haselor
	Cross Lanes Farm, Mancetter
2	Cross Leys, Ilmington
4	Cross O The Hill Farm, Stratford upon Avon
	Cross Point, Walsgrave
3	Cross Road, Alcester
	Cross Road, Keresley Newlands
	Cross Road, Keresley Newlands, Keresley
	Cross Road, Milverton, Leamington Spa
	Cross Street, Leamington Spa
	Cross Street, Long Lawford
	Cross Street, Rugby
	Cross Street, Saint Johns, Warwick
	Cross Street, Stockingford, Nuneaton
	Cross Walk, Dordon

Map ref	Address
28A43	Cross Ways Farm, Fillongley
5A24	Crossfell, Stoneydelph, Tamworth
96C32	Crossfields Road, Guys Cross Park, Warwick
147B31	Crosslands, Mountford, Wellesbourne
32A31	Crossways Farm, Burton Hastings
17C22	Crow Hall Farm, Kingsbury
54B33	Crow Thorns, Brownsover, Rugby
10B31	Crowberry Lane, Middleton
5A24	Crowden Road, Stoneydelph, Tamworth
30C22	Crowhill Road, Attleborough, Nuneaton
13B23	Crowhill Road, Baddesley Ensor
31A31	Crowhill Road, Whitestone, Nuneaton
	Crowhill, Nuneaton
91A12	Crowleys Farm, Ullenhall
117C43	Crown Close, Harbury
71A13	Crown House, Rugby
98B13	Crown Way, Lillington, Leamington Spa
45B14	Crowther Fields Farm, Anstey
40B21	Croxhall Street, Bedworth
116A23	Crutchley Drive, Whitnash
116A23	Crutchley Way, Whitnash, Leamington Spa
64A22	Cryfield Grange Farm, Gibbet Hill, Kenilworth
64B23	Cryfield Grange Road, Cryfield, Stoneleigh
64B23	Cryfield Grange Road, Gibbet Hill, Coventry
64A12	Cryfield House, Gibbet Hill, Coventry
64A22	Cryfield Lane, Stoneleigh
45B23	Ctd, Anstey
92A32	Ctd, Buckley Green, Henley in Arden
34C12	Ctd, Coleshill
87B13	Ctd, Dunchurch, Rugby
80C33	Ctd, Leek Wootton
147A21	Ctd, Wellesbourne
82B34	Cubbington Heath Farm, Cubbington
98A13	Cubbington Road, Lillington, Leamington Spa
29C11	Culpepper Close, Stockingford, Nuneaton
36C24	Culuers Lane, Green End, Fillongley
54C34	Culworth Close, Brownsover, Rugby
115C12	Culworth Close, Leamington Spa
115C12	Culworth Court, Heathcote, Whitnash
115C12	Culworth House, Whitnash
98B14	Cumberland Crescent, Lillington, Leamington Spa
29C13	Cumberland Drive, Stockingford, Nuneaton
98A41	Cumming Street, Leamington Spa
94A31	Cumsey, The
116B11	Cundall Close, Sydenham Farm Estate, Leamington
70B21	Cunningham Way, Bilton, Rugby
16B33	Curdworth Hall Farm, Curdworth
71B14	Curie Close, Rugby
128B44	Curlew Close, Stratford upon Avon

Map ref	Address
6C11	Curlew Close, Warton, Polesworth
5A33	Curlew, Stoneydelph, Tamworth
96A33	Curlieu Close, Hampton Magna, Budbrooke
94C44	Curlieu Farm, Budbrooke, Lower Norton
112C11	Curlieu Lane, Budbrooke
112C11	Curlieu Lane, Norton Curlieu, Norton Lindsey
116B21	Curran Close, Leamington Spa
98B44	Curzon Grove, Sydenham Farm Estate, Leamington
58C42	Cut Throat Lane, Earlswood, Tanworth in Arden
59A41	Cut Throat Lane, Nuthurst, Hockley Heath
111A24	Cutlers Farm, Edstone
111A22	Cutlers Farm, Edstone, Wootton Wawen
16B14	Cuttle Mill Farm, Curdworth
60C12	Cuttle Pool Lane, Dorridge
94B44	Cuttshill Farm, Claverdon
70C41	Cymbeline Way, Woodlands, Rugby
116A24	Cypress Lane, Whitnash
106B22	Cyprus Avenue, Astwood Bank
135B33	Dadglow Farm, Bishops Itchington
135B31	Dadglow Road, Bishops Itchington
28A31	Daffern Avenue, New Arley, Arley
40A31	Daffern Road, Exhall, Bedworth
81B22	Dairy Farm, Ashow
13C13	Dairy Farm, Bradley Green, Grendon
63C31	Dairy Farm, Kenilworth
36A41	Dairy Farm, Little Packington
97A13	Dairy Farm, Percy Estate, Warwick
162B41	Dairy House Farm, Ettington
75C24	Dairy House Farm, Umberslade Park, Tanworth in Arden
130B14	Daisy Hill Farm, Hampton Lucy
145B22	Dale Avenue, Stratford upon Avon
97A23	Dale Close, Percy Estate, Warwick
176B12	Dale Cottage, Radway
21C43	Dale End, Camphill, Nuneaton
46C14	Dale House Farm, Coombe Fields
97C31	Dale Street, Leamington Spa
71A11	Dale Street, Rugby
64B41	Dalehouse Lane, Kenilworth
65A14	Daleway Road, Finham
70B34	Dalkeith Avenue, Bilton, Rugby
48B43	Dallas Glebe Farm, Harborough Magna
31B31	Dalmohoy Close, Whitestone, Nuneaton
39C24	Dalton Road, Bedworth
95C34	Daly Avenue, Hampton Magna, Budbrooke
95C33	Damson Road, Hampton Magna, Budbrooke
26C34	Dandys Farm, Shawbury, Fillongley
98C43	Danesbury Crescent, Sydenham Farm Estate, Leamington Spa
89B14	Danetre Farm, Barby
29B13	Daniel Avenue, Stockingford, Nune
14C42	Daniel Road, Mancetter
75B33	Danzey Farm, Danzey Green, Tanw in Arden
75B34	Danzey Green Farm, Danzey Gree Tanworth in Arden
75B34	Danzey Green Road, Danzey Gree Tanworth in Arden
66B43	Darfield Court, Waverley Woods, Bubbenhall
106B24	Dark Lane, Astwood Bank
5C31	Dark Lane, Birchmoor, Polesworth
105C31	Dark Lane, Braunston
185A11	Dark Lane, Ebrington
39B23	Dark Lane, Goodyears End, Bedwe
94C42	Dark Lane, Hatton
105B24	Dark Lane, Little Braunston, Brau
145C11	Dark Lane, Tiddington, Stratford
60A24	Darley Green Farm, Darley Green
60B23	Darley Green Farm, Dorridge
181A23	Darlingscott Farm, Darlingscott, Tredington
181B34	Darlingscott Road, Darlingscott, Tredington
180C21	Darlingscott Road, Ilmington
181B31	Darlingscott Road, Shipston on St
185C11	Darlingscott Road, Stretton on Fo
5B23	Darnbrook, Stoneydelph, Tamwor
45A41	Darwin Close, Walsgrave on Sow
39C22	Darwin Court, Bedworth
167B31	Dassett Field Farm, Avon Dassett
167B33	Dassett Road, Avon Dassett
167C31	Dassett Road, Farnborough
151B41	Dassett Road, Northbend, Burton Dassett
101B13	Davenport Farm, Birdingbury
89B23	Daventry Road, Barby
87C23	Daventry Road, Dunchurch
87C24	Daventry Road, Grandborough
89C22	Daventry Road, Kilsby
121C24	Daventry Road, Lower Shuckbur
120B32	Daventry Road, Napton on The
119B24	Daventry Road, Southam
122C31	Daventry Road, Staverton
122A23	Daventry Road, Upper Shuckbur
119A24	Daventry Street, Southam
70C31	David Road, Bilton, Rugby
40A33	David Road, Exhall, Coventry
98A41	Davidson Avenue, Leamington :
39C34	Davies Road, Exhall, Bedworth
97B13	Davis Close, Leamington Spa
18A44	Daw Lane, Nether Whitacre
27A32	Daw Mill Colliery, Daw Mill, A
27A32	Daw Mill Colliery, Fillongley
26C32	Daw Mill Lane, Daw Mill, Fillo
27A32	Daw Mill, Daw Mill, Arley
22C44	Dawlish Close, Nuneaton
116A23	Dawson Close, Whitnash
13B43	Daybrooks Farm, Baxterley

Map ref	Address
5B23	Days Court, Stratford upon Avon
A34	De Compton Close, Keresley Newlands, Keresley
C12	De Montfort Hotel, Kenilworth
313	Deacon Street, Coten, Nuneaton
A31	Deane Road, Hillmorton, Rugby
341	Deansway, Ash Green, Bedworth
322	Deansway, Woodloes, Warwick
C21	Debden Close, Dorridge
A32	Debden Close, Mountford, Wellesbourne
C34	Debden Farm, Barford
C33	Debden Hollow, Barford
3	Deeley, Amington Ind.est., Tamworth
41	Deep Lane, Nether Whitacre
31	Deepmore Road, Bilton, Rugby
42	Deer Leap, Kenilworth
41	Deer Park Farm, Leek Wootton
31	Deerings Road, Hillmorton, Rugby
32	Deerpark Drive, Packmores, Warwick
21	Delamere Road, Bedworth
12	Delamere Way, Lillington, Leamington Spa
23	Dell Court, Henley in Arden
31	Dell House, Leamington Spa
34	Delves Crescent, Wood End, Kingsbury
1	Delves Farm, Wood End, Dordon
22	Demohun Crescent, Whichford
1	Demontfort Road, Kenilworth
3	Dempster Court, Nuneaton
1	Dempster Road, Bedworth
4	Denbigh Fork, Little Packington
2	Denby Close, Lillington, Leamington Spa
2	Dencer Drive, Kenilworth
22	Dene Close, Kineton
4	Denehurst Way, Nuneaton
2	Denewood Way, Kenilworth
1	Denham Court, Atherstone
43	Denne Close, Stratford upon Avon
2	Dennett Close, Woodloes, Warwick
1	Dennis Farm, Arbury, Nuneaton
1	Denton Close, Kenilworth
2	Dents Farm, Burton Hastings
3	Denville Road, Leamington Spa
32	Depdale Farm, Long Itchington
2	Depot Lane, Emscote, Warwick
3	Deppers Bridge Farm, Deppers Bridge, Ladbroke
1	Deppers Bridge, Bishops Itchington, Harbury
2	Deppers Bridge, Deppers Bridge, Bishops Itchington
	Derby Drive, Chelmsley Wood
	Derby Lane, Atherstone
	Dereham Court, Lillington, Leamington Spa
	Derek Avenue, Dordon
	Deronda Close, Bedworth
68A11	Derry Close, Wolston
54B33	Derwent Close, Brownsover, Rugby
97B21	Derwent Close, Leamington Spa
40A21	Derwent Road, Bedworth
22C42	Derwent Way, Saint Nicholas Park, Nuneaton
144C12	Devere Court, Stratford
39C34	Deveron Way, Exhall, Bedworth
27B23	Devitts Green Farm, Devitts Green, Arley
27B32	Devitts Green Lane, Devitts Green, Arley
29C14	Devon Close, Stockingford, Nuneaton
89C21	Devon Ox Road, Kilsby
125B24	Devonish Close, Alcester
125B22	Devonish Close, Kinwarton
40A34	Devoran Close, Exhall, Bedworth
87B13	Dew Close, Dunchurch
70B31	Dewar Close, Bilton, Rugby
71C22	Dewar Grove, Lower Hillmorton, Rugby
18B11	Dexter Court, Hurley
18A22	Dexter Lane, Foul End, Kingsbury
5C31	Dexter Way, Birchmoor
81B23	Dial House Farm, Ashow
188B33	Dickens Farm, Sutton Under Brailes
134A12	Dickens Road, Harbury
70C42	Dickens Road, Hillside, Rugby
71A21	Dickenson Court, Rugby
5C32	Dickies Hill, Polesworth
97A24	Dickins Road, All Saints, Warwick
77B31	Dicks Lane, Lapworth
77B32	Dicks Lane, Rowington
35B43	Diddington Farm, Bickenhill
35B43	Diddington Lane, Bickenhill
37B13	Didgley Lane, Fillongley
40A23	Didsbury Road, Exhall, Bedworth
24A14	Digby Crescent, Water Orton
34A44	Digby Drive, Chelmsley Wood
24C44	Digby Road, Coleshill
22A44	Dillon Court, Nuneaton
109A43	Dingewell Farm, Great Alne
75C32	Dingle House Farm, Tanworth in Arden
25C11	Dingle Lane, Hoggerills End, Nether Whitacre
129A43	Dingles Way, Stratford upon Avon
109A43	Dinglewell Farm, Alne Hills, Great Alne
41A24	Dingley Road, Bulkington, Bedworth
184B13	Dinsdale Farm, Upper Tysoe, Tysoe
79B21	Dirt Lane, Beausale
189C13	Ditchedge Lane, Lower Brailes, Brailes
186A14	Ditchford Farm, Rowborough, Stretton on Fosse
186A32	Ditchford Friary Farm, Tidmington
186B31	Ditchford Road, Stretton on Fosse
187A23	Ditchford Road, Tidmington
70B23	Ditton Close, Bilton, Rugby
170A23	Dobbie Road, Upper Quinton, Quinton

Map ref	Address
116A13	Dobson Lane, Whitnash, Leamington Spa
51C13	Dock Yard, Brinklow
169C11	Doctors Farm, Long Marston
75A23	Doctors Hill, Tanworth in Arden
92B23	Doctors Lane, Henley in Arden
97B41	Dodd Avenue, Myton, Leamington Spa
143C24	Dodwell Farm, Dodwell, Luddington
143C31	Dodwell Hill, Dodwell, Stratford upon Avon
23B32	Dodwells Road, Hinckley
120C42	Dog Lane Farm, Napton on The Hill
2A42	Dog Lane, Amington, Tamworth
152A44	Dog Lane, Fenny Compton
120C42	Dog Lane, Napton on The Hill
18A33	Dog Lane, Nether Whitacre
123C11	Dogbut Farm, Inkberrow
137C14	Doles Road, Napton on The Hill
72C31	Dollman Farm, Clifton upon Dunsmore
165B42	Dolphin Cottage, Radway
6B13	Donative Farm, Polesworth
87A14	Doncerce Close, Dunchurch
96C33	Dongan Road, Warwick
181C34	Donnington Road, Shipston on Stour
30B23	Donnithorne Avenue, Caldwell, Nuneaton
31B31	Dorcas Close, Whitestone, Nuneaton
95C34	Dorchester Avenue, Hampton Magna, Budbrooke
23A31	Dorchester Way, Saint Nicholas Park, Nuneaton
45A43	Dorchester Way, Walsgrave on Sowe
6B44	Dordon Farm, Dordon
6A42	Dordon Hayes, Dordon
5C32	Dordon Road, Dordon, Polesworth
25A31	Doris Road, Coleshill
30B31	Dorlecote Place, Caldwell, Nuneaton
30B23	Dorlecote Road, Caldwell, Nuneaton
97C22	Dormer House, Leamington Spa
97C34	Dormer Place, Leamington Spa
60A21	Dorridge Road, Dorridge
29C14	Dorset Close, Stockingford, Nuneaton
157B22	Dorsington Manor, Dorsington
157B13	Dorsington Road, Barton on The Heath, Bidford
157C41	Dorsington Road, East Hill, Pebworth
158A44	Dorsington Road, Long Marston
11B14	Dosthill Road, Kingsbury
54B41	Douglas Road, Brownsover, Rugby
147B23	Dove House Farm, Mountford, Wellesbourne
26C33	Dove House Farm, Shawbury, Fillongley
54B33	Dovedale Close, Brownsover, Rugby
24A13	Dovedale Court, Water Orton
147A23	Dovehouse Drive, Mountford, Wellesbourne
117A42	Dovehouse Lane, Harbury
134C11	Doven House Lane, Harbury

Map ref	Address
191A14	Dower Farm, Little Wolford
70C32	Down Place, Kingsway, Rugby
40B11	Downing Crescent, Bedworth
184C23	Downs Farm, Upper Tysoe, Tysoe
39B23	Dowty Avenue, Goodyears End, Bedworth
32A23	Drag Lane, Burton Hastings
123C11	Dragon Farm, Inkberrow
81B13	Draper Close, Windy Arbour, Kenilworth
76C11	Drawbridge Farm, Lapworth
86A32	Draycote Farm, Bourton And Draycote
86A23	Draycote Farm, Draycote
86A23	Draycote Farm, Marlborough Site
86B23	Draycote Fields Farm, Draycote
86B23	Draycote Fields Farm, Marlborough
86A41	Draycote Hill Farm, Bourton And Draycote
86A41	Draycote Hill Farm, Draycote
86A41	Draycote Hill Farm, Marlborough S
86A23	Draycote Lane, Draycote
87A33	Draycote Water, Draycote
73C34	Drayson Lane, Crick
144C13	Drayton Avenue, Stratford upon A
15B34	Drayton Barn Farm, Witherley
156B11	Drayton Close, Bidford
15C41	Drayton Close, Fenny Drayton
21A31	Drayton Close, Moor Wood, Harts
144B14	Drayton Close, Stratford upon Av
21A21	Drayton Court, Hartshill
96C14	Drayton Court, Woodloes, Warwi
143C21	Drayton Farm, Stratford upon Av
143B13	Drayton Field Barn Farm, Drayton
143B13	Drayton Field Barn, Stratford upo Avon
105C43	Drayton Fields Farm, Braunston
105C41	Drayton Gate Farm, Braunston
15C33	Drayton Grange Farm, Witherley
143C21	Drayton Husbandry Farm, Stratfo upon Avon
15B42	Drayton Lane, Fenny Drayton, Witherley
71A33	Drayton Leys, Hillside, Rugby
143C11	Drayton Manor Drive, Stratford t Avon
40B24	Drayton Road, Bedworth
21B33	Drayton Way, Camphill, Nuneate
81A11	Drew Crescent, Whitemore, Keni
70B21	Dreyer Close, Bilton, Rugby
45A41	Drift Road, Walsgrave on Sowe
134C12	Drinkwater Close, Harbury
107A44	Droitwich Road, Alcester
107A43	Droitwich Road, Hangingwell
119B32	Drovers Way, Southam
65A14	Droylsdon Park Road, Finham
79A13	Drum Lane, Haseley Knob
34B21	Drummond Way, Chelmsley W
71A13	Drury Lane, Rugby
162B44	Dry Bank Farm, Ettington

Map ref	Address	Map ref	Address
3C24	Drybank Farm, Upper Brailes, Brailes	34B22	Dunster Road, Chelmsley Wood
C14	Dryden Close, Kenilworth	16B32	Dunton Island, Dunton, Coleshill
A43	Dryden Close, Robinsons End, Nuneaton	17A21	Dunton Lane, Lea Marston
		16B21	Dunton Lane, Overgreen, Wishaw
C13	Dryden Place, New Bilton, Rugby	81B11	Dunvegan Close, Windy Arbour, Kenilworth
C13	Dryden Walk, Rugby		
C44	Drydon Close, Galley Common, Nuneaton	34A21	Durham Crescent, Chelmsley Wood
		194B24	Durhams Farm, Chastleton
B12	Duck Lane, Welford on Avon	90A13	Dursley Lane, Redditch
C21	Ducketts Lane, Farnborough	112B41	Duttons Close, Snitterfield
31	Dudkin Farm, Chadwick End	147C31	Duxford Close, Mountford, Wellesbourne
23	Dudley Green, Lillington, Leamington Spa		
		96C21	Dwarris Walk, Woodloes, Warwick
22	Dudley Road, Bulkington Estate, Kenilworth	58C28	Dyers Lane, Illshaw Heath, Cheswick Green
33	Dudley Square, Ryton on Dunsmore	58B32	Dyers Lane, Warings Green, Tanworth in Arden
33	Dudley Street, Atherstone		
42	Dudley Terrace, Stoneleigh	68A12	Dyers Lane, Wolston
33	Dudley Wood Farm, Bentley	72A23	Dyson Close, Hillmorton, Rugby
3	Duels Lane, Grendon	29B14	Eadie Street, Stockingford, Nuneaton
33	Duffy Place, Hillmorton, Rugby	31B31	Eagle Close, Whitestone, Nuneaton
C43	Duffus Hill, Moreton Morrell	5A12	Eagle Drive, Amington, Tamworth
44	Dugard Place, Barford	24A31	Eagle Grove, Kingshurst
11	Dugdale Avenue, Bidford	80C14	Eagle Lane, Kenilworth
43	Dugdale Avenue, Stratford upon Avon	98A43	Eagle Street, Leamington Spa
43	Dugdale Court, Leamington Spa	5A24	Ealingham, Stoneydelph, Tamworth
C43	Dugdale House, Radway	40B22	Earl Street, Bedworth
1	Dugdale Street, Nuneaton	98A24	Earl Street, Leamington Spa
4	Duke Street, Leamington Spa	71B18	Earl Street, Rugby
2	Duke Street, Nuneaton	119C14	Earles Close, Stockton
1	Duke Street, Rugby	22A43	Earls Road, Nuneaton
1	Dukes End Farm, Duke End, Maxstoke	50B43	Earls Walk, Binley Woods
3	Dukes Farm, Astley	58A24	Earlsmere, Earlswood, Tanworth in Arden
	Dukes Road, Dordon		
2	Dumble Farm, Maxstoke	58A33	Earlswood Common Road, Earlswood, Tanworth in Arden
3	Dunblane Drive, Cubbington		
2	Duncan Drive, Woodlands, Rugby	58A81	Earlswood Lakes, Earlswood
2	Dunchurch Cricket Club, Dunchurch	70C41	Earnest Cox Crescent, Woodlands, Rugby
1	Dunchurch Lodge Farm, Dunchurch		
2	Dunchurch Road, Dunchurch, Rugby	23A42	Easedale Close, Saint Nicholas Park, Nuneaton
2	Dunchurch Road, Hillside		
2	Dunchurch Road, Kingsway	53A22	Easenhall Road, Harborough Magna
	Duncombe Green, Kings Rise, Coleshill	40C21	East Avenue, Bedworth
	Duncumb Road, Sutton Coldfield	23A43	East Borough Way, Hinckley
	Dunkleys Farm, Dunchurch	63B33	East Chase Farm, Burton Green, Kenilworth
	Dunnerdale, Brownsover, Rugby		
1	Dunnington Heath Farm, Dunnington, Salford Priors	98B21	East Dene, Lillington, Leamington Spa
		118B43	East Field Farm, Deppers Bridge, Harbury
	Dunns Farm, Baxterley		
	Dunns Lane, Dordon	98A32	East Field Road, Leamington Spa
	Dunns Pits Farm, Kenilworth	22B423	East Field Road, Weddington, Nuneaton
2	Dunsden Farm, Todenham		
	Dunsmore Avenue, The Paddox, Rugby	177B33	East Gate Farm, Hornton
	Dunsmore Farm, Clifton upon	144B13	East Green Drive, Stratford upon Avon
	Dunsmore	98A43	East Grove, Leamington Spa
	Dunsmore Heath, Droitwich	18B22	East House Drive, Brook End, Hurley
	Dunsmore Home Farm, Clifton upon Dunsmore	18C13	East House Farm, Hurley, Kingsbury
		191C44	East Street, Long Compton
	Dunstall Crescent, Bishops Tachbrook	71B12	East Street, Rugby

Map ref	Address
71A21	East Union Street, Rugby
18C11	East View Road, Brook End, Hurley
2C33	East View, Shuttington
30C21	Eastborough, Attleborough, Nuneaton
106C22	Eastern Hill Farm, Sambourne
106C22	Eastern Hill, Astwood Bank
66B12	Eastern Relief Road, Willenhall Binley, Coventry
128C44	Eastfield Close, Stratford upon Avon
72C33	Eastfield Farm, Rugby
71A14	Eastfield Place, Rugby
96C41	Eastgate Mews, Warwick
177B34	Eastgate, Hornton
71B14	Eastlands Place, Rugby
71B14	Eastlands Road, Rugby
37C21	Eastlang Road, Fillongley
96A32	Eastley Crescent, Warwick
98B41	Eastnor Grove, Leamington Spa
98C43	Eastwood Close, Sydenham Farm Estate, Leamington Spa
72B33	Eastwood Green, Hillmorton, Rugby
70C14	Easy Lane, Rugby
84B41	Eathorpe Hall Farm, Eathorpe
84B34	Eathorpe Park Hotel, Eathorpe
84C21	Eathorpe Road, Princethorpe
97B13	Eaton Close, Leamington Spa
14B34	Ebbern Road, Atherstone
96C13	Eborrall Close, Woodloes, Warwick
81A12	Elmdene Road,windy Arbour, Kenilworth
179B34	Ebrington Hill Farm, Ebrington
143B31	Eccleston Court, Lower Binton
125C31	Eclipse Road, Alcester
5A24	Edale, Stoneydelph, Tamworth
107B22	Eden Close, Studley
98C21	Eden Court Flats, Lillington, Leamington Spa
98C21	Eden Court, Lillington, Leamington Spa
81A12	Eden Croft, Windy Arbour, Kenilworth
34B24	Eden Grove, Chelmsley Wood
71C24	Eden Road, Hillmorton, Rugby
45A32	Eden Road, Walsgrave on Sowe
176B21	Edge Hill Farm, Tysoe
150A11	Edge Hill Road, Lighthorne Heath, Lighthorne
92B34	Edge Lane, Henley in Arden
92C23	Edge Lane, Kite Green, Preston Bagot
92C22	Edge Lane, Preston Bagot
71C24	Edgecote Close, Hillmorton, Rugby
106C34	Edghock Lane, Astwood Bank
97C43	Edinburgh Crescent, Leamington Spa
21B42	Edinburgh Road, Camphill, Nuneaton
12B43	Edinburgh Road, Hurley, Kingsbury
65C22	Edinburgh Villas, Baginton
53A44	Edinburgh Way, Long Lawford
111A24	Edistone House, Edstone
6A31	Editha Road, Polesworth
6A22	Edithas Court, Polesworth
47C13	Ediths Close, Monks Kirby
127B24	Edkins Caravan Site, Wilmcote, Astc Cantlow
96C24	Edmondes Close, Woodloes, Warwi
170A23	Edmonds Close, Upper Quinton, Quinton
87B12	Edmondson Close, Dunchurch
97B32	Edmondscote Road, Edmonscote, Leamington Spa
59C14	Edstone Close, Dorridge
111B31	Edstone Farm, Edstone, Wootton Wawen
111A32	Edstone Hall, Edstone, Wootton Wawen
111B42	Edstone House, Edston, Wootton Wawen
40B21	Edward Road, Bedworth
24B14	Edward Road, White City, Water C
30A14	Edward Street, Coten, Nuneaton
97B23	Edward Street, Milverton, Leaming Spa
70C12	Edward Street, Rugby
96B34	Edward Street, Warwick
40A23	Edward Tyler Road, Exhall, Bedwc
81B12	Edwards Grove, Kenilworth
70C41	Edyvean Close, Shakespeare Garde Rugby
98B14	Elan Close, Lillington, Leamington
71A13	Elbrow Street, Rugby
11B32	Elder Close, Kingsbury
70A22	Elder Close, Long Lawford
73B42	Eldon Way, Crick
107C13	Eldorado Close, Studley
31A33	Elgar Close, Whitestone, Nuneato
96C13	Eliot Close, Woodloes, Warwick
70C13	Eliot Court, New Bilton, Rugby
6A21	Elizabeth Avenue, Polesworth
97A41	Elizabeth Court, Myton, Leaming Spa
97C43	Elizabeth Road, Leamington Spa
63C43	Elizabeth Way, Kenilworth
53A44	Elizabeth Way, Long Lawford
89C11	Elkington Lane, Barby
73C14	Elkington Road, Yelvertoft
73C14	Elkins Close, Yelvertoft
40A21	Elksmere Road, Bedworth
51C14	Ell Lane, Easenhall
181C34	Ellen Badger Hospital, Shipston Stour
73C41	Ellen Close, Crick
5A24	Ellerbeck, Stoneydelph, Tamwor Ellerbreck, Stoneydelph, Tamwo
40A21	Ellesmere Road, Bedworth
24A34	Ellice Drive, Kingshurst
156B11	Elliott Close, Bidford
147A13	Elliott Drive, Mountford, Welles
114A42	Elliotts Orchard, Barford
116B12	Elliston Grove, Sydenham Farm Estate, Leamington Spa
63C41	Elm Bank Road, Kenilworth

ɒ ref	Address
A34	Elm Bank, Southam
33	Elm Close, Binley Woods
B12	Elm Close, Ilmington
A31	Elm Close, Southam
B42	Elm Drive, Oversley Green, Alcester
2	Elm Farm, Austrey
24	Elm Farm, Frankton
23	Elm Grove, Arley
42	Elm Grove, Hurley, Kingsbury
14	Elm Road, Lillington, Leamington Spa
244	Elm Road, Stratford upon Avon
212	Elm Row, Stockton
42	Elm Tree Close, Kingsbury
3	Elm Tree Farm, Ullenhall
4	Elm Tree Road, Bulkington, Bedworth
11	Elmbank Close, Lillington, Leamington Spa
4	Elmdene Close, Hatton Station, Hatton
4	Elmdene Close, Wolston
2	Elmdene Road, Windy Arbour, Kenilworth
	Elmdon Airport, Elmdon, Birmingham
3	Elmdon Lane, Chelmsley Wood
3	Elmdon Road, Chelmsley Wood
43	Elmers Close, Priors Hardwick
4	Elmfield Road, Weddington, Nuneaton
4	Elmhurst Farm, Withybrook
13	Elmhurst Farm, Wootton Wawen
4	Elmore Road, Overslade, Rugby
	Elms Court, Austrey
	Elms Drive, Austrey
	Elms Drive, The Paddox, Rugby
1	Elms Farm, Bishops Itchington
3	Elms Farm, Newbold Pacey
	Elms Farm, Sheepy Magna, Sheepy
2	Elmswood Farm, Napton on The Hill
	Elmure Farm, Bedworth
	Elmwood Farm, Beausale
	Elsee Road, Rugby
1	Elsinor, Stratford upon Avon
	Elter Close, Brownsover, Rugby
	Elton Close, Lillington, Leamington Spa
	Elton Leys, Hillside, Rugby
	Elwy Circle, Keresley Newlands, Keresley
	Ely Close, Chelmsley Wood
	Ely Cottage, Stratford upon Avon
	Ely Place, Stratford upon Avon
	Ely Street, Stratford upon Avon
	Emes Walk, Gatehouse Lane, Bedworth
	Emmott Drive, Sydenham Farm Estate, Leamington
	Emperor Way, Glebe Farm Estate, Rugby
	Emscote Mills, Warwick
	Emscote Road, Emscote, Warwick
	Endesleigh Gardens, Sydenham Farm Estate, Leamington Spa

Map ref	Address
22C42	Enerdale Crescent, Saint Nicholas Park, Nuneaton
140C24	Enester Lane, Salford Priors
141A23	Enester Lane, Wixford
97C41	England Crescent, Leamington Spa
97C22	England House, Leamington Spa
97B21	Ennerdale Close, Leamington Spa
54B31	Ennerdale, Brownsover, Rugby
25A23	Ennersdale Bungalows, Coleshill
25A23	Ennersdale Close, Coleshill
25A31	Ennersdale Road, Coleshill
97C21	Enright Close, Leamington Spa
5C23	Ensor Drive, Polesworth
97C33	Epperstone Court, Leamington Spa
98B12	Epping Way, Lillington, Leamington Spa
19B14	Epps Farm, Bentley
40A12	Epsom Close, Collycroft, Bedworth
70C23	Epsom Road, Bilton, Rugby
98B11	Epsom Road, Lillington, Leamington Spa
184B14	Epwell Road, Upper Tysoe, Tysoe
14B34	Erdington Road, Atherstone
39C21	Erica Drive, Bedworth Woodlands, Bedworth
116A24	Erica Drive, Whitnash
5A32	Eringden, Stoneydelph, Tamworth
65A12	Erithway Road, Finham
40A11	Ernest Richards Road, Collycroft, Bedworth
59C22	Ernsford Close, Dorridge
54B31	Eskdale, Brownsover, Rugby
89C13	Essen Lane, Kilsby
80C21	Essex Close, Bulkington Estate, Kenilworth
96C31	Essex Court, Packmores, Warwick
150C43	Essex Gardens, Temple Herdewyke, Burton Dassett
71A11	Essex Street, Rugby
40B13	Essoldo Bingo Club, Bedworth
145B22	Eton Road, Stratford upon Avon
22A44	Etone Court, Nuneaton
30A13	Etone Sports Centre, Nuneaton
161C12	Ettingley Farm, Loxley
147A22	Ettington Close, Mountford, Wellesbourne
162B44	Ettington House Farm, Ettington
172B14	Ettington Park Hotel, Newbold on Stour, Ettington
172B12	Ettington Road, Alderminster
172C11	Ettington Road, Ettington Park, Ettington
147B31	Ettington Road, Loxley
147A22	Ettington Road, Mountford, Wellesbourne
145A22	Ettington Road, Stratford upon Avon
45A32	Eurocrest Hotel, Ansley
141A24	Eurogas, Wixford
115B11	Europa House, Whitnash, Leamington Spa

Map ref	Address
115B13	Europa Way, Greys Mallory, Warwick
97B42	Europa Way, Leamington Spa
115B11	Europa Way, Whitnash
41B24	Eustace Road, Bulkington, Bedworth
97C34	Euston Place, Leamington Spa
97C34	Euston Square, Leamington Spa
40B14	Evans Close, Bedworth
144B24	Evans Close, Stratford upon Avon
116A23	Evans Grove, Whitnash
70B21	Evans Road, Bilton, Rugby
145B23	Evenlode Close, Stratford upon Avon
55A43	Everard Close, Clifton upon Dunsmore
30C21	Everard Road, Attleborough, Nuneaton
	Everard Road, Nuneaton
70C34	Everest Road, Sharespeare Gardens, Rugby
12B21	Everglade Road, Wood End, Baddesley Ensor
12B21	Everglade Road, Wood End, Kingsbury
150A13	Everitt Road, Lighthorne Heath, Lighthorne
155A23	Eversham Road, Harvington
144C22	Evesham Place, Stratford upon Avon
124A41	Evesham Road, Arrow
106C23	Evesham Road, Astwood Bank
127A44	Evesham Road, Billesley
156A31	Evesham Road, Cleeve Prior
124A33	Evesham Road, Cook Hill, Inkberrow
106C13	Evesham Road, Dagtail End
143C32	Evesham Road, Dodwell, Luddington
140B32	Evesham Road, Dunnington
106C11	Evesham Road, Hunt End
143B31	Evesham Road, Lower Binton, Binton
155C21	Evesham Road, Salford Priors
144B24	Evesham Road, Stratford upon Avon
140A24	Evesham Road, Weethley
125A43	Evesham Street, Arrow, Alcester
71A11	Evreux Way, Rugby
134A23	Ewefields Farm, Chesterton
30C31	Exbury Way, Nuneaton
39B31	Exeter House, Goodyears End, Bedworth
145B24	Exhall Close, Stratford upon Avon
141C19	Exhall Court, Exhall
39B43	Exhall Grange Special School, Exhall, Bedworth
40A33	Exhall Green Road, Exhall, Bedworth
142A23	Exhall Lodge Farm, Ardens Grafton, Bidford
141C24	Exhall Lodge Farm, Exhall
142A22	Exhall Road, Ardens Grafton, Bidford
141C14	Exhall Road, Exhall
38C42	Exhall Road, Keresley Newlands, Keresley
141C13	Exhall Road, Wixford
40A32	Exhall, Exhall, Bedworth
96C23	Exham Close, Woodloes, Warwick
73C41	Exit 18 M1, Crick
73C41	Exit 18, M1
98B12	Exmoor Drive, Lillington, Leamingt Spa
39A41	Exton Way, Bedworth
54C34	Eydon Close, Brownsover, Rugby
167C31	Eydons Terrace, Farnborough
96B33	Eyffler Close, Warwick
85B23	Fair Close, Frankton
29C22	Fair Isle Drive, Heath End, Nuneat
45A34	Fairbanks Close, Walsgrave on Sov
80C14	Faircroft, Kenilworth
114B41	Fairfax Close, Barford
96C42	Fairfax Court, Warwick
144C13	Fairfield Walk, Stratford upon Avo
23A42	Fairfields Estate, Saint Nicholas Pa Nuneaton
5C32	Fairfields Hill, Polesworth
144C13	Fairfields Walk, Stratford upon Av
97B14	Fairhurst Drive, Leamington Spa
97B23	Fairlawn Close, Milverton, Leamir Spa
2A43	Fairview Close, Amington, Tamwe
25A41	Fairview Mews, Coleshill
125B31	Fairwater Crescent, Alcester
64C41	Fairway Rise, Kenilworth
31A32	Fairway, Whitestone, Nuneaton
31B31	Falcon Close, Whitestone, Nuneat
141C44	Falcon Crescent, Bidford
9A44	Falcon Lodge Crescent, Sutton Cc
150C44	Falkland Place, Temple Herdewy Burton Dassett
24A44	Falkland Way, Bacons End, Kings
98B41	Fallow Hill, Sydenham Farm Esta Leamington
31A11	Falmouth Close, Nuneaton
31A22	Falstaff Close, Whitestone, Nune;
145A13	Falstaff Court, Stratford upon Av
70C41	Falstaff Drive, Woodlands, Rugb
187A14	Famington Farm Road, Willingto Barcheston
141C32	Famington Farm, George Elm La Bidford
187C13	Famington Farm, Willington, Barcheston
183B43	Fant Hill Farm, Upper Brailes, B
183B43	Fant Hill, Upper Brailes, Brailes
193C44	Fanville Head Farm, Hook Nort
94C34	Far Gannaway Farm, Claverdon
90A13	Far Moor Lane, Redditch
23C33	Faraday Road, Hinckley
71B23	Faraday Road, Rugby
45A41	Farber Road, Walsgrave on Sow
71C31	Fareham Avenue, The Paddox,
134A12	Farley Avenue, Harbury
98A34	Farley Street, Leamington Spa
71B23	Farm Grove, Rugby
4A24	Farm Lane, Austrey
6C42	Farm Lane, Grendon
52C11	Farm Road, Easenhall
80B22	Farm Road, Kenilworth

p ref	Address	Map ref	Address
A14	Farm Road, Lillington, Leamington Spa	168B12	Fenny Compton Road, Claydon
B43	Farm Street, Harbury	168A11	Fenny Compton Road, Farnborough
C23	Farm Walk, Bishops Tachbrook	152C33	Fenny Compton Wharf, Fenny Compton
A12	Farmer Ward Road, Windy Arbour, Kenilworth	125B24	Fenwick Close, Kinwarton
24	Farmhurst, Rugby	72A33	Fenwick Drive, Hillmorton, Rugby
A23	Farnborough Fields Farm, Farnborough	42B12	Fern Hill Way, Wolvey
B34	Farnborough Hall, Farnborough, Banbury	22C41	Ferndale Close, Nuneaton
		81B12	Ferndale Drive, Windy Arbour, Kenilworth
C32	Farnborough Hill Farm, Farnborough	176B12	Ferndale House, Radway
B21	Farnborough Road, Farnborough	50C33	Ferndale Road, Binley Woods
A13	Farnborough Road, Fenny Compton	25A43	Ferndale Road, Coleshill
C43	Farnborough Road, Radway	70C23	Ferndown Road, Overslade, Rugby
B3	Farndon Close, Bulkington, Bedworth	63C41	Fernhill Close, Kenilworth
A22	Farriers Court, Wasperton	98A32	Fernhill Drive, Leamington Spa
B23	Farriers Ford, Alcester	80A22	Fernhill Farm, Kenilworth
22	Farriers Way, Attleborough, Nuneaton	61C13	Fernhill Lane, Frogmore
C31	Farrington Close, Mountford, Wellesbourne	79C22	Fernwood Farm, Beausale
		87B14	Ferriers Close, Dunchurch
23	Farrington Court, Mountford, Wellesbourne	68B33	Ferry Farm, Stretton on Dunsmore
		68B33	Ferry Farm, Wolston
33	Farther Sand Close, Hampton Lucy	130A41	Ferry Lane, Alveston, Stratford upon Avon
2	Farthing Lane, Curdworth		
4	Father Hudsons Home, Coleshill	97C43	Fetherston Court, Leamington Spa
33	Fathersand Close, Hampton Lucy	59C43	Fetherston House, Lapworth
1	Faultlands Close, Whitestone, Nuneaton	67A24	Fetherstone Crescent, Ryton on Dunsmore
2	Faultlands Farm, Nuneaton		
3	Fawsley Leys, Hillside, Rugby	81A32	Field Barn Farm, Chesford, Leek Wootton
22	Featherbed Lane, Aston Cantlow		
1	Featherbed Lane, Bascote Heath, Long Itchington	95C34	Field Barn Farm, Hampton Magna, Budbrooke
1	Featherbed Lane, Cherington	97A34	Field Close, Emscote, Warwick
	Featherbed Lane, Hillmorton, Rugby	64B43	Field Close, Kenilworth
4	Featherbed Lane, Ilmington	90A41	Field Farm Dairy, Washford, Studley
2	Featherbed Lane, Wilmcote	27B32	Field Farm, Arley
	Featherbed Lane, Withybrook	4B33	Field Farm, Austrey
4	Featherbow Lane, Ratley	116C42	Field Farm, Harbury
	Featherstone Close, Hilltop, Nuneaton	92C24	Field Farm, Outhill, Studley
	Featherstone Farm, Ryton on Dunsmore	90A42	Field Farm, Washford, Studley
3	Feckenham Road, Astwood Bank	110B21	Field Farm, Wootton Wawen
2	Feckenham Road, Hunt End	63C42	Field Gate Lane, Kenilworth
	Fell Grove, Lillington, Leamington Spa	63C42	Field Gate Lawn, Kenilworth
4	Fell Mill Farm, Honington	97A41	Field Head Lane, Myton, Leamington Spa
4	Fell Mill Lane, Barcheston		
4	Fell Mill Lane, Honington	40A32	Field View Close, Exhall, Bedworth
4	Fell Mill, Honington	105B21	Field View, Braunston
4	Fell Mill, Upper Brailes, Brailes	116A22	Field View, Leamington Spa
	Fellmore Grove, Sydenham Farm Estate, Leamington Spa	48A44	Fieldgate Farm, Harborough Magna
		79A14	Fieldgate Farm, Haseley Knob, Haseley
	Fellows Way, Hillmorton, Rugby	63C34	Fieldgate House, Kenilworth
	Fells Lane, Napton on The Hill	116B31	Fieldgate Lane, Whitnash
	Felspar Road, Amington Ind.est., Tamworth	92B31	Fieldhouse Close, Henley in Arden
		45A42	Fielding Close, Walsgrave on Sowe
	Fen End Farm, Frogmore	14B14	Fielding Close, Whittington, Atherstone
	Fen End Road, Frogmore	21A43	Fielding Way, Galley Common, Nuneaton
	Fen End Road, Temple Balsall		
	Fennis Close, Dorridge	21A43	Fielding Way, Robinsons End, Nuneaton
	Fennis Fields Farm, Kings Newnham		

Map ref	Address
97A34	Fields Close, Emscote, Warwick
96C32	Fields Court, Warwick
12C23	Fields Farm, Baddesley Ensor
88A41	Fields Farm, Grandborough
84C43	Fields Farm, Marton
99B21	Fields Farm, Offchurch
118C44	Fields Farm, Southam
83B23	Fields Farm, Weston Under Wetherl
125B31	Fields Park Drive, Alcester
59B42	Fieldway, Hockley Heath, Cheswick Green
30A11	Fife Street, Nuneaton
30B22	Fifield Close, Attleborough, Nuneaton
164C11	Fighting Close, Kineton
34C21	Fillingham Close, Chelmsley Wood
27B44	Fillongley Lodge, Fillongley
36C11	Fillongley Road, Fillongley
36B11	Fillongley Road, Maxstoke
36C44	Fillongley Road, Meriden
67C43	Finacre Lane, Stretton on Dunsmore
155A33	Finch Lane, Harvington
100A23	Findle Farm, Snowford, Long Itchington
41B13	Findon Close, Ryton, Bedworth
64A44	Finham Crescent, Kenilworth
64A42	Finham Flats, Kenilworth
65A22	Finham Green Road, Finham
64A42	Finham Road, Kenilworth
54C43	Finmere, Rugby
97C21	Finnings Court, Lillington, Leamington Spa
77C41	Finwood Farm, Finwood, Rowington
77C43	Finwood Hill Farm, Finwood, Rowington
77C43	Finwood Road, Finwood, Rowington
77C24	Finwood Road, Turners Green
118B11	Fir Tree Farm, Bascote, Long Itchington
105B14	Fir Tree Farm, Braunston
60B34	Fir Tree Farm, Chessetts Wood, Lapworth
37C33	Fir Tree Farm, Corley Moor, Corley
37C33	Fir Tree Farm, Fillongley
28A31	Fir Tree Farm, New Arley, Arley
30B24	Fir Tree Grove, Caldwell, Nuneaton
28A23	Fir Tree Lane, Hilltop, Arley
56B13	Fir Tree Lane, Swinford
177C14	Fir Treebarn Lane, Warmington
11B34	Fircroft, Kingsbury
125A34	Fire Station, Alcester
14C31	Fire Station, Atherstone
40A22	Fire Station, Bedworth
156B12	Fire Station, Bidford
51C13	Fire Station, Brinklow
24C42	Fire Station, Coleshill
152A42	Fire Station, Fenny Compton
92B23	Fire Station, Henley in Arden
23C33	Fire Station, Hinckley
63C44	Fire Station, Kenilworth
164B21	Fire Station, Kineton
97C31	Fire Station, Leamington Spa
22B43	Fire Station, Nuneaton
6A13	Fire Station, Polesworth
71A11	Fire Station, Rugby
181C42	Fire Station, Shipston on Stour
119B21	Fire Station, Southam
144C13	Fire Station, Stratford upon Avon
107C13	Fire Station, Studley
175B44	Fire Station, Tysoe
96B34	Fire Station, Warwick
116A32	Firethorn Crescent, Whitnash
41B14	Firleigh Drive, Ryton, Bedworth
70C22	Firs Drive, Rugby
168A33	Firs Farm, Farnborough
122B14	Firs Farm, Flecknoe, Wolfhamcote
79A32	Firs Farm, Haseley Green, Haseley
60B23	Firs Farm, Lapworth
101C31	Firs Farm, Long Itchington
79A21	Firs Lane, Haseley Green, Haseley
95A11	Firs Lane, Hatton Green, Hatton
163C32	Fish Lane, Butlers Marston
35B33	Fish Pool Lane, Little Packington
71C31	Fisher Avenue, The Paddox, Rugby
135B23	Fisher Road, Bishops Itchington
89C21	Fishers Close, Kilsby
114B12	Fishers Court, Forbes Estate, War
35B24	Fishers Hall Farm, Little Packingt
10C21	Fishers Mill Lane, Middleton
80C13	Fishponds Road, Kenilworth
85B31	Fishpool Farm, Frankton
85B23	Fishpools Road, Frankton
163C32	Fishway, Butlers Marston
174C24	Fithers Farm, Oxhill
30A14	Fitton Street, Coten, Nuneaton
38B44	Fivefield Road, Keresley, Covent
94B13	Fiveways Road, Shrewley Comm Shrewley
4A24	Flats Lane, Austrey
4A21	Flavel Court, Austrey
97C42	Flavel Crescent, Leamington Spa
4A23	Flavels House Farm, Austrey
122B14	Flecknoe Farm, Flecknoe, Wolfha
121C13	Flecknoe Fields Farm, Wolfhamc
103C44	Flecknoe House Farm, Wolfham
102C23	Flecknoe Road, Grandborough
102B14	Flecknoe Road, Leamington Has
103C41	Flecknoe Station Road, Wolfham
71C22	Fleet Crescent, Rugby
23C31	Fleming Road, Hinckley
Cov	Fletchampstead Highway, Cove
78B31	Fletchers Lane, Mousley End, Rowington
97A32	Fleur de Leys Court, Emscote R
14C21	Flint Close, Atherstone
14B24	Florence Close, Atherstone
39C31	Florence Close, Exhall, Bedwor
2A43	Florendine Street, Amington, T
144C24	Flower Court, Stratford upon A
128C42	Flower Road, Stratford upon A

Map ref	Address	Map ref	Address
B32	Flying Fields Road, Southam	100A11	Fosse Way, Hunningham
C13	Fodge Farm, Hook Norton	51C14	Fosse Way, Kings Newnham
341	Folly Farm, Great Alne	47A24	Fosse Way, Monks Kirby
C41	Folly Lane, Napton on The Hill	133A43	Fosse Way, Moreton Morrell
43	Ford Bridge Road, Kingshurst	133A34	Fosse Way, Newbold Pacey
22	Ford Farm, Cubbington	99C33	Fosse Way, Offchurch
C24	Ford Farm, Southam	84C21	Fosse Way, Princethorpe
31	Ford Hall Farm, Ullenhall	116C44	Fosse Way, Radford Semele
31	Ford Hall Lane, Tanworth in Arden	68A33	Fosse Way, Stretton on Dunsmore
C13	Ford Lane, Aston Cantlow	186A11	Fosse Way, Stretton on Fosse
C24	Ford Lane, Butlers Marston	47A33	Fosse Way, Stretton Under Fosse
12	Ford Lane, Great Alne	43C21	Fosse Way, Wibtoft
1	Ford Street, Stockingford, Nuneaton	68B11	Fosse Way, Wolston
34	Forde Hall Lane, Orchard Hill, Tamworth in Arden	99B44	Fosse Wharf Farm, Offchurch
		162C23	Fossebury Farm, Pillerton Hersey
14	Forde Hall Lane, Ullenhall	162C24	Fosseway Farm, Pillerton Hersey
11	Fordham Avenue, Stratford upon Avon	65A14	Fosseway Road, Finham
		S1c33	Fosseway, Bretford
3	Fords Foundry, Leamington Spa	148B41	Fosseway, Combrook
13	Foredraught, Studley	148B32	Fosseway, Compton Verney
41	Forest Farm, Long Marston	162B44	Fosseway, Ettington
3	Forest Road, Kenilworth	148C12	Fosseway, Lighthorne
3	Forest Way, Arbury, Nuneaton	162C24	Fosseway, Pillerton Hersey
3	Forfield Place, Leamington Spa	162C43	Fosseway, Pillerton Priors
23	Forgate Street, Astwood Bank	107C23	Foster Avenue, Tomstown, Studley
23	Forge Farm, Cook Hill, Inkberrow	53C42	Foster Road, Newbold on Avon, Rugby
31	Forge Lane, Farnborough	91C24	Fosters Farm, Ullenhall
2	Forge Road, Kenilworth	18A22	Foul End Lane, Foul End, Kingsbury
1	Forge Road, Shustoke	175B34	Fountain Farm, Lower Tysoe, Tysoe
4	Fork Hill, Morton Bagot	131B43	Fountain Gardens, Charlecote
3	Fork Hill, Spernall	145A21	Fountain Way, Stratford upon Avon
	Fornside Close, Brownsover, Rugby	59C11	Four Ashes Road, Dorridge
	Forresters Place, Hillmorton, Rugby	107B13	Four Elms Farm, Node Hill, Sambourne
	Forshaw Heath Lane, Earlswood		
	Forshaw Heath Lane, Forshaw Heath, Tamworth in Arden	92B14	Four Oaks Farm, Buckley Green, Beaudesert
	Forshaw Heath Lane, Portway, Tanworth in Arden	194A11	Four Shire Stone Farm, Little Compton
		14C32	Four Ways, Atherstone
	Forshaw Lane, Forshaw Heath, Tamworth in Arden	27C31	Fourfields Way, New Arley
		9A43	Fowler Road, Sutton Coldfield
	Forth Drive, Chelmsley Wood	22B31	Fox Avenue, Weddington, Nuneaton
	Forty Acre Lane, Nether Whitacre	134B12	Fox Close, Harbury
	Forum Drive, Glebe Farm Estate, Rugby	72A32	Fox Close, Hillmorton, Rugby
	Fosberry Close, Warwick	157B31	Fox Covert Farm, Dorsington
	Fossdale Road, Stoneydelph, Tamworth	16B11	Fox Covey Farm, Wishaw
	Fosse Crescent, Princethorpe	118B22	Fox Farm, Bascote, Long Itchington
	Fosse Farm, Offchurch	9A21	Fox Hill Road, Sutton Coldfield
	Fosse Farm, Radford Semele	92C34	Fox Lane, Wootton Wawen
	Fosse Farm, Withybrook	78A34	Foxbrook Farm, Rowington
	Fosse Farm, Wolston	60A14	Foxbury Drive, Dorridge
	Fosse Way Crescent, Tredington	179C32	Foxcote Farm, Foxcote, Ilmington
	Fosse Way Roman Road, Monks Kirby	180B13	Foxcote Hill, Ilmington
	Fosse Way Roman Road, Wibtoft	116B12	Foxdale Walk, Sydenham Farm Estate, Leamington
	Fosse Way, Brinklow		
	Fosse Way, Chesterton	96B44	Foxes Way, Lodge Wood Est, Warwick
	Fosse Way, Cloudsley Bush	54C23	Foxglove Close, Brownsover, Rugby
	Fosse Way, Darlingscott, Tredington	5A11	Foxglove, Amington, Tamworth
	Fosse Way, Eathorpe	31B23	Foxhills Close, Whitestone, Nuneaton
	Fosse Way, Harbury	34C13	Foxland Close, Chelmsley Wood

Map ref	Address
58B12	Foxland Close, Cheswick Green
87A42	Foxley Farm, Thurlaston
54B34	Foxons Barn Road, Brownsover, Rugby
15C41	Foxs Covert, Fenny Drayton, Witherley
156C42	Foxs Farm, Bickmarsh
128B44	Foxtail Close, Stratford upon Avon
5C31	Foxwood Road, Birchmoor
64B41	Framlingham Grove, Kenilworth
97A33	Frances Avenue, Emscote, Warwick
40A13	Frances Crescent, Bedworth
65C13	Frances Road, Baginton
134C12	Frances Road, Harbury
6A21	Francis Close, Polesworth
59C13	Francis Way, Dorridge
30A14	Frank Street, Nuneaton
30B24	Franklin Road, Caldwell, Nuneaton
116A21	Franklin Road, Whitnash
139B44	Franklins Lane, Church Lench
68A43	Frankton Lane, Stretton on Dunsmore
85C41	Frankton Road, Birdingbury
85C21	Frankton Road, Bourton on Dunsmore
85C21	Frankton Road, Oxley
139B44	Franlins Lane, Church Lench
29B12	Fraser Close, Stockingford, Nuneaton
158B11	Frasers Way, Welford on Avon
20C41	Freasland Farm, Galley Common, Nuneaton
5B44	Freasley Lane, Freasley, Dordon
70C14	Frederick Press Way, Rugby
28A31	Frederick Road, New Arley, Arley
70C14	Frederick Street, Rugby
67C31	Freeboard Lane, Ryton on Dunsmore
67B31	Freeboard Lane, Stretton on Dunsmore
29B12	Freeman Close, Stockingford, Nuneaton
97B22	Freemans Close, Milverton, Leamington Spa
70B21	Freemantle Road, Bilton, Rugby
30C21	Freer Street, Attleborough, Nuneaton
21A42	Freesland Rise, Whittleford, Nuneaton
34B22	Frensham Close, Chelmsley Wood
21A44	Frensham Drive, Chapel End, Nuneaton
98B42	Freshwater Grove, Sydenham Farm Estate, Leamington Spa
50C33	Friars Close, Binley Woods
14B32	Friars Gate, Atherstone
188C14	Friars Lane, Brailes
96B42	Friars Street, Forbes Estate, Warwick
95C34	Friary Close, Hampton Magna, Budbrooke
14C23	Friary Road, Atherstone
22A44	Friary Street, Nuneaton
141B44	Friday Close, Bidford
141C41	Friday Furlong, Bidford
170B13	Friday Street, Lower Quinton, Quinton
148A32	Friz Hill Farm, Wellesbourne
148A31	Friz Hill, Wellesbourne
70B21	Frobisher Road, Bilton, Rugby
180A14	Frog Lane, Ilmington
158A12	Frog Lane, Welford on Avon

Map ref	Address
61C14	Frogmore Farm, Frogmore
129B11	Frogmore Road, Snitterfield
85C41	Front Street, Birdingbury
180B12	Front Street, Ilmington
129B21	Fruit Farm, Snitterfield
64B42	Fry The Close, Kenilworth
97B14	Fryer Avenue, Leamington Spa
113C34	Fulbrook Lane, Sherbourne
57B22	Fulford Hall Road, Fulford Heath, Tidbury Green
132C43	Fuller Place, Little Morrell, Moreto Morrell
173C23	Fullready Farm, Fullready, Ettingt
71B12	Funter Street, Rugby
186C12	Furlong Meadow, Shipston on Sto
40B14	Furnace Road, Bedworth
54C33	Furness Close, Brownsover, Rugby
119B21	Furrows, The, Southam
186C11	Furze Hill Road, Shipston on Stou
90A11	Furze Lane, Redditch
82C23	Furzenhill Farm, Cubbington
21C12	Fyves Court, Nuneaton
70B32	Gable Close, Bilton, Rugby
181B13	Gables Farm, Blackwell, Tredingtc
62C13	Gables Garage, Mere End, Balsall Common
30B14	Gadsby Street, Attleborough, Nu
72A24	Gainsborough Crescent, Lower Hillmorton, Rugby
40A11	Gainsborough Drive, Collycroft, Bedworth
98B43	Gainsborough Drive, Sydenham Estate, Leamington Spa
144B24	Gainsborough Road, Shottery, Stratford upon Avon
100C34	Galanos House, Long Itchington
40A13	Gallagher Road, Bedworth
20C43	Galley Common School, Galley Common, Nuneaton
20C42	Galley Farm, Galley Common, Nuneaton
189B22	Gallow Hill Farm, Lower Brailes Brailes
97A44	Gallows Hill, Heathcote, Warwic
62C13	Gambles Garage, Frogmore
82A22	Game Show, Stoneleigh
112C11	Gannaway Court, Norton Linds
112C11	Gannaway Farm, Budbrooke
94C43	Gannaway Road, Gannaway, Cl
94C43	Gannaway Road, Shrewley
3C23	Garbour Lane, Austrey
136A21	Garden Cottage Farm, Ladbrok
97A32	Garden Court, Warwick
147B21	Garden Row, Mountford, Welle
147B21	Garden Terrace, Mountford, Wellesbourne
98A34	Garden View Cottage, Leaming
165C43	Gardners Cottage, Radway
64B41	Garlick Drive, Kenilworth

⁊ ref	Address	Map ref	Address
,44	Garnette Close, Whittleford, Nuneaton	30B21	George Eliot Street, Nuneaton
C14	Garrard Close, Salford Priors	15C42	George Foxes Lane, Fenny Drayton
44	Garratt Close, Long Lawford	97A23	George Road, Percy Estate, Warwick
21	Garrett Street, Attleborough, Nuneaton	24B14	George Road, White City, Water Orton
C23	Garrick Way, Stratford upon Avon	30B22	George Street, Attleborough, Nuneaton
2	Garrigill, Stoneydelph, Tamworth	40A14	George Street, Bedworth
14	Garway Close, Leamington Spa	98A33	George Street, Leamington Spa
31	Garyth Williams Close, Bilton	28A32	George Street, New Arley, Arley
21	Gas Plant, Coleshill	70C12	George Street, Rugby
43	Gas Pumping Station, Radford Semele	119C12	George Street, Stockton
12	Gas Street, Leamington Spa	71A31	Georges Avenue, Kingsway, Rugby
14	Gas Street, Rugby	141C31	Georges Elm Lane, George Elm Lane, Bidford
33	Gashouse Lane, Alcester		
21	Gate Farm, Bourton on Dunsmore	141B34	Georges Elm Lane, George Elm Lane, Wixford
4	Gate Farm Drive, Monks Kirby		
4	Gate Farm, Monks Kirby	95A24	Georges Farm, Hatton
1	Gate Farm, Oxley	14C23	Georges Road, Atherstone
32	Gate Farm, Sawbridge, Wolfhamcote	97C44	Georges Road, Leamington Spa
12	Gate Farm, Willoughby	125A33	Georgian Close, Alcester
4	Gate Lane, Dorridge	71C31	Gerandria Court, The Paddox, Rugby
2	Gate Lane, Nether Whitacre	40C41	Germany Farm, Bedworth
34	Gated Road, Chapel Ascote	125B32	Gerrard Road, Kinwarton
	Gated Road, Clifton upon Dunsmore	96C42	Gerrard Street, Warwick
3	Gated Road, Fenny Compton	181C44	Gerrards Road, Shipston on Stour
12	Gated Road, Hambridge	64B23	Gibbet Hill Road, Gibbet Hill, Coventry
3	Gated Road, Knightcote, Bishops Itchington	54B12	Gibbett Hill, Churchover, Rugby
		49C42	Gibbett Lane, Cotesbach
	Gatehouse, The, Tower Road, Bedworth	54B12	Gibbetts Cross, Gibbet Hill, Rugby
	Gatehouse Lane, Bedworth	82B43	Gibbs Cottage, Leamington Spa
	Gateley Close, Redditch	145C11	Gibbs Lane, Tiddington, Stratford upon Avon
	Gattax Farm, Outhill, Studley		
	Gaveston Close, Guys Cross Park, Warwick	189C44	Gibraltar Farm, Hook Norton
		102A24	Gibraltar Lane, Broadwell, Leamington Hastings
	Gaveston Island To Chesford Island, Warwick by pass	40A24	Gibson Crescent, Bedworth
	Gaveston Island, Warwick by pass	72A23	Gibson Drive, Lower Hillmorton, Rugby
	Gaveston Road, Milverton, Leamington Spa	96C21	Giffard Way, Woodloes, Warwick
		134C43	Gifford Road, Lighthorne Heath, Lighthorne
	Gaveston To Stanks Hill, Warwick by pass	144B11	Gifford Walk, Stratford upon Avon
	Gaveston To Thickthorn, Warwick by pass	77B44	Giffard Terrace, Finwood
		70B22	Gilbert Avenue, Bilton, Rugby
	Gaydon Farm, Gaydon	128C42	Gilbert Close, Stratford upon Avon
	Gaydon Fields Road, Gaydon	74C14	Gilberts Green Lane, Gilberts Green, Tanworth in Arden
	Gaydon Fields Road, Northend, Burton Dassett	120B31	Gildacre Farm, Napton on The Hill
	Gaydon Hill Farm, Gaydon	30A24	Gilfil Road, Hilltop, Nuneaton
	Gaydon Proving Ground, Lighthorne Heath, Gaydon	174C32	Gilks Street, Oxhill
		188B11	Gilletts Lane, Grove End, Brailes
	Gaydon Road, Bishops Itchington	24B32	Gilson Drive, Woodlands, Coleshill
	Gaydon Road, Chadshunt	24C31	Gilson Road, Gilson, Coleshill
	Gaydon Road, Gaydon	24C31	Gilson Road, Water Orton
	Gayle, Stoneydelph, Tamworth	24B24	Gilson Way, Gilson, Coleshill
	Geilgud Way, Anstey	24A43	Gilson Way, Kingshurst
	General Hospital, Stratford upon Avon	14B22	Gipsy Lane, Atherstone
	Gentlemans Lane Farm, Ullenhall	30C33	Gipsy Lane, Nuneaton
	George Birch Close, Brinklow	14B21	Gipsy Lane, Whittington, Grendon
	George Eliot Avenue, Bedworth	32C42	Gipsy Lane, Wolvey
	George Eliot Hospital, Nuneaton	82B43	Girvan Grove, Cubbington

Map ref	Address
96C24	Gisburn Close, Woodloes, Warwick
53C34	Gladiator Way, Glebe Farm Estate, Rugby
60A21	Gladstone Road, Dorridge
70C12	Gladstone Street, Rugby
54B34	Glaramara Close, Brownsover, Rugby
5A22	Glascote Road, Amington Ind.est., Tamworth
5B23	Glascote Road, Stoneydelph, Tamworth
81B12	Glasshouse Lane, Ashow
59C34	Glasshouse Lane, Packwood, Lapworth
81A14	Glasshouse Lane, Windy Arbour, Kenilworth
116A21	Gleave Road, Whitnash, Leamington Spa
39C23	Glebe Avenue, Goodyears End, Bedworth
156B11	Glebe Close, Bidford
119C14	Glebe Close, Stockton
116A22	Glebe Court, Leamington Spa
116A22	Glebe Court, Whitnash
70C14	Glebe Crescent, New Bilton, Rugby
81A13	Glebe Crescent, Whitemore, Kenilworth
53C32	Glebe Farm Estate, Rugby
54A33	Glebe Farm Industrial Estate, Brounsover, Rugby
53C32	Glebe Farm Industrial Estate, Glebe Farm Estate, Rugby
54A33	Glebe Farm Road, Glebe Farm Estate, Rugby
126C14	Glebe Farm, Aston Cantlow
135B43	Glebe Farm, Bishops Itchington
181B14	Glebe Farm, Blackwell, Tredington
86A32	Glebe Farm, Bourton And Draycote
157C21	Glebe Farm, Braggington, Welford on Avon
188C14	Glebe Farm, Brailes
83B12	Glebe Farm, Bubbenhall
44C11	Glebe Farm, Claybrook Parva
168C21	Glebe Farm, Claydon
98C14	Glebe Farm, Cubbington
158A31	Glebe Farm, Dorsington
86A23	Glebe Farm, Draycote
141C13	Glebe Farm, Exhall
15C44	Glebe Farm, Fenny Drayton, Witherley
53C34	Glebe Farm, Glebe Farm Estate, Rugby
48B43	Glebe Farm, Harborough Magna
79A41	Glebe Farm, Haseley
177C33	Glebe Farm, Horley
146B24	Glebe Farm, Hunscote, Charlecote
125C24	Glebe Farm, Kinwarton
133A34	Glebe Farm, Lighthorne
149A42	Glebe Farm, Lighthorne Rough, Compton Verney
101A34	Glebe Farm, Long Itchington
121B24	Glebe Farm, Lower Shuckburgh
49C11	Glebe Farm, Lutterworth
21A14	Glebe Farm, Mancetter
86A32	Glebe Farm, Marlborough Site
7C14	Glebe Farm, Orton on The Hill
165B34	Glebe Farm, Radway
78A31	Glebe Farm, Rowington
107A32	Glebe Farm, Sambourne
109A34	Glebe Farm, Shelfield Green, Great Alne
112A34	Glebe Farm, Snitterfield
119B24	Glebe Farm, Southam
146A11	Glebe Farm, Stratford upon Avon
57B34	Glebe Farm, Tanworth in Arden
7C14	Glebe Farm, Twycross
131B21	Glebe Farm, Wasperton
158B12	Glebe Farm, Weston on Avon
44C44	Glebe Farm, Willey
127B24	Glebe Farm, Wilmcote
15C12	Glebe Farm, Witherley
112B13	Glebe Farm, Wolverton
28A44	Glebe Farm, Wood End, Astley
152C12	Glebe Farm, Wormleighton
16A34	Glebe Fields, Curdworth
22C41	Glebe Lane, Nuneaton
98B33	Glebe Place, Leamington Spa
93C41	Glebe Road, Claverdon
30B12	Glebe Road, Nuneaton
119A23	Glebe Road, Southam
144B13	Glebe Road, Stratford upon Avon
96C21	Gleeson Drive, Woodloes, Warwick
181C42	Glen Close, Shipston on Stour
166C41	Glen Farm, Warmington
64A44	Glendale Avenue, Kenilworth
41B13	Glendon Gardens, Bulkington, Bedworth
145A11	Glendower, Stratford upon Avon
31B23	Gleneagles Close, Whitestone, Nuneaton
2A44	Gleneagles, Amington, Tamworth
22B33	Glenfield Avenue, Weddington, Nuneaton
75B44	Glenfields Farm, Ullenhall
93B34	Glenhurst Farm, Barnmoor Green, Claverdon
92A34	Glenhurst Road, Henley in Arden
12B31	Glenville Avenue, Wood End, Kingsbury
58B12	Glenwood Drive, Cheswick Green
40A11	Glenwood Gardens, Collycroft, Bedworth
30A43	Glenwood Gardens, Griff, Nuneaton
58A21	Gleobury Lane, Cheswick Green
63C42	Gloster Drive, Kenilworth
147A31	Gloster Gardens, Mountford, Wellesbourne
23A32	Gloucester Close, Saint Nicholas, Nuneaton
97C34	Gloucester Street, Leamington Spa
34A23	Gloucester Way, Chelmsley Wood
97B41	Glover Close, Leamington Spa
114A12	Glover Close, Warwick
9A43	Glover Road, Sutton Coldfield
14C42	Glovers Close, Mancetter
116C12	Godfrey Road, Radford Semele

Map ref	Address
31	Godsons Hill Farm, Preston Bagot
C34	Godsons Road, Napton on The Hill
31	Gofton, Stoneydelph, Tamworth
A12	Gogbrook Farm, Warwick
31	Gold Close, Nuneaton
32	Goldbys Farm, Arbury, Nuneaton
3	Goldcrest, Tamworth
33	Golden Acres Lane, Binley Woods
C24	Golden Cross Farm, Stretton on Fosse
311	Goldicote House, Goldicote
C43	Goldicote Road, Loxley
1	Goldsborough, Stoneydelph, Tamworth
43	Goldsmith Avenue, Forbes Estate, Warwick
34	Goldsmith Avenue, Hillside, Rugby
24	Golf Drive, Whitestone, Nuneaton
21	Golf Lane, Whitnash
23	Goodacres Lane, Burton Hastings
1	Goode Avenue, Myton, Leamington Spa
1	Goode Avenue, Myton, Warwick
	Goodere Avenue, Polesworth
	Goodere Drive, Polesworth
	Goodeve Walk, Sutton Coldfield
3	Goodfellow Street, Milverton, Leamington Spa
3	Goodrest Farm, Leek Wootton
2	Goods Farm, Kings Newnham
	Goodway Court, Gerard Street, Warwick
23	Goodwood Close, Stratford upon Avon
	Goodyers End Lane, Exhall, Bedworth
11	Goose Bank, Warmington
14	Goose Lane, Lower Quinton, Quinton
41	Gooseberry Hall Farm, Barford
	Gorcott Hill, Studley
	Gordon Close, Bedworth
	Gordon House, Leamington Spa
	Gordon Passage, Leamington Spa
	Gordon Street, Leamington Spa
	Gorse Close, Overslade, Rugby
	Gorse Cottage Farm, Whitestone, Nuneaton
	Gorse Cottage, Whitestone, Nuneaton
	Gorse Farm Road, Whitestone, Nuneaton
	Gorse Farm, Bearley
	Gorse Farm, Chelmsley Wood
	Gorse Farm, Nuneaton
	Gorse Farm, Rugby
4	Gorse Lane, Wootton Wawen
3	Gorse Lea, Southam
	Gorsey Close, Astwood Bank
	Gorsey Lane, Astley
	Gorsey Lane, Coleshill
	Gorsey Lane, Shustoke
	Gorsey Way, Camphill, Nuneaton
	Gorsey Way, Coleshill
	Gorsy Bank Road, Tamworth
	Gospel Oak Farm, Lapworth
	Gospel Oak Lane, Drayton

Map ref	Address
128B22	Gospel Oak Lane, Snitterfield
128B23	Gospel Oak Lane, Stratford upon Avon
166A14	Gosport Lane, Burton Dassett
105A24	Gould Close, Braunston
96A33	Gould Road, Hampton Magna, Budbrooke
165C43	Grafton Cottage, Radway
142A31	Grafton Lane, Ardens Grafton, Bidford
142A21	Grafton Lane, Ardens Grafton, Exhall
143A34	Grafton Lane, Lower Binton, Binton
71B11	Graham Road, Rugby
22B43	Graham Street, Nuneaton
14C42	Gramer Court, Mancetter, Atherstone
169C43	Granbrook Lane, Mickleton
182A11	Granby Farm, Honington
182A14	Granby Road, Honington
29C14	Granby Road, Stockingford, Nuneaton
98A22	Grandborough Court, Leamington Spa
103B23	Grandborough Fields Road, Grandborough
102C13	Grandborough Road, Leamington Hastings
65B21	Grange Avenue, Finham
63C41	Grange Avenue, Kenilworth
21A34	Grange Close, Camphill, Nuneaton
97A32	Grange Close, Emscote, Warwick
176C12	Grange Close, Ratley, Ratley And Upton
19A22	Grange Close, Southam
165C43	Grange Cottage, Radway
95C32	Grange Farm, Budbrooke
38A21	Grange Farm, Fillongley
103C21	Grange Farm, Grandborough
21B21	Grange Farm, Hartshill
23A22	Grange Farm, Hinckley
18C11	Grange Farm, Hurley, Kingsbury
151C13	Grange Farm, Knightcote, Bishops Itchington
132C42	Grange Farm, Little Morrell, Moreton Morrell
101A21	Grange Farm, Long Itchington
94B23	Grange Farm, Pinley Green, Rowington
138B44	Grange Farm, Priors Marston
67B24	Grange Farm, Ryton on Dunsmore
40B43	Grange Farm, Sutton Stop, Coventry
86B22	Grange Farm, Thurlaston
66C11	Grange Farm, Willenhall Binley, Brandon
147B21	Grange Gardens, Mountford, Wellesbourne
155A34	Grange Lane, Harvington
97B24	Grange Mews, Milverton, Leamington Spa
145A11	Grange Park, Stratford upon Avon
111A42	Grange Road, Bearley
156C12	Grange Road, Bidford
21A34	Grange Road, Camphill, Nuneaton
59C33	Grange Road, Dorridge
21B13	Grange Road, Hartshill, Nuneaton

Map ref	Address
98A32	Grange Road, Leamington Spa
53C41	Grange Road, Newbold on Avon, Rugby
120A11	Grange Road, Stockton
40B43	Grange Road, Sutton Stop, Coventry
59B34	Grange Road, Tanworth in Arden
94C11	Grangers Close, Little Shrewley
168A13	Granmore Hill Farm, Farnborough
40A31	Grant Road, Exhall, Bedworth
152A43	Grants Close, Fenny Compton
181C34	Granville Court, Shipston on Stour
60A21	Granville Road, Dorridge
147A14	Granville Road, Mountford, Wellesbourne
98A21	Granville Street, Leamington Spa
54B41	Grasmere Close, Brownsover, Rugby
145A14	Grasmere Court, Stratford upon Avon
22C34	Grasmere Crescent, Saint Nicholas Park, Nuneaton
40A22	Grasmere Road, Bedworth
12B44	Grass Yard Farm, Hurley, Kingsbury
5A31	Grassholme, Stoneydelph, Tamworth
96C24	Grassington Avenue, Woodloes, Warwick
31A22	Grassington Drive, Nuneaton
110A33	Gray Mill Lane, Aston Cantlow
110A32	Gray Mill Lane, Wootton Wawen
51C14	Grays Close, Brinklow
86C23	Grays Orchard, Thurlaston
51B14	Great Balance, Brinklow
54B31	Great Borne, Brownsover, Rugby
55A31	Great Central View, Newton And Biggin
51B14	Great Galance, Brinklow
165C41	Great Grounds Farm, Radway
123B42	Great Knighton Farm, Inkberrow
139A11	Great Nobury Farm, Inkberrow
94B23	Great Pinley Farm, Shrewley
145A13	Great William Street, Stratford upon Avon
97C21	Greatheed Road, Milverton, Leamington Spa
97B41	Greaves Close, Leamington Spa
97B41	Greaves Close, Myton, Warwick
2A44	Green Acre Close, Amington, Tamworth
150B34	Green Acres Farm, Gaydon
69C12	Green Close, Long Lawford
107C23	Green Close, Studley
116B22	Green Close, Whitnash
181C14	Green Cottage, Tredington
187A14	Green End Farm, Barcheston
188C22	Green End Farm, Brailes
37A31	Green End Farm, Newhall Green, Fillongley
37A23	Green End Lane, Green End, Fillongley
36C21	Green End Road, Green End, Fillongley
36B21	Green End Road, Maxstoke
36C23	Green End, Fillongley
101A33	Green End, Long Itchington

Map ref	Address
25C22	Green End, Shustoke
164C14	Green Farm End, Kineton
133C24	Green Farm, Chesterton
163B11	Green Farm, Combrook
12A44	Green Farm, Hurley Common, Kingsbury
12C31	Green Farm, Hurley, Baxterley
78A24	Green Farm, Rowington
104A33	Green Farm, Sawbridge, Wolfhamc
25C24	Green Farm, Shustoke
120A13	Green Farm, Stockton
188A34	Green Farm, Sutton Under Brailes
186C24	Green Farm, Tidmington
92B23	Green Gates, Henley in Arden
141B33	Green Highway, Broom, Bidford
135A14	Green Hill Farm, Harbury
70C24	Green Hill Road, Overslade, Rugb
109A23	Green Hill, Aston Cantlow
36C32	Green Lane Farm, Green End, Fill
37A31	Green Lane Farm, Newhall Green, Fillongley
107C11	Green Lane Farm, Studley
44A22	Green Lane N, Wibtoft
44A33	Green Lane S, Monks Kirby
44A24	Green Lane S, Wibtoft
37B42	Green Lane, Allesley
19B22	Green Lane, Bentley
19C31	Green Lane, Birchley Heath, Ansl
5C33	Green Lane, Birchmoor, Poleswor
51B14	Green Lane, Brinklow
102C23	Green Lane, Broadwell, Leamingt
	Hastings
21B33	Green Lane, Camphill, Nuneaton
34B14	Green Lane, Chelmsley Wood
58B12	Green Lane, Cheswick Green
52A42	Green Lane, Church Lawford
25A43	Green Lane, Coleshill
65A21	Green Lane, Finham
37A31	Green Lane, Green End, Fillongl
6C43	Green Lane, Grendon
10B43	Green Lane, Hunts Green, Midd
94C11	Green Lane, Little Shrewley
174C33	Green Lane, Oxhill
96C31	Green Lane, Packmores, Warwic
107A14	Green Lane, Sambourne
181C44	Green Lane, Shipston on Stour
5B34	Green Lane, Stoneydelph, Tamw
7B14	Green Lane, Twycross
74C13	Green Trees Farm, Tanworth in
105A24	Green Way, Braunston
96C23	Green Way, Woodloes, Warwic
34A22	Green Wood Way, Chelmsley V
41B32	Greenacres Farm, Bedworth
14C33	Greendale Close, Mancetter
14C33	Greendale Road, Mancetter
186C11	Greenfields Close, Shipston on
24A33	Greenfinch Road, Kingshurst
5A11	Greenheart, Amington, Tamwo
175A23	Greenhill Farm, Oxhill

ref	Address	Map ref	Address
333	Greenhill Farm, Sutton Under Brailes	119B13	Griffins Farm, Southam
313	Greenhill Road, Whitnash	54B33	Griffiths House, Rugby
C22	Greenhill Street, Stratford upon Avon	91B22	Grimshaw Hill Farm, Barrells Park,
22	Greenlands Road, Chelmsley Wood		Ullenhall
14	Greenmoor Road, Nuneaton	24C31	Grimstock Hill, Coleshill
41	Greens Charity Farm, Fillongley	5A31	Grindsbrook, Stoneydelph, Tamworth
1	Greens Close, Churchover	112A43	Griswolds Farm, Snitterfield
3	Greenside Close, Whitestone, Nuneaton	54C23	Gritan Way, Brownsover, Rugby
42	Greensward Close, Kenilworth	54B31	Grizedale, Brownsover, Rugby
42	Greenway Close, Shipston on Stour	139A21	Groomshill Farm, Rous Lench
3	Greenway Farm, Pailton	97C24	Grosvenor Court, Leamington Spa
42	Greenway Road, Shipston on Stour	71B13	Grosvenor Road, Rugby
	Greenway, Polesworth	116A11	Grosvenor Road, Whitnash
4	Greenway, Whitestone, Nuneaton	16A13	Grounds Farm, Grove End, Wisham
21	Greenways Estate, Braunston	80B11	Grounds Farm, Kenilworth
4	Greenways Farm, Fillongley	144B11	Grouse Close, Stratford upon Avon
4	Greenwood Close, Long Lawford	95C43	Grove Croft, Hampton on The Hill,
2	Greenwood Court, Attleborough,		Budbrooke
	Nuneaton	81C23	Grove Farm Road, Ashow
2	Greenwood Court, Leamington Spa	81C23	Grove Farm, Ashow
	Greenwood Drive, Bearley	115C21	Grove Farm, Bishops Tachbrook
2	Grendon Drive, Rugby	166B14	Grove Farm, Burton Dassett Hills,
	Grendon Fields Farm, Grendon		Burton Dassett
	Grendon House Farm, Grendon	194B23	Grove Farm, Chastleton
	Grendon Road, Saint Helena, Polesworth	38B34	Grove Farm, Corley
	Grenfell Close, Sydenham Farm Estate,	162A33	Grove Farm, Ettington
	Leamington Spa	142A13	Grove Farm, Exhall
	Grenville Close, Bilton, Rugby	85B12	Grove Farm, Frankton
	Gresham Avenue, Lillington,	90B12	Grove Farm, Gorcott, Studley
	Leamington Spa	79B12	Grove Farm, Honiley
	Gresham Place, Lillington, Leamington	43A21	Grove Farm, Wolvey
	Gresham Road, Griff, Nuneaton	131A13	Grove Field Farm, Hampton Lucy
	Gresley Farm, Sheepy Magna, Sheepy	130C13	Grove Field, Hampton Lucy
3	Greville Road, Alcester	22B31	Grove Fields, Weddington, Nuneaton
	Greville Road, Kenilworth	146C43	Grove Hill Farm, Loxley
	Greville Road, Percy Estate, Warwick	144C22	Grove House, Stratford upon Avon
	Greville Smith Avenue, Whitnash	60A13	Grove Lane, Dorridge
3	Grey Goose Lane, Chastleton	16A13	Grove Lane, Grove End, Wisham
4	Grey Mill Farm, Wootton Wawen	38C33	Grove Lane, Keresley Newlands,
	Greynolds Lane, Cheswick Green		Keresley
	Greys Road, Tomstown, Studley	60A43	Grove Lane, Packwood, Lapworth
	Griff Hill Farm, Griff, Nuneaton	95A34	Grove Park Farm, Budbrooke
	Griff Hollows, Nuneaton	98A43	Grove Place, Leamington Spa
	Griff Island To Junction 3 M6,	29B22	Grove Place, Stockingford, Nuneaton
	Bedworth by pass	45B14	Grove Road, Anstey
	Griff Island To Nuneaton Island,	14C33	Grove Road, Atherstone
	Bedworth by pass	29B22	Grove Road, Stockingford, Nuneaton
	Griff Island, Bedworth by pass	144C22	Grove Road, Stratford upon Avon
	Griff Island, Griff, Nuneaton	97C31	Grove Street, Leamington Spa
	Griff Lane, Arbury	45B14	Growner Field Farm, Anstey
	Griff Lane, Griff, Bedworth	180B13	Grump Street, Ilmington
	Griff Lodge Farm, Griff, Nuneaton	126C12	Guild Road, Aston Cantlow
	Griff Lorry Park, Griff, Bedworth	145A13	Guild Street, Stratford upon Avon
	Griff To Junction 3 M6, Bedworth by	97B24	Gulistan Court, Leamington Spa
	pass	97B24	Gulistan Road, Leamington Spa
	Griff To Junction 3 M6, Old Arley	27C42	Gun Hill Farm, Gun Hill, Arley
	Griff To Nuneaton, Bedworth by pass	28A33	Gun Hill, New Arley, Arley
	Griff To Nuneaton, Old Arley	165C43	Gunby Hall, Radway
	Griffin Road, Myton, Leamington Spa	98A41	Gundry Close, Leamington Spa

Map ref	Address
126A12	Gunn Court, Great Alne
181C34	Gunn End, Shipston on Stour
107C22	Gunners Lane, Studley
97B24	Gunnery Terrace, Milverton, Leamington Spa
125B31	Gunnings Bridge, Alcester
125B31	Gunnings Road, Alcester
24A42	Gurnsey Drive, Kingshurst
97C24	Guy Place E, Leamington Spa
97C24	Guy Place W, Leamington Spa
80C14	Guy Road, Kenilworth
96C34	Guy Street, Coten End, Warwick
97C24	Guy Street, Leamington Spa
96C32	Guys Close, Warwick
96C32	Guys Cross Park Road, Guys Cross Park, Warwick
97B24	Guyscliffe Avenue, Milverton, Leamington Spa
97B32	Guyscliffe Road, Milverton, Leamington Spa
96C34	Guyscliffe Terrace, Warwick
127B22	Gypsy Hall Farm, Wilmcote, Aston Cantlow
14B22	Gypsy Lane, Atherstone
30A41	Gypsy Lane, Griff, Nuneaton
80C22	Gypsy Lane, Kenilworth
24B22	Gypsy Lane, Water Orton
31A33	Gypsy Lane, Whitestone, Nuneaton
14B21	Gypsy Lane, Whittington, Grendon
32C42	Gypsy Lane, Wolvey
191B24	Hack Lane, Little Wolford
191C31	Hack Lane, Long Compton
120C34	Hackwell Street, Napton on The Hill
98B23	Haddon Road, Lillington, Leamington
55A43	Hadfield Close, Clifton upon Dunsmore
65B13	Hadleigh Road, Finham
11B44	Hadleys Croft, Kingsbury
98A12	Hadrian Close, Lillington, Leamington Spa
24C22	Hadrian Drive, Coleshill
125A33	Hadrians Walk, Arrow
53C34	Hadrians Way, Rugby
70C23	Haig Court, Rugby
112B41	Hales Close, Snitterfield
148C13	Hales Farm, Moreton Morrell
173A43	Halford Hill Farm, Halford
172B42	Halford Road, Armscote, Tredington
173C41	Halford Road, Idlicote
144B24	Halford Road, Stratford upon Avon
18C33	Halfway House Farm, Nether Whitacre
87A14	Halfway Lane, Dunchurch
147A31	Halifax Close, Mountford, Wellesbourne
89C14	Hall Close, Kilsby
65A42	Hall Close, Stoneleigh
184B22	Hall Close, Upper Tysoe, Tysoe
65C13	Hall Drive, Baginton
34A33	Hall Drive, Chelmsley Wood
5B42	Hall End Cottage, Dordon
75C43	Hall End Farm, Blunts Green, Ullen
5C44	Hall End Farm, Hall End, Dordon
91C14	Hall End Farm, Hall End, Ullenhall
30B22	Hall End Place, Nuneaton
30B22	Hall End, Attleborough, Nuneaton
91C11	Hall Farm Road, Ullenhall
164B31	Hall Farm, Butlers Marston
39B34	Hall Farm, Exhall, Bedworth
53B13	Hall Farm, Harborough Parva, Harborough Magna
23A12	Hall Farm, Higham, Higham on T. Hill
83C43	Hall Farm, Hunningham
136A21	Hall Farm, Ladbroke
111C13	Hall Farm, Langley
164B24	Hall Farm, Little Kineton, Kineton
52C34	Hall Farm, Little Lawford
26C12	Hall Farm, Over Whitacre
26A24	Hall Farm, Shustoke
4A31	Hall Fields Farm, Austrey
51C14	Hall Green, Brinklow
41B14	Hall Grounds Farm, Ryton, Bedw
117C44	Hall Lane, Harbury
15A33	Hall Lane, Witherley
42B12	Hall Lane, Wolvey
189B11	Hall Meadow Farm, Brailes
13B33	Hall Road, Baxterley
97C23	Hall Road, Leamington Spa
42B12	Hall Road, Wolvey
35A11	Hall Walk, Coleshill
98C42	Hallfields, Radford Semele
17C32	Halloughton Hall, Nether Whitac Kingsbury
17C31	Halloughton Lane, Halloughton, Kingsbury
17B34	Halloughton Lane, Nether Whita
121B41	Halls Barn Farm, Lower Shuckb
116B21	Halls Close, Whitnash
41C41	Hallway Drive, Shilton
5A31	Halton Lea, Stoneydelph, Tamw
99A21	Ham Farm, Cubbington
151C21	Hambridge Lane, Knightcote
135B32	Hambridge Road, Bishops Itchir
150C13	Hambridge Road, Gaydon
151C13	Hambridge Road, Knightcote, B Dassett
152B14	Hambridge Road, Watergall
3B14	Hames Lane, Newton Regis
39A24	Hamilton Close, Goodyears En Bedworth
107B22	Hamilton Drive, Studley
98C43	Hamilton Road, Radford Semel
145C13	Hamilton Road, Tiddington, St. upon Avon
97C34	Hamilton Terrace, Leamington
31A22	Hamlet Close, Whitestone, Nur
70B42	Hamlet Close, Woodlands, Rug
39C23	Hammersley Street, Goodyears Bedworth

Map ref	Address	Map ref	Address
A31	Hammerton Way, Mountford, Wellesbourne	36C21	Hardingwood Lane, Green End, Fillongley
14	Hammond Close, Attleborough, Nuneaton	96C22	Hardley Close, Woodloes, Warwick
12	Hammonds Terrace, Kenilworth	127C22	Hardwick Farm, Aston Cantlow
44	Hampden Court, Temple Herdewyke, Burton Dassett	175C13	Hardwick Farm, Tysoe
4	Hampden Way, Bilton, Rugby	90B34	Hardwick Lane, Clarkes Green, Studley
A24	Hampdon Way, Mountford, Wellesbourne	90C31	Hardwick Lane, Outhill, Studley
12	Hampton Avenue, Whittleford, Nuneaton	92C24	Hardwick Lane, Studley
31	Hampton Barn, Hampton Lucy	90A43	Hardwick Lane, Washford, Studley
3	Hampton Croft, Hampton on The Hill, Budbrooke	138B43	Hardwick Road, Priors Marston
4	Hampton Grove, Leamington Spa	70B21	Hardy Close, Bilton, Rugby
12	Hampton Hill Farm, Budbrooke	30A21	Hare And Hounds Lane, Heath End, Nuneaton
3	Hampton Road, Budbrooke	54C31	Harebell Way, Brownsover, Rugby
3	Hampton Road, Forbes Estate, Warwick	2A43	Harebell, Amington, Tamworth
3	Hampton Street, Forbes Estate, Warwick	30A32	Harefield Lane, Bermuda, Nuneaton
3	Hams Hall Power Station, Lea Marston, Coleshill	22B43	Harefield Road, Nuneaton
2	Hams Lane, Lea Marston, Curdworth	114C33	Hareway Farm, Barford
13	Hanbury Close, Kineton	114B34	Hareway Lane, Barford
	Hanbury Road, Bedworth	115B41	Hareway Lane, Bishops Tachbrook
	Hanbury Road, Dorridge	80C14	Harger Court, Kenilworth
12	Handgate Farm, Church Lench	24A14	Hargrave Close, Water Orton
	Handley Green, Woodloes, Warwick	64B43	Harlech Close, Kenilworth
	Handley Grove, Woodloes, Warwick	96B24	Harmar Close, Woodloes, Warwick
	Handleys Close, Ryton on Dunsmore	70C41	Harold Cox Place, Rugby
4	Hands Paddle, Newbold on Stour, Tredington	30B13	Harold Street, Chilvers Coton, Nuneaton
4	Hands Paddock, Newbold on Stour	119A44	Harp Farm, Southam
	Hangmans Lane, Seckington	92A34	Harpers Hill Farm, Henley in Arden
	Hangmans Lane, Shuttington	15A33	Harpers Lane, Mancetter
	Hanlith, Stoneydelph, Tamworth	96C22	Harriot Green, Woodloes, Warwick
	Hanover Gardens, Leamington Spa	115B12	Harriott Drive, Heathcote Industrial, Whitnash
	Hanover Glebe, Nuneaton	92B31	Harris Close, Henley in Arden
	Hansell Drive, Dorridge	70C32	Harris Drive, Overslade, Rugby
2	Hansells Farm, Shottery, Stratford upon Avon	92B31	Harris Mews, Henley in Arden
3	Hanson Avenue, Shipston on Stour	96B23	Harris Road, Wedgenock Industrial, Warwick
	Hanworth Close, Lillington, Leamington Spa	72B31	Harrison Close, Hillmorton, Rugby
	Hanworth Road, Packmores, Warwick	40A21	Harrison Crescent, Bedworth
	Harborough Fields Farms, Monks Kirby	76A22	Harrisons Farm, Tanworth in Arden
	Harborough Road, Rugby	174A32	Harrods Farm, Whatcote
	Harbour Close, Bidford	23C33	Harrow Brook Road, Hinckley
	Harbridges Lane, Farnborough	191C31	Harrow Hill Farm, Long Compton
	Harbridges Lane, Fenny Compton	105B23	Harrow Lane, Braunston
	Harbury Fields Farm, Harbury	116A24	Harrow Road, Whitnash
	Harbury Lane, Bishops Tachbrook	71C21	Hart Close, Rugby
	Harbury Lane, Harwoods House, Chesterton	5A31	Hartley Burn, Stoneydelph, Tamworth
	Harbury Lane, Ufton	20B23	Hartshill Lane, Oldbury
	Harbury Lane, Warwick	147A32	Harvard Close, Mountford, Wellesbourne
	Harbury Lane, Whitnash, Leamington Spa	116B12	Harvest Hill Close, Sydenham Farm Estate, Leamington
		63B33	Harvest House, Burton Green, Kenilworth
		133B23	Harwoods House Farm, Harwoods House, Chesterton
		116B11	Haseley Close, Whitnash
		170A14	Haseley Court, Lower Quinton
		78C32	Haseley Grange, Haseley

Map ref	Address
79A22	Haseley Green Farm, Haseley Knob, Haseley
78C32	Haseley Hall Farm, Haseley
79A21	Haseley Knob, Haseley
79A12	Haseley Knob, Haseley Knob, Haseley
95A12	Haseley Manor, Haseley Knob, Hatton
79B33	Haseley Mill, Waste Green, Haseley
125B32	Haselor Close, Kinwarton
126B21	Haselor Grounds Farm, Haselor
115B34	Hassell Close, Bishops Tachbrook
147B11	Hastings Road, Charlecote, Wellesbourne
71B21	Haswell Close, Rugby
34B23	Hatchford Grove, Chelmsley Wood
31A24	Hathaway Drive, Whitestone, Nuneaton
96C13	Hathaway Drive, Woodloes, Warwick
147A32	Hathaway Gardens, Mountford, Wellesbourne
144A14	Hathaway Green Lane, Stratford upon Avon
144B22	Hathaway Lane, Shottery, Stratford upon Avon
98C43	Hatherell Road, Radford Semele
193C32	Hathway Lane, Hook Norton
14B14	Hatters Drive, Atherstone
130A21	Hatton Bank Farm, Hampton Lucy
130A31	Hatton Bank Lane, Hampton Lucy
130A22	Hatton Bank Lane, Snitterfield
95C21	Hatton Close, Hatton
95B24	Hatton Farm, Hatton
94C12	Hatton Farm, Shrewley
95A14	Hatton Hill, Hatton, Warwick
95A13	Hatton Lane Farm, Hatton
95A13	Hatton Road, Hatton
130A31	Hatton Rock Trout Farm, Hatton Rock, Hampton Lucy
94C23	Hatton Station, Hatton
95C21	Hatton Terrace, Budbrooke
17A33	Haunch Lane, Lea Marston
28C11	Haunchwood Park Drive, Whittleford, Nuneaton
29C13	Haunchwood Road, Stockingford, Nuneaton
70C13	Haven Court, New Bilton, Rugby
46C11	Haven Farm, Withybrook
5A43	Hawfinch, Tamworth
31B31	Hawk Close, Whitestone, Nuneaton
115C12	Hawkes Cottage, Whitnash
115B12	Hawkes Drive, Heathcote Industrial, Leamington
115B14	Hawkes Farm, Whitnash
100A22	Hawkes Meadow, Hatton Junction
40B33	Hawkesbury Colliery Farm, Exhall, Bedworth
40B34	Hawkesbury Hall Farm, Bedworth Hill, Bedworth
40C41	Hawkesbury Lane, Bedworth
40B44	Hawkesbury Lane, Parrots Grove
54B34	Hawkeshead, Brownsover, Rugby
35B13	Hawkeswell Farm, Coleshill
35A14	Hawkeswell Lane, Coleshill
64A41	Hawkesworth Drive, Kenilworth
70C23	Hawkins Close, Rugby
5A32	Hawkside, Stoneydelph, Tamworth
64A41	Hawksworth Drive, Kenilworth
54B41	Hawlands, Brownsover, Rugby
97C43	Hawthorn Road, Leamington Spa
70A22	Hawthorn Way, Bilton, Rugby
12B44	Hawthorne Avenue, Hurley, Kings
28A34	Hawthorne Avenue, New Arley, A
125A24	Hawthorne Close, Alcester
51A43	Hawthorne Close, Wolston
21C42	Hawthorne Terrace, Camphill, Nuneaton
53B21	Hawthorne Terrace, Harborough [Magna], Harborough Magna
167C23	Hay Pool, Farnborough
144B24	Haydock Close, Stratford upon Av[on]
107C34	Haydon Way Farm, Sambourne
107C42	Haydon Way, Coughton
107C34	Haydon Way, Spernall, Sambourn[e]
90A23	Haye Farm, Mappleborough Green, Studley
90B21	Haye Lane, Mappleborough Green, Studley
54B34	Hayes Close, Brownsover, Rugby
39C23	Hayes Green Lane, Exhall, Bedwo[rth]
37A33	Hayes Hall Farm, Newhall Green, Fillongley
40A33	Hayes Lane, Exhall, Bedworth
21A31	Hayes Road, Moor Wood, Harts[hill]
97A21	Hayle Avenue, Woodloes, Warw[ick]
31A11	Hayle Close, Nuneaton
53C32	Haynes Way, Cosford
73B32	Haythog Farm, Crick
95C34	Hayward Close, Hampton Magn[a], Budbrooke
102C23	Hayway Lane, Broadwell, Leami[ngton] Hastings
193C32	Hayway Lane, Hook Norton
95C33	Haywood Close, Hampton Magn[a]
61A44	Haywood Farm, Baddesley Clint[on]
78B33	Haywood Lane, Mousley End, Rowington
98B22	Hazard Close, Lillington, Leami[ngton] Spa
98A21	Hazel Close, Leamington Spa
105B21	Hazel Croft, Braunston
34A24	Hazel Croft, Chelmsley Wood
40B14	Hazel Grove, Bedworth
59B41	Hazel Grove, Hockley Heath, C[hadwick] Green
30A23	Hazel Road, Bermuda
21B44	Hazel Road, Camphill, Nuneato[n]
30A21	Hazel Way, Bermuda, Nuneato[n]
11B32	Hazelcroft, Kingsbury
5A32	Hazelgarth, Stoneydelph, Tamw[orth]
27B23	Hazells Hill, Devitts Green, Ar[ley]

ref	Address	Map ref	Address
A33	Hazelwood Close, Arrow	115B12	Heathcote Way, Heathcote Industrial, Whitnash
21	Hazelwood Close, Dunchurch	29C22	Heather Close, Heath End, Nuneaton
21	Hazelwood Green Farm, Preston Bagot	24A31	Heather Close, Kingshurst
A33	Hazelwood Close, Arrow	70C23	Heather Close, Overslade, Rugby
A12	Headland Close, Welford on Avon	119A22	Heather Close, Southam
A12	Headland Rise, Welford on Avon	144B14	Heather Close, Stratford upon Avon
A12	Headland Road, Welford on Avon	14C23	Heather Court, Atherstone
C11	Headlands Farm, Chapel Green, Napton on The Hill	39C13	Heather Drive, Bedworth Woodlands, Bedworth
3	Healey Close, Brownsover, Rugby	50C33	Heather Road, Binley Woods
32	Healey Court, Emscote, Warwick	58C42	Heathfield Farm, Tanworth in Arden
1	Heanley Farm, Hurley, Kingsbury	71C31	Heathway, Ashlawn Estate, Rugby
2	Heanley Lane, Hurley, Kingsbury	96C24	Hebden Avenue, Woodloes, Warwick
3	Heath Avenue, Goodyears End, Bedworth	5A32	Hebden, Stoneydelph, Tamworth
41	Heath End Farm, Fulbrook	134B11	Heber Drive, Harbury
4	Heath End Farm, Heath End, Nuneaton	40A33	Heckley Fields, Exhall, Bedworth
43	Heath End Lane, Marraway Turn, Fulbrook	40A33	Heckley Road, Exhall, Bedworth
		21C41	Hedgerows, The, Nuneaton
4	Heath End Road, Stockingford, Nuneaton	34B21	Hedgetree Croft, Chelmsley Wood
32	Heath End, Snitterfield	34B22	Hedingham Grove, Chelmsley Wood
22	Heath Farm Road, Lighthorne	98A21	Heemstede Lane, Leamington Spa
4	Heath Farm, Bascote Heath, Long Itchington	6A32	Helena, Polesworth
	Heath Farm, Bourton on Dunsmore	30B23	Helena Close, Nuneaton
	Heath Farm, Chelmsley Wood	98A21	Hellidon Close, Lillington, Leamington Spa
	Heath Farm, Churchover	138B34	Hellidon Road, Priors Marston
4	Heath Farm, Lighthorne	94C34	Hells Kitchen Farm, Claverdon
	Heath Farm, New Arley, Arley	54C42	Helmdon Close, Brownsover, Rugby
	Heath Farm, Oxley	98A12	Helmsdale Road, Lillington, Leamington Spa
2	Heath Farm, Sibford Gower	34B24	Helmswood Drive, Chelmsley Wood
	Heath Farm, Stoneleigh	31A11	Helston Close, Nuneaton
1	Heath Farm, Stratford upon Avon	54B34	Helvellyn Way, Brownsover, Rugby
	Heath Farm, Ullenhall	82A44	Hemesdale Road, Leamington Spa
	Heath Farm, Wolvey	17B12	Hemlingsford Road, Kingsbury
	Heath Green Close, Chelmsley Wood	98C43	Hemmings Close, Radford Semele
	Heath Grove, Woodloes, Warwick	114A42	Hemmings Mill, Barford
	Heath Lane, Brinklow	165C43	Hemp Cottage, Radway
	Heath Road, Dunchurch	41A14	Hemsworth Drive, Bulkington, Bedworth
	Heath Road, Exhall, Bedworth	188B14	Henbrook Lane, Grove End, Brailes
	Heath Terrace, Beausale	22C32	Henley Close, Saint Nicholas Park, Nuneaton
	Heath Terrace, Haseley	125B31	Henley Court, Alcester
	Heath Terrace, Milverton, Leamington Spa	93A13	Henley Road, Bushwood
	Heathcote Farm, Wasperton	93B34	Henley Road, Claverdon
	Heathcote Farm, Wolvey Heath, Wolvey	126C11	Henley Road, Great Alne
	Heathcote Home Farm, Heathcote, Whitnash	113C11	Henley Road, Hampton on The Hill, Budbrooke
	Heathcote Hospital, Heathcote, Warwick	93A14	Henley Road, Lowsonford, Rowington
	Heathcote Lane, Warwick	91A12	Henley Road, Ullenhall
	Heathcote Lane, Whitnash, Leamington Spa	116A12	Henley Road, Whitnash, Leamington Spa
	Heathcote Park, Warwick	125B31	Henley Street, Alcester
	Heathcote Road, Whitnash, Leamington Spa	145A13	Henley Street, Stratford upon Avon
	Heathcote Terrace, Leamington Spa	170B13	Henneys Farm, Lower Quinton, Quinton
		3B13	Henneys Pond Farm, Newton Regis

Map ref	Address	Map ref	Address
30B21	Henry Street, Coten, Nuneaton	93C12	High Cross Farm, Sibson, Rowington
64A43	Henry Street, Kenilworth	93C12	High Cross Lane, Sibson, Rowington
71A12	Henry Street, Rugby	9A32	High Heath Farm, Sutton Coldfield
97B24	Henry Tandey Court, Leamington Spa	63B43	High House Farm, Burton Green,
86C41	Hensborough Farm, Kites Hardwick,		Kenilworth
	Thurlaston	38A14	High House Farm, Corley
39B24	Henson Road, Goodyears End,	36C14	High House Farm, Fillongley
	Bedworth	103B41	High House Farm, Grandborough
27B14	Henwood Farm, Arley	90A21	High House Farm, Redditch
50B23	Hepworth Road, Binley Woods	188B13	High Lane, Grove End, Brailes
47A34	Her Majestys Prision Service College,	138A43	High Lane, Priors Hardwick
	Newbold Revel	151B22	High Ledge Farm, Knightcote, Bu
50A31	Herald Way, Binley		Dassett
97A31	Heralds Court, Warwick	74A14	High Park Farm, Tanworth in Ard
175B44	Herbers Farm, Middle Tysoe, Tysoe	125A34	High Street, Alcester
29C13	Herbert Street, Stockingford, Nuneaton	106C23	High Street, Astwood Bank
175B44	Herberts Farm, Middle Tysoe, Tysoe	114B34	High Street, Barford
64A43	Herberts Lane, Kenilworth	40A22	High Street, Bedworth
93C33	Hercules Farm, Claverdon	156B14	High Street, Bidford
164A44	Herdhill Farm, Butlers Marston	143A21	High Street, Binton
29C13	Hereford Close, Stockingford, Nuneaton	135A24	High Street, Bishops Itchington
97B44	Hermes Close, Leamington Spa	188C13	High Street, Brailes
36A32	Hermitage Farm, Great Packington	105B23	High Street, Braunston
5C23	Hermitage Farm, Polesworth	141B33	High Street, Broom
5C24	Hermitage Hill, Polesworth	25A34	High Street, Coleshill
5C31	Hermitage Lane, Birchmoor, Polesworth	73C44	High Street, Crick
81A14	Hermitage Way, Windy Arbour,	82C43	High Street, Cubbington
	Kenilworth	11B14	High Street, Dosthill, Tamworth
125A24	Heron Close, Alcester	152A42	High Street, Fenny Compton
60C24	Heron Field Farm, Chadwick End	134B12	High Street, Harbury
128B43	Heron Lane, Stratford upon Avon	92B23	High Street, Henley in Arden
30B11	Heron Precinct, Nuneaton	72A31	High Street, Hillmorton
58B12	Heron Walk, Cheswick Green	18B12	High Street, Hurley
22B43	Heron Way, Nuneaton	63C42	High Street, Kenilworth
95C13	Hertford Hill Hospital, Hertford Hill,	11B13	High Street, Kingsbury
	Hatton	97C42	High Street, Leamington Spa
95C24	Hertford Hill, Hatton, Warwick	84C43	High Street, Marton
125B23	Hertford Road, Alcester	120C33	High Street, Napton on The Hil'
125B23	Hertford Road, Kinwarton	30A12	High Street, Nuneaton
144C23	Hertford Road, Stratford upon Avon	6A23	High Street, Polesworth
5A32	Hesleden, Stoneydelph, Tamworth	177A13	High Street, Ratley, Ratley And
96C22	Hetton Close, Woodloes, Warwick	71A13	High Street, Rugby
97C24	Hewitts Buildings, Leamington Spa	67A24	High Street, Ryton on Dunsmor
71A41	Heyford Leys, Hillside, Rugby	181C44	High Street, Shipston on Stour
81B13	Heyville Croft, Kenilworth	119A24	High Street, Southam
81A11	Hibberd Court, Kenilworth	119C12	High Street, Stockton
71A31	Hibbert Close, Rugby	145A21	High Street, Stratford upon Av
28C13	Hickman Road, Galley Common,	107C13	High Street, Studley
	Nuneaton	56A13	High Street, Swinford
96C22	Hicks Close, Woodloes, Warwick	96C41	High Street, Warwick
116C13	Hidcote Close, Leamington Spa	143A44	High Street, Welford on Avon
34A42	Hidcote Grove, Chelmsley Wood	73C21	High Street, Yelvertoft
64B41	Hidcote Road, Kenilworth	39A34	High View Close, Keresley Ne
179A42	Hidcote Road, Mickleton		Keresley
24C34	High Brink Road, Cole End, Coleshill	39A34	High View Drive, Keresley Ne
101B42	High Clays Farm, Long Itchington		Keresley
130A11	High Close Farm, Snitterfield	18B12	High View, Hurley, Kingsbury
194C24	High Corner, Little Compton	22C43	Higham Lane, Nuneaton
33C44	High Cross Barn, Copston Magna	39C34	Highash Close, Exhall, Bedwo

p ref	Address	Map ref	Address
33	Highbury Green, Camphill, Nuneaton	161A41	Hill Farm, Alderminster
22	Highcroft Crescent, Milverton, Leamington Spa	28B12	Hill Farm, Ansley, Nuneaton
33	Highcroft, Claverdon	4B13	Hill Farm, Austrey
A34	Highdown Farm, Bishops Tachbrook	195A11	Hill Farm, Barton on The Heath
43	Highdown Road, Sydenham Farm Estate, Leamington Spa	118C11	Hill Farm, Bascote, Long Itchington
3	Highfield Avenue, Amington, Tamworth	79B22	Hill Farm, Beausale
11	Highfield Close, Kenilworth	86A21	Hill Farm, Bourton on Dunsmore
1	Highfield Close, Sheepy Magna, Sheepy	51B32	Hill Farm, Brandon
343	Highfield Close, Snitterfield	51B32	Hill Farm, Bretford
4	Highfield Farm, Appleby Magna	177C11	Hill Farm, Camp Lane, Warmington
34	Highfield Farm, Corley Ash, Corley	194C42	Hill Farm, Chastleton
33	Highfield Farm, Curdworth	38B34	Hill Farm, Corley
23	Highfield Farm, Frankton	75C31	Hill Farm, Danzey Green, Tanworth in Arden
11	Highfield Farm, Sibson, Rowington	86A12	Hill Farm, Draycote
23	Highfield House Farm, Bedworth	109B43	Hill Farm, Great Alne
4	Highfield Lane, Corley	102C12	Hill Farm, Hill, Leamington Hastings
4	Highfield Road, Attleborough, Nuneaton	26A11	Hill Farm, Hoggerills End, Nether Whitacre
41	Highfield Road, Stratford upon Avon	180A12	Hill Farm, Ilmington
14	Highfield Road, Studley	65A22	Hill Farm, Kings Hill, Stoneleigh
3	Highfield Terrace, Milverton, Leamington Spa	111B14	Hill Farm, Langley
		133B44	Hill Farm, Lighthorne
11	Highfields Farm, Great Alne	69C11	Hill Farm, Long Lawford
3	Highfields Farm, Middleton	86A21	Hill Farm, Marlborough Site
43	Highfields Farm, Southam	26B43	Hill Farm, Maxstoke
43	Highfields Poultry Farm, Feckenham	9C34	Hill Farm, Middleton
1	Highland Close, Warwick	148B21	Hill Farm, Moreton Paddox, Moreton Morrell
1	Highland Hill Farm, Clerks Green, Studley	120C32	Hill Farm, Napton on The Hill
3	Highland Road, Crackley, Kenilworth	98B12	Hill Farm, New Cubbington, Leamington Spa
4	Highland Road, Lillington, Leamington Spa	21C31	Hill Farm, Nuneaton
13	Highpoint, Blackhill, Snitterfield	85A11	Hill Farm, Princethorpe
2	Highview Hospital, Goodyears End, Bedworth	138C31	Hill Farm, Priors Marston
		116C13	Hill Farm, Radford Semele
3	Highview Road, Cubbington	28B12	Hill Farm, Robinsons End, Nuneaton
4	Highwood Farm, Brinklow	26B32	Hill Farm, Shawbury, Fillongley
	Highwood Farm, Brinklow	8A13	Hill Farm, Sheepy
2	Hilary Bevins Close, Higham, Higham on The Hill	176B44	Hill Farm, Shennington
		2C33	Hill Farm, Shuttington
	Hilary Farm, Hill Wootton, Leek Wootton	118C34	Hill Farm, Southam
		142C31	Hill Farm, Temple Grafton
2	Hill Barn Farm, Leamington Hastings	74C32	Hill Farm, Traps Green, Tanworth in Arden
1	Hill Barn Farm, Rollright	118A34	Hill Farm, Ufton
	Hill Close, Dorridge	184C13	Hill Farm, Upper Tysoe, Tysoe
	Hill Close, Lillington, Leamington Spa	84A23	Hill Farm, Wappenbury
2	Hill Close, Northend, Burton Dassett	152B13	Hill Farm, Watergall
2	Hill Cottage, Radway	31B21	Hill Farm, Whitestone, Nuneaton
	Hill Crescent, Stretton on Dunsmore	15C12	Hill Farm, Witherley
	Hill Crest Farm, Newton And Biggin	110C23	Hill Farm, Wootton Wawen
	Hill Crest, Cubbington	45B42	Hill Fields Farm, Coombe Fields
	Hill Farm Avenue, Whitestone, Nuneaton	102B21	Hill House Farm, Broadwell, Leamington Hastings
	Hill Farm Cottage, Hatton, Warwick	133B22	Hill House Farm, Chesterton
	Hill Farm Cottage, Hunts Green, Middleton	9A22	Hill Lane, Bassetts Pole, Middleton
		188B11	Hill Lane, Upper Brailles
	Hill Farm Road, Hatton	170A23	Hill Lane, Upper Quinton, Quinton

Map ref	Address
77A24	Hill Park Farm, Lapworth
103B21	Hill Road, Grandborough
99A12	Hill Road, Hunningham
38C34	Hill Road, Keresley Newlands, Keresley
102C13	Hill Road, Leamington Hastings
188B43	Hill Road, Stourton
105B33	Hill Row, Braunston
120C31	Hill Side, Napton on The Hill
97A32	Hill Street, All Saints, Warwick
30A44	Hill Street, Collycroft, Bedworth
98A23	Hill Street, Leamington Spa
71A11	Hill Street, Rugby
29B14	Hill Street, Stockingford, Nuneaton
167A31	Hill Top Farm, Avon Dassett
55C11	Hill Top Farm, Shawell
13B21	Hill Top, Baddesley Ensor
28A24	Hill Top, Hilltop, Arley
146C41	Hill Top, Lexley
84C22	Hill Top, Princethorpe
122B14	Hill View Farm, Flecknoe, Wolfhamcote
141C41	Hill View Road, Bidford
81B43	Hill Wootton Farm, Hill Wootton, Leek Wootton
81C33	Hill Wootton Road, Blackdown
81B34	Hill Wootton Road, Hill Wootton, Leek Wootton
21C44	Hillary Road, Camphill, Nuneaton
70C32	Hillary Road, Kingsway, Rugby
142B43	Hillborough Farm, Temple Grafton
142C42	Hillborough Farm, Welford on Avon
142B41	Hillborough Lane, Temple Grafton
90A31	Hillcrest Farm, Mappleborough Green, Studley
21B43	Hillcrest Road, Camphill, Nuneaton
6A33	Hillcrest Road, Dordon
21B43	Hillcrest, Aa45, Nuneaton
145A11	Hillcrest, Stratford upon Avon
70B24	Hillfield Road, Bilton, Rugby
120B34	Hillhani Farm, Napton on The Hill
40A13	Hilliard Close, Bedworth
40A23	Hilliard Close, Collycroft, Bedworth
55C43	Hillmorton Lane, Lilbourne
73B22	Hillmorton Lane, Yelvertoft
55A44	Hillmorton Road, Clifton upon Dunsmore
71A14	Hillmorton Road, Rugby
120C31	Hillside Croft, Napton
21B31	Hillside Drive, Camphill, Nuneaton
167A23	Hillside Farm, Avon Dassett
190B24	Hillside Farm, Great Wolford
117A44	Hillside Farm, Harbury
144B13	Hillside Road, Stratford upon Avon
17B12	Hillside, Kingsbury
21A31	Hillside, Moor Wood, Hartshill
119A23	Hilltop Close, Southam
61C31	Hilltop Close, Wroxhall
76B43	Hilltop Farm, Liveridge Hill, Beaudesert
30B31	Hilltop, Nuneaton
36C42	Hillwood Cottage Farm, Meriden
119A21	Hillyard Road, Southam
21A42	Hilton Avenue, Whittleford, Nunea
114A22	Hilton National Hotel, Warwick by pass, Warwick
39B21	Himley Road, Market End, Bedwor
23C33	Hinckley Fire Station, Hinckley
23A12	Hinckley Lane, Higham, Higham o The Hill
23B13	Hinckley Lane, Hinckley
45A32	Hinckley Road, Anstey
32A31	Hinckley Road, Burton Hastings
32B12	Hinckley Road, Hinckley
23A43	Hinckley Road, Long Shoot, Nune
45A32	Hinckley Road, Walsgrave on Sow
32C14	Hinckley Road, Wolvey
96C22	Hind Close, Woodloes, Warwick
54B33	Hinde Close, Brownsover, Rugby
12C41	Hipsley Farm, Hurley, Kingsbury
12C43	Hipsley Lane, Hurley, Kingsbury
97C13	Hirsel Gardens, Leamington Spa
53A44	Hirst Close, Long Lawford
116A11	Hitchman Mews, Leamington Spa
116A11	Hitchman Road, Leamington Spa
130C33	Hithersand Close, Hampton Lucy
19B41	Hoar Park Farm, Ansley
31A34	Hoarstone Avenue, Whitestone, Nuneaton
62C12	Hob Farm, Balsall Common
63A12	Hob Lane, Burton Green, Kenilw
40B13	Hobb Lane, Bedworth
37C22	Hobgoblin Lane, Fillongley
70B32	Hobley Close, Bilton, Rugby
103C21	Hockley Close, Grandborough
84C33	Hockley House Farm, Eathorpe
162B41	Hockley Lane, Ettington
20C41	Hockley Lane, Galley Common, Nuneaton
11C12	Hockley Road, Dosthill, Tamwor
95A13	Hockley Road, Hatton
156A34	Hoden Lane, Cleeve Prior
2A42	Hodge Lane, Amington, Tamwo
128C44	Hodgson Road, Stratford upon A
119b34	Hodnell Drive, Southam
64B43	Hodnet Close, Kenilworth
144B24	Hogarth Road, Shottery, Stratfor upon Avon
133A21	Hogbrook Farm Cottage, Bishop Tachbrook
133A21	Hogbrook Farm, Bishops Tachbr
25B12	Hoggrills End Lane, Hoggerills Nether Whitacre
96C22	Holbache Walk, Woodloes, War
167C13	Holbech Hill, Farnborough
37C13	Holbeche Crescent, Fillongley
9A44	Holbeche Road, Sutton Coldfiel
40A12	Holbein Close, Collycroft, Nune
71A12	Holbrook Avenue, Rugby
53A44	Holbrook Road, Long Lawford

Map ref	Address	Map ref	Address
B13	Holbrook Road, Stratford upon Avon	57A41	Holly Lane, Portway, Tanworth in Arden
33	Holcote Leys, Hillside, Rugby	14B23	Holly Lane, Whittington, Grendon
C43	Holder Close, Bidford	9C43	Holly Lane, Wishaw
324	Hole Farm, Astwood Bank	147B21	Holly Lodge, Mountford, Wellesbourne
32	Hole Farm, Preston Bagot	21C42	Holly Stitches Road, Camphill, Nuneaton
23	Hole House Farm, Lapworth	98A24	Holly Street, Leamington Spa
31	Hole House Lane, Lapworth	178A44	Holly Tree Farm, Horley
A22	Holego Farm, Halford	31A22	Holly Walk, Attleborough, Nuneaton
11	Holgarth Road, Collycroft, Bedworth	65C13	Holly Walk, Baginton
42	Holioake Drive, Myton, Warwick	98A31	Holly Walk, Leamington Spa
13	Holl Bank Farm, Preston Bagot	144B12	Holly Walk, Stratford upon Avon
12	Holland Close, Bidford	4A22	Hollybank Estate, Austrey
14	Holland Meadow, Welford on Avon	90A11	Hollyberry Close, Redditch
11	Hollaway Farm, Wasperton	38B44	Hollyfast Lane, Keresley, Coventry
14	Hollaway Hill, Lower Brailes	24B22	Hollyhurst, White City, Water Orton
22	Holliars Farm, Shustoke	25C23	Hollyland Lane, Shustoke
31	Hollick Crescent, New Arley, Arley	93C24	Hollywell Farm, Holywell, Rowington
	Hollies Farm, Dordon	30B14	Holman Way, Nuneaton
22	Hollies Farm, Marston, Lea Marston	54B33	Holme Close, Brownsover, Rugby
	Hollies Road, Saint Helena, Polesworth	89B24	Holme Way, Barby
4	Hollinwell Close, Whitestone, Nuneaton	116B23	Holmes Road, Whitnash
	Hollis Farm, Twycross	64A44	Holmewood Close, Kenilworth
3	Hollis Lane, Kenilworth	120C41	Holroyd Farm, Napton on The Hill
1	Hollis Lane, Stoneleigh	22C44	Holsworth Close, Nuneaton
3	Hollow Farm, Nuneaton	115B33	Holt Avenue, Bishops Tachbrook
44	Hollow Meadow Farm, Priors Hardwick	181A41	Holt Farm, Darlingscott, Tredington
	Hollow Oak Farm, Corley	123A21	Holt Farm, Inkberrow
33	Hollow Way, Napton on The Hill	11C22	Holt Farm, Kingsbury
	Holloway Farm, Nuneaton	137B14	Holt Farm, Napton on The Hill
22	Holloway Hill, Brailes	119C44	Holt Farm, Southam
21	Holloway Lane, Lower Brailes, Brailes	107C32	Holt Farm, Studley
	Hollowell Way, Brownsover, Rugby	107C31	Holt Gardens, Studley
4	Hollows, Long Compton	19A41	Holt Hall Farm, Over Whitacre
	Holly Bush Farm, Astley	11C22	Holt Hall Farm, Whately, Kingsbury
4	Holly Bush Farm, Dunnington, Salford Priors	119B32	Holt Leys, Southam
4	Holly Bush Lane, Priors Marston	164B32	Holt Road, Little Kineton, Kineton
	Holly Drive, Hurley, Kingsbury	107C31	Holt Road, Studley
	Holly Farm, Beausale	14C23	Holte Road, Atherstone
	Holly Farm, Corley	144C24	Holtom Street, Stratford upon Avon
	Holly Farm, Hurley, Kingsbury	5A32	Holwick, Stoneydelph, Tamworth
	Holly Farm, Pinley Green, Rowington	110A33	Holy Oak Farm, Aston Cantlow
	Holly Farm, Portway, Tanworth in Arden	70B31	Holyoak Close, Bilton, Rugby
	Holly Grange Farm, Balsall Common	39C23	Holyoak Close, Exhall, Bedworth
	Holly Hurst Farm, Hawkesbury, Bedworth	119A23	Holywell Road, Southam
	Holly Lane Farm, Balsall Common	66B41	Home Close, Bubbenhall
	Holly Lane Farm, Wishaw	181C14	Home Close, Tredington
	Holly Lane Industrial Estate, Grendon, Atherstone	15A32	Home Farm Close, Witherley
	Holly Lane, Allen End	32B12	Home Farm Cottage, Stretton Baskerville
	Holly Lane, Atherstone	116B21	Home Farm Crescent, Whitnash, Leamington Spa
	Holly Lane, Baddesley Ensor	176B24	Home Farm Drive, Ratley And Upton
	Holly Lane, Balsall Common	173C43	Home Farm Road, Idlecote
	Holly Lane, Frogmore	171A23	Home Farm, Admington
	Holly Lane, Merevale	45B14	Home Farm, Anstey
		142A22	Home Farm, Ardens Grafton, Bidford
		166B41	Home Farm, Arlescote, Warmington

Map ref	Address	Map ref	Address
65C21	Home Farm, Baginton	160B41	Home Farm, Wimpstone, Whitchur-
190C42	Home Farm, Barton on The Heath	15A34	Home Farm, Witherley
181B11	Home Farm, Blackwell, Tredington	42C42	Home Farm, Withybrook
85C24	Home Farm, Bourton on Dunsmore	70A14	Home Fields Farm, Long Lawford
188C22	Home Farm, Brailes	147B31	Home Furlong, Mountford,
105B32	Home Farm, Braunston		Wellesbourne
102B23	Home Farm, Broadwell, Leamington	30B13	Home Park Road, Nuneaton
	Hastings	41C24	Home Pastures Farm, Wolvey
54B24	Home Farm, Brownsover, Rugby		Homers Yard, Gatehouse Lane, Bec
188A43	Home Farm, Cherington	87B11	Homestead Farm Cottage, Dunchu-
1C12	Home Farm, Chilcote		Rugby
54B24	Home Farm, Churchover	87A12	Homestead Farm, Dunchurch
168B24	Home Farm, Claydon	156C23	Honeybourne Road, Barton, Bidfor
159C12	Home Farm, Clifford Chambers	54C31	Honeysuckle Close, Brownsover, R
72A13	Home Farm, Clifton upon Dunsmore	62A34	Honiley Airfield, Honiley, Kenilwc
184A24	Home Farm, Compton Wynyates	62A34	Honiley Proving Ground, Honiley,
124A23	Home Farm, Cook Hill, Inkberrow		Kenilworth
60C11	Home Farm, Dorridge	79B23	Honiley Road, Beausale
37B21	Home Farm, Fillongley	62A23	Honiley Road, Frogmore
161B11	Home Farm, Goldicote, Alderminster	62A44	Honiley Road, Honiley
6C34	Home Farm, Grendon	182A21	Honington Hall Drive, Honington
53A14	Home Farm, Harborough Magna	182A21	Honington Hall, Honington
21B23	Home Farm, Hartshill	182A23	Honington Road, Shipston on Stor
95B13	Home Farm, Hatton	134A12	Honiwell Close, Harbury
115B14	Home Farm, Heathcote, Whitnash	125C23	Hoo Mill Road, Kinwarton
182A24	Home Farm, Honington	27C12	Hood Lane Farm, Ansley
177B41	Home Farm, Hornton	27C14	Hood Lane, Ansley
12B33	Home Farm, Hurley, Kingsbury	70B22	Hoods Way, Bilton, Rugby
173C43	Home Farm, Idlicote	123C11	Hookeys Farm, Inkberrow
80C42	Home Farm, Leek Wootton	106C23	Hoopers Lane, Astwood Bank
166B11	Home Farm, Little Dassett, Burton	39A33	Hope Close, Bedworth
	Dassett	176C32	Hope Farm, Ratley And Upton
35C33	Home Farm, Little Packington	175C34	Hopkins Farm, Lower Tysoe, Tys-
114A22	Home Farm, Longbridge, Warwick	125B23	Hopkins Precinct, Alcester
175B34	Home Farm, Lower Tysoe, Tysoe	147B11	Hoppers Lane, Mountford, Charl-
146C42	Home Farm, Loxley	46B11	Hopsford Old Hall Farm, Withyb-
175B43	Home Farm, Middle Tysoe, Tysoe	46B11	Hopsford Spring Farm, Withybro-
120C41	Home Farm, Napton on The Hill	89B24	Hopthorne Farm, Barby
55A23	Home Farm, Newton And Biggin	97B13	Hopton Crofts, Leamington Spa
85C24	Home Farm, Oxley	114A22	Horgans Manor Farm, Longbridg-
48A32	Home Farm, Pailton		Warwick
176B32	Home Farm, Ratley And Upton	194A44	Horn Farm, Chastleton
53B41	Home Farm, Rugby	98B44	Hornbeam Grove, Sydenham Fa-
119B34	Home Farm, Southam		Estate, Leamington Spa
118B24	Home Farm, Stoneythorpe, Long	5A11	Hornbeam, Amington, Tamwort-
	Itchington	72A32	Horne Close, Hillmorton, Rugby
68C41	Home Farm, Stretton on Dunsmore	181C43	Horniblow Close, Shipston on St
47B33	Home Farm, Stretton Under Fosse	177A32	Hornton Hill Farm, Hornton
56C22	Home Farm, Swinford	181C43	Horsefair, Shipston on Stour
59A43	Home Farm, Tanworth in Arden	92B31	Horsefair, The, Henley in Arden
1A41	Home Farm, Thorpe Constantine	186C22	Horseley Farm Road, Tidmingto-
120C21	Home Farm, Tomlow, Napton on The	186B22	Horseleys Farm, Tidmington
	Hill	182A43	Horseshoe Close, Shipston on St-
117C23	Home Farm, Ufton	95A41	Horsesley House Farm, Budbro-
121C32	Home Farm, Upper Shuckburgh	119A24	Horsewell, Southam
184B22	Home Farm, Upper Tysoe, Tysoe	9A43	Horsfall Road, Sutton Coldfield
147C32	Home Farm, Walton, Wellesbourne	125B24	Horton Close, Kinwarton
187A22	Home Farm, Willington, Barcheston	71A21	Horton Crescent, Rugby
104B14	Home Farm, Willoughby	40B22	Hosiery Street, Bedworth

Map ref	Address
:32	Hoskyn Close, Hillmorton, Rugby
B31	Hospital Farm, Broadwell, Leamington Hastings
11	Hospital Farm, Harborough Magna
13	Hospital Farm, Hatton
31	Hospital Lane, Goodyears End, Bedworth
22	Hospital Saint Cross, Rugby
A24	Hotchkiss Close, Mountford, Wellesbourne
:32	Houghtons Farm, Napton on The Hill
:14	House Farm, Inkberrow
A12	House Farm, Red Hill, Binton
41	Houston Road, Brownsover, Rugby
A12	Howard Close, Bidford
2	Howard Close, Dunchurch
43	Howard Road, Nuneaton
2	Howard Walk, Leamington Spa
33	Howat Road, Keresley Newlands, Keresley
33	Howcombe Lane, Napton on The Hill
3	Howe Green Lane, Astley
4	Howe Green Lane, Fillongley
3	Howells Close, Goodyears End, Bedworth
1	Howes Lane, Finham
1	Howkins Road, Brownsover, Rugby
4	Hoylake Close, Whitestone, Nuneaton
	Hoylake, Amington, Tamworth
31	Huckson Road, Bishops Itchington
1	Huddison Close, Warwick
3	Hudson Avenue, Coleshill
3	Hudson Road, Overslade, Rugby
34	Hughes Close, Harvington
	Hughes Close, Woodloes, Warwick
	Hughes Hill, Shrewley Common, Shrewley
34	Hughes Lane, Harvington
	Hughes, The, Warwick
4	Humber Farm, Blackdown
	Humphrey Davy Road, Goodyears End, Bedworth
	Humphris Street, All Saints, Warwick
	Hungerfield Farm, Preston Bagot
	Hungerley Farm, Brownshill Green
	Hungerley Hall Farm, Binley
2	Hunningham Hill Farm, Hunningham
	Hunningham Lodge Farm, Hunningham
	Hunningham Road, Hunningham
	Hunningham Road, Offchurch
	Hunningham Road, Weston Under Wetherley
	Hunscote Lane, Hunscote, Charlecote
	Hunscote Lane, Hunscote, Wellesbourne
	Hunt Close, Hampton Magna, Budbrooke
	Hunt End Farm, Hunt End
	Hunt Hall Farm, Welford on Avon
158A13	Hunt Hall Lane, Welford on Avon
15A34	Hunt Lane, Witherley
71B12	Hunter Street, Rugby
15C42	Hunters Lane, Fenny Drayton
54A43	Hunters Lane, Rugby
13B23	Hunters Park, Baddesley Ensor
80C23	Huntfield Drive, Kenilworth
29C13	Huntingdon Way, Stockingford, Nuneaton
10B33	Hunts Green Dairy Farm, Hunts Green, Middleton
10B33	Hunts Green Farm, Hunts Green, Middleton
145A24	Hunts Road, Stratford upon Avon
115B11	Hurbutt Road, Heathcote, Whitnash
134C22	Hurdiss Farm, Harbury
98A24	Hurley Close, Leamington Spa
12B41	Hurley Common, Hurley Common, Kingsbury
12B33	Hurley Farm, Hurley, Kingsbury
19B21	Hurley Lane, Bentley
18B22	Hurley Lane, Brook End, Kingsbury
18C33	Hurley Lane, Nether Whitacre
18C43	Hurley Lane, Whitacre Fields, Over Whitacre
1C12	Hurst Farm, Chilcote
119A33	Hurst Farm, Southam
63C12	Hurst Farm, Stoneleigh
59C12	Hurst Green Road, Dorridge
40A14	Hurst Road, Bedworth
119A33	Hurst Road, Southam
181C34	Husbandmans Lane, Shipston on Stour
181C32	Husbandsman Close, Shipston on Stour
142B13	Hutch Hill Farm, Temple Grafton
192C42	Hutton Grange Farm, Great Rollright
193A43	Hutton Grange Farm, Rollright
97B32	Hyde Place, Milverton, Leamington Spa
64A41	Hyde Road, Kenilworth
31B14	Hydes Lane, Stretton Baskerville
156C11	Icknield Close, Bidford
156C12	Icknield Court, Bidford
125A31	Icknield Row, Alcester
156C11	Icknield Street, Bidford
182C14	Idlicote Hill Farm, Idlicote
173A34	Idlicote Road, Halford
182B21	Idlicote Road, Honington
173C43	Idlicote Road, Idlicote
174A41	Idlicote Road, Whatcote
176B12	Idunno, Radway
64B43	Ilam Park, Kenilworth
97A33	Ilex Court, Emscote, Warwick
40A11	Ilford Close, Bedworth
58C24	Illshaw Heath Farm, Illshaw Heath, Cheswick Green
58C23	Illshaw Heath Road, Illshaw Heath, Cheswick Green
172A42	Ilmington Road, Armscote, Tredington
180C21	Ilmington Road, Blackwell

Map ref	Address
180C21	Ilmington Road, Ilmington
170B21	Ilmington Road, Lower Quinton
90A11	Ilshaw Close, Redditch
24C22	Imperial Rise, Coleshill
92A12	Impsley Farm, Ullenhall
64B33	Inchbrook Road, Crackley, Kenilworth
96C21	Inchford Avenue, Woodloes, Warwick
79B42	Inchford Brook Farm, Kites Nest, Beausale
31A23	Inchford Close, Attleborough, Nuneaton
89C14	Independent Street, Kilsby
30C11	Industrial Estate, Nuneaton
97C33	Ingle Court, Leamington Spa
31A22	Ingleton Close, Nuneaton
98A14	Inglewood Close, Lillington, Leamington Spa
129B34	Ingon Bank Farm, Ingon, Hampton Lucy
129B22	Ingon Grange Farm, Snitterfield
129B34	Ingon Lane, Ingon, Hampton Lucy
129B23	Ingon Lane, Snitterfield
129B34	Ingon Lane, Stratford upon Avon
129B31	Ingon Manor Farm, Ingon, Hampton Lucy
190B31	Ingram Close, Great Wolford
2A43	Ingrams Pits Lane, Amington, Tamworth
98A34	Innage Close, Leamington Spa
14B32	Innage Terrace, Atherstone
81B11	Inverary Close, Windy Arbour, Kenilworth
71A43	Inwoods Farm, Dunchurch
34A22	Ipswich Walk, Chelmsley Wood
76C44	Irelands Farm, Lapworth
150B42	Irelands Farm, Temple Herdewyke
140B43	Iron Cross, Salford Priors
127B34	Iron Gate Farm, Aston Cantlow
24B21	Island Close, Water Orton
117B21	Island Farm, Ufton
12B24	Islington Crescent, Wood End, Kingsbury
12B24	Islington Farm, Wood End, Kingsbury
30C23	Ivanhoe Avenue, Nuneaton
14C34	Ivor Road, Atherstone
51A42	Ivy House Farm, Brandon
59C31	Ivy House Farm, Dorridge
37A44	Ivy House Farm, Meriden
5A42	Ivy House Farm, Tamworth
6C11	Ivy House Farm, Warton, Polesworth
44A12	Ivy House Farm, Wibtoft
162A42	Ivy Lane, Ettington
134B42	Ivy Lane, Harbury
165C43	Ivy Lodge Cottage, Radway
165C43	Ivy Lodge, Radway
6C11	Ivycroft Road, Warton, Poleswortk
77C33	Ivyhouse Farm, Rowington
155C13	Jack Thomson Croft, Salford Priors
65B13	Jacklin Drive, Finham
95C41	Jackson Close, Hampton Magna, Budbrooke

Map ref	Address
39A33	Jackson Close, Keresley Newlands, Keresley
72A23	Jackson Road, Hillmorton, Rugby
109A34	Jacksons Farm, Shelfield Green, Grं Alne
64B43	Jacox Crescent, Kenilworth
71A14	James Court, Rugby
96C34	James Court, Warwick
92A12	James Farm, Ullenhall
24C32	James Road, Coleshill
28A32	James Street, New Arley, Arley
22A43	James Street, Nuneaton
71A12	James Street, Rugby
71A14	James Walk, Rugby
50B34	Janewood Road, Binley Woods
24B23	Jaques Close, Water Orton
165C43	Jasmine Cottage, Radway
98A21	Jasmine Grove, Leamington Spa
2A43	Jasmine Road, Amington, Tamwoं
13B23	Jean Street, Baddesley Ensor
39B31	Jeffrey Close, Goodyears End, Bedं
33A42	Jeffreys Barn, Wolvey
188C13	Jeffs Close, Brailes
72A23	Jenkins Road, Hillmorton, Rugby
98B43	Jenton Road, Sydenham Farm Estं Leamington
125C31	Jephcott Close, Alcester
97C24	Jephson Gardens, Leamington Spं
97C34	Jephson House, Leamington Spa
98A34	Jephson Place, Leamington Spa
24A42	Jersey Croft, Kingshurst
9A43	Jesson Road, Sutton Coldfield
107A14	Jill Lane, Sambourne
65B13	Joanna Drive, Finham
98B43	Joans Close, Sydenham Farm Estं Leamington
173C14	Jobs Close, Pillerton Priors
22A42	Jodrell Street, Nuneaton
40A33	John Haynes Court, Exhall, Bedv
40A12	John Knight Road, Collycroft, Be
80C14	John Nash Square, Kenilworth
80C21	John O Gaunt Road, Kenilworth
68A13	John Simpson Close, Wolston
30A22	John Street, Coten, Nuneaton
97C31	John Street, Leamington Spa
29C13	John Street, Stockingford, Nuneं
145A13	John Street, Stratford upon Avoं
70C22	John Thwaites Close, Rugby
53A43	Johns Avenue, Long Lawford
71C31	Johns Avenue, The Paddox, Rugं
20C33	Johns Road, Ansley Common, A
81A13	Johns Street, Kenilworth
13A22	Johns, Baddesley Ensor
70B22	Johnson Avenue, New Bilton, R
92B21	Johnson Place, Henley in Ardenं
40B13	Johnson Road, Bedworth
12B23	Johnson Street, Wood End, Kinं
145A11	Jolyffe Park Road, Stratford upं Avon

p ref	Address
44	Jonathans Farm, Tanworth in Arden
31	Jones Road, Exhall, Bedworth
43	Jonkel Avenue, Tamworth
14	Jordan Close, Kenilworth
12	Jordan Close, Windy Arbour, Kenilworth
11	Joseph Luckman Road, Collycroft, Bedworth
C43	Joseph Way, Stratford upon Avon
34	Joyce Pool, Warwick
324	Jubilee Avenue, Lower Shuckburgh
C44	Jubilee Close, Bidford
A12	Jubilee Cottage, Clifford Chambers
44	Jubilee Cottage, Lapworth
323	Jubilee Court, Alcester
44	Jubilee Court, Kingsbury
2	Jubilee Farm, Ryton on Dunsmore
33	Jubilee Gardens, Long Itchington
11	Jubilee Street, New Bilton, Rugby
1	Jubilee Terrace, Collycroft, Bedworth
3	Judd Close, Bedworth Woodlands, Bedworth
3	Judge Close, Long Lawford
4	Juggins Lane, Forshaw Heath, Tanworth in Arden
4	Juggins Lane, Portway, Tanworth in Arden
2	Juliet Close, Whitestone, Nuneaton
2	Juliet Drive, Woodlands, Rugby
1	Julius Drive, Coleshill
3	Junction 1 M45 To Junction 17 M1, M1
3	Junction 1 M45 To Junction 17 M1, M45
4	Junction 1 M6 To Junction 19 M1, M1
	Junction 1 M6 To Junction 19 M1, M6
2	Junction 1 M69 To Junction 2 M6, M69
	Junction 1 To Junction 2, M6
	Junction 1 To Junction 2, M69
2	Junction 1 To Junction 2, Warwick by pass
	Junction 1 To 2, M6
	Junction 1 To 2, M69
2	Junction 1 To 2, Warwick by pass
	Junction 1, M45
	Junction 1, M6
	Junction 1, M69
2	Junction 1, Warwick by pass
	Junction 10 To Junction 11, M42
	Junction 10 To Junction 9, M42
	Junction 10, M42
1	Junction 15 To Junction 16, M40
1	Junction 15, M40
	Junction 16 M40 To Junction 3A M42, M40
	Junction 16 M40 To Junction 3A M42, M42
	Junction 16 M40 To Junction 4 M42, M40
	Junction 16 M40 To Junction 4 M42, M42

Map ref	Address
76B14	Junction 16 To Junction 15, M40
	Junction 16 To Junction 17, M1
	Junction 16, M1
76B14	Junction 16, M40
87A13	Junction 17 M1 To Junction 1 M45, M1
87A13	Junction 17 M1 To Junction 1 M45, M45
87A13	Junction 17 M1 To Junction 1, M45
45A22	Junction 2 M6 To Junction 1 M69, M6
45A22	Junction 2 M6 To Junction 1 M69, M69
45A22	Junction 2 To Junction 1, M6
45B21	Junction 2 To Junction 1, M69
96A32	Junction 2 To Junction 1, Warwick by pass
	Junction 2 To Junction 3, M42
45A23	Junction 2 To Junction 3, M6
96A32	Junction 2 To Junction 3, Warwick by pass
54B13	Junction 2 To 1, M6
45B21	Junction 2 To 1, M69
96A32	Junction 2 To 1, Warwick by pass
	Junction 2 To 3, M42
45A23	Junction 2 To 3, M6
96A42	Junction 2 To 3, Warwick by pass
	Junction 2, M42
45A22	Junction 2, M6
45B21	Junction 2, M69
96A32	Junction 2, Warwick by pass
57A33	Junction 3 To Junction 2, M42
39C41	Junction 3 To Junction 2, M6
96C12	Junction 3 To Junction 2, Warwick by pass
57A34	Junction 3 To Junction 3A, M42
57A41	Junction 3 To Junction 4, M42
39C33	Junction 3 To Junction 4, M6
96C12	Junction 3 To Junction 4, Warwick by pass
96C12	Junction 3 To 2, Warwick by pass
39C33	Junction 3 To 4, M6
57A33	Junction 3, M42
39C33	Junction 3, M6
96C12	Junction 3, Warwick by pass
58C43	Junction 3A M42 To Junction 16 M40, M40
58C43	Junction 3A M42 To Junction 16 M40, M42
58C43	Junction 3A To Junction 3, M42
57A41	Junction 3A To Junction 4, M42
58C43	Junction 3A, M42
58C43	Junction 4 M42 To Junction 16 M40, M40
35A21	Junction 4 M6 To Junction 3 M42, M42
35A21	Junction 4 M6 To Junction 3 M42, M6
35A21	Junction 4 M6 To Junction 7 M42, M42
35A21	Junction 4 M6 To Junction 7 M42, M6
59A12	Junction 4 To Junction 3, M42
35A21	Junction 4 To Junction 3, M6
81A24	Junction 4 To Junction 3, Warwick by pass
59A12	Junction 4 To Junction 3A, M42

Map ref	Address
35A21	Junction 4 To Junction 4A, M6
35A21	Junction 4 To Junction 5, M6
81A24	Junction 4 To Junction 5, Warwick by pass
37A12	Junction 4 To Junction 7 M42, M42
39C33	Junction 4 To 3, M6
81A24	Junction 4 To 3, Warwick by pass
81A24	Junction 4 To 5, Warwick by pass
35A21	Junction 4, M6
81A24	Junction 4, Warwick by pass
24A32	Junction 4A M6 To Junction 7 M42, M42
24A32	Junction 4A M6 To Junction 7 M42, M6
24A32	Junction 4A M6 To Junction 8 M42, M42
24A32	Junction 4A M6 To Junction 8 M42, M6
24A32	Junction 4A M6 To Junction 9 M42, M42
24A32	Junction 4A M6 To Junction 9 M42, M6
24A34	Junction 4A To Junction 4, M6
24A32	Junction 4A, M6
64C32	Junction 5 To Junction 4, Warwick by pass
64C32	Junction 5 To Junction 6, Warwick by pass
64C32	Junction 5 To 4, Warwick by pass
64C32	Junction 5 To 6, Warwick by pass
64C32	Junction 5, Warwick by pass
65B12	Junction 6 To Junction 5, Warwick by pass
65B12	Junction 6 To 5, Warwick by pass
65B12	Junction 6, Warwick by pass
34C22	Junction 7 To Junction 6, M42
34C22	Junction 7 To Junction 7A, M42
34C22	Junction 7 To Junction 8, M42
34C13	Junction 7A M42 To Junction 4 M6, M42
34C14	Junction 7A M42 To Junction 4 M6, M6
34C11	Junction 7A To Junction 7, M42
34C13	Junction 7A To Junction 8, M42
34C13	Junction 7A, M42
18B32	Junction 8 M42 To Junction 4A M6, M42
18B32	Junction 8 M42 To Junction 4A M6, M6
24C34	Junction 8 To Junction 7, M42
24C34	Junction 8 To Junction 7A, M42
24C34	Junction 8 To Junction 9, M42
24C34	Junction 8, M42
16B32	Junction 9 M42 To Junction 4A M6, M42
18B32	Junction 9 M42 To Junction 4A M6, M6
16B32	Junction 9 To Junction 10, M42
16B32	Junction 9 To Junction 8, M42
16B32	Junction 9, M42
54C31	Junewood Close, Brownsover, Rugby
5A11	Junifer, Amington, Tamworth
39A21	Juniper Close, Bedworth
96C41	Jury Court, Warwick
96C41	Jury Street, Warwick
128C43	Justins Avenue, Stratford upon Avon
50B33	Kareen Green, Binley Woods
21C33	Karen Close, Tuttle Hill, Nuneaton
39B24	Kathleen Avenue, Goodyears End, Bedworth
137B14	Katkins, Napton on The Hill
54B33	Kay Close, Brownsover, Rugby
68A41	Kaysbrook Drive, Stretton on Dunsr
36A42	Keatleys Lane, Great Packington
29A11	Keats Close, Galley Common, Nune
21A43	Keats Close, Robinsons End, Nunea
145A24	Keats Road, Stratford upon Avon
64A44	Keeling Road, Kenilworth
39B23	Keenan Drive, Goodyears End, Bedworth
39B21	Keepers Close, Bedworth
35A11	Keepers Close, Coleshill
186C11	Keetley Close, Shipston on Stour
98A21	Keir Close, Leamington Spa
98A12	Keith Road, Lillington, Leamington
30C14	Kelsey Close, Attleborough, Nunea
67C14	Kelseys Close, Wolston
34A21	Kelsull Crescent, Chelmsley Wood
82B43	Kelvin Road, Cubbington
30B22	Kem Street, Attleborough, Nuneatc
97A33	Kemp Close, Emscote, Warwick
76A21	Kemps Green Farm, Kemps Green, Tanworth in Arden
76A23	Kemps Green Road, Kemps Green, Tanworth in Arden
98B14	Kempton Crescent, Lillington, Leamington Spa
71A24	Ken Marriott Sports Centre, Rugby
24C34	Kendal Avenue, Coleshill
97B21	Kendal Avenue, Leamington Spa
90A13	Kendal Close, Redditch
23A41	Kendal Close, Saint Nicholas Park Nuneaton
144C12	Kendall Avenue, Stratford upon A
63B44	Kenil Court, Kenilworth
63C43	Kenilworth Common, Kenilworth
63B42	Kenilworth Court, Kenilworth
30A13	Kenilworth Drive, Nuneaton
15B44	Kenilworth Farm, Mancetter
63C42	Kenilworth Mews, Kenilworth
35A31	Kenilworth Road A446, Little Packington
62B14	Kenilworth Road, Balsall Commo
35B41	Kenilworth Road, Bickenhill
81C33	Kenilworth Road, Blackdown
62C22	Kenilworth Road, Burton Green
81B32	Kenilworth Road, Chesford
35A23	Kenilworth Road, Coleshill
64B31	Kenilworth Road, Crackley, Keni
82A42	Kenilworth Road, Cubbington
62C21	Kenilworth Road, Frogmore
64B22	Kenilworth Road, Gibbet Hill, C
97C22	Kenilworth Road, Leamington S
150A11	Kenilworth Road, Lighthorne H Lighthorne
35A31	Kenilworth Road, Little Packing
97C32	Kenilworth Street, Leamington S
97C42	Kennan Avenue, Leamington Sp
116A22	Kennard Road, Whitnash
70B21	Kennedy Drive, Bilton, Rugby

ref	Address
23	Kennedy Square, Leamington Spa
34	Kennel Farm, Witherley
42	Kennel Lane, Witherley
12	Kenpass Highway, Finham, Coventry
334	Kents Farm, Kineton
A34	Kents Lane, Ettington
32	Kenwyn Green, Exhall, Bedworth
21	Keppel Close, Bilton, Rugby
34	Keresley Recreation Ground, Keresley
A13	Kerns Terrace, Stratford upon Avon
2	Kerria Centre, Amington, Tamworth
2	Kerria Road, Amington, Tamworth
A43	Kestrel Close, Stratford upon Avon
4	Kestrel, Tamworth
41	Keswick Close, Saint Nicholas Park, Nuneaton
4	Keswick Green, Milverton, Leamington Spa
2	Kettlewell Close, Woodloes, Warwick
3	Kew Close, Kenilworth
2	Kew Road, Rugby
3	Keys Drive, Bilton, Rugby
3	Keys Hill, Baddesley Ensor
32	Keys Lane, Priors Marston
41	Keytes Lane, Barford
42	Keytes Road, Ilmington
12	Kiblers Lane, Pillerton Priors
4	Kiddles Farm, Baxterley
2	Kidpile Farm, Fulford Heath, Tidbury Green
2	Kielder Drive, Arbury, Nuneaton
3	Kilby Court, Leamington Spa
2	Kilby Grove, Sydenham Farm Estate, Leamington
2	Kildwick Way, Woodloes, Warwick
2	Kiln Close, Leamington Spa
	Kiln Close, Nuneaton
	Kiln Way, Bulkington
	Kiln Way, Polesworth
	Kilnsey Grove, Woodloes, Warwick
	Kilsby Lane, Hillmorton, Rugby
	Kilsby Road, Barby
	Kilsby Road, Crick
	Kilworth Road, Hillmorton, Rugby
	Kilworth Road, Swinford
	Kimberley Drive, Baginton
	Kimberley Road, Bedworth
	Kimberley Road, Rugby
	Kimble Close, Knightcote
	Kineton Grange Farm, Chadshunt
	Kineton Lane, Cheswick Green
	Kineton Road, Butlers Marston
	Kineton Road, Chadshunt
	Kineton Road, Gaydon
	Kineton Road, Oxhill
	Kineton Road, Pillerton Hersey
	Kineton Road, Pillerton Priors
	Kineton Road, Radway
	Kineton Road, Southam

Map ref	Address
147B14	Kineton Road, Wellesbourne Hastings, Wellesbourne
81B13	Kineton Road, Windy Arbour, Kenilworth
95C23	King Edward Hospital, Hertford Hill, Warwick
30B12	King Edward Road, Nuneaton
71A12	King Edward Road, Rugby
192C21	King Edward Terrace, Whichford
95C23	King Edward The Seventh Hospital, Hertford Hill, Warwick
30A44	King Georges Avenue, Collycroft, Bedworth
130B34	King Georges Field, Hampton Lucy
164B14	King John Road, Kineton
176B14	King Johns Lane, Tysoe
51C33	King Newnham Lane, Bretford
195C12	King Stone Farm, Long Compton
40B21	King Street, Bedworth
98A23	King Street, Leamington Spa
71A11	King Street, Rugby
21B43	Kingfisher Avenue, Whittleford, Nuneaton
24A31	Kingfisher Drive, Kingshurst
125A24	Kingfisher Way, Alcester
5A43	Kingfisher, Tamworth
90A11	Kingham Close, Redditch
97A22	Kingland Drive, Milverton, Leamington Spa
125B23	Kingley Avenue, Alcester
14C31	Kings Avenue, Atherstone
191B31	Kings Brake Farm, Little Wolford
90A23	Kings Close, Mappleborough Green, Studley
125A21	Kings Coughton Lane, Kings Coughton, Alcester
40B21	Kings Gardens, Bedworth
141B41	Kings Lane, Broom, Bidford
13B21	Kings Lane, Grendon Common, Grendon
3B14	Kings Lane, Newton Regis
129A23	Kings Lane, Snitterfield
128C33	Kings Lane, Stratford upon Avon
73C21	Kings Lane, Yelvertoft
147A11	Kings Mead Farm, Mountford, Wellesbourne
52A42	Kings Newnham Road, Church Lawford
52A34	Kings Newnham Road, Kings Newnham
22B42	Kingsbridge Road, Weddington, Nuneaton
11B34	Kingsbury Colliery Sidings, Kingsbury
11A44	Kingsbury Country Park, Kingsbury
19A13	Kingsbury Hall Farm, Kingsbury
11C33	Kingsbury Oil Terminal, Kingsbury
16B31	Kingsbury Road, Dunton, Curdworth
17B12	Kingsbury Road, Kingsbury
17A22	Kingsbury Road, Marston, Lea Marston
11C43	Kingsbury Road, Piccadilly

Map ref	Address
11A44	Kingsbury Water Park, Kingsbury
59C21	Kingscote Road, Dorridge
65A22	Kingshill Lane, Finham
65A23	Kingshill Lane, Kings Hill, Stoneleigh
26B42	Kingshill Lane, Maxstoke
26B34	Kingshill Lane, Shawbury, Fillongley
64C23	Kingshill Lane, Stoneleigh
98C41	Kingshurst, Radford Semele
71C31	Kingsley Avenue, Rugby
50B32	Kingsley Court, Binley Woods
115C33	Kingsley Court, Bishops Tachbrook
41A14	Kingsley Crescent, Bulkington, Bedworth
115C33	Kingsley Road, Bishops Tachbrook
79C44	Kingstanding Farm, Beausale
134B42	Kingston Farm, Chesterton, Chesterton
134A41	Kingston Fields Farm, Chesterton, Chesterton
134A44	Kingston Grange Farm, Chesterton, Chesterton
134B43	Kingston Holt Farm, Chesterton, Chesterton
134B33	Kingston Manor Farm, Chesterton
116B12	Kingston Mews, Sydenham Farm Estate, Leamington Spa
73C42	Kingstyle Close, Crick
11B41	Kingsway, Kingsbury
71A31	Kingsway, Kingsway, Rugby
97C44	Kingsway, Leamington Spa
150A14	Kingsway, Lighthorne Heath, Lighthorne
30A11	Kingsway, Nuneaton
38A34	Kingswood Avenue, Corley
77B12	Kingswood Close, Lapworth
94B12	Kingswood Cottage, Rowington
29B12	Kingswood Court, Grove Farm Estate, Nuneaton
64C33	Kingswood Farm, Kenilworth
77B12	Kingswood Farm, Lapworth
29B12	Kingswood Road, Stockingford, Nuneaton
111B11	Kington Cottage Farm, Tattle Bank, Langley
93B43	Kington Farm, Claverdon
93B34	Kington Lane, Barnmoor Green, Claverdon
111B12	Kington Lane, Tattle Bank, Langley
111B11	Kington Rise, Tattle Bank
29C22	Kinross Close, Heath End, Nuneaton
98A12	Kinross Road, Lillington, Leamington Spa
29B12	Kinswood Road, Stockingford, Nuneaton
36C34	Kinwalsey Farm, Newhall Green, Fillongley
36C42	Kinwalsey Lane, Little Packington, Meriden
36C31	Kinwalsey Lane, Newhall Green, Fillongley

Map ref	Address
125C21	Kinwarton Farm Road, Kinwarton
125C23	Kinwarton Farm, Kinwarton
125B24	Kinwarton Road, Kinwarton, Alces
114B11	Kipling Avenue, Forbes Estate, Warwick
21A43	Kipling Close, Galley Common, Nuneaton
145A32	Kipling Road, Stratford upon Avon
96C22	Kirby Avenue, Woodloes, Warwick
51A41	Kirby Close, Brandon
174B44	Kirby Farm, Compton Wynyates
43C31	Kirby Lane, Monks Kirby
42C4	Kirby Lane, Withybrook
71C24	Kirby Road, Hillmorton, Rugby
54C34	Kirkby Drive, Brownsover, Rugby
71C24	Kirkby Road, Rugby
98A42	Kirkland Court, Leamington Spa
175B44	Kirkland Farm, Middle Tysoe, Tys
40A21	Kirkstone Road, Bedworth
54C33	Kirkstone, Brownsover, Rugby
119A32	Kirkwall, Southam
4A24	Kirtland Close, Austrey
116B23	Kirton Close, Whitnash
6B22	Kisses Barn Lane, Polesworth
130A41	Kissing Tree Lane, Alveston, Strat upon Avon
194B21	Kitebrook End Farm, Kitebrook, Chastleton
194B14	Kitebrook Farm, Kitebrook, Little Compton
96C21	Kites Close, Woodloes, Warwick
79B34	Kites Nest Farm, Kites Nest, Beau
79B23	Kites Nest Lane, Beausale
79B34	Kites Nest Lane, Kites Nest, Beau
5C43	Kitwood Avenue, Dordon
31A23	Klevedon Close, Whitestone, Nu
161B31	Knavenhill Farm, Alderminster
30B23	Knebley Crescent, Caldwell, Nun
144C22	Knight Court, Stratford upon Av
150A21	Knight Road, Lighthorne Heath, Lighthorne
151B14	Knightcote Bottom, Knightcote, P Dassett
97B32	Knightcote Drive, Milverton, Leamington Spa
135A34	Knightcote Road, Bishops Itching
82C44	Knightley Close, Cubbington
81B11	Knightlow Close, Windy Arbour Kenilworth
135A42	Knightlow Farm, Bishops Itching
67C32	Knightlow Hill, Stretton on Dun
134B12	Knightlow Way, Harbury
82C44	Knightly Close, Cubbington
123B42	Knighton Farm, Inkberrow
166C32	Knights Farm, Avon Dassett
145C11	Knights Lane, Tiddington, Strat
40B11	Knightsbridge Avenue, Collycro Bedworth

Map ref	Address
31	Knightsbridge House, Goodyears End, Bedworth
A43	Knob Hill, Stretton on Dunsmore
A33	Knobbs Farm, Long Harston
21	Knoll Drive, Woodloes, Warwick
C41	Knollands Farm, Honington
B13	Knottesfield Close, Studley
B13	Knottesford Close, Studley
B23	Knowle Barn Farm, Inkberrow
11	Knowle Hill, Hurley, Kingsbury
41	Knowle Hill, Kenilworth
22	Knowle Hill, Kingsbury
22	Knowle Wood Road, Dorridge
11	Knowles Avenue, Whittleford, Nuneaton
32	Knox Crescent, Saint Nicholas Park, Nuneaton
32	Kyneer Way, Binley Woods
21	Kyte Green Farm, Kite Green, Preston Bagot
41	Labrador Farm, Shelfield Green, Great Alne
1	Labunham Close, Bedworth
2	Laburnam Close, Kingsbury
24	Laburnam Drive, Whitnash
2	Laburnam Grove, Percy Estate, Warwick
2	Laburnum Avenue, Windy Arbour, Kenilworth
1	Laburnum Grove, Bilton, Rugby
1	Laburnum Grove, Camphill, Nuneaton
3	Lacell Close, Woodloes, Warwick
23	Ladbroke Grove Farm, Ladbroke
2	Ladbroke Hall Farm, Tanworth in Arden
13	Ladbroke Hill Farm, Ladbroke
23	Ladbroke Road, Bishops Itchington
4	Lady Lane Farm, Cheswick Green
1	Lady Lane, Cheswick Green
1	Lady Lane, Kenilworth
	Lady Warwick Avenue, Bedworth
1	Lady Wood Farm, Oldbury
	Ladycroft, Cubbington
	Lair, The, Birchmoor, Polesworth
	Lakeland House, Warwick
	Lakeside, Bedworth
2	Lakeside, Wotton Wawen
	Lakin Court, Packmores, Warwick
2	Lakin Drive, Bishops Itchington
	Lakin Road, Packmores, Warwick
	Lamb Farm, Hints
2	Lambcote Farm, Ettington
3	Lambert Court, Barford
2	Lambert Court, Bidford
	Lambert Court, Warwick
	Lambeth Croft, Chelmsley Wood
	Lambourne Crescent, Sydenham Farm Estate, Leamington
	Lamintone Drive, Milverton, Leamington Spa

Map ref	Address
96B42	Lammas Court, Warwick
68A12	Lammas Court, Wolston
116A13	Lammas Croft, Whitnash, Leamington Spa
96B34	Lammas Walk, Warwick
30C12	Lamorna Close, Nuneaton
28A43	Lamp Lane, Fillongley
27C13	Lamp Lane, Gun Hill, Arley
14C21	Lancaster Close, Atherstone
147A32	Lancaster Close, Mountford, Wellesbourne
80C21	Lancaster Place, Bulkington Estate, Kenilworth
71A11	Lancaster Road, Rugby
41B22	Lancing Road, Ryton, Bedworth
34A33	Land Lane, Chelmsley Wood
116A23	Landor House, Whitnash, Leamington Spa
96B32	Landor Road, Packmores, Warwick
116A21	Landor Road, Whitnash
107B22	Landsdowne Crescent, Studley
98A23	Landsdowne Street, Leamington Spa
72A24	Landseer Close, Lower Hillmorton, Rugby
175B34	Lane End Farm, Lower Tysoe, Tysoe
175C33	Lane End, Lower Tysoe, Tysoe
79B31	Lane Farm, Beausale
188B43	Lanes End Farm, Stourton
96C24	Langcliffe Avenue, Woodloes, Warwick
54B34	Langdale Close, Brownsover, Rugby
98C21	Langdale Close, Lillington, Leamington Spa
23A41	Langdale Drive, Saint Nicholas Park, Nuneaton
165B42	Langdon Lane, Radway
9C31	Langley Brook Farm, Middleton
111C21	Langley Farm, Langley
128B32	Langley Farm, Stratford upon Avon
111C24	Langley Green Farm, Langley
9A42	Langley Hall, Sutton Coldfield
9B34	Langley Hill Farm, Sutton Coldfield
93C34	Langley Road, Claverdon
111B12	Langley Road, Langley
116A14	Langley Road, Whitnash
111B12	Langmoor Poultry Farm, Tattle Bank, Langley
195A24	Langston Farm, Little Compton
195A24	Langston Terrace, Little Compton
71C23	Langton Road, Rugby
98A31	Lansdowne Circus, Leamington Spa
40A14	Lansdowne Close, Bedworth
98A31	Lansdowne Crescent, Leamington Spa
107B22	Lansdowne Crescent, Studley
60B13	Lansdowne Farm, Dorridge
71C13	Lansdowne Place, Rugby
98A23	Lansdowne Road, Leamington Spa
107B22	Lansdowne Road, Studley
98A23	Lansdowne Street, Leamington Spa
98A31	Lansdowne Terrace, Leamington Spa

Map ref	Address
5A41	Lapwing, Tamworth
76B14	Lapworth Farm, Lapworth
76B14	Lapworth Hill Farm, Lapworth
76C33	Lapworth Lodge Farm, Lapworth
76C34	Lapworth Park Farm, Lapworth
77A32	Lapworth Street, Bushwood
77B44	Lapworth Street, Lowsonford, Lapworth
125A24	Larch Close, Alcester
70A22	Larch Close, Long Lawford
145A11	Larch Close, Stratford upon Avon
34B21	Larch Croft, Chelmsley Wood
97A21	Larch Grove, Percy Estate, Warwick
51A44	Larch Ways, Wolston
51A44	Larchfields, Wolston
40A32	Larchwood Road, Blackbank, Bedworth
41A14	Larkin Close, Bulkington, Bedworth
54C23	Larkspur, Brownsover, Rugby
11B12	Larkspur, Dosthill, Tamworth
179B33	Larkstoke Road, Ebrington
179B22	Larkstoke Road, Mickleton
80C22	Latimer Close, Bulkington Estate, Kenilworth
53B43	Lauderdale Close, Rugby
73C44	Lauds Road, Crick
30C12	Launceston Drive, Nuneaton
78C11	Laundry Cottage, Wroxhall
2B34	Laundry Lane, Tamworth
6A33	Laurel Avenue, Dordon
70A22	Laurel Drive, Long Lawford
176B32	Laurel Drive, Ratley And Upton
87B14	Laurel Farm, Dunchurch
102B13	Laurel Farm, Leamington Hastings
178B32	Laurel Farm, Shotteswell
119C13	Laurel Farm, Stockton
70C34	Laurel Gardens, Rugby
39B21	Laurels, The, Bedworth
54C23	Lavender Close, Brownsover, Rugby
145A11	Lavender Gardens, Stratford upon Avon
31B31	Lavenham Close, Whitestone, Nuneaton
70A14	Lawford Field Farm, Long Lawford
69B32	Lawford Heath Farm, Lawford Heath, Long Lawford
69C14	Lawford Heath Lane, Lawford Heath, Long Lawford
69C22	Lawford Hill Farm, Lawford Heath, Long Lawford
70A24	Lawford Lane, Bilton, Rugby
69A24	Lawford Lodge Farm, Church Lawford
70A12	Lawford Road, Long Lawford
70C14	Lawford Road, New Bilton, Rugby
116A14	Lawford Road, Whitnash
70A24	Lawford Way, Rugby
39B21	Lawns, The, Bedworth
109B24	Lawnsbrook Farm, Shelfield, Aston Cantlow
24C34	Lawnsdale Close, Kings Rise, Coleshill
40A31	Lawrence Road, Exhall, Bedworth
64A41	Lawrence Road, Kenilworth
71B14	Lawrence Road, Rugby
71A13	Lawrence Sherriff Street, Rugby
145C11	Lawson Avenue, Tiddington, Stratfe upon Avon
27A13	Laxe Farm, Over Whitacre
98C44	Lay Gardens, Radford Semele
39A34	Le Hanche Close, Keresley Newlan Keresley
70A22	Le Stock Close, Bilton, Rugby
125B23	Lea Close, Alcester
144A12	Lea Close, Stratford upon Avon
144C23	Lea Court, Stratford upon Avon
53B42	Lea Crescent, Newbold on Avon, F
144C23	Lea Crescent, Stratford upon Avon
17A32	Lea Farm, Lea Marston
16A12	Lea Farm, Wishaw
27A12	Lea Lane Farm, Monwode Lea, Ar
26B13	Lea Lane, Over Whitacre
65B12	Leaf Lane Island, Warwick by pass
65B12	Leaf Lane To Stoneleigh, Warwick pass
65B12	Leaf Lane, Warwick by pass
114B14	Leafields Farm, Lodge Wood Est, Warwick
64B31	Leagh Close, Kenilworth
83C33	Leam Bank Farm, Wappenbury
31A23	Leam Close, Attleborough, Nunea
104A32	Leam Farm, Sawbridge, Wolfham
104A24	Leam Farm, Willoughby
97B41	Leam Road, Leamington Spa
150A11	Leam Road, Lighthorne Heath, Lighthorne
98A34	Leam Street, Leamington Spa
98A34	Leam Terrace E, Leamington Spa
98A33	Leam Terrace, Leamington Spa
116C42	Leamington Hall Farm, Harbury
85C43	Leamington Hastings Road, Birdi
83B11	Leamington Road, Bubbenhall
134A13	Leamington Road, Harbury
100A22	Leamington Road, Hunningham
81A13	Leamington Road, Kenilworth
81A24	Leamington Road, Leek Wootton
101A33	Leamington Road, Long Itchingte
84A23	Leamington Road, Princethorpe
98C41	Leamington Road, Radford Seme
67A33	Leamington Road, Ryton on Du
65B41	Leamington Road, Stoneleigh
35A34	Leamington Road, Stoneythorpe
117B13	Leamington Road, Ufton
83A13	Leamington Road, Waverley Wo Bubbenhall
40A13	Leas Close, Bedworth
182A43	Leason Road, Barcheston
154A34	Leasow Farm, Church Lench
192C21	Leasow Farm, Whichford
99A44	Leasowe Farm, Radford Semele
96A41	Leasowes Farm, Budbrooke
65A11	Leasowes Farm, Finham, Coven
174C13	Leasowes Farm, Pillerton Herse

Map ref	Address	Map ref	Address
4C13	Leasowes Farm, Pillerton Priors	97C42	Leycester Place, Leamington Spa
C11	Leather Mill Cottage, Hartshill	96C41	Leycester Place, Warwick
312	Leather Mill Farm, Hartshill	80C22	Leycester Road, Kenilworth
313	Leather Mill Lane, Hartshill	79A22	Leyend Farm, Haseley Knob, Haseley
C21	Leaward Close, Heath End, Nuneaton	64B44	Leyes Lane, Kenilworth
C43	Ledbrook Road, Cubbington	114B12	Leyfields Crescent, Lodge Wood Est, Warwick
344	Ledbury Road, Sydenham Farm Estate, Leamington	41A24	Leyland Road, Bulkington, Bedworth
C13	Lee Close, Woodloes, Warwick	30C23	Leyland Road, Nuneaton
C41	Lee Road, Leamington Spa	24B21	Leys Court, Water Orton
C12	Leek Wootton Island To Chesford Island, Warwick by pass	190C41	Leys Farm, Barton on The Heath
		168B24	Leys Farm, Claydon
C12	Leek Wootton Island To Stanks Hill, Warwick by pass	159A14	Leys Farm, Clifford Chambers
		154B24	Leys Road, Church Lench
C12	Leek Wootton Island, Warwick by pass	154C32	Leys Road, Harvington
C43	Lees House, Radway	72B33	Leys Road, Hillmorton, Rugby
24	Leicester Court, Leamington Spa	31A13	Liberty Close, Nuneaton
21	Leicester Crescent, Atherstone	31A13	Liberty Way, Nuneaton
23	Leicester Croft, Bulkington, Bedworth	27C31	Lichfield Close, New Arley
14	Leicester Grange Farm, Wolvey	23A32	Lichfield Close, Saint Nicholas Park, Nuneaton
A12	Leicester House Farm, Harbury		
23	Leicester House, Leamington Spa	16B21	Lichfield Road, Coleshill
42	Leicester Lane, Cubbington	24B12	Lichfield Road, Curdworth
43	Leicester Lane, Lillington, Leamington Spa	16B21	Lichfield Road, Moxhull, Wishaw
		24C11	Lichfield Road, Water Orton
24	Leicester Lane, Stoneleigh	101A42	Liegh Crescent, Long Itchington
14	Leicester Road, Bedworth	149C42	Lighthorne Road, Chadshunt
43	Leicester Road, Brownsover, Rugby	149B43	Lighthorne Road, Kineton
1	Leicester Road, Churchover	149A23	Lighthorne Road, Lighthorne Rough, Kineton
1	Leicester Road, Nuneaton		
14	Leicester Road, Shilton	148B21	Lighthorne Rough, Lighthorne Rough, Lighthorne
3	Leicester Road, Wolvey Heath, Wolvey		
4	Leicester Street, Bedworth	70A22	Lilac Drive, Long Lawford
1	Leicester Street, Bulkington	97A21	Lilac Grove, Percy Estate, Warwick
3	Leicester Street, Leamington Spa	56A42	Lilbourne Fields Farm, Lilbourne
3	Leigh Avenue, Finham	56B13	Lilbourne Lane, Swinford
42	Leigh Crescent, Long Itchington	55B43	Lilbourne Road, Dunsmore, Clifton upon Dunsmore
	Leigh Road, Sutton Coldfield		
2	Leighton Close, Gibbet Hill, Coventry	97C21	Lillington Avenue, Leamington Spa
2	Leighton Close, Lillington, Leamington Spa	98A14	Lillington Close, Lillington, Leamington Spa
34	Lench Farm, Inkberrow	98A13	Lillington Road, Leamington Spa
	Lennon Close, Hillmorton, Rugby	98A14	Lime Avenue, Lillington, Leamington Spa
2	Lentons Lane Farm, Walsgrave on Sowe		
	Lentons Lane, Sutton Stop, Coventry	21C41	Lime Grove, Camphill, Nuneaton
	Leo House, Warwick	34B23	Lime Grove, Chelmsley Wood
	Leonards Close, Dordon	18B11	Lime Grove, Hurley, Kingsbury
	Leonards View, Polesworth	3B14	Lime Grove, Newton Regis
1	Lever Hill, Halford	81A12	Lime Grove, Windy Arbour, Kenilworth
	Lever Road, Hillmorton, Rugby	68C41	Lime Kiln Farm, Stretton on Dunsmore
	Levett Road, Amington, Tamworth	119B21	Lime Road, Southam
	Levy Close, Rugby	70B33	Lime Tree Avenue, Bilton, Rugby
	Lewis Close, Mancetter	70A34	Lime Tree Avenue, Dunchurch
	Lewis Road, Radford Semele	58B23	Limekiln Lane, Cheswick Green
	Lexington Court, Nuneaton	6A32	Limekilns, St Helena, Polesworth
	Leyburn Close, Woodloes, Warwick	144B23	Limes Avenue, Stratford upon Avon
	Leycester Close, Harbury	28A12	Limes Coppice, Ansley
	Leycester Court, Leamington Spa	69A13	Limestone Hall Farm, Church Lawford
	Leycester Court, Warwick	52A43	Limestone Hall Lane, Church Lawford

Map ref	Address
21A34	Lincoln Avenue, Bucks Hill, Nuneaton
147A32	Lincoln Close, Mountford, Wellesbourne
96C23	Lincoln Close, Woodloes, Warwick
34A34	Lincoln Croft, Chelmsley Wood
34A31	Lincoln Grove, Chelmsley Wood
54B34	Lindale, Brownsover, Rugby
147C22	Linden Avenue, Wellesbourne Hasting, Wellesbourne
96C13	Linden Close, Woodloes, Warwick
40A14	Linden Lea, Bedworth
2A43	Lindera, Amington, Tamworth
81B11	Lindisfarne Drive, Windy Arbour, Kenilworth
39B21	Lindley Road, Market End, Bedworth
97B32	Lindon Court, Milverton, Leamington Spa
42B33	Lindon Farm, Withybrook
9B41	Lindridge Road, Sutton Coldfield
81A23	Lindsey Crescent, Kenilworth
150C34	Lindsey Walk, Temple Herdewyke, Burton Dassett
96B42	Linen Street, Warwick
9A43	Lingard Road, Sutton Coldfield
22A34	Lingfield Farm, Nuneaton
128B42	Lings Lane, Bishopton, Stratford upon Avon
29C22	Lingwood Drive, Heath End, Nuneaton
97B42	Linkway, Leamington Spa
22C22	Linley Lodge Farm, Higham, Higham on The Hill
119A22	Linley Road, Southam
71C22	Linnell Road, Lower Hillmorton, Rugby
90A13	Linridge Close, Redditch
123C14	Linsey Farm, Inkberrow
5A32	Lintly, Stoneydelph, Tamworth
70C43	Lion Farm, Dunchurch
31A11	Liskeard Close, Nuneaton
98A43	Lisle Court, Leamington Spa
115B32	Lisle Gardens, Bishops Tachbrook
14C21	Lister Road, Atherstone
30B14	Lister Street, Attleborough, Nuneaton
129A23	Little Acre Farm, Ingon, Hampton Lucy
13B21	Little Brum, Grendon
71A13	Little Church Street, Rugby
195A32	Little Compton Manor, Little Compton
190C43	Little Compton Road, Barton on The Heath
195A23	Little Compton Road, Little Compton
143C11	Little Drayton Farm, Stratford upon Avon
30A12	Little Duke Street, Nuneaton
71A13	Little Elborow Street, Rugby
71B23	Little Farm, Rugby
57B21	Little Fulford Farm, Fulford Heath, Tidbury Green
71B23	Little Grove, Rugby
143C34	Little Hall Farm, Dodwell, Luddington
131B42	Little Hill Farm, Charlecote
176A21	Little Kineton Road, Tysoe
123C41	Little Knighton Farm, Inkberrow
74B11	Little Ladbroke Farm, Tanworth in Arden
53A34	Little Lawford Lane, Harborough Magna
52B33	Little Lawford Lane, Kings Newnha
52C33	Little Lawford Lane, Little Lawford
53B33	Little Lawford Lane, Rugby
55A31	Little London Lane, Newton And Biggin
144A34	Little Luddington Farm, Luddingto
123B24	Little Mearse Farm, Inkberrow
95A31	Little Nunhold Farm, Hatton
119A24	Little Park, Southam
71A13	Little Pennington Street, Rugby
94A24	Little Pinley Farm, Pinley Green, Rowington
74B11	Little Rushbrook Farm, Tanworth i Arden
57A22	Little Tankers Green Farm, Tanner Green, Wythall
63C43	Little Virginia, Kenilworth
49A12	Little Walton Lodge Farm, Monks
6C14	Little Warton Road, Little Warton, Polesworth
6C14	Little Warton Road, Warton
159B41	Little Willicote Farm, High Cross, Claybrook
159B41	Little Willicote Farm, Quinton
107C31	Littlewood Green Farm, Spernall, Sambourne
107B24	Littlewood Green, Littlewood Gre Studley
183A24	Littleworth Farm, Honington
113A11	Littleworth Farm, Norton Lindsey
5B31	Litton, Stoneydelph, Tamworth
76B44	Liveridge Hill, Henley in Arden
97C32	Livery Street, Leamington Spa
69C12	Livingstone Avenue, Long Lawfo
54B31	Liza Court, Brownsover, Rugby
116A11	Llewellyn Road, Leamington Spa
95C34	Lloyd Close, Hampton Magna, Budbrooke
54B34	Lloyd Road, Brownsover, Rugby
163B24	Lobbingtonn Hall Farm, Butlers Marston
145A13	Lock Close, Stratford upon Avor
96B24	Lock Lane, The Cape, Warwick
81A11	Lockhart Close, Whitemore, Ken
115C12	Lockheed Close, Leamington Sp
114B14	Lodge Crescent, Lodge Wood Es Warwick
3C32	Lodge Farm, Austrey
134A21	Lodge Farm, Chesterton
11B11	Lodge Farm, Dosthill, Tamwort
78C23	Lodge Farm, Five Ways, Shrewl

Map ref	Address	Map ref	Address
B33	Lodge Farm, Forshaw Heath, Tanworth in Arden	41B21	Long Street, Bulkington
A34	Lodge Farm, Grandborough	6A41	Long Street, Dordon
A21	Lodge Farm, Harborough Magna	14B23	Long Street, Innage Park Estate, Grendon
C21	Lodge Farm, Lawford Heath, Long Lawford	41B21	Long Street, Ryton, Bedworth
B23	Lodge Farm, Monks Kirby	112B14	Long Thatch Cottage, Norton Curlieu, Claverdon
C23	Lodge Farm, Nuneaton	179B42	Longbridge Farm, Ebrington
B11	Lodge Farm, Rugby	114B23	Longbridge Farm, Warwick
4	Lodge Farm, Sheepy	114A22	Longbridge Island To Stanks Hill Island, Warwick by pass
B41	Lodge Farm, Snitterfield	114A22	Longbridge Island, Warwick by pass
23	Lodge Farm, Street Ashton, Stretton Under Fosse	114A22	Longbridge To Stanks Hill, Warwick by pass
A34	Lodge Farm, Withybrook	180C31	Longdon Manor Road, Longdon, Tredington
12	Lodge Road, Rugby	180C23	Longdon Road Farm, Longdon, Tredington
C14	Lodge Road, Stratford upon Avon	89B31	Longdown Lane, Barby
31	London Gate, Nuneaton	88C44	Longdown Lane, Willoughby
C22	London Road, Braunston	98B43	Longfield Road, Sydenham Farm Estate, Leamington Spa
11	London Road, Dunchurch	141C44	Longford Close, Bidford
B1	London Road, Dunton, Curdworth	60A14	Longford Close, Dorridge
4	London Road, Hints	40A33	Longford Road, Exhall
C24	London Road, Little Compton	Cov	Longford Road, Longford, Coventry
	London Road, Middleton	90A13	Longhope Close, Redditch
13	London Road, Ryton on Dunsmore	116C11	Longleat Grove, Sydenham Farm Estate, Leamington Spa
C12	London Road, Shipston on Stour	179B42	Longridge Farm, Ebrington
2	London Road, Stretton on Dunsmore	70B34	Longrood Road, Bilton, Rugby
1	London Road, Thurlaston	2C11	Lonkshill Farm, Thorpe Constantine
12	London Road, Willoughby	98A12	Lonsdale Road, Lillington, Leamington Spa
1	London Road, Wishaw	68B13	Lordhill Farm, Wolston
31	Lone Acre Farm, Wilmcote, Aston Cantlow	107B24	Lords Lane, Littlewood Green, Studley
3	Long Brook Lane, Frogmore	21A44	Lorina Close, Whittleford, Nuneaton
23	Long Compton Road, Whichford	5B31	Lothersdale, Stoneydelph, Tamworth
1	Long Fellow Avenue, Forbes Estate, Warwick	5B31	Loughshaw, Stoneydelph, Tamworth
3	Long Furlong, Hillside, Rugby	84C44	Louisa Ward Close, Marton
22	Long Itchington Road, Birdingbury	14C13	Loveday Close, Atherstone
14	Long Itchington Road, Hunningham	51C12	Loveitts Farm, Brinklow
	Long Itchington Road, Offchurch	40A13	Lovell Road, Bedworth
3	Long Itchington Road, Snowford, Long Itchington	71C22	Loverock Crescent, Hillmorton, Rugby
4	Long Lane, Gaydon	41C33	Lovitts Farm, Shilton
4	Long Lane, Northend	5B31	Lowdham, Stoneydelph, Tamworth
	Long Lawford Lodge Farm, Long Lawford	116A43	Lowdown Farm, Bishops Tachbrook
	Long Leys Court, Water Orton	146C13	Lowe Farm, Hunscote, Wellesbourne
	Long Leys Croft, Water Orton	172A14	Lower Andrews Farm, Crimscote, Whitchurch
	Long Marston Airfield, Long Marston	97C34	Lower Avenue, Leamington Spa
	Long Marston Road, Mickleton	139B22	Lower Barn Farm, Abbots Moreton
	Long Marston Road, Pebworth	143B31	Lower Binton Court, Lower Binton
	Long Marston Road, Rumer Hill, Welford on Avon	143B32	Lower Binton Farm, Lower Binton, Binton
	Long Meadow Barn Farm, Burton Green, Kenilworth	112B22	Lower Blacon Farm, Lower Norton, Wolverton
	Long Meadow Farm, Burton Green, Kenilworth	112B22	Lower Blacon Farm, Norton Lindsey
	Long Orchard Farm, Welford on Avon	123B13	Lower Bouts Farm, Inkberrow
	Long Shoot, Long Shoot, Nuneaton		
	Long Street, Atherstone		

Map ref	Address
194A21	Lower Brookend Farm, Evenlode
96B32	Lower Cape, The Cape, Warwick
123C14	Lower Cladswell Farm, Inkberrow
123C21	Lower Cladswell Lane, Inkberrow
169C34	Lower Clopton Farm, Quinton
128C34	Lower Clopton Farm, Stratford upon Avon
184A21	Lower Compton Farm, Compton Wynyates
130A41	Lower End, Alveston, Stratford upon Avon
167A23	Lower End, Avon Dassett
66B43	Lower End, Bubbenhall
37C33	Lower Farm Betterage, Fillongley
178C12	Lower Farm Lane, Mollington
166C32	Lower Farm, Avon Dassett
151B12	Lower Farm, Bishops Itchington
181B11	Lower Farm, Blackwell, Tredington
10C42	Lower Farm, Bodymoor Heath, Middleton
122A42	Lower Farm, Catesby
120C43	Lower Farm, Chapel Green, Napton on The Hill
37C33	Lower Farm, Corley Moor, Corley
181A23	Lower Farm, Darlingscott, Tredington
95B14	Lower Farm, Hatton
118B32	Lower Farm, Long Itchington
179A31	Lower Farm, Mickleton
178C14	Lower Farm, Mollington
110B43	Lower Farm, Newnham, Aston Cantlow
160A32	Lower Farm, Preston on Stour
155B11	Lower Farm, Salford Priors
118B32	Lower Farm, Stoneythorpe
186B42	Lower Farm, Todenham
7B14	Lower Farm, Twycross
22B32	Lower Farm, Weddington, Nuneaton
174A44	Lower Farm, Whatcote
152C12	Lower Farm, Wormleighton
120A31	Lower Fields Farm, Napton on The Hill
120A33	Lower Fields Farm, Southam
162C32	Lower Fosse Farm, Pillerton Hersey
117A23	Lower Fosse Farm, Radford Semele
96B44	Lower Friars, Forbes Estate, Warwick
103B34	Lower Grandborough Fields Farm, Grandborough
115B14	Lower Heathcote Farm, Warwick
71B13	Lower Hillmorton Road, Rugby
13A13	Lower House Farm, Baddesley Ensor
90A13	Lower House Farm, Redditch
146B24	Lower Hunscote Farm, Hunscote, Charlecote
129B32	Lower Ingon Farm, Ingon, Hampton Lucy
64A41	Lower Ladyes Hill, Kenilworth
166C32	Lower Lane, Avon Dassett
148A14	Lower Lea Farm, Wellesbourne

Map ref	Address
76A34	Lower Liveridge Hill Farm, Mows H Beaudesert
54B23	Lower Lodge Farm, Brownsover, Ru
146C33	Lower Meer Hill Farm, Loxley
170B24	Lower Meon Farm, Lower Meon, Quinton
183B22	Lower Nineveh Farm, Idlicote
125B41	Lower Oversley Lodge Farm, Oversl Wood, Alcester
106C44	Lower Park Farm, Feckenham
184A44	Lower Qynton Farm, Winderton, Brailes
136C41	Lower Radbourne Farm, Lower Radbourne
71B43	Lower Rainsbrook Farm, Rugby
41A42	Lower Road, Barnacle, Shilton
71B23	Lower Road, Rugby
38B34	Lower Rock Farm, Corley
108A32	Lower Spernall Farm, Morgrove Coppice, Spernall
72A32	Lower Street, Lower Hillmorton, R
104B12	Lower Street, Willoughby
175C41	Lower Tysoe Road, Lower Tysoe
175C41	Lower Tysoe Road, Lower Tysoe, Tysoe
114C41	Lower Watchbury Farm, Barford
129A31	Lower Welcombe Farm, Ingon, Hampton Lucy
117B41	Lower West Fields Farm, Harbury
113A24	Lowerhouse Farm, Norton Lindsey
96C21	Lowes Avenue, Woodloes, Warwic
147B21	Lowes Lane, Mountford, Wellesbo
23A42	Loweswater Close, Saint Nicholas Nuneaton
5B31	Lowforce, Stoneydelph, Tamworth
40A11	Lowry Close, Collycroft, Bedworth
93B12	Lowsonford Farm, Lowsonford, Rowington
147A21	Loxley Close, Mountford, Wellesbourne
146C42	Loxley Farm, Loxley
147A41	Loxley Paddocks, Loxley
145A22	Loxley Road, Stratford upon Avo
147A22	Loxley Road, Wellesbourne
98A22	Loxley Way, Lillington, Leamingt
62A31	Lucas Aerospace, Honiley
37B42	Luckmans Farm, Corley Moor
37B42	Luckmans Farm, Corley Moor, C
110C21	Lucys Farm, Wootton Wawen
144B23	Luddington Road, Drayton, Strat upon Avon
144A34	Luddington Road, Luddington
28A12	Ludford Close, Ansley
144B11	Ludford Close, Stratford upon A
21B44	Ludford Road, Camphill, Nunea
24A13	Ludgate Close, Water Orton
34B22	Ludlow Close, Chelmsley Wood
34B22	Lumley Grove, Chelmsley Wood
24A42	Lundy View, Bacons End, Kings

Map ref	Address	Map ref	Address
?21	Lunn Avenue, Kenilworth	70B34	Magnet Lane, Bilton, Rugby
C32	Luscombe Farm, Snitterfield	5A11	Magnolia, Amington, Tamworth
?23	Lutterworth Road, Attleborough	31A31	Magyar Crescent, Whitestone, Nuneaton
?23	Lutterworth Road, Attleborough	54C23	Maidenhair Drive, Brownsover, Rugby
?33	Lutterworth Road, Bramcote	145A11	Maidenhead Close, Stratford on Avon
?12	Lutterworth Road, Brinklow	129A43	Maidenhead Road, Stratford upon Avon
?43	Lutterworth Road, Churchover		
12	Lutterworth Road, Monks Kirby	148B21	Main Drive, Moreton Paddox, Moreton Morrell
?23	Lutterworth Road, Pailton		
?11	Lutterworth Road, Shawell	45B14	Main Road, Anstey
?2	Lutterworth Road, Shelford, Burton Hastings	4A21	Main Road, Austrey
		13B42	Main Road, Baxterley
?41	Lutterworth Road, Stretton Under Fosse	188A43	Main Road, Cherington
?12	Lutterworth Road, Swinford	73C43	Main Road, Crick
?31	Lutterworth Road, Whitestone, Nuneaton	173A31	Main Road, Halford
		89C13	Main Road, Kilsby
?11	Lutterworth Road, Wolvey	172B24	Main Road, Newbold on Stour, Tredington
?3	Lycroft Avenue, Chelmsley Wood		
?12	Lydgate Court, Bedworth	3B14	Main Road, Newton Regis
?4	Lydgate Court, Coten, Nuneaton	1C41	Main Road, No Mans Heath, Newton Regis
?2	Lydstep Grove, Sydenham Farm Estate, Leamington Spa		
		15A13	Main Road, Ratcliffe Culey, Witherley
	Lye Corner, Gatehouse Lane, Bedworth	3A23	Main Road, Seckington
?4	Lye Green Road, Holywell, Rowington	8A41	Main Road, Sheepy Magna, Sheepy
?4	Lye Green Road, Lye Green, Claverdon	2C41	Main Road, Shuttington
?3	Lyle Court, Leamington Spa	188A42	Main Road, Stourton
?4	Lyndhurst Road, Hillmorton, Rugby	145B12	Main Road, Tiddington, Stratford upon Avon
?2	Lyndon Court, Milverton, Leamington Spa		
		7B12	Main Road, Twycross
?1	Lyndons Farm, Tanworth in Arden	188B14	Main Road, Upper Brailes, Brailes
?3	Lynmouth Close, Nuneaton	42C41	Main Road, Withybrook
?3	Lynton Close, Woodloes, Warwick	141A24	Main Road, Wixford
1	Lynwood Walk, Sydenham Farm Estate, Leamington Spa	12B23	Main Road, Wood End, Kingsbury
		45B14	Main Street, Anstey
	Lyon Farm, Beausale	70B31	Main Street, Bilton, Rugby
?3	Lyons Farm, Rowington	85C41	Main Street, Birdingbury
?1	Lysander Close, Mountford, Wellesbourne	85C13	Main Street, Bourton on Dunsmore
		66B41	Main Street, Bubbenhall
?1	Lysander Court, Stratford upon Avon	188A41	Main Street, Cherington
	Lyster Close, Warwick	156A34	Main Street, Cleeve Prior
	Lythall Close, Radford Semele	55A43	Main Street, Clifton upon Dunsmore
	Lytham Road, Overslade, Rugby	52C11	Main Street, Easenhall
	Lyttleton Road, Packmores, Warwick	85B24	Main Street, Frankton
?1	Mables Farm, Ilmington	53A21	Main Street, Harborough Magna
	Macaulay Road, Shakespeare Gardens, Rugby	22C14	Main Street, Higham, Higham on The Hill
	Macbeth Close, Woodlands, Rugby	191C34	Main Street, Long Compton
	Macbrae Poultry Farm, Stretton on Dunsmore	70A11	Main Street, Long Lawford
		170A13	Main Street, Lower Quinton, Quinton
	Macdonnell Drive, Exhall, Bedworth	175C43	Main Street, Middle Tysoe, Tysoe
	Mackley Way, Harbury	178C13	Main Street, Mollington
	Madden Place, Bilton, Rugby	53C33	Main Street, Newbold on Avon, Rugby
	Madrona, Amington, Tamworth	55A31	Main Street, Newton And Biggin
	Maerose, Radway	151B33	Main Street, Northend, Burton Dassett
	Maffey Court, Rugby	112C14	Main Street, Norton Lindsey
	Magdalen Close, Lower Quinton, Quinton	174C32	Main Street, Oxhill
		85C13	Main Street, Oxley
	Magdalen Road, Willoughby, Magna Park, Bitteswell	55B11	Main Street, Shawell
		188A42	Main Street, Stourton

Map ref	Address	Map ref	Address
47B24	Main Street, Street Ashton, Monks Kirby	29A14	Malvern Avenue, Stockingford, Nuneaton
185C23	Main Street, Stretton on Fosse	97B24	Malvern Court, Leamington Spa
47A3	Main Street, Stretton Under Fosse	102A31	Malvern Hall Farm, Broadwell, Leamington Hastings
86C22	Main Street, Thurlaston		
145B12	Main Street, Tiddington, Stratford upon Avon	20B11	Mancetter Hill Farm, Mancetter
91B13	Main Street, Ullenhall	21B32	Mancetter Road, Hartshill
84B33	Main Street, Wappenbury	14C34	Mancetter Road, Mancetter
44C43	Main Street, Willey	21C33	Mancetter Road, Tuttle Hill, Nunea
104C13	Main Street, Willoughby	116B14	Mancliffe Drive, Sydenham Farm Estate, Leamington Spa
46C11	Main Street, Withybrook		
68A11	Main Street, Wolston	114A12	Mander Grove, Warwick
103C13	Main Street, Woolscott, Grandborough	26C42	Mandykes Farm, Shawbury, Fillon;
96C22	Makepeace Avenue, Woodloes, Warwick	71A13	Manning Walk, Rugby
		67A32	Manns Close, Ryton on Dunsmore
5B31	Malham Road, Stoneydelph, Tamworth	13A22	Manor Close, Baddesley Ensor
96C24	Malham Road, Woodloes, Warwick	22A44	Manor Court Avenue, Nuneaton
125A32	Malin Court, Alcester	30A11	Manor Court Hospital, Nuneaton
21B43	Mallard Avenue, Whittleford, Nuneaton	30A11	Manor Court Road, Nuneaton
128B42	Mallard Close, Stratford upon Avon	97C33	Manor Court, Leamington Spa
107C22	Mallard Road, Studley	91A33	Manor Drive, Morton Bagot
21A44	Mallerin Croft, Whittleford, Nuneaton	67C44	Manor Drive, Stretton on Dunsmo
184B12	Malletts Close, Middle Tysoe, Tysoe	127C31	Manor Drive, Wilmcote
39C41	Mallory Drive, Bedworth	68A11	Manor Estate, Wolston
96B33	Mallory Drive, Warwick	89B22	Manor Farm Drive, Barby
115C31	Mallory Road, Bishops Tachbrook	142A22	Manor Farm Road, Ardens Grafto Bidford
150A11	Mallory Road, Lighthorne Heath, Lighthorne	181C13	Manor Farm Road, Tredington
25C11	Malt House Farm, Hoggerills End, Nether Whitacre	142A23	Manor Farm, Ardens Grafton, Bid
		172A42	Manor Farm, Armscote, Tredingt
93A21	Malt House Farm, Preston Bagot	126C12	Manor Farm, Aston Cantlow
34A31	Malt House Lane, Chelmsley Wood	106B42	Manor Farm, Astwood Bank
47B33	Malt Kiln Farm, Stretton Under Fosse	187A11	Manor Farm, Barcheston
89C22	Malt Mill Close, Kilsby	118C12	Manor Farm, Bascote
89C22	Malt Mill Green, Kilsby	135A31	Manor Farm, Bishops Itchington
125B33	Malt Mill Lane, Alcester	128B33	Manor Farm, Bishopton, Stratford upon Avon
28A12	Malthouse Close, Ansley		
155A33	Malthouse Close, Harvington	181B13	Manor Farm, Blackwell, Tredingt
151B42	Malthouse Close, Northend, Burton Dassett	169A23	Manor Farm, Broad Marston, Pebworth
144C12	Malthouse Close, Stratford upon Avon	32A31	Manor Farm, Burton Hastings
28A12	Malthouse Farm, Ansley	55C23	Manor Farm, Catthorpe
19B21	Malthouse Farm, Bentley	58A23	Manor Farm, Cheswick Green
124A31	Malthouse Farm, Cook Hill, Inkberrow	1C13	Manor Farm, Chilcote
59C44	Malthouse Farm, Lapworth	20A41	Manor Farm, Church End, Ansle
91B12	Malthouse Farm, Ullenhall	168B31	Manor Farm, Claydon
57C33	Malthouse Lane, Clowes Wood, Tanworth in Arden	53C14	Manor Farm, Cosford
		73C33	Manor Farm, Crick
57C33	Malthouse Lane, Earlswood	172A13	Manor Farm, Crimscote, Whitch
63C41	Malthouse Lane, Kenilworth	60A33	Manor Farm, Darley Green
191C34	Malthouse Lane, Long Compton	59B14	Manor Farm, Dorridge
151B41	Malthouse Lane, Northend	86A31	Manor Farm, Draycote
151B42	Malthouse Lane, Northend, Burton Dassett	52C11	Manor Farm, Easenhall
		122B14	Manor Farm, Flecknoe, Wolfhan
57C33	Malthouse Lane, Terrys Green, Tanworth in Arden	18B23	Manor Farm, Foul End, Kingsbi
		85B31	Manor Farm, Frankton
91B14	Malthouse Lane, Ullenhall	173C23	Manor Farm, Fulready, Ettingto
107B14	Maltings, The, Studley	150B23	Manor Farm, Gaydon
71B24	Malvern Avenue, Rugby	88A31	Manor Farm, Grandborough

Map ref	Address	Map ref	Address
5A14	Manor Farm, Great Alne	37A22	Manor House Farm, Fillongley
9B22	Manor Farm, Great Wolford	53A14	Manor House Farm, Harborough Magna
A14	Manor Farm, Harborough Magna	138B34	Manor House Farm, Priors Marston
9B33	Manor Farm, Haselor	24A14	Manor House Lane, Water Orton
C24	Manor Farm, Holywell, Rowington	102A13	Manor House, Leamington Hastings
9A11	Manor Farm, Inkberrow	195A23	Manor House, Little Compton
5A13	Manor Farm, Ladbroke	94A33	Manor Lane, Claverdon
C21	Manor Farm, Langley	55A43	Manor Lane, Clifton upon Dunsmore
A23	Manor Farm, Little Rollright	162A42	Manor Lane, Ettington
A13	Manor Farm, Little Wolford	62A43	Manor Lane, Honiley
A33	Manor Farm, Long Itchington	164C21	Manor Lane, Kineton
B11	Manor Farm, Long Marston	146C42	Manor Lane, Loxley
A22	Manor Farm, Mickleton	94A32	Manor Lane, Pinley Green, Rowington
14	Manor Farm, Monks Kirby	181C42	Manor Lane, Shipston on Stour
34	Manor Farm, Morton Bagot	107C22	Manor Mews, Studley
C32	Manor Farm, Napton on The Hill	134B11	Manor Orchard, Harbury
A42	Manor Farm, Norton	61A43	Manor Park Farm, Baddesley Clinton
23	Manor Farm, Offchurch	22A43	Manor Park Road, Nuneaton
31	Manor Farm, Pailton	168B24	Manor Park, Claydon
34	Manor Farm, Pinley Green, Claverdon	135A32	Manor Road, Cross Green, Bishops Itchington
4	Manor Farm, Princethorpe	59C13	Manor Road, Dorridge
13	Manor Farm, Ratcliffe Culey, Witherley	134B12	Manor Road, Harbury
A13	Manor Farm, Ratley, Ratley And Upton	64A41	Manor Road, Kenilworth
1	Manor Farm, Ryton on Dunsmore	89C14	Manor Road, Kilsby
A31	Manor Farm, Sawbridge, Wolfhamcote	98A14	Manor Road, Lillington, Leamington Spa
	Manor Farm, Sheepy Parva, Sheepy	146C43	Manor Road, Loxley
31	Manor Farm, Shotteswell	14C41	Manor Road, Mancetter
	Manor Farm, Shuttington	71A12	Manor Road, Rugby
14	Manor Farm, Stockton	119C14	Manor Road, Stockton
3	Manor Farm, Stretton Baskerville	145B21	Manor Road, Stratford upon Avon
2	Manor Farm, Stretton on Dunsmore	185C23	Manor Road, Stretton on Fosse
4	Manor Farm, Tanners Green, Wythall	107C22	Manor Road, Studley
43	Manor Farm, Todenham	40A32	Manse Close, Exhall, Bedworth
43	Manor Farm, Upper Brailes, Brailes	172B31	Mansell Farm, Newbold on Stour, Tredington
3	Manor Farm, Upper Tysoe, Tysoe	160A42	Mansell Farm, Preston on Stour
24	Manor Farm, Walcote, Haselor	144C14	Mansell Street, Stratford upon Avon
14	Manor Farm, Warmington	171C43	Mansill Farm, Tredington
21	Manor Farm, Wasperton	135B31	Mansion Close, Bishops Itchington
2	Manor Farm, Welford on Avon	147A24	Manston Drive, Mountford, Wellesbourne
	Manor Farm, Wibtoft	145A11	Mantua, Stratford upon Avon
	Manor Farm, Willey	20A43	Maor Farm, Church End, Ansley
2	Manor Farm, Willington, Barcheston	40A32	Maple Avenue, Exhall, Bedworth
3	Manor Farm, Willoughby	11B32	Maple Drive, Kingsbury
	Manor Farm, Withybrook	97A21	Maple Grove, Percy Estate, Warwick
	Manor Farm, Wolston	71A11	Maple Grove, Rugby
4	Manor Farm, Wolverton	128C44	Maple Grove, Stratford upon Avon
4	Manor Farm, Wootton Wawen	21C44	Maple Road, Camphill, Nuneaton
	Manor Farm, Wroxhall	97C44	Maple Road, Leamington Spa
	Manor Fields Farm, Stoneleigh	34A22	Maple Way, Chelmsley Wood
2	Manor Green, Stratford upon Avon	126A13	Maples, The, Great Alne
	Manor Hall School, Blackdown, Leamington Spa	107C13	Marble Alley, Studley
	Manor Hospital, Nuneaton	178B11	March Road, Mollington
	Manor House Close, Newbold on Avon, Rugby	31A21	Marchfront Close, Attleborough, Nuneaton
	Manor House Farm, Ansley		
	Manor House Farm, Cliff, Kingsbury		
	Manor House Farm, Dorsington		

Map ref	Address	Map ref	Address
98C43	Marcroft Place, Sydenham Farm Estate, Leamington Spa	38A42	Marsland Farm, Corley
40A13	Margaret Avenue, Bedworth	73C44	Marsons Drive, Crick
134C13	Margaret Close, Harbury	150A13	Marston Avenue, Lighthorne Heath Lighthorne
14C33	Margaret Road, Mancetter	98B23	Marston Close, Lillington, Leaming▪ Spa
80C13	Margetts Close, Kenilworth		
15A33	Marie Close, Mancetter	34A34	Marston Curley Farm, Chelmsley W▪
65C22	Market Corner, Baginton	24A43	Marston Drive, Kingshurst
97C44	Market Corner, Leamington Spa	147A24	Marston Drive, Mountford, Wellesbourne
39B21	Market End Close, Bedworth		
39B22	Market End Farm, Market End, Bedworth	30C43	Marston Hall Farm, Marston Jabbe▪ Nuneaton
119A32	Market Hill, Southam	51A44	Marston Hall Farm, Wolston
71A13	Market Mall, Rugby	40B12	Marston Lane Park, Bedworth
40B21	Market Place, Bedworth	16C23	Marston Lane, Curdworth
30B11	Market Place, Nuneaton	40B11	Marston Lane, Marston Jabbett, Bedworth
71A13	Market Place, Rugby		
181C42	Market Place, Shipston on Stour	30C23	Marston Lane, Nuneaton
96C41	Market Place, Warwick	68B11	Marston Maples Farm, Wolston
164B14	Market Square, Kineton	158B31	Marston Road, Rumer Hill, Welfo▪ on Avon
14B32	Market Street, Atherstone		
6A23	Market Street, Polesworth	158C14	Marston Road, Weston on Avon
71A12	Market Street, Rugby	158C14	Marstons Road, Weston Sands, Weston on Avon
96B42	Market Street, Warwick		
116B23	Markham Drive, Whitnash	96A33	Marten Close, Hampton Magna, Budbrooke
70B34	Marks Avenue, Bilton, Rugby		
96C41	Marks Mews, Warwick	129A41	Martin Close, Stratford upon Avo
116C13	Marlborough Drive, Radford Semele	70B34	Martin Lane, Bilton, Rugby
116C11	Marlborough Drive, Sydenham Farm Estate, Leamington Spa	40B33	Martindale Road, Exhall, Bedwort
		14C21	Martins Drive, Atherstone
30A12	Marlborough Road, Nuneaton	39C23	Martins Road, Goodyears End, Bedworth
70C23	Marlborough Road, Overslade, Rugby		
37A44	Marlbrook Hall Farm, Meriden	100C11	Marton Fields Farm, Marton
141C43	Marleigh Road, Bidford	101C13	Marton Glebe Farm, Birdingbury
34B24	Marlene Croft, Chelmsley Wood	85B44	Marton Road, Birdingbury
98B41	Marloes Walk, Sydenham Farm Estate, Leamington	101A34	Marton Road, Long Itchington
		85B43	Marton Road, Marton
21A43	Marlow Close, Robinsons End, Nuneaton	127C24	Mary Ardens House, Wilmcote
		96B32	Marys Close, Packmores, Warwi▪
18B12	Marlow Road, Hurley, Kingsbury	14C31	Marys Road, Atherstone
20C44	Marlowe Close, Galley Common, Nuneaton	37C13	Marys Road, Fillongley
		16A42	Marys Walk, Curdworth
20C44	Marlowe Walk, Galley Common, Nuneaton	114B11	Masefield Avenue, Forbes Estate Warwick
41B14	Marlpit Lane, Ryton, Bedworth	145A24	Masefield Road, Stratford upon ▪
40A13	Marner Road, Bedworth	98B21	Mason Avenue, Lillington, Leam▪ Spa
30A24	Marner Road, Hilltop, Nuneaton		
156A11	Marriage Hill Farm, Bidford	57C24	Mason Lane, Tanworth in Arder▪
39B21	Marriott Road, Market End, Bedworth	144C13	Masons Road, Stratford upon A▪
29C14	Marsdale Drive, Nuneaton	144C13	Masons Way, Stratford upon Av
73C44	Marsh Close, Crick	116A14	Masters Road, Whitnash, Leami▪ Spa
140C42	Marsh Farm, Salford Priors		
16B44	Marsh Lane, Curdworth	85C41	Masters Yard, Birdingbury
24B12	Marsh Lane, Water Orton	116B14	Mathecroft, Sydenham Farm Es▪ Leamington
127B23	Marsh Road, Wilmcote, Aston Cantlow		
181C43	Marshall Avenue, Shipston on Stour	54B33	Matlock Close, Brownsover, Ru▪
39C32	Marshall Road, Exhall, Bedworth	145A11	Matthews Close, Stratford upor▪
97A24	Marsham Close, All Saints, Warwick	24B22	Maud Road, White City, Water
64B22	Marshfield Drive, Gibbet Hill, Coventry	39B23	Mavor Drive, Goodyears End, ▪

p ref	Address	Map ref	Address
A32	Mawnan Close, Exhall, Bedworth	133B41	Meadow Close, Redlands Brake, Lighthorne
C11	Maxons Farm, Stretton Baskerville	3A32	Meadow Close, Sheepy Magna, Sheepy
C34	Maxstoke Castle, Maxstoke, Coleshill	144B14	Meadow Close, Stratford upon Avon
11	Maxstoke Close, Dosthill, Tamworth	68A41	Meadow Close, Stretton on Dunsmore
A11	Maxstoke Court, Coleshill	42B14	Meadow Close, Wolvey
C11	Maxstoke Farm, Maxstoke	130B11	Meadow Court Farm, Snitterfield
43	Maxstoke Gardens, Leamington Spa	22A44	Meadow Court, Nuneaton
12	Maxstoke Hall Farm, Maxstoke	27C23	Meadow Croft, Arley
42	Maxstoke Lane, Coleshill	135B23	Meadow Crofts, Bishops Itchington
32	Maxstoke Lane, Great Packington	3C33	Meadow Farm, Austrey
43	Maxstoke Lane, Maxstoke	62C11	Meadow Farm, Balsall Common
43	Maxstoke School Farm, Maxstoke	134C12	Meadow Farm, Harbury
22	May Lane, Bilton, Rugby	68A41	Meadow Farm, Stretton on Dunsmore
21	May Tree Crescent, Chelmsley Wood	13B31	Meadow Gardens, Baddesley Common, Baddesley Ensor
C12	Maybird Centre, Stratford upon Avon	171B43	Meadow Hill Farm, Ilmington
C11	Maybrook Industrial Estate, Stratford upon Avon	125A24	Meadow Road, Alcester
C34	Mayd Road, Shipston on Stour	97A33	Meadow Road, Emscote, Warwick
2	Mayfair Drive, Galley Common, Nuneaton	92B32	Meadow Road, Henley in Arden
11	Mayfield Avenue, Stratford upon Avon		Meadow Road, Hollbrooks
4	Mayfield Close, Bedworth	12B43	Meadow Road, Hurley, Kingsbury
11	Mayfield Close, Sydenham Farm Estate, Leamington Spa	77B12	Meadow Road, Kingswood, Lapworth
11	Mayfield Court, Stratford upon Avon	21A33	Meadow Road, Moor Wood, Hartshill
4	Mayfield Drive, Henley in Arden	53B42	Meadow Road, Newbold on Avon, Rugby
3	Mayfield Drive, Windy Arbour, Kenilworth	119B23	Meadow Road, Southam
	Mayfield Grove, Overslade, Rugby	51A43	Meadow Road, Wolston
	Mayfield Road, Attleborough, Nuneaton	14B34	Meadow Street, Atherstone
	Mayfield Road, Overslade, Rugby	22A44	Meadow Street, Nuneaton
21	Mayfield Road, Southam	155C22	Meadow View, Abbotts Salford, Salford Priors
	Maynard Avenue, Emscote, Warwick	53A22	Meadow Way, Harborough Parva, Harborough Magna
	Maynard Avenue, Goodyears End, Bedworth	23B31	Meadowcroft Farm, Nuneaton
	Maynard Close, Budbrooke	77B44	Meadowhill Farm, Lowsonford, Lapworth
	Mayne Close, Hampton Magna, Budbrooke	31B23	Meadowside, Whitestone, Nuneaton
	Mayo Drive, Windy Arbour, Kenilworth	128B44	Meadowsweet Road, Stratford upon Avon
4	Mayo Road, Shipston on Stour	163B41	Mears Farm, Pillerton Hersey
	Maypole Lane, Grendon Common, Grendon	123B22	Mearse Farm, Inkberrow
	Maypole Road, Warton, Polesworth	31A31	Meddleburg Close, Whitestone, Nuneaton
	Mays Hill Farm, Mays Wood, Wootton Wawen	87B21	Medhurst Close, Dunchurch
	Mays Wood Road, Mays Wood, Wootton Wawen	145A13	Meer Street, Stratford upon Avon
	Mcdonnell Drive, Exhall, Bedworth	125B31	Meeting Lane, Alcester
	Mckinnell Crescent, Rugby	31C31	Melbourne Close, Nuneaton
	Mcmahon Road, Goodyears End, Bedworth	39C22	Melbourne Court, Bedworth
	Meadow Bank, Marton	39C14	Melbourne Court, Bedworth Woodlands, Bedworth
	Meadow Close, Anstey	150C43	Meldrum Court, Temple Herdewyke, Burton Dassett
	Meadow Close, Hockley Heath, Cheswick Green	29B14	Meldrum Road, Stockingford, Nuneaton
	Meadow Close, Kingsbury	70C24	Melish Road, Overslade, Rugby
	Meadow Close, Lillington, Leamington Spa	70C23	Mellish Court, Rugby
		72A32	Mellor Road, Hillmorton, Rugby
		5B31	Mellwaters, Stoneydelph, Tamworth
		5B32	Melmerby, Stoneydelph, Tamworth

Map ref	Address
39B31	Melrose Avenue, Goodyears End, Bedworth
98A12	Melton Road, Lillington, Leamington Spa
40A31	Melville Close, Exhall, Bedworth
70C23	Melville Close, Rugby
152A42	Memorial Road, Fenny Compton
34A12	Menai Walk, Chelmsley Wood
29A14	Mendip Drive, Stockingford, Nuneaton
169C43	Meon Road, Mickleton
24A13	Mercer Avenue, Water Orton
97A33	Mercia Way, Emscote, Warwick
5A21	Mercian Way, Amington Ind. Est., Tamworth
158B13	Mere Barn Farm, Welford on Avon
62B24	Mere End Farm, Frogmore
62B22	Mere End Road, Frogmore, Mere End
43A11	Mere Lane, Cloudesley Bush Lane, Copston Magna
48A11	Mere Lane, Copston Magna
60C24	Meres Farm, Chadwick End
30A11	Merevale Avenue, Nuneaton
14A24	Merevale Hall, Merevale, Atherstone
14B23	Merevale House, Merevale, Grendon
13C33	Merevale Lane, Baxterley
14A24	Merevale Lane, Merevale, Atherstone
14B33	Merevale View, Atherstone
57C34	Merewood Farm, Clowes Wood, Tanworth in Arden
5A41	Merganiser, Tamworth
90A13	Meriden Close, Redditch
24A41	Meriden Drive, Kingshurst
37B33	Meriden Road, Chapel Green, Fillongley
21A44	Merlin Avenue, Whittleford, Nuneaton
73C22	Merrycot Lane, Yelvertoft
91B44	Merryfield Farm, Wootton Wawen
41A13	Mersey Road, Bulkington, Bedworth
70C22	Merttens Drive, Rugby
72A31	Mews, The, Hillmorton, Rugby
97B32	Mews Road, Milverton, Leamington Spa
5A22	Mica Road, Amington Ind. Est., Tamworth
14C24	Michaels Close, Atherstone
93C41	Michaels Close, Claverdon
135A32	Michaels Close, Cross Green, Bishops Itchington
96B32	Michaels Road, Packmores, Warwick
33C12	Mickle Hill Farm, Hinckley
68B31	Mickle Hill Farm, Wolston
24A22	Mickle Meadow, Water Orton
171A43	Mickleton Road, Admington
171A44	Mickleton Road, Ilmington
179A11	Mickleton Wood Farm, Mickleton
35A41	Middle Bickenhill Lane, Bickenhill
123B21	Middle Bouts Farm, Inkberrow
194A23	Middle Brookend Farm, Chastleton
115C42	Middle Farm, Bishops Tachbrook
122B41	Middle Farm, Catesby
146C42	Middle Farm, Loxley

Map ref	Address
131C31	Middle Hill Farm, Charlecote
146B14	Middle Hunscote Farm, Hunscote, Charlecote
17B42	Middle Lane, Nether Whitacre
178B32	Middle Lane, Shotteswell
95B21	Middle Lock Lane, Hatton
30A23	Middle March Road, Bermuda
30A24	Middle March Road, Hilltop, Nune
117A41	Middle Road Farm, Ufton
116C34	Middle Road, Harbury
108B32	Middle Spernall Farm, Morgrove Coppice, Spernall
108B32	Middle Spernall Farm, Spernall
172B41	Middle Street, Armscote, Tredingto
180B12	Middle Street, Ilmington
89C14	Middle Street, Kilsby
114B42	Middle Watchbury Farm, Barford
31A31	Middleburg Close, Whitestone, Nuneaton
172B24	Middlefield Lane, Newbold on Sto Tredington
186B11	Middlehurst Farm, Shipston on St
107B22	Middlemore Close, Studley
184B12	Middleton Close, Middle Tysoe, T
10B44	Middleton House Farm, Middleto
10B31	Middleton Lane, Hunts Green, Middleton
172B23	Middleton Lane, Newbold on Sto Tredington
9C23	Middleton Wood Farm, Middleto
107B24	Middletown, Studley
107B24	Middletown Lane, Littlewood Gr Sambourne
107B24	Middletown Lane, Middletown, Sambourne
107B23	Middletown Lane, Sambourne
132C43	Middletown, Little Morrell, More Morrell
22A44	Midland Road, Nuneaton
23B31	Midland Shire Farmers, Nuneato
102A43	Midland Shire Farmers, Stockton
64B32	Milburn Grange Farm, Stoneleig
5B33	Milburn, Stoneydelph, Tamwort
22C32	Milby Drive, Saint Nicholas Parl Nuneaton
144B42	Milcote Hall Farm, Milcote
144C41	Milcote Hall, Milcote, Stratford Avon
159A11	Milcote Manor Farm, Milcote
144C42	Milcote Road, Clifford Chamber
158C14	Milcote Road, Weston Sands, W on Avon
145B32	Mildmay Close, Stratford upon
40C34	Mile Tree Farm, Carroway Hea Bedworth
40C34	Mile Tree Lane, Bedworth
70C32	Milestone Drive, Kingsway, Ru
42B31	Milethorn Farm, Hopsford, Wo
98A33	Milford Court, Leamington Spa

p ref	Address
A22	Milford Street, Nuneaton
31	Milking Lane, Henley in Arden
A22	Mill Bank, Percy Estate, Warwick
A24	Mill Close, Braunston
A34	Mill Close, Broom, Bidford
C13	Mill Close, Norton Lindsey
A23	Mill Close, Southam
C14	Mill Close, Tredington
31	Mill Close, Whitestone, Nuneaton
C44	Mill Court, Shipston on Stour
C13	Mill Crescent, Kineton
12	Mill Crescent, Kingsbury
A24	Mill Crescent, Southam
42	Mill End, Kenilworth
42	Mill Farm Caravan Park, Bedworth
1	Mill Farm Close, Dunchurch
2	Mill Farm, Great Packington
1	Mill Farm, Marston Jabbett
4	Mill Farm, Maxstoke
42	Mill Farm, Middle Tysoe, Tysoe
34	Mill Farm, Newbold Pacey
1	Mill Farm, Newton And Biggin
31	Mill Farm, Upper Shuckburgh
23	Mill Farm, Walton, Wellesbourne
43	Mill Farm, Wolfhamcote
	Mill Hill, Baginton
	Mill Hill, Finham
	Mill House Close, Edmonscote, Leamington Spa
3	Mill House, Fenny Compton
41	Mill Lane, Alveston
	Mill Lane, Ansley
1	Mill Lane, Aston Cantlow
2	Mill Lane, Barford
4	Mill Lane, Broom, Bidford
	Mill Lane, Bulkington, Bedworth
	Mill Lane, Burton Hastings
1	Mill Lane, Cleeve Prior
4	Mill Lane, Crimscote, Whitchurch
	Mill Lane, Cubbington
	Mill Lane, Dorridge
2	Mill Lane, Fenny Compton
	Mill Lane, Fillongley
	Mill Lane, Forshaw Heath, Tanworth in Arden
	Mill Lane, Halford
	Mill Lane, Harbury
	Mill Lane, Hartshill
	Mill Lane, Haselor
	Mill Lane, Kineton
	Mill Lane, Kingswood, Lapworth
	Mill Lane, Little Shrewley
	Mill Lane, Lowsonford, Lapworth
	Mill Lane, Mancetter
	Mill Lane, Newbold on Stour
	Mill Lane, Oversley Green, Alcester
	Mill Lane, Oversley Wood
	Mill Lane, Rowington
	Mill Lane, Sheepy Magna, Sheepy

Map ref	Address
	Mill Lane, Shrewley
144C24	Mill Lane, Stratford upon Avon
57A24	Mill Lane, Tanners Green, Wythall
143A43	Mill Lane, Welford on Avon
160C43	Mill Lane, Whitchurch
15A31	Mill Lane, Witherley
32C44	Mill Lane, Wolvey Heath, Wolvey
135B34	Mill Pit Farm, Hambridge, Bishops Itchington
60B33	Mill Pool Lane, Chessetts Wood, Packwood
60A32	Mill Pool Lane, Darley Green
14B14	Mill Race View, Atherstone
98A33	Mill Road, Leamington Spa
54B43	Mill Road, Rugby
119A21	Mill Road, Southam
182A43	Mill Street, Barcheston
40A14	Mill Street, Bedworth
87B14	Mill Street, Dunchurch
117B43	Mill Street, Harbury
164C21	Mill Street, Kineton
98A33	Mill Street, Leamington Spa
30B11	Mill Street, Nuneaton
182A43	Mill Street, Shipston on Stour
96C42	Mill Street, Warwick
30A44	Mill Terrace, Collycroft, Bedworth
30B13	Mill Walk, Nuneaton
40A12	Millais Close, Collycroft, Bedworth
64A42	Millbank Mews, Kenilworth
54C31	Millbeck, Brownsover, Rugby
64A44	Millbrook Grange Special School, Kenilworth
64A44	Millbrook Grange, Kenilworth
64B24	Millburn Grange Farm, Kenilworth
14B32	Milleners Court, Atherstone
87A11	Millers Close, Dunchurch
158B11	Millers Close, Welford on Avon
54B33	Millers Dale Close, Brownsover, Rugby
177B31	Millers Lane, Hornton
47B13	Millers Lane, Monks Kirby
96B32	Millers Road, Packmores, Warwick
92B22	Millfield Court, Henley in Arden
174A12	Millfield Farm, Pillerton Priors
98A33	Millfield, Leamington Spa
71C24	Millfields Avenue, Hillmorton, Rugby
97B31	Millhouse Drive, Edmonscote, Leamington Spa
101C11	Millhouse Farm, Birdingbury
97B31	Millhouse Terrace, Edmonscote, Leamington Spa
107B24	Millpeck, Studley
115C31	Millway Drive, Bishops Tachbrook
41B14	Milner Close, Ryton, Bedworth
2C31	Milner Drive, Shuttington
96B43	Milton Avenue, Forbes Estate, Warwick
40B24	Milton Close, Bedworth
59C12	Milton Close, Dorridge
59C12	Milton Road, Dorridge
97B32	Milverton Court, Leamington Spa

Map ref	Address
97B24	Milverton Crescent, Milverton, Leamington Spa
97B24	Milverton Crescent, W.milverton, Leamington Spa
97B32	Milverton Hill, Milverton, Leamington Spa
97B34	Milverton Lodge, Leamington Spa
97B32	Milverton Terrace, Milverton, Leamington Spa
5C31	Miners Walk, Polesworth
40B21	Miners Welfare Park, Bedworth
27B24	Mines Recue, Arley
14B34	Minions Close, Atherstone
161A44	Minits Lane, Alderminster
95C34	Minster Close, Hampton Magna, Budbrooke
188B13	Mint Row, Brailes
24A13	Minworth Road, Water Orton
22B14	Mira Drive, Higham, Higham on The Hill
22C11	Mira Proving Ground, Nuneaton
22A11	Mira, Redgate, Nuneaton
78C32	Miseltoe Farm, Shrewley
40B21	Mitchell Road, Bedworth
187A34	Mitford Bridge Farm, Burmington
187A33	Mitford Bridge, Burmington, Shipston on Stour
37C33	Moar Farm Stables, Corley Moor
37C33	Moar House Farm, Corley Moor
66B41	Moat Close, Bubbenhall
90A31	Moat Close, Mappleborough Green, Studley
86C21	Moat Close, Thurlaston
34A21	Moat Crescent, Chelmsley Wood
39A24	Moat Farm Drive, Goodyears End, Bedworth
72A34	Moat Farm Drive, Hillmorton, Rugby
39B31	Moat Farm Kennels, Goodyears End, Bedworth
91B12	Moat Farm Lane, Ullenhall
155B32	Moat Farm, Abbotts Salford, Salford Priors
63A13	Moat Farm, Burton Green, Kenilworth
59B12	Moat Farm, Dorridge
103C13	Moat Farm, Grandborough
72A34	Moat Farm, Hillmorton, Rugby
78C31	Moat Farm, Shrewley
114A23	Moat Green, Sherbourne
90A31	Moat House Court, Mappleborough Green
157C31	Moat House Farm, Dorsington
37B34	Moat House Farm, Fillongley
26A23	Moat House Farm, Shustoke
145A14	Moat House Hotel, Stratford upon Avon
35B32	Moat House Lane, Little Packington
26A23	Moat House Lane, Shustoke
32C42	Moat Lane, Wolvey Heath, Wolvey
35B24	Moathouse Farm, Little Packington
91B12	Moathouse Farm, Ullenhall
46B21	Mobbs Wood Farm, Coombe Fields
75B42	Mockley Manor Farm, Ullenhall
75B43	Mockley Wood Farm, Ullenhall
135B24	Model Farm, Bishops Itchington
134C14	Model Farm, Harbury
101A43	Model Farm, Model Village, Long Itchington
101A44	Model Village, Long Itchington
165C43	Mole End, Radway
167C31	Mollington Lane, Farnborough
167C41	Mollington Lane, Mollington
178A12	Mollington Lane, Warmington
178B14	Mollington Road, Mollington
178B32	Mollington Road, Shotteswell
116A22	Mollington Road, Whitnash
182B34	Monastry Farm, Honington
116B14	Moncrieff Drive, Whitnash
118B34	Monkey Barn Farm, Ufton
107B14	Monks Drive, Studley
160A12	Monks Farm, Clifford Chambers
43C33	Monks Kirby Grounds Farm, Monks Kirby
47C11	Monks Kirby Lane, Monks Kirby
50B34	Monks Road, Binley Woods
96B42	Monks Way, Forbes Estate, Warwick
29C13	Monmouth Gardens, Stockingford, Nuneaton
129C43	Monroe Devis Maternity Hospital, Tiddington, Stratford
25B31	Monsard Court, Shustoke
97A23	Montague Road, Percy Estate, Warwick
70C41	Montague Road, Woodlands, Rugby
29C14	Montana Walk, Nuneaton
25A43	Montfort Road, Coleshill
95C41	Montgomery Avenue, Hampton Magna, Budbrooke
144B22	Montgomery Close, Stratford upon Avon
70B23	Montgomery Drive, Bilton, Rugby
48B42	Montilo Farm, Harborough Magna
53A14	Montilo Lane, Harborough Parva, Harborough Magna
48C31	Montilo Lane, Pailton Pastures,
5B33	Montley, Stoneydelph, Tamworth
63C44	Montpelier House, Kenilworth
98A11	Montrose Avenue, Lillington, Leamington Spa
29C22	Montrose Drive, Heath End, Nuneaton
71A31	Montrose Road, Kingsway, Rugby
6A32	Monument View, Saint Helena, Polesworth
129A43	Monument Way, Stratford upon Avon
27A22	Monwode House Farm, Monwode, Ansley
27A12	Monwode Lea Farm, Over Whitacre
27A12	Monwode Lea Lane, Monwode, Ansley

Map ref	Address
C34	Moor Farm Close, Stretton on Dunsmore
B34	Moor Farm Stables, Wilmcote, Aston Cantlow
34	Moor Farm, Chapel Green, Fillongley
42	Moor Farm, Corley Moor, Corley
42	Moor Farm, Stretton on Dunsmore
B14	Moor Lane, Amington, Tamworth
41	Moor Lane, Willoughby
24	Moor Park Close, Whitestone, Nuneaton
33	Moor Poultry Farm, Corley Moor
31	Moor Road, Moor Wood, Hartshill
23	Moor Wood Farm, Hartshill
41	Moorash Farm, Kingsbury
12	Moorbarns Farm, Lutterworth
23	Moorcroft Close, Whitestone, Nuneaton
13	Moore Close, Woodloes, Warwick
33	Moore Walk, Myton, Warwick
11	Moorend Avenue A452, Chelmsley Wood
3	Moorend Avenue, Chelmsley Wood
32	Moorfield Road, Alcester
	Moorfields Farm, Stoneydelph
21	Moorhill Road, Whitnash
3	Moors Lane, Clifton upon Dunsmore
2	Moors Lane, Hillmorton, Rugby
31	Moorwood Crescent, Moor Wood, Hartshill
3	Moorwood Lane, Moor Wood, Hartshill
2	Mop Meadow Farm, Lowsonford, Rowington
12	Mordaunt Road, Charlecote
4	Moreall Meadows, Canley
3	Morelands Avenue, Kenilworth
22	Moreton Close, Stratford upon Avon
44	Moreton Hill, Moreton Morrell
12	Moreton Morrell Agricultural College, Moreton Morrell
1	Moreton Morrell Road, Lighthorne
4	Moreton Morrell Road, Little Morrell, Moreton Morrell
3	Moreton Morrell Road, Newbold Pacey
1	Moreton Morrell Road, Oakley Wood, Bishops Tachbrook
	Morgan Close, New Arley
2	Morgan Close, Norton Curlieu
1	Morgan Close, Studley
	Morland Close, Ryton, Bedworth
	Mornington Court, Coleshill
1	Morrell Farm, Little Morrell, Moreton Morrell
	Morrell Street, Leamington Spa
	Morris Drive, Caldwell, Nuneaton
4	Morris Drive, Whitnash
	Morris Hill, Dordon
	Morsdale Drive, Nuneaton
4	Morse Road, Whitnash
	Morson Crescent, Rugby
	Morston, Dosthill, Tamworth
80C14	Mortimer Road, Bulkington Estate, Kenilworth
108B14	Morton Common Farm, Morton Bagot
145A14	Morton Court, Stratford upon Avon
90C34	Morton Farm, Morton Bagot
97C24	Morton Street, Leamington Spa
139B31	Morton Woods Farm, Abbots Morton
54C31	Mosedale, Brownsover, Rugby
81A14	Moseley Road, Windy Arbour, Kenilworth
70C23	Moss Close, Overslade, Rugby
172B23	Moss Lane, Newbold on Stour, Tredington
74B31	Moss Lane, Pink Green, Beoley
98A41	Moss Street, Leamington Spa
29C21	Mossdale Crescent, Heath End, Nuneaton
5B33	Mossdale, Stoneydelph
97B14	Mosspaul Close, Leamington Spa
126A13	Mother Huffcap, Great Alne, Alcester
65B43	Motslow Hill, Stoneleigh
71A14	Moultrie Road, Rugby
144B13	Mount Crescent, Stratford upon Avon
40A13	Mount Drive, Bedworth
167C31	Mount Farm, Farnborough
177A11	Mount Farm, Ratley
181B44	Mount Farm, Shipston on Stour
119C12	Mount Pleasant Close, Stockton
36C21	Mount Pleasant Farm, Fillongley
18B44	Mount Pleasant Farm, Over Whitacre
144B14	Mount Pleasant Farm, Stratford upon Avon
91B14	Mount Pleasant Farm, Ullenhall
162B12	Mount Pleasant Farm, Walton Park, Wellesbourne
91B22	Mount Pleasant Lane, Ullenhall
40A14	Mount Pleasant Road, Bedworth
21C42	Mount Pleasant Terrace, Camphill, Nuneaton
135A24	Mount Pleasant, Bishops Itchington
119C12	Mount Pleasant, Stockton
144B13	Mount Pleasant, Stratford upon Avon
92B32	Mount Road, Henley in Arden
63C42	Mount Royal, Kenilworth
190B21	Mount Sorrell Farm, Great Wolford
30A11	Mount Street, Nuneaton
81B13	Mountbatten Avenue, Windy Arbour, Kenilworth
144B24	Mountbatten Close, Stratford upon Avon
119B23	Mountfield Gardens, Southam
147C11	Mountford Close, Wellesbourne Hasting, Wellesbourne
76C13	Mountford Farm, Lapworth
149B12	Mountford Rise, Lighthorne
78B34	Mousley End House Farm, Mousley End, Rowington
78B31	Mousley Hill Farm, Mousley End, Rowington

Map ref	Address
76A31	Mows Hill Farm, Mows Hill, Tanworth in Arden
76B33	Mows Hill Road, Beaudesert
76A34	Mows Hill Road, Mows Hill, Tanworth in Arden
16A14	Moxhull Hall, Moxhull
24A43	Moxhull Road, Kingshurst
23C43	Moxons Farm, Stretton Baskerville
71C31	Moyeady Avenue, The Paddox, Rugby
140B33	Mudwalls Farm, Salford Priors
31B24	Muirfield Close, Whitestone, Nuneaton
2A44	Muirfield, Amington, Tamworth
145A13	Mulberry Court, Stratford upon Avon
70A22	Mulberry Road, Bilton, Rugby
98A22	Mulberry Close, Leamington Spa
145A13	Mulberry Street, Stratford upon Avon
24A34	Mull Croft, Kingshurst
116B24	Mullard Drive, Whitnash
16C23	Mullensgrove Farm, Curdworth
24A43	Mullensgrove Road, Kingshurst
40B33	Murco Petroleum, Exhall, Bedworth
116A22	Murcott Court, Leamington Spa
116A21	Murcott Road E, Whitnash
116A21	Murcott Road W, Whitnash
116A22	Murcott Road, Whitnash, Leamington Spa
71B13	Murray Road, Rugby
5B33	Murton, Stoneydelph, Tamworth
37A23	Musson Hall Farm, Green End, Fillongley
37A23	Musson Hall, Fillongley
155A31	Myatt Fields, Harvington
155A31	Myatts Field, Harvington
120A31	Myer Bridge Farm, Napton on The Hill
72B31	Myers Road, Hillmorton, Rugby
65B14	Mylgrove, Finham
15A23	Mythe Lane, Witherley
14C21	Mythe View, Atherstone
97B41	Myton Crescent, Myton, Leamington Spa
97B42	Myton Crofts, Leamington Spa
97B44	Myton Farm, Whitnash, Leamington Spa
97A42	Myton Gardens, Myton, Leamington Spa
97A34	Myton Hamlet, Warwick
97A42	Myton Hospice, Myton, Warwick
97A42	Myton Lane, Myton, Warwick
97B41	Myton Park, Myton, Leamington Spa
97B42	Myton Road, Leamington Spa
97A42	Myton Road, Warwick
24A13	Myton Road, Water Orton
59C21	Nailsworth Road, Dorridge
29C22	Nairn Close, Heath End, Nuneaton
98A21	Napton Drive, Lillington, Leamington Spa
119C24	Napton Fields Farm, Southam
121A24	Napton Road, Lower Shuckburgh
120A14	Napton Road, Napton on The Hill
119C12	Napton Road, Stockton
97B31	Narborough Court, Leamington Spa
70C23	Nares Close, Rugby
93C11	Narrow Lane, Lowsonford
93C11	Narrow Lane, Sibson, Rowington
144C24	Narrow Lane, Stratford upon Avon
71B23	Naseby Road, Rugby
179B44	Nash Lane, Ebrington
145A22	National Farmers Union, Stratford upon Avon
145B12	National Farmers Union, Tiddington Stratford upon Avon
131B34	National Vegetable Research Station Wellesbourne
27C23	Ncb Central Rescue Station, Arley
22B43	Ndhq, Nuneaton
41B23	Neal Close, Bulkington, Bedworth
134C11	Neales Close, Harbury
179C14	Nebsworth Lane, Nebsworth, Ilmington
138A23	Nedge Hill Farm, Priors Marston
107C12	Needle Close, Studley
48C11	Neham Fields Farm, Monks Kirby
98A41	Neilson Street, Leamington Spa
180B14	Nelands Close, Ilmington
180B14	Nellands Close, Ilmington
97A23	Nelson Avenue, Percy Estate, War
162B33	Nelson Close, Ettington
96C32	Nelson Lane, Warwick
70B23	Nelson Way, Bilton, Rugby
5A12	Nemisia, Amington, Tamworth
70B11	Nene Court, Rugby
104B44	Nethercote Farm, Nethercot, Wolfhamcote
41A44	Nethergreen Farm, Barnacle, Shil
1A11	Netherseal Lane, Clifton Campvil
6A21	Nethersole Street, Polesworth
108C12	Netherstead Farm, Netherstead, Morton Bagot
50C34	Netherwood Heath Farm, Badde Clinton
14C24	Netherwood Industrial Estate, Atherstone
60C44	Netherwood Lane, Baddesley Cl
61A33	Netherwood Lane, Chadwick En
46A22	Nettle Hill Farm, Coombe Fields
34B24	Nevada Way, Chelmsley Wood
97C43	Nevill Close, Leamington Spa
96C24	Neville Grove, Woodloes, Warw
54B13	New Ash Tree Farm, Churchove Rugby
37C22	New Barn Farm, Fillongley
111C13	New Barn Farm, Langley
113B24	New Barn Farm, Sherbourne
188C23	New Barn Farm, Sutton Under]
181A11	New Bridges Farm, Blackwell, Tredington
144C24	New Broad Street, Stratford up Avon

ref	Address	Map ref	Address
12	New Century Way, Nuneaton	24B21	New Road, Water Orton
34	New Close, Hampton Magna, Budbrooke	170A13	New Row, Lower Quinton, Quinton
11	New Enclosure Farm, Combrook	144B21	New Row, Shottery
41	New End Farm, Coughton	54A44	New Station, Rugby
41	New End Farm, Great Barr, Coughton	13B23	New Street, Baddesley Ensor
1	New End Road, Maxstoke	5C33	New Street, Birchmoor, Polesworth
2	New Farm, Blackdown	41B22	New Street, Bulkington, Bedworth
13	New Farm, Blackwell, Tredington	82C44	New Street, Cubbington
12	New Farm, Chadshunt	6A43	New Street, Dordon
11	New Farm, Marton	63C42	New Street, Kenilworth
2	New Farm, Wolston	98A33	New Street, Leamington Spa
22	New Fields Farm, Long Itchington	120C41	New Street, Napton on The Hill
4	New House Farm, Cubbington	70C13	New Street, New Bilton, Rugby
31	New House Farm, Dorsington	181C44	New Street, Shipston on Stour
31	New House Farm, Edstone, Wootton Wawen	144C24	New Street, Stratford upon Avon
		145C11	New Street, Tiddington
1	New House Farm, Foul End, Kingsbury	96C41	New Street, Warwick
3	New House Farm, Greys Mallory, Bishops Tachbrook	132C22	New Wiggerland Farm, Newbold Pacey
3	New House Farm, Grove End, Brailes	120A14	New Zealand Farm, Napton on The Hill
4	New House Farm, Knightcote, Burton Dassett	54C44	Newall Close, Rugby
		122B42	Newbold Grounds, Catesby
32	New House Farm, Ladbroke	98A32	Newbold Lawn, Leamington Spa
2	New House Farm, Langley	147B12	Newbold Place, Charlecote
	New House Farm, Over Whitacre	97C34	Newbold Place, Leamington Spa
4	New House Farm, Pathlow, Aston Cantlow	147B12	Newbold Place, Wellesbourne
		47A42	Newbold Revel College, Newbold Revel, Stretton Under Fosse
	New House Farm, Stoneleigh		
	New House Farm, Weston Under Wetherley	47A34	Newbold Revel Road, Stretton Under Fosse
	New House Farm, Yelvertoft	53C33	Newbold Road, Newbold on Avon, Rugby
4	New Inn Farm, Rushford, Salford Priors	147B12	Newbold Road, Wellesbourne Hasting, Wellesbourne
	New Inn Lane, Abbotts Salford, Salford Priors	53B42	Newbold Rugby Football Club, Newbold on Avon
2	New Inn Lane, Salford Priors	98A31	Newbold Street, Leamington Spa
	New Kingswood Farm, Kenilworth	98A32	Newbold Terrace E, Leamington Spa
	New Land Farm, Bentley	97C34	Newbold Terrace, Leamington Spa
	New Manor Farm, Cubbington	174C13	Newborough Farm, Pillerton Priors
	New Park Cottage, Brailes	97C31	Newbrook Street, Leamington Spa
	New Park Farm, Ansley	4A23	Newburgh Close, Austrey
	New Road, Ash Green, Exhall	96B32	Newburgh Crescent, Packmores, Warwick
	New Road, Astley		
	New Road, Astwood Bank	98B44	Newbury Close, Sydenham Farm Estate, Leamington Spa
	New Road, Atherstone		
	New Road, Budbrooke	34B11	Newby Grove, Chelmsley Wood
	New Road, Ebrington	87B13	Newcombe Close, Dunchurch
	New Road, Gaydon	39B31	Newcomen Road, Goodyears End, Bedworth
	New Road, Goldicote, Alderminster		
	New Road, Henley in Arden	40A11	Newdegate Close, Bedworth
	New Road, Keresley Newlands, Keresley	30B11	Newdegate Place, Nuneaton
		30B11	Newdegate Street, Nuneaton
	New Road, Lowsonford, Rowington	39B21	Newdigate Colliery, Bedworth
	New Road, Norton Lindsey	30B11	Newdigate Place, Nuneaton
	New Road, Ratley, Ratley And Upton	40A13	Newdigate Road, Bedworth
	New Road, Shotteswell	9A43	Newdigate Road, Sutton Coldfield
	New Road, Shuttington	30B11	Newdigate Street, Nuneaton
	New Road, Tomstown, Studley		

Map ref	Address
116B14	Newdigate, Sydenham Farm Estate, Leamington
90A13	Newent Close, Redditch
64C24	Newera Farm, Stoneleigh
39B23	Newey Avenue, Goodyears End, Bedworth
81B13	Newfield Road, Windy Arbour, Kenilworth
98B41	Newgale Walk, Sydenham Farm Estate, Leamington Spa
37B31	Newhall Lane, Newhall Green, Fillongley
21B33	Newham Green, Camphill, Nuneaton
4A21	Newhouse Farm, Austrey
120B12	Newhouse Farm, Calcutt, Grandborough
17A21	Newhouse Farm, Marston, Lea Marston
10C24	Newhouse Farm, Middleton
74C43	Newhouse Farm, Oldberrow
38C33	Newland Farm House, Keresley Newlands, Keresley
39A34	Newland Hall Farm, Bedworth
39B33	Newland Lane, Keresley Newlands, Bedworth
70C13	Newland Street, New Bilton, Rugby
175B34	Newlands Farm House, Lower Tysoe, Tysoe
106C31	Newlands Farm, Astwood Bank
112B13	Newlands Farm, Norton Curlieu, Claverdon
94C12	Newlands Farm, Shrewley
39A34	Newlands Hall Farm, Keresley Newlands, Keresley
34A44	Newlands Lane, Chelmsley Wood
39B33	Newlands Lane, Keresley Newlands, Keresley
13B23	Newlands Road, Baddesley Ensor
59C11	Newlands Road, Dorridge
98B22	Newlands Road, Lillington, Leamington Spa
108C42	Newlands, Shelfield Green, Great Alne
107C21	Newlands, Studley
30C12	Newlyn Close, Nuneaton
39B31	Newlyn House, Goodyears End, Bedworth
40B11	Newman Close, Collycroft, Bedworth
144B24	Newmarket Close, Stratford upon Avon
48C11	Newnham Fields Farm, Monks Kirby, Willey
52A21	Newnham Lane, Kings Newnham
110B43	Newnham Lane, Newnham
110C41	Newnham Lane, Newnham, Aston Cantlow
44B41	Newnham Lodge Farm, Monks Kirby
98B13	Newnham Road, Lillington, Leamington Spa
9B31	Newpark Farm, Middleton
125A42	Newport Drive, Alcester

Map ref	Address
125A42	Newport Drive, Arrow
30C12	Newquay Close, Nuneaton
96C24	Newsholme Close, Woodloes, War~
32B12	Newstead Avenue, Hinckley
31A21	Newstead Close, Attleborough, Nuneaton
119A31	Newstead Drive, Southam
3C13	Newton Close Farm, Newton Regi~
21A21	Newton Close, Hartshill
1C33	Newton Field Farm, Appleby Mag~
54C24	Newton House Farm, Newton An~ Biggin
3C22	Newton Lane, Austrey
55A11	Newton Lane, Churchover
55A23	Newton Lane, Newton And Biggi~
3A13	Newton Lane, Seckington
26C31	Newton Lane, Shawbury, Fillongl~
1C43	Newton Lodge Farm, No Mans H~ Newton Regis
54C34	Newton Manor House Farm, New~ And Biggin
54B32	Newton Manor Lane, Brownsover Rugby
39C14	Newton Road, Bedworth Woodla~ Bedworth
23C31	Newton Road, Hinckley
55A33	Newton Road, Rugby
26C31	Newtown Lane, Shawbury, Fillor~
40A14	Newtown Road, Bedworth
22B43	Newtown Road, Nuneaton
105B23	Nibbits Lane, Braunston
13B13	Nicholas Estate, Grendon
22C34	Nicholas Park, Nuneaton
96C22	Nicholson Close, Woodloes, War
24A31	Nightingale Avenue, Kingshurst
14C21	Nightingale Close, Atherstone
126A11	Nightingale Close, Great Alne
98A34	Nightingale Court, Leamington ~
5A41	Nightingale, Tamworth
19A21	Nightingales Farm, Kingsbury
145C11	Nights Lane, Tiddington, Stratfo~ upon Avon
11B12	Nimbus, Dosthill, Tamworth
34A21	Nineacres Drive, Chelmsley Wo~
183A14	Nineveh Farm, Idlicote
22B42	Niton Road, Weddington, Nune~
4A21	No Mans Heath Lane, Austrey
96B44	Noble Close, Forbes Estate, Wa~
107B24	Node Hill, Littlewood Green, S~
107B22	Node Hill Close, Studley
174C23	Nolands Road, Pillerton Priors
188B14	Nook Farm, Grove End, Braile~
45B11	Noonhill Farm, Anstey
29C13	Norfolk Crescent, Stockingford~ Nuneaton
98A23	Norfolk Street, Leamington Sp~
181C34	Norluck Court, Shipston on St~
50B33	Norman Ashman Coppice, Bin~ Woods

Map ref	Address	Map ref	Address
A12	Norman Avenue, Nuneaton	170A14	Norton Drive, Lower Quinton, Quinton
C42	Norman Road, Newbold on Avon, Rugby	96C13	Norton Drive, Woodloes, Warwick
A33	Normandy Close, Hampton Magna, Budbrooke	60A24	Norton Green Lane, Darley Green
		60A24	Norton Green Lane, Dorridge
'23	Normandy Farm, Clifton upon Dunsmore	169A43	Norton Hall Farm, Mickleton
'21	North Avenue, Bedworth	4A24	Norton Hill, Austrey
B24	North Close, Braunston	4B24	Norton Hill, Twycross
43	North Close, Cubbington	58A23	Norton Lane, Cheswick Green, Earlswood
43	North Division Headquarters, Nuneaton	57C13	Norton Lane, Tidbury Green
B11	North Drive, Wootton Wawen	4B44	Norton Lane, Twycross
333	North End, Long Marston	112B14	Norton Lea, Lower Norton, Wolverton
C31	North Farm Road, Cherington	24C21	Norton Leas Estate, Coleshill
C23	North Farm, Cherington	71A33	Norton Leys, Hillside, Rugby
B12	North Farm, Priors Marston	24C24	Norton Road, Coleshill
A43	North Four Shire Stone Farm, Little Compton	164B23	Norton School Farm, Little Kineton, Kineton
21	North Lodge Farm, Arbury, Nuneaton	151B41	Nortons Close, Northend, Burton Dassett
33	North Lodge Farm, Wolston		
43	North Road, Clifton upon Dunsmore	23A31	Norwich Close, Saint Nicholas Park, Nuneaton
43	North Rock, Warwick	39C13	Norwood Farm, Bedworth Woodlands, Bedworth
1	North Rookery Farm, Rookery, Rowington	44B33	Norwood Farm, Willey
1	North Street, Atherstone	97C22	Norwood House, Leamington Spa
3	North Street, Kilsby	4A21	Nove Haven, Austrey
2	North Street, Marton	97C13	Nova Lodge, Leamington Spa
3	North Street, Rugby	39C42	Novotel, Exhall, Bedworth
4	North Street, Stockingford, Nuneaton	23C31	Nuffield Road, Hinckley
3	North Street, Swinford	58B12	Nugent Grove, Cheswick Green
2	North View, Walsgrave on Sowe	30A11	Nuneaton Borough Football Ground, Nuneaton
3	North Villiers Street, Leamington Spa	31A12	Nuneaton Fields, Nuneaton
12	North Way, Chelmsley Wood	30A22	Nuneaton Island To Griff Island, Bedworth by pass
3	North Way, Leamington Spa		
	Northampton Lane, Dunchurch	22C22	Nuneaton Lane, Higham, Higham on The Hill
	Northampton Lane, Thurlaston		
3	Northampton Road, Ryton on Dunsmore	20B33	Nuneaton Road, Ansley
		41B21	Nuneaton Road, Bulkington
	Northcote Road, Rugby	40A12	Nuneaton Road, Collycroft, Bedworth
	Northcote Street, Leamington Spa	37C13	Nuneaton Road, Fillongley
	Northcote Walk, Whittington, Atherstone	21B13	Nuneaton Road, Hartshill
		15A41	Nuneaton Road, Mancetter
2	Northdown House, Long Compton	27B11	Nuneaton Road, Monwode Lea, Ansley
4	Northend Farm, Northend, Burton Dassett	26C13	Nuneaton Road, Over Whitacre
		30B14	Nuneaton Rugby Football Ground, Nuneaton
2	Northend Road, Fenny Compton		
2	Northfield Farm, Stretton on Fosse	30A22	Nuneaton To Griff, Bedworth by pass
3	Northfield Road, Southam	30A22	Nuneaton To Griff, Old Arley
4	Northfields Farm, Priors Marston	95A31	Nunhold Farm Business Centre, Hatton
	Northgate Street, Warwick	95A23	Nunhold Farm Cottage, Hatton
	Northumberland Avenue, Stockingford, Nuneaton	95A31	Nunhold Farm, Hatton
		61C34	Nunley Farm, Wroxhall
	Northumberland Court, Leamington Spa	83C12	Nunwood Lane, Bubbenhall
	Northumberland Road, Leamington Spa	83C14	Nunwood Lane, Wappenbury
	Northvale Close, Kenilworth	35B32	Nursery Farm, Little Packington
	Nortoft Farm, Kilsby	116A12	Nursery Lane, Whitnash
	Nortoft Lodge Farm, Kilsby	20C33	Nursery Road, Ansley Common, Ansley
	Norton Culieu Lane, Claverdon		

Map ref	Address
14C33	Nursery Road, Atherstone
28B11	Nuthurst Crescent, Ansley
76B23	Nuthurst Farm, Tanworth in Arden
76B11	Nuthurst Grange Lane, Nuthurst, Tanworth in Arden
28C33	Nuthurst Lane, Astley
76B34	Nuthurst Lane, Beaudesert
76A24	Nuthurst Lane, Kemps Green, Tanworth in Arden
28B14	Nuthurst Lane, Nuneaton
91C31	Nutlands Farm, Ullenhall
23C42	Nutts Lane, Hinckley
27C23	Oak Avenue, Arley
65C22	Oak Close, Baginton
40B12	Oak Close, Bedworth
65C21	Oak Farm, Baginton
50A23	Oak Farm, Binley Woods
38B13	Oak Farm, Fillongley
107A13	Oak Farm, Sambourne
112A41	Oak Farm, Snitterfield
70C22	Oak Field Road, Rugby
167C14	Oak House Farm, Farnborough
194B12	Oak House Farm, Kitebrook
73C34	Oak Lane, Crick
59A24	Oak Lodge Farm, Cheswick Green
98A34	Oak Place, Leamington Spa
24C44	Oak Rise, Coleshill
145C13	Oak Road, Tiddington, Stratford upon Avon
71A21	Oak Street, Rugby
24A43	Oak Thorpe Drive, Kingshurst
59C11	Oak Tree Close, Dorridge
11B42	Oak Tree Close, Kingsbury
98A21	Oak Tree Close, Leamington Spa
132B44	Oak Tree Close, Little Morrell, Moreton Morrell
47B32	Oak Tree Cottage, Stretton Under Fosse
124A24	Oak Tree Lane, Cook Hill, Inkberrow
107A21	Oak Tree Lane, Sambourne
154C32	Oak Tree Road, Harvington
97A21	Oak Wood Grove, Percy Estate, Warwick
50B31	Oakdale Road, Binley Woods
93C41	Oakdene Close, Claverdon
94C23	Oakdene Crescent, Hatton Station, Hatton
22B34	Oakdene Crescent, Weddington, Nuneaton
14C33	Oakfield Gardens, Atherstone
97C21	Oakfield House, Leamington Spa
70C22	Oakfield Place, Rugby
8A33	Oakfield Way, Sheepy Magna, Sheepy
41B22	Oakham Crescent, Ryton, Bedworth
179B44	Oakham Farm, Ebrington
162A12	Oakham Farm, Loxley
195A24	Oakham Road, Little Compton
194B12	Oakhouse Farm, Little Compton
98A13	Oakhurst, Leamington Spa
110C33	Oakland Farm, Wootton Wawen

Map ref	Address
74A21	Oakland Poultry Farm, Bransons Cr● Beoley
81A13	Oaklands Court, Kenilworth
45B22	Oaklands Farm, Anstey
95C24	Oaklands Farm, Budbrooke
16A44	Oaklands, Curdworth
128C43	Oakleigh Road, Stratford upon Avc●
150A12	Oakleigh, Lighthorne Heath
39B33	Oakley Court, Exhall, Bedworth
66A33	Oakley Hill Farm, Baginton
115B43	Oakley Wood Farm, Oakley Wood, Bishops Tachbrook
115C43	Oakley Wood Road, Oakley Wood, Bishops Tachbrook
61C24	Oakley, Frogmore
72A12	Oakridge Farm, Clifton upon Dun●
98B11	Oakridge Road, Lillington, Leamir● Spa
21B34	Oakroyd Crescent, Camphill, Nun●
97C22	Oaks Corner, Leamington Spa
80B14	Oaks Farm, Kenilworth
80C14	Oaks Road, Bulkington Estate, Kenilworth
94C21	Oakslade Farm, Hatton Station, H●
111A42	Oaktree Close, Bearley
93C23	Oaktree Farm, Yarningale, Claver●
13B24	Oakwood Close, Grendon
74C31	Oakwood Farm, Tanworth in Ard●
30B12	Oasten Road, Nuneaton
22C43	Oaston Road, Nuneaton
168C44	Oat Hill Farm, Claydon
193B23	Oatleyhill Farm, Hook Norton
30A21	Oban Drive, Heath End, Nuneat●
76A12	Obelisk Farm, Tanworth in Arde●
31A22	Oberon Close, Whitestone, Nune●
70B42	Oberon Close, Woodlands, Rugb●
21A14	Occupation Lane, Hartshill, Nun●
74C32	Ockwood Farm, Traps Green, Tanworth in Arden
100C34	Odingsell Drive, Long Itchingto●
81A11	Offa Drive, Whitemore, Kenilwc●
116A12	Offa Road, Leamington Spa
99A32	Offchurch Bury, Offchurch
99C34	Offchurch Fruit Farm, Offchurc●
99A34	Offchurch House, Offchurch
98C42	Offchurch Lane, Radford Semel●
98C11	Offchurch Road, Cubbington
98B41	Ogmore Road, Sydenham Farm, Leamington
96B34	Oken Court, Warwick
96B32	Oken Road, Packmores, Warwi●
45A34	Olaf Place, Walsgrave on Sowe●
147A31	Old Airfield Estate, Loxley, Wellesbourne
158C34	Old Airfield, Long Marston
55C24	Old Barn Farm, Catthorpe
135C22	Old Barn Farm, Ladbroke
176B12	Old Barn House, Radway

Map ref	Address
7A14	Old Brook Cottage, Willington, Barcheston
A31	Old Budbrooke Road, Budbrooke
A31	Old Budbrooke Road, Hampton Magna, Budbrooke
C43	Old Butt Road, Shipston on Stour
A14	Old Church Road, Water Orton
22	Old Coventry Lane, Brook End, Kingsbury
41	Old Edwardians Rugby Ground, Nuneaton
12	Old Farm Lane, Hoggerills End, Nether Whitacre
42	Old Farm Road, Mancetter
44	Old Farm, Grandborough
A22	Old Farm, Honington
A23	Old Ford Avenue, Southam
42	Old Forge Road, Fenny Drayton
2	Old Grove Farm, Tanworth in Arden
A42	Old Halford Road, Ettington
4	Old Hall Court, Newton Regis
3	Old Hall Farm, Fillongley
42	Old Hall Farm, Great Packington
4	Old Hall Farm, Seckington
14	Old Hill, Long Compton
4	Old Hinckley Road, Nuneaton
4	Old Holly Lane, Grendon, Atherstone
3	Old Holly Lane, Whittington, Grendon
3	Old House Farm, Ansley
1	Old House Farm, Bubbenhall
21	Old House Farm, Hill, Leamington Hastings
1	Old House Farm, Hoggerills End, Nether Whitacre
41	Old House Farm, Marraway Turn, Fulbrook
31	Old House Farm, Sawbridge, Wolfhamcote
2	Old House Farm, Snitterfield
	Old House Farm, Weston Under Wetherley
	Old House Lane, Corley Ash, Corley
	Old Leicester Road, Glebe Farm Estate, Rugby
	Old Leicester Road, Swift Valley Estate, Rugby
	Old Lodge Farm, Binley Woods
1	Old Lodge Farm, Lower Tysoe, Tysoe
	Old Meeting Yard, Bedworth
	Old Mill Court, Coleshill
	Old Mill Road, Cole End, Coleshill
	Old Milverton Lane, Blackdown
	Old Milverton Lane, Milverton, Leamington Spa
	Old Milverton Road, Milverton, Leamington Spa
	Old Park Farm, Beausale
	Old Pasture Farm, Hampton Lucy
	Old Penns Yard, Gatehouse Lane, Bedworth

Map ref	Address
74B32	Old Perrymill Farm, Pink Green, Beoley
14C31	Old Plough Close, Atherstone
96C33	Old Pound, Warwick
12A44	Old Rail Farm, Hurley Common, Kingsbury
49B41	Old Rectory Close, Churchover
125A34	Old Rectory Gardens, Alcester
135B24	Old Road, Bishops Itchington
105A32	Old Road, Braunston
195C12	Old Road, Long Compton
176C12	Old Road, Ratley
181C44	Old Road, Shipston on Stour
119A34	Old Road, Southam
176B12	Old School House, Radway
95C43	Old School Lane, Hampton on The Hill, Budbrooke
149C11	Old School Lane, Lighthorne
127C31	Old School Lane, Wilmcote, Drayton
98A14	Old School Mews, Lillington, Leamington Spa
75B43	Old Spinney Farm, Ullenhall
96C33	Old Square, Warwick
112C14	Old Stables, Norton Lindsey
125B33	Old Stratford Road, Oversley Wood, Alcester
112A13	Old Thatched Cottage, Norton Curlieu, Claverdon
135B43	Old Town Farm, Bishops Itchington
144C32	Old Town Mews, Stratford upon Avon
145A23	Old Town, Stratford upon Avon
145A22	Old Tramway Lane, Stratford upon Avon
184B12	Old Tree Lane, Upper Tysoe, Tysoe
162A34	Old Warwick Road, Ettington
59B41	Old Warwick Road, Hockley Heath, Cheswick Green
59B44	Old Warwick Road, Lapworth
97C41	Old Warwick Road, Leamington Spa
94C13	Old Warwick Road, Shrewley
94B12	Old Warwick Road, Shrewley Common, Rowington
15B41	Old Watling Street, Merevale, Atherstone
38A41	Old Winnings Road, Keresley Newlands, Keresley
29C22	Oldany Way, Heath End, Nuneaton
91B23	Oldberrow Court Farm, Oldberrow
74C43	Oldberrow Hill Farm, Oldberrow
74B42	Oldberrow Lane Farm, Gorcott Hill, Oldberrow
21A24	Oldberry View, Hartshill
146B23	Oldbrough Farm, Stratford upon Avon
20C24	Oldbury Road, Hartshill
21A31	Oldbury Road, Oldbury, Ansley
104A12	Olde Farm, Willoughby
78B43	Oldfield Farm, Rowington
78B43	Oldfield Hill Farm, Rowington
53A44	Oldham Way, Long Lawford
70A12	Oldham Way, Rugby

Map ref	Address
61A22	Oldwich Farm, Chadwick End
61B24	Oldwich House Farm, Chadwick End
61C23	Oldwich Lane E, Frogmore
61B23	Oldwich Lane, Chadwick End
61C23	Oldwich Lane, Frogmore
70C14	Oliver Street, Rugby
45A32	Oliver Way, Anstey
32A31	Olton Close, Burton Hastings
30A11	Olton Place, Nuneaton
97B44	Olympus Avenue, Leamington Spa
152A23	Ongar Farm, Knightcote, Burton Dassett
88C13	Onley Fields Farm, onley
71B44	Onley Fields Farm, Rugby
88C11	Onley Lane, onley
71B41	Onley Lane, Rugby
97C13	Onslow Croft, Leamington Spa
24B21	Openfield Close, Water Orton
24B21	Openfield Croft, Water Orton
96C44	Orchard, The, Warwick
174B41	Orchard, The, Whatcote
4A21	Orchard Close, Austrey
156B12	Orchard Close, Bidford
135B32	Orchard Close, Bishops Itchington
188C13	Orchard Close, Brailes
21A33	Orchard Close, Chapel End, Hartshill
25A33	Orchard Close, Coleshill
16A34	Orchard Close, Curdworth
18B11	Orchard Close, Hurley, Kingsbury
6A13	Orchard Close, Polesworth
181C44	Orchard Close, Shipston on Stour
158B13	Orchard Close, Welford on Avon
15A31	Orchard Close, Witherley
42B14	Orchard Close, Wolvey
14B34	Orchard Court, Atherstone
97C21	Orchard Court, Leamington Spa
170A21	Orchard Court, Quinton
125A42	Orchard Drive, Alcester
155A12	Orchard Drive, Rushford, Salford Priors
39B22	Orchard Farm, Market End, Bedworth
119C12	Orchard Grove, Stockton
145A42	Orchard Hill Farm, Stratford upon Avon
81B13	Orchard Lane, Windy Arbour, Kenilworth
144C44	Orchard Place, Clifford Chambers
155A31	Orchard Place, Harvington
90A33	Orchard Place, Mappleborough Green, Studley
143A23	Orchard Rise, Binton
59B33	Orchard Road, Hockley Heath, Cheswick Green
40B11	Orchard Street, Collycroft, Bedworth
30B12	Orchard Street, Nuneaton
70B32	Orchard Way, Bilton, Rugby
66B42	Orchard Way, Bubbenhall
21B41	Orchard Way, Camphill, Nuneaton
101A33	Orchard Way, Long Itchington

Map ref	Address
119B21	Orchard Way, Southam
144C21	Orchard Way, Stratford upon Avon
67C41	Orchard Way, Stretton on Dunsmo
107C31	Orchard Way, Studley
147B14	Orford Close, Wellesbourne Hastin Wellesbourne
28C11	Orford Rise, Galley Common, Nun
165C43	Oriel Cottage, Radway
30A21	Orkney Close, Heath End, Nuneato
24A34	Orkney Croft, Kingshurst
70B42	Orlando Close, Woodlands, Rugby
15A12	Ormes Lane, Ratcliffe Culey, Withe
128B44	Orrian Close, Stratford upon Avon
71A33	Orson Leys, Hillside, Rugby
24A13	Orton Close, Water Orton
4C31	Orton House Farm, Twycross
4A32	Orton Lane, Austrey
4B44	Orton Lane, Twycross
6C13	Orton Road, Little Warton, Polesw
55A43	Orwell Close, Clifton upon Dunsn
21A43	Orwell Close, Galley Common, Nuneaton
116A13	Osborne Court, Whitnash, Leamin Spa
45A33	Oslo Gardens, Walsgrave on Sow
31B31	Osprey Close, Whitestone, Nunea
5A41	Osprey, Tamworth
93B32	Ossetts Hole Lane, Yarningale, Claverdon
97B32	Oswald Road, Milverton, Leamin Spa
70B14	Oswald Way, New Bilton, Rugby
70B44	Othello Close, Woodlands, Rugby
37C13	Ousterne Lane, Fillongley
90C23	Outhill Farm, Outhill, Studley
14B43	Outwards Farm, Mancetter
14B41	Outwoods Close, Atherstone
36B33	Outwoods Farm, Outwoods, Gre Packington
36A34	Outwoods Lane, Outwoods, Gre Packington
40B22	Oval Football Ground, Bedworth
71B32	Oval Road, Rugby
75A23	Overbare Close, Tanworth in Ar
115B32	Overberry Orchard, Bishops Tac
97B13	Overell Green, Leamington Spa
8B22	Overfield Farm, Sheepy
16A23	Overgreen Farm, Overgreen
12B13	Overhouse Farm, Freasley, King
70C31	Overslade Lane, Bilton, Rugby
70C32	Overslade Manor Drive, Kingsv Rugby
141A22	Oversley Farm, Wixford
125C42	Oversley Hill Farm, Alcester
125B31	Oversley House, Alcester
125B24	Oversley House, Kinwarton, A
42C41	Overstone Road, Withybrook
24B13	Overton Drive, Water Orton
98C44	Overtons Close, Radford Seme

Map ref	Address
43	Overwoods Road, Tamworth
334	Owen Square, Atherstone
334	Owen Street, Atherstone
A32	Ox Hayes Farm, Ansley
C32	Oxford Close, Saint Nicholas Park, Nuneaton
24	Oxford Place, Leamington Spa
C31	Oxford Road, Frankton
C12	Oxford Road, Long Compton
A13	Oxford Road, Marton
21	Oxford Road, Princethorpe
34	Oxford Road, Ryton on Dunsmore
43	Oxford Road, Stretton on Dunsmore
24	Oxford Row, Leamington Spa
24	Oxford Street, Leamington Spa
13	Oxford Street, Rugby
A32	Oxford Street, Southam
A31	Oxford Way, Mountford, Wellesbourne
443	Oxhill Bridle Road, Pillerton Hersey
A24	Oxhill Farm, Oxhill
A24	Oxhill Hill Farm, Oxhill
443	Oxhill Road, Middle Tysoe
12	Oxhill Road, Middle Tysoe, Tysoe
24	Oxhouse Farm, Butlers Marston
3	Oxley Drive, Finham
22	Oxstalls Farm, Admington
3	Oxstalls Farm, Tanworth in Arden
42	Oxstals Farm, Stratford upon Avon
42	Oxway Close, Shipston on Stour
1	Packington Farm, Coleshill
3	Packington Hall, Little Packington, Coleshill
4	Packington Lane, Bickenhill
2	Packington Lane, Coleshill
4	Packington Lane, Little Packington
2	Packington Lane, Maxstoke
3	Packington Place, Leamington Spa
	Packington Tip, Little Packington
	Packmore Street, Packmores, Warwick
42	Packsaddle Hill, Hampton Lucy
	Packwood Avenue, Hillmorton, Rugby
	Packwood Close, Dorridge
3	Packwood Close, Sydenham Farm Estate, Leamington Spa
	Packwood Court, Kenilworth
	Packwood Farm, Packwood, Lapworth
	Packwood House Special School, Packwood, Lapworth
	Packwood House, Packwood, Lapworth
	Packwood Lane, Packwood, Lapworth
	Packwood Road, Darley Green
	Packwood Road, Dorridge
	Packwood Road, Packwood, Lapworth
	Packwood Special School, Packwood, Lapworth
	Paddiford Place, Stockingford, Nuneaton
	Paddock Close, Napton on The Hill
	Paddock Close, Polesworth
	Paddock Close, Wolston

Map ref	Address
38B14	Paddock Farm, Astley
38B14	Paddock Farm, Corley
144B24	Paddock Lane, Stratford upon Avon
145B23	Paddock Place, Stratford upon Avon
60A21	Paddock Road, Dorridge
71C31	Paddox Court, Hillmorton, Rugby
98B43	Padmore Court, Sydenham Farm Estate, Leamington Spa
145A11	Padua, Stratford upon Avon
177B34	Pages Lane, Hornton
83C11	Pagets Lane, Blue Lias
66B44	Pagets Lane, Bubbenhall
48A22	Pailton Fields Farm, Pailton
47C23	Pailton House, Pailton
48B24	Pailton Pastures Farm, Pailton Pastures, Pailton
53A14	Pailton Road, Harborough Magna
23A33	Pallett Drive, Saint Nicholas Park, Nuneaton
145A21	Palmer Court, Stratford upon Avon
116B21	Palmer Road, Whitnash
72A32	Palmers Close, Hillmorton, Rugby
128B44	Pampas Close, Stratford upon Avon
23A31	Pangbourne Close, Saint Nicholas Park, Nuneaton
53C33	Pantolf Place, Newbold on Avon, Rugby
97C24	Parade, Leamington Spa
96C31	Paradise Street, Packmores, Warwick
71B13	Paradise Street, Rugby
45A32	Paradise Way, Walsgrave on Sowe
40B34	Paragon Way, Exhall, Bedworth
11B12	Parbury, Dosthill, Tamworth
30C13	Park Avenue, Attleborough, Nuneaton
25A41	Park Avenue, Coleshill
6A34	Park Avenue, Saint Helena, Polesworth
107C23	Park Avenue, Studley
132B12	Park Barn Farm, Oakley Wood, Bishops Tachbrook
166C32	Park Close, Avon Dassett
93C42	Park Close, Claverdon
64A44	Park Close, Kenilworth
97B41	Park Close, Myton, Warwick
127C31	Park Close, Wilmcote, Drayton
64A41	Park Court, Kenilworth
144C11	Park Court, Stratford upon Avon
30B14	Park Drive, Attleborough, Nuneaton
93C42	Park Drive, Claverdon
97C33	Park Drive, Leamington Spa
37B21	Park Farm Cottage, Fillongley
29A24	Park Farm, Arbury, Nuneaton
74B24	Park Farm, Aspley Heath, Tanworth in Arden
166C32	Park Farm, Avon Dassett
61A43	Park Farm, Baddesley Clinton
41A41	Park Farm, Barnacle, Shilton
92A22	Park Farm, Beaudesert
35A42	Park Farm, Bickenhill
115A24	Park Farm, Bishops Tachbrook
93C42	Park Farm, Claverdon

Map ref	Address
148B43	Park Farm, Compton Verney
173A21	Park Farm, Ettington
129C13	Park Farm, Hampton Lucy
10B33	Park Farm, Hunts Green, Middleton
121C42	Park Farm, Lower Shuckburgh
6A24	Park Farm, Polesworth
160A23	Park Farm, Preston on Stour
82B14	Park Farm, Stareton, Stoneleigh
128C31	Park Farm, Stratford upon Avon
69A41	Park Farm, Stretton on Dunsmore
74B43	Park Farm, Studley
56B13	Park Farm, Swinford
121C42	Park Farm, Upper Shuckburgh
84A34	Park Farm, Wappenbury
160C43	Park Farm, Whitchurch
110A21	Park Farm, Wootton Wawen
119A24	Park Fields, Southam
10B24	Park Gate Farm, Middleton
24B21	Park Grove, Water Orton
140C43	Park Hall Farm, Salford Priors
155B12	Park Hall Mews, Salford Priors
155B12	Park Hall, Salford Priors
161B12	Park Hill Farm, Goldicote, Loxley
173A42	Park Hill Farm, Halford
64A43	Park Hill, Kenilworth
121B24	Park Hill, Lower Shuckburgh
121C24	Park Hill, Upper Shuckburgh
37B22	Park House Farm, Fillongley
129B11	Park House, Snitterfield
121C23	Park Lane Farm, Lower Shuckburgh
28A44	Park Lane Farm, Wood End, Astley
134B12	Park Lane Terrace, Harbury
170C41	Park Lane, Admington
27B44	Park Lane, Fillongley
28C12	Park Lane, Galley Common, Nuneaton
126A12	Park Lane, Great Alne
134B12	Park Lane, Harbury
170A21	Park Lane, Lower Quinton, Quinton
121C23	Park Lane, Lower Shuckburgh
29A13	Park Lane, Robinsons End, Nuneaton
129C11	Park Lane, Snitterfield
119A24	Park Lane, Southam
29A13	Park Lane, Stockingford, Nuneaton
28A44	Park Lane, Wood End, Nuneaton
161B22	Park Leys Farm, Goldicote, Alderminster
164B21	Park Piece, Kineton
13A24	Park Road, Baddesley Ensor
40A22	Park Road, Bedworth
24C42	Park Road, Coleshill
64A41	Park Road, Kenilworth
97C12	Park Road, Leamington Spa
71A11	Park Road, Rugby
6A34	Park Road, Saint Helena, Polesworth
144C11	Park Road, Stratford upon Avon
96C33	Park Side, Warwick
30B14	Park Street, Attleborough, Nuneaton
97C32	Park Street, Leamington Spa
40A33	Park View Close, Exhall, Bedworth

Map ref	Address
172B24	Park View Lane, Newbold on Stour, Tredington
124C44	Park View, Arrow
59B42	Park View, Hockley Heath, Cheswic Green
29B12	Park View Court, Nuneaton
8A34	Park View, Sheepy Magna, Sheepy
96C34	Park View, Warwick
71A11	Park Walk, Rugby
45A32	Park Way, Anstey
184B12	Parke Row, Middle Tysoe, Tysoe
96B34	Parkes Court, Warwick
96B34	Parkes Street, Warwick
64A44	Parkfield Drive, Kenilworth
107C4	Parkfield House Farm, Coughton
25A41	Parkfield Road, Coleshill
39A42	Parkfield Road, Keresley Newlands Keresley
53C43	Parkfield Road, Newbold on Avon, Rugby
14C13	Parkinson Drive, Atherstone
98B11	Parklands Avenue, Lillington, Leamington Spa
163B34	Parkslade Farm, Pillerton Hersey
97C22	Parmiter House, Leamington Spa
70C14	Parnell Close, Rugby
40B44	Parrots Grove, Sutton Stop, Coven
40B44	Parrotts Grove, Bedworth
21B34	Parrs Piece, Camphill, Nuneaton
115C31	Parsonage Close, Bishops Tachbro
36B32	Parsonage Farm, Outwoods, Grea Packington
196A41	Parsonage Farm, Salford
186C11	Parsons Close, Shipston on Stour
44C41	Parsons Close, Willey
134C24	Parsons Farm, Bishops Itchington
34B14	Partridge Close, Chelmsley Wood
144B11	Partridge Road, Stratford upon A
146B44	Pastures Farm Lane, Loxley
146B44	Pastures Farm, Loxley
128A24	Pathlow Farm, Pathlow, Aston Cantlow
128B21	Pathlow Paddock Farm, Pathlow, Aston Cantlow
97A22	Pattens Road, Percy Estate, Warw
54B32	Patterdale, Brownsover, Rugby
98A21	Payne Close, Leamington Spa
70B14	Paynes Lane, Rugby
145A13	Payton Street, Stratford upon Av
34B23	Peace Walk, Chelmsley Wood
147B22	Peacock Court, Mountford, Wellesbourne
93C21	Peacock Farm, Holywell, Claver
175C43	Peacock Lane, Middle Tysoe, Ty
22C34	Peak Avenue, Saint Nicholas Pa Nuneaton
21A41	Peak Farm, Robinsons End, Nu
21C41	Pear Tree Avenue, Camphill, N
11B44	Pear Tree Avenue, Kingsbury

p ref	Address	Map ref	Address
B41	Pear Tree Close, Long Marston	71B24	Percival Road, Rugby
31	Pear Tree Close, Shuttington	80C21	Percy Crescent, Kenilworth
C43	Pear Tree Cottage, Farnborough	80C21	Percy Road, Kenilworth
14	Pear Tree Farm, Dorridge	96C31	Percy Road, Packmores, Warwick
31	Pear Tree Farm, Frogmore	145A11	Percy Street, Stratford upon Avon
C44	Pear Tree Gardens, Aston Cantlow	97B24	Percy Terrace, Milverton, Leamington
31	Pear Tree Way, Bilton		Spa
21	Pear Tree Way, Rugby	177A42	Perkins Close, Hornton
B41	Pear Trees, Northend, Burton Dassett	155C11	Perkins Close, Salford Priors
42	Pears Close, Kenilworth	71C24	Perkins Grove, Hillmorton, Rugby
23	Peat Close, Overslade, Rugby	63B44	Perlieu Lane, Kenilworth
4	Pebble Close, Amington, Tamworth	91B11	Perry Mill Lane, Ullenhall
C33	Pebworth Road, Dorsington	107A24	Perrymill Lane, Sambourne
31	Peel Road, Packmores, Warwick	46A41	Peter Hall Farm, Coombe Fields
3	Peggs Farm, Twycross	24B21	Peters Close, Water Orton
22	Pelham Close, Milverton, Leamington	158A43	Pettifers Farm, Pebworth Pastures
	Spa	92C34	Pettiford Lane, Wootton Wawen
31	Pelham Lane, Haselor	72A31	Pettiver Crescent, Hillmorton, Rugby
24	Pembroke Close, Goodyears End,	66B14	Peugeot Talbot Cars, Ryton on
	Bedworth		Dunsmore
3	Pembroke Close, Guys Cross Park,	39B21	Pheasant Close, Bedworth
	Warwick	144B11	Pheasant Close, Stratford upon Avon
1	Pembroke Court, Leamington Spa	38C24	Pheasants Nest Farm, Bedworth
31	Pembroke Gardens, Mountford,	97C43	Philip Court, Leamington Spa
	Wellesbourne	97A21	Phillipes Road, Warwick
4	Pembroke Way, Nuneaton	190A13	Phillips Farm, Todenham
32	Pendicke Court, Southam	71C24	Phipps Avenue, Hillmorton, Rugby
23	Pendicke Street, Southam	40A34	Phoenix Park, Bedworth
2	Pendine Court, Leamington Spa	34B24	Picadilly Close, Chelmsley Wood
3	Pendred Road, New Bilton, Rugby	11C33	Picadilly Lane, Kingsbury
13	Penelope Close, Harbury	11C32	Piccadilly Crescent, Piccadilly,
4	Penfold Close, Bishops Tachbrook		Kingsbury
	Penisula Farm, Rugby	11C33	Piccadilly Lane, Kingsbury
	Penmire Close, Suckle Green,	17C13	Piccadilly Way, Piccadilly, Kingsbury
	Baddesley Ensor	11C32	Piccadilly, Piccadilly, Kingsbury
	Penn Lane, Monks Kirby	54C34	Pickard Close, Newton Biggin, Rugby
	Penn Lane, Tanworth in Arden	97A33	Pickard Street, Emscote, Warwick
	Penn Lane, Wibtoft	31A21	Pickford Close, Attleborough, Nuneaton
	Pennine Way, Stockingford, Nuneaton	34B22	Picton Crescent, Chelmsley Wood
	Pennine Way, Stoneydelph, Tamworth	104B11	Pie Court, Willoughby
	Pennington Mews, Rugby	66B43	Piece Barn Farm, Bubbenhall
	Pennington Street, Rugby	96C32	Piers Close, Guys Cross Park, Warwick
	Penns Close, Cubbington	186C14	Pig Brook Farm, Shipston on Stour
	Penns Lane, Coleshill	58A22	Pig Farm, Cheswick Green
	Penns Lane, Eathorpe	180A22	Pig Lane, Ilmington
	Pennyford Hall Farm, Wootton Wawen	112C41	Pigeon Green, Snitterfield
	Pennyford Lane, Wootton Wawen	75B31	Pigtrot Lane, Danzey Green, Tanworth
	Pennymore Road, Stoneydelph,		in Arden
	Tamworth	75C24	Pigtrot Lane, Umberslade Park,
	Pennystone Close, Sydenham Farm		Tanworth in Arden
	Estate, Leamington Spa	34B21	Pike Drive, Chelmsley Wood
	Penrhyn Close, Kenilworth	102B41	Pike Hall Farm, Broadwell,
	Penrith Close, Leamington Spa		Leamington Hastings
	Penrith Grove, Chelmsley Wood	194C24	Pill Lane, Little Compton
	Penryhn Close, Kenilworth	120C41	Pillory Green Farm, Napton on The
	Penryn Close, Nuneaton		Hill
	Pentire Close, Nuneaton	145C41	Pimlico Lane, Alveston, Stratford
	Pepperwell Farm, Little Wolford	195A21	Pinchester Close, Little Compton
	Perch Avenue, Chelmsley Wood	175B22	Pincock Farm, Lower Tysoe, Tysoe

Map ref	Address	Map ref	Address
97C32	Pindars Court, Leamington Spa	181A23	Pleasure Farm, Darlingscott, Tredington
71A14	Pinders Court, Rugby		
71A12	Pinders Lane, Rugby	115A43	Plestowes Farm, Barford
144B24	Pine Close, Shottery, Stratford upon Avon	70B24	Plexfield Road, Bilton, Rugby
		70B23	Plomer Close, Bilton, Rugby
98A14	Pine Court, Leamington Spa	67C41	Plott Lane, Stretton on Dunsmore
72A24	Pine Green, Lower Hillmorton, Rugby	21A41	Plough Hill Farm, Robinsons End, Nuneaton
	Pine Tree Court, Pine Tree Road, Bedworth		
119B21	Pine Tree Crescent, Southam	21A33	Plough Hill Road, Chapel End, Nuneaton
39B21	Pines, The, Market End, Bedworth	20C44	Plough Hill Road, Galley Common
134C11	Pineham Avenue, Harbury	135A32	Plough Lane, Cross Green, Bishops Itchington
134C13	Pineham Farm, Harbury		
82C42	Pinehurst, Cubbington	134C21	Plough Lane, Harbury
40B12	Pinetree Road, Bedworth	119A14	Ploughmans Holt, Southam
12B21	Pinewood Avenue, Wood End, Baddesley Ensor	125A24	Plover Close, Alcester
		128B44	Plover Close, Stratford upon Avon
12B21	Pinewood Avenue, Wood End, Kingsbury	70C14	Plowman Street, Rugby
		188C22	Plumtrees Farm, Brailes
50B33	Pinewood Drive, Binley Woods	98A33	Plymouth Place, Leamington Spa
70C11	Pinfold Street, New Bilton, Rugby	2C41	Polesworth Road, Shuttington
30B22	Pingle Court, Attleborough, Nuneaton	5B23	Polesworth Road, Stoneydelph, Tamworth
30B22	Pingles Sports Centre, Nuneaton		
74A34	Pink Green Farm, Pink Green, Beoley	80C33	Police Headquarters, Leek Wootton
76A34	Pinks Farm, Mows Hill, Beaudesert	87A33	Police Training College, Ryton on Dunsmore
94B31	Pinley Abbey Farm, Rowington		
94B23	Pinley Lane, Great Pinley	183C22	Policemans Tree Corner, Upper Brailes, Brailes
94C31	Pinley Farm, Claverdon		
7C41	Pinwall Hall Farm, Pinwall, Sheepy	5C13	Pond Cottage Farm, Polesworth
7B44	Pinwall Lane, Pinwall, Sheepy	30A12	Pool Bank Street, Nuneaton
7B12	Pipe Lane, Twycross	70B32	Pool Close, Bilton, Rugby
78C33	Pipers Cottage Farm, Shrewley	35A11	Pool Farm, Coleshill
42B14	Pipers End, Wolvey	107C42	Pool Farm, Sambourne
134C42	Pipers Hill Farm, Bishops Itchington	78C42	Pool Farm, Shrewley
20B32	Pipers Lane, Ansley Common, Ansley	58C34	Pool Farm, Tanworth in Arden
81A12	Pipers Lane, Whitemore, Kenilworth	62C12	Pool House Farm, Balsall Common
107C11	Pipers Road, Park Farm South, Redditch	21C44	Pool Road, Camphill, Nuneaton
		107C13	Pool Road, Studley
70B23	Pipewell Close, Bilton, Rugby	107C13	Poole Road, Studley
134C12	Pirie Close, Harbury	5C21	Pooley Lane, Polesworth
146C22	Pit Farm, Mountford, Wellesbourne	6A21	Pooley View, Polesworth
66B43	Pit Hill, Waverley Woods, Bubbenhall	184B13	Poolgate, Upper Tysoe, Tysoe
120A14	Pitams Farm, Napton on The Hill	57C43	Poolhead Farm, Tanworth in Arden
169A34	Pitchell Farm, Mickleton	57B33	Poolhead Lane, Earlswood
155A11	Pitchill, Iron Cross, Harvington	57B33	Poolhead Lane, Forshaw Heath, Tanworth in Arden
94A14	Pits Farm, Rowington		
164A13	Pittern Hill Farm, Brookhampton, Kineton	10B32	Poolhouse Farm, Hunts Green, Middleton
89B23	Pittoms Lane, Barby		
94A14	Pitts Farm, Shrewley Common, Rowington	57A43	Poolhouse Farm, Portway, Tanworth in Arden
		60C43	Poor Clares Convent, Baddesley
181C41	Pittway Avenue, Shipston on Stour	70C13	Pope Street, New Bilton, Rugby
34B23	Plane Grove, Chelmsley Wood	86A22	Popehill, Draycote
24A22	Plank Lane, Water Orton	106C21	Popes Lane, Astwood Bank
30C14	Plantaganet Drive, Attleborough, Nuneaton	40B24	Poplar Avenue, Bedworth
		34B31	Poplar Avenue, Chelmsley Wood
70C41	Plantagenet Drive, Woodlands, Rugby	151B22	Poplar Close, Knightcote, Burton Dassett
63A42	Pleasance Farm, Burton Green, Kenilworth		
98A22	Pleasant Way, Leamington Spa	125B42	Poplar Close, Oversley Green, A

Map ref	Address
B11	Poplar Drive N, Wootton Wawen
B12	Poplar Drive S, Wootton Wawen
B12	Poplar Farm, Harbury
2	Poplar Farm, Shuttington
C33	Poplar Gardens, Napton on The Hill
11	Poplar Grove, Rugby
331	Poplar Road, Bishops Itchington
14	Poplar Road, Dorridge
C33	Poplar Road, Napton on The Hill
332	Poplars Farm, Gaydon
C23	Poplars Farm, Knightcote, Burton Dassett
1	Poplars Farm, Seckington
A31	Poplars Farm, Sherbourne
2	Poplars Farm, Wood End, Kingsbury
3	Poppy Drive, Brownsover, Rugby
23	Pork Hill, Spernall
23	Portia Close, Whitestone, Nuneaton
1	Portland Court, Leamington Spa
3	Portland Drive, Whittleford, Nuneaton
1	Portland Mews, Leamington Spa
1	Portland Place E, Leamington Spa
1	Portland Place W, Leamington Spa
1	Portland Place, Leamington Spa
4	Portland Place, Rugby
1	Portland Road, Leamington Spa
3	Portland Road, Rugby
4	Portland Row, Leamington Spa
4	Portland Street, Leamington Spa
3	Portleys Lane, Drayton Bassett
2	Portlow Lane, Crick
12	Portobello Farm, Rowborough, Stretton on Fosse
4	Portway Close, Sydenham Farm Estate, Leamington Spa
	Portway Farm, Pink Green, Beoley
	Portway Farm, Portway, Tanworth in Arden
2	Posher Farm, Ufton
	Post Office Lane, Astley
2	Post Office Lane, Lighthorne
2	Post Office Lane, Stockton
	Post Office Lane, Witherley
	Post Office Road, Baddesley Ensor
4	Post Office Row, Little Compton
	Post Office Yard, Brinklow
	Postal Management College, Churchover, Rugby
	Postle Close, Kilsby
4	Potash Farm, Priors Marston
	Potsford Dam Farm, Dunchurch
	Potters Close, Brinklow
4	Potters Lane, Darlingscott, Tredington
	Potters Lane, Polesworth
	Potters Road, Goodyears End, Bedworth
	Potts Close, Kenilworth
	Poulton Farm, Pillerton Hersey
	Poultry Farm, Bishopton, Stratford upon Avon

Map ref	Address
157C22	Poultry Farm, Braggington, Welford on Avon
37B33	Poultry Farm, Chapel Green, Fillongley
59A34	Poultry Farm, Cheswick Green
168A23	Poultry Farm, Farnborough
83C32	Poultry Farm, Wappenbury
143A41	Poultry Farm, Welford on Avon
51A44	Poultry Farm, Wolston
116C23	Pounce Hill Farm, Radford Semele
57A32	Pound Close Farm, Forshaw Heath, Tanworth in Arden
77A14	Pound Close, Lapworth
181C32	Pound Close, Shipston on Stour
75C11	Pound House Lane, Umberslade Park, Tanworth in Arden
25A43	Pound Lane, Coleshill
26B12	Pound Lane, Furnace End, Over Whitacre
98A22	Pound Lane, Lillington, Leamington Spa
106C21	Poverty, Astwood Bank
30A12	Powell Way, Nuneaton
97C23	Powers Court, Leamington Spa
64B43	Powis Grove, Kenilworth
30B23	Poyser Road, Caldwell, Nuneaton
149C11	Pratts Farm, Lighthorne
90A31	Pratts Lane, Mappleborough Green, Studley
53A42	Prentice Close, Long Lawford
29A14	Prescelly Close, Stockingford, Nuneaton
64A41	Prescelly Court, Kenilworth
90A13	Prestbury Close, Redditch
93A34	Preston Bagot Farm, Preston Bagot
93A23	Preston Field Farm, Preston Bagot
160A23	Preston Fields Lane, Clifford Chambers
93A24	Preston Fields Lane, Preston Bagot
110C12	Preston Hill Farm, Preston Bagot
160B23	Preston Lane, Alscot Park, Preston on Stour
54A33	Pretorian Way, Glebe Farm Estate, Rugby
98C11	Price Road, Cubbington
61B41	Priests Park Farm, Baddesley Clinton
54C23	Primrose Close, Brownsover, Rugby
166A42	Primrose Farm, Arlescote
166A42	Primrose Farm, Warmington
125B41	Primrose Hill, Oversley Wood, Alcester
96C13	Primrose Hill, Woodloes, Warwick
125B43	Primrose Lane, Oversley Green, Alcester
92B31	Prince Harry Close, Henley in Arden
97C44	Prince Regent Court, Leamington Spa
30B24	Princes Drive, Caldwell, Nuneaton
64A34	Princes Drive, Crackley, Kenilworth
97B31	Princes Drive, Edmonscote, Leamington Spa
18B11	Princes Road, Hurley, Kingsbury
6A22	Princes Road, Polesworth
98A24	Princes Street, Leamington Spa
30A14	Princess Avenue, Nuneaton

Map ref	Address
14C23	Princess Road, Atherstone
30A14	Princess Street, Nuneaton
71A11	Princess Street, Rugby
84B21	Princethorpe College, Princethorpe
84B21	Princethorpe Priory, Princethorpe
100A44	Print Farm, Bascote, Southam
100A44	Print Farm, Long Itchington
138A41	Priors Hardwick Road, Priors Marston
175A11	Priors Lea Farm, Pillerton Hersey
120C41	Priors Marston Road, Chapel Green, Napton on The Hill
63B42	Priorsfield Road, Kenilworth
174A12	Priory Bungalows, Pillerton Priors
25A43	Priory Close, Coleshill
77B12	Priory Close, Lapworth
107C14	Priory Court, Studley
81A11	Priory Croft, Kenilworth
169A23	Priory Farm, Broad Marston, Pebworth
124A31	Priory Farm, Cook Hill, Inkberrow
60C43	Priory Farm, Lapworth
36A22	Priory Farm, Maxstoke
5B22	Priory Farm, Polesworth
84B22	Priory Farm, Princethorpe
138C23	Priory Farm, Priors Marston
107C11	Priory Farm, Studley
174A12	Priory Lane, Pillerton Priors
96C33	Priory Mews, Warwick
96C33	Priory Park, Warwick
123A31	Priory Piece Farm, Inkberrow
125A34	Priory Road, Alcester
81A11	Priory Road, Kenilworth
96C32	Priory Road, Warwick
51A44	Priory Road, Wolston
107C13	Priory Square, Studley
97C42	Priory Street, Leamington Spa
29B14	Priory Street, Stockingford, Nuneaton
97C34	Priory Terrace, Leamington Spa
14C42	Priory Walk, Mancetter
96C34	Priory Walk, Saint Johns, Warwick
47A43	Prison Service College, Newbold Revel, Stretton Under Fosse
50A31	Progress Close, Binley Woods
50A31	Progress Way, Binley
96A12	Prospect Farm, Leek Wootton
96A12	Prospect Farm, Warwick
116A12	Prospect Road, Whitnash, Leamington Spa
174A12	Prospect Row, Pillerton Priors
54B44	Prospect Way, Butlers Leap Estate, Rugby
25A34	Prossers Walk, Coleshill
60A11	Prunells Way, Dorridge
31A13	Ptarmigon Close, Nuneaton
31A13	Ptarmigon Place, Nuneaton
96B42	Puckerings Lane, Warwick
181C22	Puckpits Farm, Tredington
118C11	Pudding Bag Lane, Bascote, Long Itchington
86C22	Pudding Bag Lane, Thurlaston
5A21	Pulman Close, Amington Ind.est., Tamworth
12C34	Pump House Farm, Hurley, Baxterl…
37B14	Pump Lane, Fillongley
26C33	Pump Lane, Shawbury, Fillongley
31A33	Purcell Avenue, Whitestone, Nunea…
98A31	Purcell Close, Leamington Spa
114A12	Purser Drive, Warwick
116B12	Purion Mews, Sydenham Farm Est. Leamington
20A22	Purley Chase Lane, Mancetter, Atherstone
20A22	Purley Chase Lane, Oldbury
20A22	Purley Chase Lane, Ridge Lane
14C42	Purley View, Mancetter
63B43	Purlieu Lane, Burton Green, Kenilv…
125B22	Purton Close, Kinwarton
116B12	Purton Mews, Sydenham Farm Est… Leamington
34A12	Putney Walk, Chelmsley Wood
40A23	Putters Road, Bedworth
71B23	Pytchley Road, Rugby
144B11	Quail Close, Stratford upon Avon
15C33	Quaker Close, Fenny Drayton
29A14	Quantock Drive, Stockingford, Nuneaton
80C34	Quarry Close, Leek Wootton
53C42	Quarry Close, Newbold on Avon, Rugby
184C24	Quarry Farm, Epwell
177A31	Quarry Farm, Hornton
81C43	Quarry Farm, Milverton, Leaming… Spa
78A24	Quarry Farm, Rowington
80C34	Quarry Fields, Leek Wootton
78A13	Quarry Lane, Baddesley Clinton
156A34	Quarry Lane, Cleeve Prior
15A43	Quarry Lane, Mancetter
78B33	Quarry Lane, Mousley End, Row…
30C24	Quarry Lane, Nuneaton
78B44	Quarry Lane, Shrewley
63C41	Quarry Road, Kenilworth
97B23	Quarry Street, Milverton, Leamin… Spa
21B44	Queen Elizabeth Road, Camphill Nuneaton
30B43	Queen Marys Road, Collycroft, Bedworth
106C23	Queen Street, Astwood Bank
40B22	Queen Street, Bedworth
82B44	Queen Street, Cubbington
173A31	Queen Street, Halford
98A23	Queen Street, Leamington Spa
71A13	Queen Street, Rugby
71B13	Queen Victoria Street, Rugby
181C41	Queens Avenue, Shipston on St…
117C44	Queens Close, Harbury
80C14	Queens Close, Kenilworth
181C43	Queens Close, Shipston on Stou…

ref	Address	Map ref	Address
C32	Queens Court, Stratford upon Avon	72C23	Radio Station C Building, Hillmorton, Rugby
23	Queens Drive, Rowington	55B24	Radio Station, Hillmorton, Rugby
23	Queens Ferry Close, Bilton, Rugby	30A21	Radley Drive, Heath End, Nuneaton
43	Queens Park, Leamington Spa	29C21	Radnor Drive, Arbury, Nuneaton
31	Queens Road, Atherstone	165C43	Radway Cottage, Radway
14	Queens Road, Kenilworth	165C43	Radway Fields, Radway
42	Queens Road, Nuneaton	165C43	Radway House, Radway
C13	Queens Road, Tredington	166A14	Radway Road, Burton Dassett
44	Queens Square, Forbes Estate, Warwick	165C43	Radway Stables, Radway
2	Queensway Crescent, Weddington, Nuneaton	30B14	Raglan Close, Nuneaton
		64B43	Raglan Grove, Kenilworth
2	Queensway Trading Estate, Leamington Spa	34C21	Raglan Way, Chelmsley Wood
12	Queensway, Bidford	140C11	Ragley Hall, Arrow, Alcester
	Queensway, Dordon	125A31	Ragley Mill Lane, Alcester
3	Queensway, Hurley, Kingsbury	155A34	Ragley Road, Harvington
2	Queensway, Leamington Spa	30C22	Ragley Way, Attleborough, Nuneaton
	Quince, Amington, Tamworth	107B14	Railway Close, Studley
44	Quineys Leys, Welford on Avon	70A11	Railway Street, Long Lawford
21	Quineys Road, Stratford upon Avon	20C34	Railway Terrace, Ansley Common
11	Quinneys Court, Bidford	14B34	Railway Terrace, Atherstone
42	Quinneys Lane, Bidford	40B22	Railway Terrace, Bedworth
13	Quinnies Oak Farm, Sambourne	71A14	Railway Terrace, Rugby
44	Quinton House Farm, Winderton, Brailes	181C42	Rainbow Field, Shipston on Stour
		181C42	Rainbow Fields, Shipston on Stour
43	Quinton House Nursing Home, Lower Quinton	71C31	Rainsbrook Avenue, The Paddox, Rugby
	Quorn House, Leamington Spa	31A21	Rainsbrook Drive, Attleborough, Nuneaton
	Rabbit Lane, Bedworth Woodlands, Bedworth	145A43	Rainsford Close, Clifford Chambers
		5A34	Rainstar, Stoneydelph
	Race Meadow Road, Atherstone	22C32	Raison Avenue, Saint Nicholas Park, Nuneaton
4	Radbourne Close, Southam		
2	Radbourne Lane, Hodnell	14C24	Rale Meadow, Atherstone
2	Radbourne Lane, Ladbroke	11B41	Ralph Crescent, Kingsbury
3	Radbourne Manor Farm, Upper Radbourne, Southam	75B44	Rams Hill Lane, Ullenhall
		21B34	Ramsden Avenue, Camphill, Nuneaton
	Radbrook Farm, Corley	15A33	Ramsden Road, Mancetter
3	Radbrook Farm, Radbrook, High Cross Claybrook	98B41	Ramsey Road, Sydenham Farm Estate, Leamington
3	Radbrook Farm, Radbrook, Quinton	80C14	Randall Road, Kenilworth
	Radbrook Way, Sydenham Farm Estae, Leamington	29B14	Randle Road, Stockingford, Nuneaton
	Radcliffe Gardens, Leamington Spa	98B43	Randolph Close, Sydenham Farm Estate, Leamington Spa
	Radcliffe House, Gibbet Hill, Coventry	98A41	Ranelagh Street, Leamington Spa
4	Radcote Farm, Ingon, Hampton Lucy	97C44	Ranelagh Terrace, Leamington Spa
	Radford Close, Atherstone	97B13	Range Meadow Close, Leamington Spa
	Radford Cottage, Leamington Spa	17B12	Range Way, Kingsbury
	Radford Hall Farm, Radford Semele	53C33	Rankin Close, Newbold on Avon, Rugby
	Radford Hall, Radford Semele		
	Radford Hall, Radford Semele, Leamington Spa	28A33	Ransome Road, New Arley, Arley
	Radford Hill, Radford Semele	29B14	Ratcliffe Court, Stockingford, Nuneaton
	Radford Road, Leamington Spa	8A41	Ratcliffe Lane, Sheepy Magna, Sheepy
	Radford Road, Offchurch	14C31	Ratcliffe Road, Atherstone
	Radford Road, Radford Semele	70C34	Ratcliffe Road, Shakespeare Gardens, Rugby
	Radio Station A Building, Hillmorton, Rugby	14C31	Ratcliffe Street, Atherstone
		72A31	Rathbone Close, Hillmorton, Rugby
	Radio Station B Building, Hillmorton, Rugby	39A41	Rathbone Close, Keresley Newlands, Keresley

Map ref	Address
24A42	Rathlin Croft, Kingshurst
30B24	Raveloe Drive, Caldwell, Nuneaton
54C33	Ravenglass, Brownsover, Rugby
97B21	Ravensdale Avenue, Leamington Spa
5A34	Ravenstone, Stoneydelph, Tamworth
24C34	Ravenswood Hill, Kings Rise, Coleshill
98B23	Rawlinson Road, Lillington, Leamington Spa
14C42	Rawn View, Mancetter
64B41	Rawnsley Drive, Kenilworth
145B12	Rayford Caravan Park, Tiddington, Stratford
5A34	Raygill, Stoneydelph, Tamworth
39B23	Raynor Crescent, Goodyears End, Bedworth
96B24	Raynsford Walk, Woodloes, Warwick
22C32	Reading Avenue, Saint Nicholas Park, Nuneaton
145B12	Reading Court, Tiddington, Stratford upon Avon
96C21	Reardon Court, Woodloes, Warwick
96C21	Reardun Court, Warwick
89B23	Rectory Close, Barby
73C41	Rectory Close, Crick
40A24	Rectory Close, Exhall, Bedworth
155A34	Rectory Close, Harvington
119C14	Rectory Close, Stockton
116B21	Rectory Close, Whitnash
27C21	Rectory Cottage, Arley
40A24	Rectory Drive, Exhall, Bedworth
152A43	Rectory Farm Court, Fenny Compton
190C43	Rectory Farm, Barton on The Heath
188C14	Rectory Farm, Brailes
144C43	Rectory Farm, Clifford Chambers
190C31	Rectory Farm, Great Wolford
12C33	Rectory Farm, Hurley, Baxterley
135C22	Rectory Farm, Ladbroke
119C14	Rectory Farm, Stockton
185C14	Rectory Farm, Stretton on Fosse
188C31	Rectory Farm, Sutton Under Brailes
174A31	Rectory Farm, Whatcote
125B33	Rectory Gardens, Alcester
174A31	Rectory House Farm, Whatcote
89B23	Rectory Lane, Barby
188C14	Rectory Lane, Brailes
174A42	Rectory Lane, Whatcote
27C21	Rectory Road, Arley
188C14	Rectory Road, Brailes
9B41	Rectory Road, Sutton Coldfield
30B32	Red Deeps Caravan Site, Caldwell, Nuneaton
30B32	Red Deeps, Caldwell, Nuneaton
90A43	Red Hill Close
38A21	Red Hill Farm, Fillongley
79B23	Red House Farm Lane, Beausale
115A34	Red House Farm, Greys Mallory, Bishops Tachbrook
164B32	Red House Farm, Little Kineton, Kineton

Map ref	Address
121C23	Red House Farm, Lower Shuckburg
137C24	Red House Farm, Priors Marston
63B24	Red Lane Farm, Burton Green, Kenilworth
63B24	Red Lane Farm, Stoneleigh
63B13	Red Lane Poultry Farm, Burton Gre Kenilworth
28C33	Red Lane, Astley
63B31	Red Lane, Burton Green, Kenilwor
70C31	Red Lodge Drive, Rugby
150A21	Red Road, Lighthorne Heath, Lighthorne
164B24	Red Road, Little Kineton, Kineton
98A43	Redberry Court, Leamington Spa
98B13	Redcar Close, Lillington, Leamingt Spa
18A43	Redding Lane, Nether Whitacre
79B22	Reddings, Beausale
107C13	Redditch Road, Studley
64A44	Redfern Avenue, Kenilworth
62C13	Redfern Farm, Frogmore
22A11	Redgate, Caldecote
147A32	Redhill Close, Mountford, Wellesbourne
143A11	Redhill Farm, Red Hill, Binton
112C44	Redhill Farm, Snitterfield
90A41	Redhill Farm, Studley
143A11	Redhill Road, Red Hill, Binton
143A11	Redhill, Alcester
19C41	Redhouse Farm, Ansley
79B31	Redhouse Farm, Beausale
116B11	Redland Road, Whitnash
144B13	Redlands Crescent, Stratford upo Avon
195A24	Redlands Farm, Little Compton
110B44	Redlands Farm, Newnham, Aston Cantlow
133B33	Redlands Farm, Redlands Brake, Lighthorne
30C12	Redruth Close, Nuneaton
5A41	Redwing, Tamworth
128B43	Redwing Close,. Stratford on Av
30A23	Redwood Croft, Heath End, Nur
11B32	Redwood Drive, Kingsbury
195A23	Reed College, Little Compton
117C23	Reeds Park, Ufton
65B13	Rees Drive, Finham
70C21	Refley Club, Rugby
144C12	Regal Industrial Estate, Stratford Avon
144C12	Regal Road, Stratford upon Avo
97C31	Regency Arcade, Leamington Sp
22B42	Regency Close, Weddington, Nu
80C14	Regency Drive, Kenilworth
125A21	Regency Drive, Kings Coughton Alcester
98A31	Regency House, Leamington Sp
97C33	Regent Arcade, Leamington Spa
97C32	Regent Grove, Leamington Spa

Map ref	Address	Map ref	Address
24	Regent Place, Leamington Spa	6A33	Ridings Gardens, Dordon
12	Regent Place, Rugby	18A43	Ridley Lane, Nether Whitacre
32	Regent Square House, Leamington Spa	115B12	Rigby Close, Heathcote Industrial, Whitnash
12	Regent Street, Bedworth		
32	Regent Street, Leamington Spa	81B14	Riley Close, Kenilworth
43	Regent Street, Nuneaton	172B31	Rimell Close, Newbold on Stour, Tredington
14	Regent Street, Rugby		
33	Regina Crescent, Walsgrave on Sowe	40A14	Ringway, Bedworth
22	Reins Farm, Sambourne	2A41	Ringwood Rise, Amington, Tamworth
24	Reinswood Court, Sambourne	98C43	Rinill Grove, Sydenham Farm Estate, Leamington
32	Remburn Gardens, Guys Cross Park, Warwick		
		97C14	Riplingham, Leamington Spa
23	Renison Road, Goodyears End, Bedworth	97B21	Risdale Close, Leamington Spa
		155C11	Risdale Close, Salford Priors
2	Repington Avenue, Atherstone	60C43	Rising Lane, Baddesley Clinton
2	Repington Road, Amington, Tamworth	60B43	Rising Lane, Lapworth
2	Repington Way, Sutton Coldfield	22A44	Ritz Bingo, Nuneaton
2	Reservoir Drive, Shustoke, Coleshill	97B33	River Close, Edmondscote, Leamington Spa
1	Reservoir Road, Brownsover, Rugby		
4	Retail Park, Whitnash, Leamington Spa	39C31	River Close, Exhall, Bedworth
44	Retreat Farm, Newnham, Aston Cantlow	14B14	River Drive, Atherstone
		58B11	River Walk, Cheswick Green
23	Retreat Street, Astwood Bank	156B11	Rivermead Close, Bidford on Avon
4	Reynolds Close, Lower Hillmorton, Rugby	145C11	Rivermead Drive, Tiddington, Stratford upon Avon
1	Reynolds Road, Collycroft, Bedworth	14C32	Riversdale Road, Atherstone
2	Ribble Close, Bulkington, Bedworth	97B32	Riversdale, Leamington Spa
	Ribblesdale, Stoneydelph, Tamworth	8A32	Riverside Close, Sheepy
4	Rich Close, Emscote, Warwick	25A34	Riverside Court, Coleshill
3	Richards Close, Kenilworth	110B12	Riverside Drive, Wootton Wawen
2	Richardson Close, Woodloes, Warwick	92B31	Riverside Gardens, Beaudesert
4	Richmond Court, Leamington Spa	92B31	Riverside Gardens, Henley in Arden
	Richmond Road, Atherstone	125B32	Riverside, Alcester
	Richmond Road, Nuneaton	144A34	Riverside, Luddington
	Richmond Road, Rugby	107C14	Riverside, Studley
	Richmond Way, Chelmsley Wood	145B12	Riverside, Tiddington, Stratford upon Avon
2	Riddell Close, Kinwarton		
	Riddings Farm, Grendon	110B13	Riverside, Wootton Wawen
	Riddings Lane, Grendon Common, Grendon	97A22	Riversleigh Road, Milverton, Leamington Spa
	Riddles Hill, Tanworth in Arden	30B13	Riversley Park, Nuneaton
	Ridge Lane, Atherstone	30B13	Riversley Road, Nuneaton
	Ridge Lane, Oldbury, Mancetter	34B13	Roach Close, Chelmsley Wood
	Ridge Lane, Ridge Lane	121A23	Roadside Farm, Napton on The Hill
4	Ridge Way Close, Littlewood Green, Studley	40A22	Roadway Close, Bedworth
		30A12	Roanne Ringway, Nuneaton
2	Ridge Way, Cook Hill, Inkberrow	71C31	Robbins Court, Rugby
	Ridgeley Close, Woodloes, Warwick	66B11	Robert Close, Coventry
2	Ridgeway Farm, Arrow	72A23	Robert Hill Close, Lower Hillmorton, Rugby
	Ridgeway Farm, Rugby		
	Ridgeway Farm, Wolvey	40A33	Robert Road, Exhall, Coventry
3	Ridgeway Lane, Hunningham	67C33	Roberts Close, Stretton on Dunsmore
4	Ridgeway Lane, Offchurch	55A43	Robertson Close, Clifton upon Dunsmore
3	Ridgeway Lane, Snowford, Long Itchington		
		5B14	Robeys Lane, Alvecote, Shuttington
2	Ridgeway, Astwood Bank	5B24	Robeys Lane, Polesworth
	Ridgewood Close, Milverton, Leamington Spa	24A31	Robin Close, Kingshurst
		75B23	Robin Hoods Farm, Tanworth in Arden
	Ridings Farm, Grendon	98A24	Robinia Close, Leamington Spa

Map ref	Address
29A13	Robins Way, Stockingford, Nuneaton
39B23	Robinson Road, Goodyears End, Bedworth
39A33	Robinsons Close, Keresley Newlands, Keresley
28C22	Robinsons End Farm, Robinsons End, Nuneaton
53C42	Robotham Close, Newbold on Avon, Rugby
70C32	Rocheberie Way, Kingsway, Rugby
30A13	Rochester Close, Nuneaton
97C33	Rochford Court, Leamington Spa
28C12	Rock Close, Galley Common, Nuneaton
65C32	Rock Farm Lane, Baginton
66A32	Rock Farm, Baginton
38B32	Rock House Farm, Corley
38B32	Rock Lane, Corley
59C13	Rockingham Close, Dorridge
97B31	Rockmill Lane, Milverton, Leamington Spa
126B11	Rockwell Maudslay, Great Alne, Alcester
81B14	Rocky Lane, Ashow
81B14	Rocky Lane, Kenilworth
59C13	Rodborough Road, Dorridge
147B22	Roddis Croft, Mountford, Wellesbourne
70B23	Rodney Close, Bilton, Rugby
96C31	Roe Close, Packmores, Warwick
4B11	Roe House Lane, Austrey
4B11	Roe House Lane, Twycross
96C31	Roe Street, Packmores, Warwick
125A23	Roebuck Park, Alcester
162B41	Rogers Lane, Ettington
70C34	Rokeby Court, Kingsway, Rugby
71B14	Rokeby Street, Rugby
45C33	Rolls Royce, Coombe Fields, Anstey
126B43	Rollswood Farm, Haselor
156C23	Roman Road, Barton, Bidford
84B32	Roman Road, Eathorpe
100A11	Roman Road, Hunningham
133A43	Roman Road, Moreton Morrell
133A34	Roman Road, Newbold Pacey
84C21	Roman Road, Princethorpe
141A24	Roman Road, Wixford
192B22	Roman Row, Whichford
125A33	Roman Way, Arrow
24C22	Roman Way, Coleshill
6A41	Roman Way, Dordon
65B14	Roman Way, Finham
54A33	Roman Way, Glebe Farm Estate, Rugby
172C34	Roman Way, Halford
119B32	Roman Way, Southam
22B32	Romsey Avenue, Weddington, Nuneaton
62B31	Rook Farm, Frogmore
68C22	Rookers Hill Farm, Church Lawford
15C34	Rookery Close, Fenny Drayton
15C33	Rookery Farm, Fenny Drayton
152C34	Rookery Farm, Wormleighton

Map ref	Address
162A41	Rookery Lane Farm, Ettington
162A42	Rookery Lane, Ettington
93B12	Rookery Lane, Lowsonford, Rowin
172B24	Rookery Lane, Newbold on Stour, Tredington
93A22	Rookery Lane, Preston Bagot
93B13	Rookery Lane, Rookery, Rowingto
144C12	Rookes Court, Stratford upon Avo
70B23	Rooney Close, Bilton, Rugby
125A32	Rope Walk, Alcester
72A31	Roper Close, Hillmorton, Rugby
92B21	Rose Avenue, Henley in Arden
84A13	Rose Cottage Farm, Princethorpe
165C43	Rose Cottage, Radway
96C31	Rose Cottage, Warwick
63C41	Rose Croft, Kenilworth
55B11	Rose Farm, Shawell
184B14	Rose Farm, Upper Tysoe, Tysoe
30B13	Rose Lane, Chilvers Coton, Nunea
24C31	Rose Road, Coleshill
11B14	Rosebery Road, Dosthill, Tamwor
97C34	Rosefield Place, Leamington Spa
97C34	Rosefield Street, Leamington Spa
69B33	Rosegrove Farm, Lawford Heath, Lawford
14C34	Rosehill, Mancetter
80C14	Roseland Road, Kenilworth
61B24	Rosemary Farm, Chadwick End
63C44	Rosemary Hill, Kenilworth
40A32	Rosemullion Close, Exhall, Bedw
29B24	Rosendale Way, Arbury, Nuneato
71A31	Rosewood Avenue, Kingsway, R
98A24	Rosewood Crescent, Leamington
31A34	Ross Way, Whitestone, Nuneator
23C32	Roston Drive, Hinckley
144C22	Rother Street, Stratford upon Av
98A34	Rotherfield Close, Leamington S
13B31	Rotherhams Hill, Baddesley Enso
58C32	Rotherhams Oak Farm, Illshaw F Cheswick Green
58C42	Rotherhams Oak Lane, Tanwort Arden
181C42	Rotherwick Court, Shipston on S
30A21	Rothesay Close, Heath End, Nu
96B23	Rothwell Road, Wedgenock Ind Warwick
60B13	Rotten Row Farm, Dorridge
160C21	Rough Farm Old Airfield, Ailsto Preston on Stour
160C21	Rough Farm, Ailstone, Preston c Stour
80B32	Rouncil Farm, Kenilworth
80C22	Rouncil Lane, Kenilworth
53A44	Round Avenue, Long Lawford
128C31	Round House Farm, Stratford u Avon
70C12	Round Street, Rugby
183A43	Roundhill Farm, Honington
178C12	Roundhill Road, Mollington

Map ref	Address	Map ref	Address
12	Rounds Gardens, Rugby	72B42	Rugby Road, Kilsby
21	Rounds Hill, Bulkington Estate, Kenilworth	102B14	Rugby Road, Leamington Hastings
32	Roundshill Farm, Kenilworth	55C41	Rugby Road, Lilbourne
32	Rouses Lane, Oxhill	70A12	Rugby Road, Long Lawford
34	Rowan Close, Binley Woods	97B31	Rugby Road, Milverton, Leamington Spa
12	Rowan Close, Kingsbury	98B11	Rugby Road, New Cubbington
42	Rowan Close, Stratford upon Avon	48A31	Rugby Road, Pailton
22	Rowan Grove, Bilton, Rugby	84C21	Rugby Road, Princethorpe
31	Rowan Road, Camphill, Nuneaton	54C44	Rugby Road, Rugby
4	Rowan Way, Chelmsley Wood	119A14	Rugby Road, Southam
13	Rowborough Farm, Rowborough, Stretton on Fosse	119B13	Rugby Road, Stockton
41	Rowcroft Road, Walsgrave on Sowe	46C11	Rugby Road, Withybrook
3	Rowland Avenue, Polesworth	71A13	Rugby Shopping Centre, Rugby
23	Rowland Avenue, Studley	71A24	Rugby Sports Centre, Rugby
3	Rowland Court, Arley	71A14	Rugby Theatre, Rugby
2	Rowland Street, Rugby	57C21	Rumbush Farm, Rumbush, Tidbury Green
1	Rowland Way, Atherstone	57C21	Rumbush Lane, Earlswood
43	Rowlands Way, Whatcote	57C21	Rumbush Lane, Rumbush, Tidbury Green
11	Rowley Crescent, Stratford upon Avon	158B41	Rumer Close, Long Marston
1	Rowley Drive, Coventry	158B24	Rumer Hill Farm, Rumer Hill, Welford on Avon
3	Rowley Lane, Coventry	34B11	Runcorn Close, Chelmsley Wood
3	Rowley Road, Baginton	29C14	Runymeade Gardens, Whittleford, Nuneaton
23	Rowley Road, Whitnash, Leamington Spa	70C33	Rupert Brooke Road, Shakespeare Gardens, Rugby
3	Rowse Close, Brownsover, Rugby	135B23	Rupert Kettle Drive, Bishops Itchington
3	Roxburgh Croft, Cubbington	11B14	Rush Lane, Whately, Kingsbury
3	Roxburgh Road, Nuneaton	74B14	Rushbrook Farm, Tanworth in Arden
1	Royal Meadow Drive, Atherstone	74B22	Rushbrook Lane, Aspley Heath, Tanworth in Arden
3	Royal Oak Lane, Ash Green, Bedworth	145B23	Rushbrook Road, Stratford upon Avon
2	Royal Priors, Leamington Spa	98A42	Rushmore Place, Leamington Spa
4	Royal Show Ground, Stoneleigh	98A42	Rushmore Street, Leamington Spa
2	Ruby Cottage, Radway	98A42	Rushmore Terrace, Leamington Spa
	Rudfyn Manor, Burton Green, Kenilworth	187A22	Rushway Farm, Willington, Barcheston
2	Rufford Close, Kinwarton	97C44	Rusina Court, Leamington Spa
	Rugby Cricket Club, Rugby	21A43	Ruskin Close, Galley Common, Nuneaton
	Rugby Football Club, Rugby	70C42	Ruskin Close, Hillside, Rugby
	Rugby Lane, Stretton on Dunsmore	71A21	Russelheim Way, Rugby
	Rugby Post House, Crick	87B12	Russell Avenue, Dunchurch
	Rugby Radio Station A Building, Hillmorton, Rugby	97C44	Russell Court, Leamington Spa
	Rugby Radio Station B Building, Hillmorton, Rugby	97C23	Russell Street, Leamington Spa
	Rugby Radio Station C Building, Hillmorton, Rugby	98A34	Russell Terrace, Leamington Spa
	Rugby Road, Barby	119C31	Russells Farm, Southam
	Rugby Road, Binley	102B23	Rusty Butts, Broadwell, Leamington Hastings
	Rugby Road, Binley Woods	31A31	Rutherford Glen, Nuneaton
	Rugby Road, Brandon	29C14	Rutland Avenue, Stockingford, Nuneaton
	Rugby Road, Bulkington, Bedworth	67A41	Rutland Row, Ryton on Dunsmore
	Rugby Road, Crick	22C42	Rydal Avenue, Saint Nicholas Park, Nuneaton
	Rugby Road, Cubbington	54B34	Rydal Close, Brownsover, Rugby
	Rugby Road, Dunchurch	22B42	Ryde Avenue, Weddington, Nuneaton
	Rugby Road, Easenhall		
	Rugby Road, Harborough Parva, Harborough Magna		
	Rugby Road, Hinckley		

Map ref	Address
95C34	Ryder Close, Hampton Magna, Budbrooke
28A31	Ryder Row, New Arley, Arley
21B33	Ryders Hill Crescent, Camphill, Nuneaton
128C43	Rye Close, Stratford upon Avon
16A22	Rye Farm, Overgreen, Wishaw
115B32	Rye Fields, Bishops Tachbrook
130C31	Rye Hill Barn, Hampton Lucy
179A44	Rye Piece Farm, Ebrington
40B21	Rye Piece Ringway, Bedworth
34B14	Ryeclose Croft, Chelmsley Wood
16A22	Ryefield Lane, Overgreen, Wishaw
87A14	Ryehill Farm, Dunchurch
189C31	Ryehill Farm, Sibford Gower
39A24	Ryhope Close, Goodyears End, Bedworth
141A24	Ryknild Street, Wixford
116B11	Ryland Close, Sydenham Farm Estate, Leamington
114C33	Ryland Road, Barford
145C32	Ryland Street, Stratford upon Avon
69B33	Rylands, Lawford Heath, Long Lawford
96C23	Rylstone Way, Woodloes, Warwick
129C33	Ryon Hill Farm, Hampton Lucy
67B41	Ryton Heath Farm, Ryton on Dunsmore
67B41	Ryton Heath Farm, Stretton on Dunsmore
67B41	Ryton Heath Road, Stretton on Dunsmore
67B23	Ryton Island To Blue Boar Island, Park Farm South
67B23	Ryton Island To Coventry Island, Park Farm South
67B23	Ryton Island, Park Farm South
66C31	Ryton Lodge Farm, Ryton on Dunsmore
66C14	Ryton Mill Lane, Ryton
66B41	Ryton Road, Ryton on Dunsmore
100C34	Sabin Close, Long Itchington
144B11	Sackville Close, Stratford upon Avon
112B13	Saddlebow Lane, Norton Curlieu, Claverdon
112B13	Saddlebow Lane, Wolverton
175A33	Saddledon Street, Middle Tysoe, Tysoe
181C41	Saddlers Close, Shipston on Stour
128C42	Sadler Close, Stratford upon Avon
181C43	Sadlers Avenue, Shipston on Stour
59A42	Sadlerswell Lane, Tanworth in Arden
54C23	Saffron Close, Brownsover, Rugby
144C23	Saffron Meadow, Stratford upon Avon
144C32	Saffron Walk, Stratford on Avon
5A12	Saffron, Amington, Tamworth
30C12	Saint Agnes Way, Nuneaton
97B21	Saint Albans Close, Milverton, Leamington Spa
97C31	Saint Albans House, Leamington Spa
71A31	Saint Andrews Crescent, Kingsway, Rugby
144C21	Saint Andrews Crescent, Stratford upon Avon
31B23	Saint Andrews Drive, Whitestone, Nuneaton
82A44	Saint Andrews Road, Lillington, Leamington Spa
71B34	Saint Andrews Rugby Football Clu Rugby
98B42	Saint Annes Close, Sydenham Far Estate, Leamington Spa
70C23	Saint Annes Road, Overslade, Rug
107B12	Saint Asaphs Avenue, Studley
31A11	Saint Austell Close, Nuneaton
14B34	Saint Benedicts Close, Atherstone
24B21	Saint Blaise Avenue, Water Orton
98B42	Saint Brides Close, Sydenham Far Estate, Leamington Spa
116A21	Saint Catherines Crescent, Whitna
77B14	Saint Chads Mews, Lapworth
115B32	Saint Chads Road, Bishops Tachb
107B11	Saint Chads Road, Studley Comm Studley
96B32	Saint Christophers Close, Packmo Warwick
71A22	Saint Cross Hospital, Rugby
98B41	Saint Davids Close, Sydenham Fa Estate, Leamington Spa
37B12	Saint Davids Farm, Fillongley
183A24	Saint Dennis Farm, Honington
182A34	Saint Dennis Road, Honington
183A24	Saint Dennis Road, Upper Braile Brailes
6A31	Saint Editha Road, Polesworth
97A32	Saint Ediths Green, All Saints, W
97A31	Saint Ediths, Warwick
12B43	Saint Edmunds Road, Hurley, Kingsbury
125B23	Saint Faiths Road, Alcester
71A31	Saint Georges Avenue, Kingswa Rugby
156B14	Saint Georges Close, Bidford
144C13	Saint Georges Close, Stratford u Avon
14C23	Saint Georges Road, Atherstone
97C44	Saint Georges Road, Leamingto
30A34	Saint Georges Way, Griff, Nune
25A41	Saint Gerards Hospital, Coleshi
16A14	Saint Gerrards Orthopaedic Hos Coleshill
108B22	Saint Giles Farm, Spernall
39B42	Saint Giles Road Park, Ash Gre
39B42	Saint Giles Road, Ash Green, B
150B31	Saint Giles Road, Gaydon
98B42	Saint Govans Close, Sydenham Estate, Leamington Spa
145A14	Saint Gregorys Court, Stratford Avon
145A11	Saint Gregorys Road, Stratford Avon

p ref	Address	Map ref	Address
32	Saint Helena Road, Saint Helena, Polesworth	91B13	Saint Marys Close, Ullenhall
C12	Saint Helens Road, Leamington Spa	98A34	Saint Marys Court, Leamington Spa
12	Saint Ives Way, Nuneaton	98B41	Saint Marys Crescent, Leamington Spa
B12	Saint James Avenue, Charlecote	3B14	Saint Marys Grove, Newton Regis
A23	Saint James Crescent, Southam	97B24	Saint Marys Mews, Milverton, Leamington Spa
B12	Saint James Road, Charlecote	48B44	Saint Marys Nursing Home, Harborough Magna
A22	Saint James Road, Southam	37C13	Saint Marys Road, Fillongley
11	Saint John Street, Rugby	125C31	Saint Marys Road, Kinwarton
14	Saint Johns Avenue, Kenilworth	98A42	Saint Marys Road, Leamington Spa
31	Saint Johns Avenue, The Paddox, Rugby	22A44	Saint Marys Road, Nuneaton
A41	Saint Johns Close, Cherington	145A11	Saint Marys Road, Stratford upon Avon
32	Saint Johns Close, Henley in Arden	98A42	Saint Marys Terrace, Leamington Spa
21	Saint Johns Close, Stratford upon Avon	16A42	Saint Marys Walk, Curdworth
14	Saint Johns Court, Coten End, Warwick	155B12	Saint Matthews Close, Salford Priors
23	Saint Johns Court, Stratford upon Avon	71A13	Saint Matthews Street, Rugby
11	Saint Johns Lane, Long Lawford	14C24	Saint Michaels Close, Atherstone
3	Saint Johns Road, Ansley Common, Ansley	93C42	Saint Michaels Close, Claverdon
41	Saint Johns Road, Cherington	135A32	Saint Michaels Close, Cross Green, Bishops Itchington
3	Saint Johns Road, Leamington Spa	28A33	Saint Michaels Close, New Arley, Arley
4	Saint Johns Street, Kenilworth	29B11	Saint Michaels Close, Stockingford, Nuneaton
4	Saint Johns Terrace, Leamington Spa	117C24	Saint Michaels Close, Ufton
2	Saint Johns, Baddesley Ensor	83B31	Saint Michaels Close, Weston Under Wetherley
3	Saint Johns, Warwick	12B23	Saint Michaels Close, Wood End, Kingsbury
4	Saint Judes Avenue, Studley	119C14	Saint Michaels Crescent, Stockton
3	Saint Judes Avenue, Studley Common, Studley	93C42	Saint Michaels Road, Claverdon
	Saint Lawrence Avenue, Forbes Estate, Warwick	96B32	Saint Michaels Road, Packmores, Warwick
4	Saint Lawrence Close, Napton on The Hill	80C14	Saint Nicholas Avenue, Kenilworth
	Saint Lawrence Close, Turners Green, Rowington	96C42	Saint Nicholas Church Street, Warwick
	Saint Lawrence Road, Ansley	4A22	Saint Nicholas Close, Austrey
	Saint Leonards Close, Chelmsley Wood	96C42	Saint Nicholas Court, Warwick
	Saint Leonards Close, Dordon	13B13	Saint Nicholas Estate, Grendon
	Saint Leonards Close, Priors Marston	116C12	Saint Nicholas Hill Terrace, Radford Semele
	Saint Leonards View, Polesworth	22C34	Saint Nicholas Park Drive, Saint Nicholas Park, Nuneaton
	Saint Leonards Walk, Ryton on Dunsmore	96C42	Saint Nicholas Park, Warwick
	Saint Lukes Hospital, Rugby	92B32	Saint Nicholas Road, Beaudesert, Henley in Arden
	Saint Margarets Road, Whitnash	22B44	Saint Nicholas Road, Nuneaton
	Saint Marks Close, Gaydon	116C12	Saint Nicholas Road, Radford Semele
	Saint Marks Close, Ullenhall	25A34	Saint Paul Crescent, Coleshill
	Saint Marks Court, Bilton, Rugby	96B42	Saint Pauls Close, Warwick
	Saint Marks Road, Milverton, Leamington Spa	47A34	Saint Pauls College, Newbold Revel, Stretton Under Fosse
	Saint Martins Avenue, Studley	98A31	Saint Pauls Court, Leamington Spa
	Saint Martins Avenue, Studley Common, Studley	29B14	Saint Pauls Road, Stockingford, Nuneaton
	Saint Martins Close, Stratford upon Avon	96B42	Saint Pauls Terrace, Warwick
	Saint Martins Road, Finham	15A34	Saint Peters Avenue, Witherley
	Saint Marys Acre, Bearley	24B21	Saint Peters Close, Water Orton
	Saint Marys Close, Packmores, Warwick	15A34	Saint Peters Close, Witherley
	Saint Marys Close, Priors Hardwick		
	Saint Marys Close, Southam		

Map ref	Address
28C11	Saint Peters Drive, Galley Common, Nuneaton
11B43	Saint Peters Place, Kingsbury
164C11	Saint Peters Road, Kineton
97C33	Saint Peters Road, Leamington Spa
15A33	Saint Peters Road, Mancetter
71B14	Saint Peters Road, Rugby
147B12	Saint Peters Road, Wellesbourne
170A14	Saint Swithins Drive, Lower Quinton, Quinton
27C13	Saint Wilfreds Cottage, Arley
27C22	Saint Wilfreds Road, Arley
119B23	Saint Wulstan Court, Southam
119B23	Saint Wulstan Way, Southam
145B24	Saintbury Close, Stratford upon Avon
22B44	Saints Way, Nuneaton
23A43	Salcombe Close, Nuneaton
140B43	Salford Farm, Iron Cross, Salford Priors
155B24	Salford Hall, Abbotts Salford
154C22	Salford Lodge Farm, Salford Priors
141C43	Salford Priors Road, Bidford
141C43	Salford Road, Bidford
156B12	Salford Road, Marriage Hill, Bidford
21A34	Salisbury Drive, Bucks Hill, Nuneaton
24B13	Salisbury Drive, Water Orton
67A33	Salop Square, Ryton on Dunsmore
120A43	Salt Spring Farm, Southam
1C41	Salt Street, Appleby Magna
4B11	Salt Street, Austrey
1C41	Salt Street, No Mans Heath, Newton Regis
106B44	Salt Way, Astwood Bank
125A32	Saltbox Row, Alcester
58B23	Salter Street Farm, Warings Green, Tanworth in Arden
58B23	Salter Street, Cheswick Green
58B31	Salter Street, Warings Green, Tanworth in Arden
110A41	Salters Lane, Aston Cantlow
110C41	Salters Lane, Bearley Cross, Wootton Wawen
194C22	Salters Well Farm, Little Compton
96B32	Saltisford Gardens, Packmores, Warwick
96B34	Saltisford, Warwick
10C12	Salts Lane, Drayton Bassett
189A13	Saltway Lane, Lower Brailes
184A44	Saltway Lane, Winderton, Brailes
106C24	Sambourne Lane, Astwood Bank
107A24	Sambourne Lane, Sambourne
106C32	Sambourne Warren Farm, Sambourne
144C24	Sanctus Court, Stratford upon Avon
144C24	Sanctus Drive, Stratford upon Avon
144C23	Sanctus Road, Stratford upon Avon
144C23	Sanctus Street, Stratford upon Avon
130A13	Sand Barn Lane, Blackhill, Snitterfield
59B44	Sand Farm, Lapworth
59B44	Sand Lane, Lapworth
93C12	Sandall House Farm, High Cross, Rowington

Map ref	Address
40A12	Sandby Close, Collycroft, Bedworth
144C13	Sandel Close, Stratford upon Avon
14C23	Sanders Close, Atherstone
105A22	Sanders Close, Braunston
97A31	Sanders Court, Warwick
40B41	Sanders Road, Exhall, Bedworth
155C14	Sanders Road, Salford Priors
144C23	Sandfield Court, Stratford upon Avon
143C33	Sandfield Farm, Luddington
144C23	Sandfield Road, Stratford upon Avon
87B13	Sandford Way, Dunchurch
93C12	Sandle House Farm, Sibson, Rowington
22A44	Sandon Road, Nuneaton
98B13	Sandown Close, Lillington, Leamington Spa
54B43	Sandown Road, Rugby
5A43	Sandpiper, Tamworth
128B43	Sandpiper Close, Stratford on Avon
101A13	Sandpit Farm, Long Itchington
174A13	Sandpit Farm, Pillerton Priors
16A34	Sandpits Close, Curdworth
184B11	Sandpits Close, Middle Tysoe, Tysoe
175B44	Sandpits Road, Middle Tysoe, Tysoe
24A42	Sandra Croft, Kingshurst
21C42	Sandringham Court, Camphill, Nuneaton
97C11	Sandy Lane Farm, Milverton
81C41	Sandy Lane, Blackdown
38A13	Sandy Lane, Fillongley
98A11	Sandy Lane, Lillington, Leamington
85A43	Sandy Lane, Marton
97B11	Sandy Lane, Milverton
47C11	Sandy Lane, Monks Kirby
70C13	Sandy Lane, New Bilton, Rugby
1B42	Sandy Lane, Newton Regis
26C13	Sandy Lane, Over Whitacre
6B33	Sandy Way Lane, Dordon
5A12	Sandy Way, Amington ind.est., Tamworth
114B43	Sandy Way, Barford
93C11	Santan Farm, Sibson, Rowington
97C41	Sargeaunt Street, Leamington Spa
24A42	Sark Drive, Kingshurst
97C32	Satchwell Court, Leamington Spa
98A33	Satchwell Place, Leamington Spa
97B41	Saumur Way, Myton, Warwick
40A22	Saunders Avenue, Bedworth
70C22	Saunton Road, Overslade, Rugby
115C32	Savages Close, Bishops Tachbrook
64B43	Saville Grove, Kenilworth
103C24	Sawbridge Grange Farm, Grandborough
103C21	Sawbridge Road, Grandborough
104A32	Sawbridge Road, Sawbridge, Wolfhamcote
104B21	Sawbridge Road, Willoughby
50B34	Saxon Close, Binley Woods
5C31	Saxon Close, Polesworth
145A22	Saxon Close, Stratford upon Avon

Map ref	Address	Map ref	Address
C11	Saxon Court, Bidford	147B13	School Road, Charlecote
312	Saxon Fields, Bidford	163B11	School Road, Combrook
12	Saxon Wood Road, Cheswick Green	126A13	School Road, Great Alne
34	Scafell, Brownsover, Rugby	92B31	School Road, Henley in Arden
4	Scammerton, Stoneydelph, Tamworth	59B41	School Road, Hockley Heath, Cheswick Green
23	Scar Bank, Packmores, Warwick		
41	Schofield Road, Keresley Newlands, Keresley	58C34	School Road, Illshaw Heath, Cheswick Green
22	Scholars Court, Stratford on Avon	140B43	School Road, Iron Cross, Salford Priors
22	Scholars Lane, Stratford upon Avon	129B11	School Road, Snitterfield
13	School Avenue, Salford Priors	147B14	School Road, Wellesbourne Hasting, Wellesbourne
23	School Close, Braunston	52A44	School Street, Church Lawford
13	School Close, Great Alne	49B41	School Street, Churchover
41	School Close, Kingshurst	87B13	School Street, Dunchurch
44	School Close, Long Compton	72A32	School Street, Hillmorton, Rugby
2	School Close, Yelvertoft	70A11	School Street, Long Lawford
2	School Croft, Beausale	119B23	School Street, Southam
3	School Farm, Bentley	119C12	School Street, Stockton
1	School Farm, Churchover	68A12	School Street, Wolston
3	School Hill, Chapel End, Hartshill	30C21	School Walk, Attleborough, Nuneaton
42	School Hill, Fenny Compton	22B32	Scott Avenue, Weddington, Nuneaton
41	School Hill, Flecknoe, Wolfhamcote	80C21	Scott Road, Kenilworth
42	School Hill, Mollington	98A44	Scott Road, Leamington Spa
43	School Hill, Napton on The Hill	70B33	Scotts Close, Rugby
2	School Hill, Offchurch	70C14	Seabroke Avenue, Rugby
4	School House Lane, Walsgrave on Sowe	74A21	Seafield Farm, Bransons Cross, Beoley
	School House Mews, Henley in Arden	74A24	Seafield Lane, Bransons Cross, Beoley
1	School Lane, Bearley	164C11	Seagrave Close, Kineton
	School Lane, Bentley	1A12	Seal Fields Farm, Clifton Campville
3	School Lane, Brailes	40A13	Sealand Drive, Bedworth
	School Lane, Dosthill, Tamworth	54B32	Seathwaite, Brownsover, Rugby
2	School Lane, Ettington	23A43	Seaton Close, Nuneaton
	School Lane, Exhall, Bedworth	63B11	Seatons Field, Burton Green, Kenilworth
1	School Lane, Farnborough	3B14	Seckington Lane, Newton Regis
2	School Lane, Fenny Compton	3A13	Seckington Old Hall Farm, Seckington
	School Lane, Galley Common, Nuneaton	70C32	Seddlescombe Park, Kingsway, Rugby
	School Lane, Haseley Knob, Haseley	66B11	Sedgemoor Road, Coventry
	School Lane, Hunningham	29B21	Seeswood Close, Stockingford, Nuneaton
	School Lane, Kenilworth		
2	School Lane, Ladbroke	11B12	Sefton Road, Dosthill, Tamworth
	School Lane, Lea Marston	125A34	Seggs Lane, Alcester
	School Lane, Lighthorne	70C31	Selborne Road, Bilton, Rugby
	School Lane, Little Packington	21A44	Selby Way, Whittleford, Nuneaton
	School Lane, Middle Tysoe, Tysoe	66B11	Selsey Close, Coventry
	School Lane, Nether Whitacre	54B34	Selside, Brownsover, Rugby
	School Lane, Priors Marston	98C43	Semele Close, Radford Semele
	School Lane, Radford Semele	31A11	Sennen Close, Nuneaton
	School Lane, Shuttington	97C31	Service Headquarters, Leamington Spa
	School Lane, Stretton on Dunsmore	115B31	Seven Acre Close, Bishops Tachbrook
	School Lane, Tiddington, Stratford upon Avon	145B12	Seven House, Tiddington
		145A31	Seven Meadows Road, Stratford on Avon
	School Lane, Turners Green, Rowington		
	School Lane, Warmington	98B14	Severn Close, Lillington, Leamington Spa
	School Lane, Wolvey		
	School Lane, Wroxhall	41A13	Severn Road, Bulkington, Bedworth
	School Lane, Yelvertoft	24C13	Severn Trent Water Authority, Whitacre Heath, Coleshill
	School Road, Alcester		
	School Road, Bulkington, Bedworth	144B11	Sevincott Close, Stratford upon Avon

Map ref	Address
95C42	Seymour Close, Bampton Magna, Budbrooke
97B41	Seymour Grove, Myton, Warwick
30B14	Seymour Road, Attleborough, Nuneaton
54B43	Seymour Road, Brownsover, Rugby
125B24	Seymour Road, Kinwarton
144B24	Seymour Road, Stratford upon Avon
39A42	Shaftsbury Avenue, Keresley Newlands, Keresley
100C21	Shakers Lane, Long Itchington
165C43	Shakesfield, Radway
40C23	Shakespeare Avenue, Bedworth
96B43	Shakespeare Avenue, Forbes Estate, Warwick
145A13	Shakespeare Court, Stratford upon Avon
31A22	Shakespeare Drive, Whitestone, Nuneaton
70C34	Shakespeare Gardens, Shakespeare Gardens, Rugby
155A33	Shakespeare Lane, Harvington
145A13	Shakespeare Street, Stratford upon Avon
22B42	Shanklin Drive, Weddington, Nuneaton
66B11	Shanklin Road, Coventry
54C33	Shap Fell, Brownsover, Rugby
117A24	Sharmer Farm, Harbury
96C31	Sharpe Close, Packmores, Warwick
2A43	Sharpe Street, Amington, Tamworth
193B12	Sharps Hill, Hook Norton
39C22	Sharratt Road, Bedworth
22B33	Shaw Avenue, Weddington, Nuneaton
26B23	Shawberry Approved School, Shustoke
26C32	Shawberry Farm, Shawbury, Fillongley
26B21	Shawberry Lane, Church End, Shustoke
26B31	Shawberry Lane, Shawbury, Fillongley
26B21	Shawbury Lane, Shustoke, Over Whitacre
56A12	Shawell Road, Swinford
78C34	Shaws Lane, Shrewley
34A13	Sheep Close Drive, Chelmsley Wood
84C13	Sheep Dip Lane, Princethorpe
71A13	Sheep Street, Rugby
181C44	Sheep Street, Shipston on Stour
145A21	Sheep Street, Stratford upon Avon
98A24	Sheepcote Close, Leamington Spa
2A43	Sheepcote Lane, Amington, Tamworth
159B21	Sheepleys Farm, Clifford Chambers
24A44	Sheepy Drive, Bacons End, Kingshurst
8B33	Sheepy Parva Farm, Sheepy Parva, Sheepy
14B22	Sheepy Road Farm, Atherstone
14B32	Sheepy Road, Atherstone
7B44	Sheepy Road, Pinwall, Sheepy
144A12	Shelbourne Road, Stratford upon Avon
96C22	Sheldon Green, Woodloes, Warwick
181C44	Sheldon House, Shipston on Stour
145A21	Sheldon House, Stratford upon Avon
108C42	Shelfield Lane, Great Alne

Map ref	Address
109A22	Shelfield Lodge Farm, Shelfield, Aston Cantlow
109B24	Shelfield Park Farm, Shelfield, Aston Cantlow
109B23	Shelfield Square Farm, Shelfield, Aston Cantlow
32B41	Shelford Cottage Farm, Shelford, Burton Hastings
32B33	Shelford Farm, Shelford, Burton Hastings
32B44	Shelford Farm, Wolvey
32B33	Shelford House Farm, Shelford, Burton Hastings
114B11	Shelley Avenue, Forbes Estate, Warwick
40B24	Shelley Close, Bedworth
145A24	Shelley Road, Stratford upon Avon
161B22	Shenington Farm, Coldicote, Alderminster
161B22	Shenington House, Goldicote, Alderminster
184C14	Shenington Road, Upper Tysoe, T
73B21	Shenley Farm, Yelvertoft
71C31	Shenstone Avenue, Rugby
84C42	Shepherd Street, Marton
119B32	Shepherds Hill, Southam
164B22	Shepherds Place, Kineton
36A42	Sheppards Lane, Great Packingto
30B21	Shepperton Court, Nuneaton
30B21	Shepperton Street, Nuneaton
21A44	Sherbourne Avenue, Whittleford, Nuneaton
35A11	Sherbourne Close, Coleshill
114A31	Sherbourne Court, Sherbourne
114A23	Sherbourne Farm, Sherbourne
114A22	Sherbourne Island To Stanks Hi Island, Warwick by pass
114A22	Sherbourne Island, Warwick by
98A23	Sherbourne Place, Leamington S
114A33	Sherbourne Priors, Sherbourne
144A12	Sherbourne Road, Drayton, Stra upon Avon
98A23	Sherbourne Terrace, Leamingto
114A22	Sherbourne To Stanks Hill, Wa by pass
70C34	Sheridan Close, Hillside, Rugby
21A43	Sheridan Drive, Robinsons End Nuneaton
20C44	Sheriden Close, Galley Commo Nuneaton
21A43	Sheriden Drive, Galley Commo Nuneaton
154A43	Sheriffs Lench Farm, Church L
30C21	Sheringham Close, Attleboroug Nuneaton
71B14	Sherriff Road, Rugby
125A33	Sherwell Drive, Alcester
12B21	Sherwood Close, Wood End, E Ensor

ap ref	Address
B21	Sherwood Close, Wood End, Kingsbury
A43	Sherwood Farm, Stretton on Dunsmore
312	Sherwood Walk, Lillington, Leamington Spa
C22	Shetland Drive, Heath End, Nuneaton
311	Shetland Road, Coventry
A42	Shetland Walk, Kingshurst
C42	Shilton Farm, Shilton Fields, Shilton
A33	Shilton Fields Farm, Shilton Fields, Shilton
C44	Shilton House Farm, Shilton
43	Shilton Lane, Barnacle, Shilton
22	Shilton Lane, Bulkington, Bedworth
A34	Shilton Lodge Farm, Shilton Fields, Shilton
11	Shilton Road, Withybrook
C21	Shipston Fields, Upper Brailes, Brailes
C41	Shipston Road, Armscote, Tredington
A14	Shipston Road, Atherstone on Stour
A12	Shipston Road, Clifford Chambers
B24	Shipston Road, Long Compton
B14	Shipston Road, Newbold on Stour, Ettington
C31	Shipston Road, Newbold on Stour, Tredington
A22	Shipston Road, Stratford upon Avon
B14	Shipston Road, Upper Tysoe, Tysoe
C34	Shipston Rugby Club, Shipston on Stour
B3	Shire Hall, Warwick
2	Shires Retail Park, Leamington Spa
B3	Shirley Road, Walsgrave on Sowe
13	Shirleys Farm, Little Wolford
	Shirrall Drive, Drayton Bassett
21	Short Acres, Kineton
42	Short Lane, Ettington
34	Short Lane, Long Itchington
4	Short Street, Stockingford, Nuneaton
4	Shortlands, Ash Green, Bedworth
21	Shottery Road, Shottery, Stratford upon Avon
14	Shoulderway Lane, Tidmington
1	Shq, Leamington Spa
21	Shreeves Walk, Stratford upon Avon
	Shrewley Common, Rowington
	Shrewley Common, Shrewley
	Shrewley Farm, Shrewley
2	Shrubland Street, Leamington Spa
3	Shuckborough Road, Napton on The Hill
	Shuckburgh Crescent, Ashlawn Estate, Rugby
	Shuckburgh Crescent, Bourton on Dunsmore
	Shuckburgh Crescent, Oxley
	Shuckburgh Grove, Lillington, Leamington Spa
2	Shuckburgh Hall, Lower Shuckburgh
2	Shuckburgh Road, Priors Marston

Map ref	Address
58A24	Shutt Lane, Cheswick Green
58A32	Shutt Lane, Earlswood, Tanworth in Arden
3A32	Shuttington Fields Farm, Shuttington
2C41	Shuttington Lane, Shuttington
2A42	Shuttington Road, Amington, Tamworth
2C31	Shuttington Road, Shuttington
55A43	Shuttleworth Road, Clifton upon Dunsmore
66A12	Sibree Road, Coventry
8B33	Sibson Road, Sheepy Parva, Sheepy
15B12	Sibson Road, Witherley
80C13	Siddeley Avenue, Kenilworth
144B14	Sidelands Road, Stratford upon Avon
58C22	Sidenhales Farm, Illshaw Heath, Cheswick Green
23A43	Sidmouth Close, Nuneaton
71B32	Sidney Road, Rugby
5A21	Signal Walk, Amington Ind.est., Tamworth
5A22	Silica Road, Amington Ind.est., Tamworth
110B34	Sillesbourne Farm, Wootton Wawen
39C21	Silver Birch Avenue, Bedworth Woodlands, Bedworth
14B32	Silver Street, Atherstone
55A31	Silver Street, Newton And Biggin
41A12	Silver Trees Drive, Bulkington, Bedworth
29C14	Silver Walk, Heath End, Nuneaton
39B44	Silverstone Drive, Rowleys Green
10A24	Simmonds Close, Middleton
147B13	Simmonds Court, Wellesbourne
14C21	Simmonds Way, Atherstone
30B22	Simon Close, Attleborough, Nuneaton
186C11	Simpson Road, Shipston on Stour
50B33	Sir Winston Churchill Place, Binley Woods
66B13	Siskin Drive, Baginton, Coventry
66B13	Siskin Drive, Coventry
101A42	Sitwell Avenue, Long Itchington
183C32	Six Bells Lane, Lower Chelmscote, Brailes
188B43	Six Bells Lane, Upper Brailes, Brailes
183C32	Six Bells Lane, Upper Chelmscote, Brailes
193C21	Sixash Farm, Hook Norton
156C31	Sixteen Acres Lane, Bickmarsh
156B32	Sixteen Acres Lane, Bidford
23A41	Skelwith Rise, Saint Nicholas Park, Nuneaton
32A12	Sketchley Lane, Hinckley
15A12	Sketchley Lane, Ratcliffe Culey, Witherley
54B31	Skiddaw, Brownsover, Rugby
90B11	Skilts School, Gorcott Hill
51B14	Skipwith Close, Brinklow
50B23	Skipworth Road, Binley Woods
29C22	Skye Close, Heath End, Nuneaton

Map ref	Address	Map ref	Address
24A34	Skye Close, Kingshurst	100C41	Snowford Hill Farm, Long Itchingto
14B42	Slacks Avenue, Atherstone	100A22	Snowford House, Snowford,
20B32	Slacks Farm, Ansley		Hunningham
31B32	Slade Close, Nuneaton	58B12	Snowshill Drive, Cheswick Green
9A13	Slade Farm, Sutton Coldfield	178B31	Snuff Lane, Shotteswell
95C34	Slade Hill, Hampton Magna, Budbrooke	29A44	Soar End Farm, Bedworth
11B11	Slade Lane, Dosthill, Tamworth	67A23	Sodens Avenue, Ryton on Dunsmo
9A13	Slade Lane, Sutton Coldfield	29A43	Sole End Farm, Astley
98C43	Slade Meadow, Radford Semele	186A41	Solloways Farm, Todenham
9A11	Slade Road, Hints	36C22	Solomon Temple Lane, Green End,
71B22	Slade Road, Rugby		Fillongley
11B24	Slateley Farm, Cliff, Kingsbury	36C22	Solomons Temple Farm, Green End
11C23	Slateley Hall Farm, Kingsbury		Fillongley
59C12	Slater Road, Dorridge	98B44	Solway Close, Sydenham Farm Est:
	Sleets Yard, Gatehouse Lane, Bedworth		Leamington
145A11	Slingates Road, Stratford upon Avon	97C31	Somers Place, Leamington Spa
30C22	Slingsby Close, Attleborough, Nuneaton	39A41	Somers Road, Keresley Newlands,
12B24	Slington Crescent, Wood End,		Keresley
	Kingsbury	35C44	Somers Road, Little Packington,
12B24	Slington Farm, Wood End, Kingsbury		Stonebridge
27A32	Slowley Green Farm, Arley	70C13	Somers Road, New Bilton, Rugby
27B41	Slowley Hall Farm, Arley	29C13	Somerset Drive, Stockingford, Nur
27A24	Slowley Hill Farm, Devitts Green, Arley	97B23	Somerville Mews, Leamington Spa
27A32	Slowley Hill, Arley	5A12	Sorbus, Amington, Tamworth
57B42	Small Lane Farm, Tanworth in Arden	54C23	Sorrel Drive, Brownsover, Rugby
57C33	Small Lane, Clowes Wood, Tanworth	11B32	Sorrel Drive, Kingsbury
	in Arden	2A44	Sorrel, Amington, Tamworth
80C11	Smalley Place, Kenilworth	30B23	Sorrell Road, Caldwell, Nuneaton
89C14	Smarts Estate, Kilsby	80C12	South Bank Road, Kenilworth
184B13	Smarts Lane, Upper Tysoe, Tysoe	63B33	South Chase Farm, Burton Green,
39C23	Smarts Road, Exhall, Bedworth		Kenilworth
46B41	Smeaton Lane, Coombe Fields, Stretton	105B24	South Close, Braunston
	Under Fosse	96A31	South Division Headquarters,
39B21	Smercote Close, Bedworth		Budbrooke, Warwick
47C14	Smite Close, Monks Kirby	24C41	South Drive, Woodlands, Coleshil
39C23	Smith Street, Goodyears End, Bedworth	22B42	South Field Close, Weddington,
97C34	Smith Street, Leamington Spa		Nuneaton
96C42	Smith Street, Warwick	64A33	South Field Drive, Crackley, Ken
12B21	Smith Street, Wood End, Kingsbury	144B21	South Green Drive, Stratford upo
129B11	Smiths Lane, Snitterfield		Avon
125B23	Smiths Way, Alcester	4B11	South Hill Farm, Austrey
24A13	Smiths Way, Water Orton	195C13	South Hill Farm, Long Compton
165C43	Smithy Cottage, Radway	78A42	South Lawn Road, Rowington
13B41	Smithy Lane, Baxterley	69A41	South Lodge Farm, Wolston
52A42	Smithy Lane, Church Lawford	186C12	South Lynn Gardens, Shipston o
7A42	Smithy Lane, Grendon		Stour
33B31	Smockington Lane, Smockington,	134C11	South Parade, Harbury
	Hinckley	55A43	South Road, Clifton upon Dunsn
32C42	Smockington Lane, Wolvey	144C32	South Stratford Relief, Stratford
38C23	Smorrall Lane, Corley		Avon
39C23	Smorrall Lane, Marret End, Bedworth	14B32	South Street, Atherstone
96C23	Smythe Green, Woodloes, Warwick	71B12	South Street, Rugby
111A41	Snitterfield Road, Bearley	116A22	South Terrace, Leamington Spa
112C24	Snitterfield Lane, Norton Lindsey	116A22	South Terrace, Whitnash
112C32	Snitterfield Road, Snitterfield	69C12	South View Road, Long Lawfor
130C34	Snitterfield Street, Hampton Lucy	82B43	South View Road, New Cubbin
29A14	Snowden Close, Stockingford, Nuneaton		Leamington
100A22	Snowford Hall Farm, Snowford,	51C14	South View, Brinklow
	Hunningham		

Map ref	Address	Map ref	Address
A33	South View, Hampton Magna, Budbrooke	116B13	Spa View, Whitnash
312	South View, Kingsbury	54A41	Sparta Close, Glebe Farm Estate, Rugby
A14	Southam by pass, Southam	115C11	Spartan Close, Heathcote Industrial, Leamington
A12	Southam Crescent, Lighthorne Heath, Lighthorne	50C32	Speedway Lane, Brinklow
A41	Southam Drive, Southam	54C31	Speedwell Close, Brownsover, Rugby
A13	Southam Fields Farm, Southam	13A24	Speedwell Lane, Baddesley Ensor
C44	Southam Holt Farm, Southam	40A24	Speedwell Lane, Blackbank, Bedworth
C12	Southam Road, Farnborough	144C23	Spencer Court, Stratford upon Avon
A44	Southam Road, Long Itchington	97C34	Spencer Street, Leamington Spa
C42	Southam Road, Mollington	108C41	Spernal Lane, Great Barr, Coughton
C32	Southam Road, Napton on The Hill	107C34	Spernal Lane, Studley
21	Southam Road, Princethorpe	107C31	Spernall Ash Farm, Morgrove Coppice, Spernall Ash
42	Southam Road, Radford Semele	108A24	Spernall Hall Farm, Morgrove Coppice, Spernall
34	Southam Road, Thurlaston		
24	Southam Road, Toft, Dunchurch	108B24	Spernall House, Morgrove Coppice, Spernall
C24	Southam Road, Ufton	108C41	Spernall Lane, Coughton
C21	Southam Street, Kineton	108C42	Spernall Lane, Great Alne
12	Southbank Close, Kenilworth	108B32	Spernall Lane, Morgrove Coppice, Spernall
12	Southbank Court, Kenilworth		
41	Southborough Terrace, Leamington Spa	107C34	Spernall Lane, Studley
A13	Southbourne House, Stratford upon Avon	108C21	Spernall Park, Morgrove Coppice, Spernall
31	Southbrook Road, Kingsway, Rugby	108C42	Spernall Road, Great Barr, Great Alne
23	Southerly Park Farm, Temple Grafton	70B24	Spicer Place, Bilton, Rugby
21	Southern Court, Lillington, Leamington Spa	97C13	Spilsbury Close, Leamington Spa
21	Southern Lane, Stratford upon Avon		Spinney, The, Tower Road, Bedworth
21	Southern Leamington Relief Road, Bishops Tachbrook	115C32	Spinney Bank, Bishops Tachbrook
11	Southern Leamington Relief Road, Warwick	50C33	Spinney Close, Binley Woods
		5C31	Spinney Close, Birchmoor, Polesworth
21	Southern Relief Road, Stratford upon Avon	27C32	Spinney Close, New Arley, Arley
3	Southey Road, Shakespeare Gardens, Rugby	133B41	Spinney Close, Redlands Brake, Lighthorne
24	Southfield Farm, Ilmington	58B12	Spinney Drive, Cheswick Green
3	Southfield Road, Rugby	115A32	Spinney Farm, Greys Mallory, Bishops Tachbrook
41	Southfield Road, Southam	129B42	Spinney Farm, Stratford upon Avon
3	Southfields Close, Coleshill	4C23	Spinney Farm, Twycross
4	Southfields Drive, Crick	105B24	Spinney Hill, Braunston
2	Southfields Farm, Bickenhill	97A21	Spinney Hill, Percy Estate, Warwick
3	Southfields Farm, Coleshill	29B11	Spinney Lane, Whittleford, Nuneaton
3	Southfields, Leamington Spa	119B33	Spire Bank, Southam
4	Southlands, Leamington Spa	166B34	Splash Leys Farm, Avon Dassett
3	Southlands, Mancetter	37C41	Splash Pits Farm, Allesley
4	Southlea Avenue, Leamington Spa	13B12	Spon Lane, Grendon
	Southlea Close, Leamington Spa	66B41	Spring Close, Bubbenhall
	Southlea Crescent, Leamington Spa	162A42	Spring Close, Ettington
2	Southmead Gardens, Studley	60A13	Spring Coppice Road, Dorridge
	Southorn Court, Lillington, Leamington Spa	66B41	Spring Court, Bubbenhall
		150C12	Spring Farm, Bishops Itchington
	Southurst Farm, Kenilworth	129C21	Spring Farm, Blackhill, Snitterfield
	Southurst Farm, Stoneleigh	16B44	Spring Farm, Curdworth
	Southview Farm, Princethorpe	63C31	Spring Farm, Kenilworth
2	Southway, Whitnash	91A32	Spring Farm, Oldberrow
	Sovereign Close, Kenilworth	44B31	Spring Farm, Willey
	Sowe Fields Farm, Barnacle, Shilton	37B44	Spring Field Cottage Farm, Allesley
		60C12	Spring Field Farm, Dorridge

Map ref	Address
162C43	Spring Field Lodge, Pillerton Hersey, Pillerton Priors
21A31	Spring Hill Moor Wood, Hartshill
21B44	Spring Hill Road, Camphill, Nuneaton
148C44	Spring Hill, Compton Verney
27C24	Spring Hill, Gun Hill, Arley
21A31	Spring Hill, Moor Wood, Hartshill
71A24	Spring Hill, Rugby
66B43	Spring Hill, Waverley Woods, Bubbenhall
148B43	Spring Lane, Combrook
64A43	Spring Lane, Kenilworth
59A44	Spring Lane, Nuthurst, Hockley Heath
98C43	Spring Lane, Radford Semele
76A11	Spring Lane, Tanworth in Arden
96C33	Spring Pool, Warwick
41A42	Spring Road, Barnacle, Shilton
71A12	Spring Street, Rugby
57C34	Springbrook Farm, Clowes Wood, Tanworth in Arden
57C34	Springbrook Lane, Earlswood, Tanworth in Arden
30B14	Springdale Court, Attleborough, Nuneaton
186C11	Springfield Close, Shipston on Stour
37B44	Springfield Cottage Farm, Corley Moor, Corley
40A24	Springfield Crescent, Bedworth
19B44	Springfield Farm, Ansley
162A31	Springfield Farm, Ettington
103A22	Springfield Farm, Grandborough
175B13	Springfield Farm, Oxhill
84C14	Springfield Farm, Princethorpe
158B31	Springfield Farm, Rumer Hill, Welford on Avon
186C11	Springfield Farm, Shipston on Stour
183C41	Springfield Farm, Upper Brailes, Brailes
119A14	Springfield Grove, Southam
30C21	Springfield Road, Attleborough, Nuneaton
186C11	Springfield Road, Shipston on Stour
9B41	Springfield Road, Sutton Coldfield
125A24	Springfields Road, Alcester
125A24	Springfields, Alcester
25A43	Springfields, Coleshill
71B33	Springhill Farm, Rugby
119A22	Springs Crescent, Southam
119A22	Springs Cresent, Southam
98B42	Springwell Road, Sydenham Farm Estate, Leamington Spa
5A12	Spruce, Amington, Tamworth
115C24	Squab Hall Poultry Farm, Bishops Tachbrook
116A31	Squabs Hall Farm, Bishops Tachbrook
38A24	Square Lane, Corley
97C23	Square Street, Leamington Spa
152A42	Squire Place, Fenny Compton
67C41	Squires Road, Stretton on Dunsmore

Map ref	Address
107B13	St Agnes Close, Studley
53A43	St Georges Court, Long Lawford
70B32	St Marks Court, Bilton, Rugby
125B24	St Moholan Close, Alcester
25A34	St Philips Court, Coleshill
165C43	Stable Cottage, Radway
31A21	Stable Walk, Attleborough, Nuneato
70C41	Stacey Court, Woodlands, Rugby
41B21	Stafford Close, Bulkington, Bedwor
14C33	Stafford Street, Atherstone
67A33	Stafford Walk, Ryton on Dunsmore
65C34	Stags Head Farm, Baginton
85C11	Staight Mile, Oxley
22C34	Staines Close, Saint Nicholas Park, Nuneaton
38B32	Staines Farm, Corley
31A22	Stainforth Close, Nuneaton
97C23	Stamford Gardens, Milverton, Leamington Spa
162C33	Stamford Hall Farm, Pillerton Prior
30B12	Stan Williams Court, Nuneaton
96B44	Stand Street, Forbes Estate, Warwi
5A34	Standedge, Stoneydelph, Tamwort
116B14	Standlake Mews, Sydenham Farm Estate, Leamington Spa
162C33	Stanford Hall Farm, Pillerton Prior
56B14	Stanford Road, Swinford
96A33	Stanks Farm, Hampton Magna, Budbrooke
96A32	Stanks Hill Island To Sherbourne Island, Warwick by pass
96A42	Stanks Hill To Gaveston, Warwick pass
96A42	Stanks Hill To Leek Wootton Isla Warwick by pass
96A32	Stanks Hill To Longbridge, Warw by pass
96A32	Stanks Hill To Sherbourne, Warw by pass
96A32	Stanks Hill, Warwick by pass
98B41	Stanley Court, Leamington
98B41	Stanley Court, Sydenham Farm E Leamington Spa
14B34	Stanley Road, Atherstone
22A43	Stanley Road, Nuneaton
71C23	Stanley Road, Rugby
156C12	Stanley Villas, Bidford
144B31	Stannells Close, Stratford upon A
81B12	Stansfield Grove, Kenilworth
98B44	Stanton Road, Sydenham Farm E Leamington
96B24	Stanton Walk, Woodloes, Warwi
118B44	Stapenhall Farm, Deppers Bridge Harbury
148A13	Staple Hill Farm, Wellesbourne
150C43	Stapledon Gardens, Temple Herdewyke, Burton Dassett
41B13	Staples Close, Bulkington, Bedw
107B22	Stapleton Close, Studley

Map ref	Address	Map ref	Address
B22	Stapleton Road, Studley	181C42	Station Road, Shipston on Stour
23	Star Corner, Barby	94C31	Station Road, Shrewley
A43	Star Lane, Claverdon	25A21	Station Road, Shustoke, Nether Whitacre
32	Star Lane, Lye Green, Claverdon	102A44	Station Road, Stockton
11	Starbold Crescent, Dorridge	144C14	Station Road, Stratford upon Avon
A11	Starbold Farm, Southam	107B14	Station Road, Studley
A32	Starbold Road, Bishops Itchington	96C34	Station Road, Warwick
14	Stareton Lane, Stareton, Stoneleigh	17B44	Station Road, Whitacre Heath, Nether Whitacre
22	Starkey Croft, Chelmsley Wood	127C23	Station Road, Wilmcote, Aston Cantlow
13	Starmer Place, Hatton Green, Hatton	51A43	Station Road, Wolston
13	Start Barn, Hinckley	14B32	Station Street, Atherstone
14	Start Farm, Hinckley	152B42	Station Works, Fenny Compton
34	Startin Close, Exhall, Bedworth	94C21	Station Yard, Hatton Station, Hatton
2	Statfold Barn Farm, Tamworth	22B43	Station 20, Nuneaton
4	Statfold Farm, Thorpe Constantine	40A22	Station 21, Bedworth
33	Station Approach, Leamington Spa	24C42	Station 22, Coleshill
43	Station Approach, Rugby	6A13	Station 23, Polesworth
32	Station Avenue, Warwick	14C31	Station 24, Atherstone
4	Station Drive, Tanworth in Arden	51C13	Station 25, Brinklow
14	Station Drive, Water Orton	71A11	Station 26, Rugby
43	Station Farm, Dunchurch	63C44	Station 27, Kenilworth
42	Station Farm, Leamington Hastings	96B34	Station 28, Warwick
4	Station Farm, Polesworth	97C31	Station 29, Leamington Spa
3	Station Lane, Baddesley Clinton	119B21	Station 30, Southam
4	Station Lane, Ringswood, Lapworth	152A42	Station 31, Fenny Compton
43	Station Mill, Stockton	164B21	Station 32, Kineton
43	Station Road Farm, Harbury	175B44	Station 33, Tysoe
31	Station Road, Alcester	181C42	Station 34, Shipston on Stour
3	Station Road, Arley	144C13	Station 35, Stratford upon Avon
22	Station Road, Bishops Itchington	156B12	Station 36, Bidford
3	Station Road, Brandon	125A34	Station 37, Alcester
3	Station Road, Catthorpe	107C14	Station 38, Studley
3	Station Road, Chelmsley Wood	92B23	Station 39, Henley in Arden
3	Station Road, Clifton upon Dunsmore	116A12	Stauton Road, Whitnash
1	Station Road, Coleshill	47A14	Stave Hall Farm, Monks Kirby
3	Station Road, Deppers Bridge	54C34	Staveley Way, Brownsover, Rugby
4	Station Road, Dorridge	71A33	Staverton Leys, Hillside, Rugby
42	Station Road, Fenny Compton	191C31	Steel Lane, Long Compton
	Station Road, Fillongley	192A23	Steel Lane, Whichford
	Station Road, Furnace End, Over Whitacre	70C13	Steele Street, New Bilton, Rugby
	Station Road, Gannaway, Claverdon	53B43	Steeping Road, Rugby
2	Station Road, Harbury	34B23	Stella Croft, Chelmsley Wood
4	Station Road, Harvington	70C14	Stephen Street, Rugby
	Station Road, Hatton	5A23	Stephenson Close, Amington Ind.est., Tamworth
	Station Road, Hatton Station, Hatton	97B21	Stephenson Close, Milverton, Leamington Spa
	Station Road, Henley in Arden	40B33	Stephenson Road, Exhall, Bedworth
	Station Road, Higham, Higham on The Hill	23C33	Stephenson Road, Hinckley
	Station Road, Kenilworth	141A44	Steppes Piece, Bidford
	Station Road, Kilsby	14C43	Steppy Lane, Mancetter
2	Station Road, Leamington Hastings	172C33	Stepstones Farm, Halford
	Station Road, Lilbourne	30C31	Sterling Way, Nuneaton
	Station Road, Long Marston	97C23	Stewart Court, Leamington Spa
	Station Road, Marton	28A33	Stewart Court, New Arley, Arley
	Station Road, Node Hill, Sambourne	30A14	Stewart Street, Coten, Nuneaton
2	Station Road, Norton		
	Station Road, Polesworth		
	Station Road, Salford Priors		

Map ref	Address
98C43	Stidfall Grove, Sydenham Farm Estate, Leamington
170A21	Stileman Close, Lower Quinton, Quinton
6B22	Stipers Hill Farm, Polesworth
6B21	Stipers Hill, Polesworth
82A44	Stirling Avenue, Lillington, Leamington Spa
47C14	Stocking Meadow Close, Monks Kirby
86C14	Stocks Lane, Thurlaston
98A21	Stockton Court, Leamington Spa
101C43	Stockton Fields Farm, Stockton
98A21	Stockton Grove, Lillington, Leamington Spa
101C44	Stockton Hill Farm, Stockton
101C34	Stockton Road, Birdingbury Wharf, Birdingbury
101C43	Stockton Road, Blue Lias, Stockton
101B42	Stockton Road, Long Itchington
67A33	Stoke Avenue, Ryton on Dunsmore
10A33	Stoke End Farm, Allen End, Middleton
30A13	Stokesay Close, Nuneaton
9A44	Stone Avenue, Sutton Coldfield
66A12	Stonebridge Highway, Coventry
35B41	Stonebridge Island, Bickenhill, Coleshill
100A33	Stonebridge Lane, Snowford, Long Itchington
24C41	Stonebridge Road Bypass, Coleshill
24C44	Stonebridge Road, Coleshill
134A43	Stonebridge Road, Lighthorne
24A11	Stonecross, Water Orton
65A22	Stonehaven Drive, Finham
11B21	Stonehill Farm, Cliff, Kingsbury
54B33	Stonehills, Brownsover, Rugby
82B44	Stonehouse Close, Cubbington
132B32	Stonehouse Farm, Ashorne, Newbold Pacey
37C42	Stonehouse Farm, Corley Moor, Corley
37A13	Stonehouse Farm, Fillongley
56A41	Stonehouse Farm, Lilbourne
37C34	Stonehouse Lane, Corley Moor, Corley
66B11	Stonehouse Lane, Coventry
27C23	Stonehouse Lane, Gun Hill, Arley
81C14	Stoneleigh Abbey, Stoneleigh, Kenilworth
64A44	Stoneleigh Avenue, Kenilworth
21A21	Stoneleigh Close, Hartshill
65A42	Stoneleigh Close, Stoneleigh
82B12	Stoneleigh Deer Park
21A13	Stoneleigh Glebe Farm, Mancetter
64C32	Stoneleigh Island To A45 Island, Warwick by pass
64C32	Stoneleigh Island To Chesford Island, Warwick by pass
64C32	Stoneleigh Island, Warwick by pass
82A24	Stoneleigh Road, Ashow
82A33	Stoneleigh Road, Bericote, Ashow
81C42	Stoneleigh Road, Blackdown
66A41	Stoneleigh Road, Bubbenhall
64B23	Stoneleigh Road, Gibbet Hill, Coven
64A41	Stoneleigh Road, Kenilworth
65B41	Stoneleigh Road, Stoneleigh
64C32	Stoneleigh To Leaf Lane, Warwick pass
64C32	Stoneleigh To Thickthorn, Warwick pass
119B34	Stoneton Close, Southam
153B12	Stoneton Farm, Stoneton
153C22	Stoneton Lane, Stoneton
153C23	Stoneton Moat Farm, Stoneton
116B12	Stoneway Grove, Sydenham Farm Estate, Leamington Spa
31A32	Stonewell Crescent, Whitestone, Nuneaton
36C24	Stoney Lane, Green End, Fillongley
95A11	Stoney Lane, Hatton
95A11	Stoney Lane, Little Shrewley
22A41	Stoney Road, Nuneaton
5A33	Stoneydelph Lane, Stoneydelph, Tamworth
118B32	Stoneythorpe Hall, Long Itchington
118B32	Stoneythorpe Riding Stables, Stoneythorpe, Long Itchington
181C44	Stour Court, Shipston on Stour
188A42	Stourton Farm, Stourton
192B13	Stourton Hill Barn Farm, Stourton
192B21	Stourton Hill Farm, Stourton
188A42	Stourton Road, Stourton
188B41	Stourton Road, Sutton Under Brai
173A33	Stourview, Halford
119B31	Stowe Drive, Southam
97C21	Strachey Avenue, Leamington Sp
85B14	Straight Mile, Bourton on Dunsm
85C11	Straight Mile, Carroway Head
85C11	Straight Mile, Oxley
86A11	Straight Mile, Princethorpe
97B24	Stratbearn Road, Milverton, Leamington Spa
14B41	Stratford Avenue, Atherstone
14B33	Stratford Avenue, Merevale
144A12	Stratford by pass, Drayton, Stratf upon Avon
112B44	Stratford by pass, Hampton Lucy
113A44	Stratford by pass, Marraway Tur Norton Lindsey
129B14	Stratford by pass, Snitterfield
129B13	Stratford by pass, Wilmcote
144C14	Stratford General Hospital, Strat upon Avon
113B41	Stratford Northern by pass, Fulb
169C33	Stratford Road A46, Mickleton
125B33	Stratford Road, Alcester
172B21	Stratford Road, Alderminster
130A32	Stratford Road, Bampton Lucy
142A43	Stratford Road, Bidford
127A43	Stratford Road, Billesley
59B43	Stratford Road, Cheswick Green
59B33	Stratford Road, Dorridge

Map ref	Address	Map ref	Address
B41	Stratford Road, Haselor	145A13	Summer Court, Stratford upon Avon
33	Stratford Road, Henley in Arden	142A33	Summer Hill Farm And Barns, Bidford
43	Stratford Road, Hockley Heath, Dorridge	162B42	Summerfields House Farm, Ettington
B31	Stratford Road, Ilmington	116A21	Summerton Road, Whitnash
34	Stratford Road, Lapworth	95C34	Sumner Close, Hampton Magna, Budbrooke
A11	Stratford Road, Lighthorne Heath, Lighthorne	25A41	Sumner Road, Coleshill
332	Stratford Road, Loxley	71B12	Sun Street, Rugby
C33	Stratford Road, Mickleton	165C43	Sunbeam Cottage, Radway
A22	Stratford Road, Mountford, Wellesbourne	71B12	Sunbridge Terrace, Rugby
		66B11	Sunbury Road, Coventry
321	Stratford Road, Newbold on Stour, Ettington	80C22	Suncliffe Drive, Kenilworth
		147A31	Sunderland Place, Mountford, Wellesbourne
242	Stratford Road, Ratley And Upton	6A32	Sunfields Close, Dordon
A13	Stratford Road, Salford Priors	23C32	Sunneydale Road, Hinckley
244	Stratford Road, Shennington	81A12	Sunningdale Avenue, Windy Arbour, Kenilworth
234	Stratford Road, Shipston on Stour		
A42	Stratford Road, Temple Grafton	31A24	Sunningdale Close, Whitestone, Nuneaton
13	Stratford Road, Warwick		
14	Stratford Road, Wootton Wawen	2A44	Sunningdale, Amington, Tamworth
1	Stratford Street, Nuneaton	37C41	Sunny Side Farm, Allesley
3	Stratton Street, Atherstone	69C11	Sunny View Farm, Long Lawford
1	Streetfield Farm, Monks Kirby	66B11	Sunnybank Avenue, Coventry
4	Stretton Court, Brownsover, Rugby	80C42	Sunnyside Cottage, Leek Wootton
13	Stretton Crescent, Whitnash	29C14	Sunnyside Court, Stockingford, Nuneaton
3	Stretton Fields Farm, Stretton Baskerville		
		37B33	Sunnyside Farm, Chapel Green, Fillongley
2	Stretton House Farm, Stretton on Dunsmore	120B11	Sunnyside Farm, Napton on The Hill
		176B31	Sunrising Farm, Sunrising Hill, Tysoe
3	Stretton Road, Nuneaton	176A24	Sunrising Hill, Lower Tysoe, Tysoe
1	Stretton Road, Princethorpe	6A32	Sunset Close, Saint Helena, Polesworth
2	Stretton Road, Stretton on Dunsmore	80C22	Sunshine Close, Kenilworth
11	Stretton Road, Stretton on Fosse	144B22	Sunshine Cottage, Shottery, Stratford upon Avon
3	Stretton Road, Wolston		
	Stripes Farm, Dorridge	29C21	Surrey Close, Stockingford, Nuneaton
2	Stroma Way, Heath End, Nuneaton	96C31	Surrey Court, Packmores, Warwick
	Stuart Close, Warwick	29C21	Sussex Close, Stockingford, Nuneaton
3	Stuart Gardens, Temple Herdewyke, Burton Dassett	96C31	Sussex Court, Woodloes, Warwick
		161A41	Sutcliffe Avenue, Alderminster
	Stubbs Close, Collycroft, Bedworth	134B11	Sutcliffe Drive, Harbury
2	Stud Farm Drive, Moreton Paddox, Moreton Morrell	96C22	Sutherland Close, Woodloes, Warwick
		40A11	Sutherland Drive, Collycroft, Nuneaton
	Studland Avenue, Hillmorton, Rugby	9A14	Sutton by pass, Bassetts Pole
1	Studley College, Studley	9A14	Sutton Coldfield by pass, Middleton
	Sturley Close, Kenilworth	70B23	Sutton House, Rugby
	Styles Avenue, Hampton Magna, Budbrooke	188B14	Sutton Lane, Brailes
		188A34	Sutton Lane, Stourton
	Styles Close, Leamington Spa	188B32	Sutton Lane, Sutton Under Brailes
	Styles Place, Yelvertoft	188B43	Sutton Mill, Stourton
	Sudbury Close, Lillington, Leamington Spa	21A34	Sutton Park, Bucks Hill, Nuneaton
		188B41	Sutton Road, Stourton
	Sudeley Road, Caldwell, Nuneaton	188B41	Sutton Road, Sutton Under Brailes
	Suffolk Close, Bedworth	40B43	Sutton Stop, Sutton Stop, Coventry
	Suffolk Close, Stockingford, Nuneaton	97C41	Swadling Street, Leamington Spa
	Suffolk Street, Leamington Spa	98B43	Swaincrofts, Sydenham Farm Estate, Leamington
	Sugarswell Farm, Hook Norton		
	Sugarswell Lane, Shenington	129A41	Swallow Close, Stratford upon Avon
	Sugarswell Lane, Sunrising Hill, Tysoe		

Map ref	Address
24A31	Swallow Drive, Kingshurst
13B11	Swan Farm, Dordon
127B24	Swan Fold, Wilmcote, Aston Cantlow
125A34	Swan Street, Alcester
98A23	Swan Street, Leamington Spa
96C41	Swan Street, Warwick
145A21	Swan Theatre, Stratford upon Avon
145A22	Swans Nest Lane, Stratford upon Avon
13C34	Swans Wood Farm, Merevale
102B13	Sweedish Houses, Hill, Leamington Hastings
171A12	Sweet Knowle Farm, Preston on Stour
171A12	Sweet Knowle Farm, Wimpstone
12C22	Sweethours Farm, Baddesley Ensor
53C24	Swift House, Cosford
54A33	Swift Park, Swift Valley Estate, Rugby
53C22	Swift Point, Cosford
129A43	Swift Road, Stratford upon Avon
54A32	Swift Valley Estate, Rugby
54A32	Swift Valley Industrial Estate, Rugby
54A32	Swift Valley, Rugby
145A14	Swimming Baths, Stratford upon Avon
21A43	Swinburne Close, Galley Common, Nuneaton
5A34	Swindale, Stoneydelph, Tamworth
73C21	Swinertons Lane, Yelvertoft
55C11	Swinford Road, Shawell
6A32	Sycamore Avenue, Saint Helena, Polesworth
129A41	Sycamore Close, Stratford upon Avon
147C22	Sycamore Close, Wellesbourne Hasting, Wellesbourne
28A34	Sycamore Corner, New Arley, Arley
28A34	Sycamore Crescent, New Arley, Arley
97A22	Sycamore Grove, Percy Estate, Warwick
71A11	Sycamore Grove, Rugby
119B13	Sycamore Grove, Southam
21B42	Sycamore Road, Camphill, Nuneaton
11B34	Sycamore Road, Kingsbury
39B21	Sycamores, The, Bedworth
98B41	Sydenham Drive, Sydenham Farm Estate, Leamington Spa
98A42	Sydenham Road, Sydenham Farm Estate, Leamington Spa
39C22	Sydney Court, Bedworth
54B33	Sydraway House, Rugby
158A12	Sykes Cottage, Welford on Avon
5A34	Sykesmere, Stoneydelph, Tamworth
167C23	Sylvan Court, Farnborough
160A32	Sylvester Cottage, Preston on Stour
39A42	Synkere Close, Keresley Newlands, Keresley
71A33	Sywell Leys, Hillside, Rugby
62A24	Table Oak Farm, Mere End
62A22	Table Oak Lane, Frogmore, Mere End
97C43	Tachbrook Court, Leamington Spa
115B42	Tachbrook Hill Farm, Bishops Tachbrook
97B44	Tachbrook Park Drive, Leamington Spa

Map ref	Address
115C12	Tachbrook Park, Whitnash, Leamington Spa
115C22	Tachbrook Road, Bishops Tachbroo
115C12	Tachbrook Road, Heathcote, Whitn
97C42	Tachbrook Road, Leamington Spa
115C12	Tachbrook Street, Leamington Spa
38C14	Taffs Farm, Astley
39A22	Taffs Farm, Market End, Bedworth
64A41	Tainters Hill, Kenilworth
66B14	Talbot Cars, Ryton on Dunsmore
98A32	Talbot Court, Leamington Spa
145A11	Talbot Road, Stratford upon Avon
80C13	Talisman Close, Kenilworth
80C14	Talisman Square, Kenilworth
172A22	Talton Farm, Tredington
172B21	Talton Road, Newbold on Stour, Tredington
41A22	Tamar Road, Bulkington, Bedwort
11B41	Tame Bank, Kingsbury
2A41	Tamworth Road, Amington, Tamv
27A32	Tamworth Road, Arley
9A14	Tamworth Road, Bassetts Pole
11B31	Tamworth Road, Cliff
11B33	Tamworth Road, Cole End
38A24	Tamworth Road, Corley
11B14	Tamworth Road, Dosthill
37C13	Tamworth Road, Fillongley
9A14	Tamworth Road, Hints
38B41	Tamworth Road, Keresley
11B31	Tamworth Road, Kingsbury
9A22	Tamworth Road, Littleworth End Middleton
18A41	Tamworth Road, Nether Whitacr
6A23	Tamworth Road, Polesworth
9A22	Tamworth Road, Sutton Coldfiel
91B22	Tamworth Road, Ullenhall
91B22	Tamworth Road, Ullenhall
12B21	Tamworth Road, Wood End
76A44	Tanworth Lane, Beaudesert
5A34	Tanhill, Stoneydelph, Tamworth
185A21	Tankards Hill, Ebrington
185B21	Tankards Hill, Paxford
185C23	Tankards Hill, Stretton on Fosse
98C13	Tanners Farm, Lillington, Leami Spa
57B21	Tanners Green Lane, Fulford He Tidbury Green
57A24	Tanners Green Lane, Tanners G Wythall
80C12	Tannery Court, Kenilworth
87A14	Tanser Court, Dunchurch
92B11	Tanworth Lane, Beaudesert
75C42	Tanworth Lane, Ullenhall
91B14	Tanworth Road, Ullenhall
81A11	Tanyards Mews, Kenilworth
81B12	Tappinger Grove, Kenilworth
77A21	Tapster Farm, Lapworth
77A33	Tapster Lane, Copt Green, Lap'
76C24	Tapster Lane, Lapworth

Map ref	Address
A21	Tarn Close, Bedworth
5A21	Taskers Way, Stratford upon Avon
332	Tatnall Green, Packmores, Warwick
A34	Tattle Bank, Southam
B22	Tavern Lane, Shottery, Stratford upon Avon
34	Taverners Lane, Atherstone
34	Taverners Walk, Atherstone
31	Tavistock House, Goodyears End, Bedworth
23	Tavistock Street, Leamington Spa
43	Tavistock Way, Nuneaton
11	Tay Croft, Chelmsley Wood
21	Taylor Avenue, Lillington, Leamington Spa
44	Taylor Close, Kenilworth
34	Taylor Court, Warwick
A23	Taylors Lane, Upper Quinton, Quinton
43	Teal Close, Stratford upon Avon
22	Teal Road, Studley
42	Telegraph Street, Shipston on Stour
44	Telford Avenue, Leamington Spa
44	Telford Avenue, New Cubbington, Leamington Spa
3	Telford Road, Exhall, Bedworth
21	Telons Road, Heath End, Nuneaton
3	Temley Hall Farm, Shawell
43	Temperance Cottage, Radway
4	Templar Cottage, Warwick
11	Temple End, Harbury
4	Temple Farm, Frogmore
2	Temple Farm, Temple Balsall
4	Temple Green, Lodge Wood Est., Warwick
1	Temple Hill, Wolvey
1	Temple Lane, Fillongley
3	Temple Lane, Temple Balsall
3	Temple Road, Dorridge
4	Temple Street, Rugby
2	Temple Way, Coleshill
4	Ten Acres, Kinwarton, Alcester
4	Tenby Close, Goodyears End, Bedworth
4	Tenby Court, Leamington Spa
1	Tenlons Road, Heath End, Nuneaton
4	Tennant Street, Attleborough, Nuneaton
	Tennyson Avenue, Forbes Estate, Warwick
	Tennyson Avenue, Shakespeare Gardens, Rugby
	Tennyson Close, Kenilworth
2	Tennyson Road, Stratford upon Avon
	Tenter Street, Atherstone
	Terets Farm, Lapworth
	Terrace Road, Atherstone
	Terry Avenue, Milverton, Leamington Spa
	Tewkesbury Drive, Bedworth
	Thackeray Close, Galley Common, Nuneaton

Map ref	Address
70C34	Thackeray Close, Hillside, Rugby
170A21	Thackery Close, Lower Quinton, Quinton
41A21	Thames Close, Bulkington, Bedworth
107C14	Thane Close, Studley
30A41	The Abbey Theatre, Nuneaton
119B34	The Airfield, Southam
39C21	The Alders, Bedworth
40A12	The Alex Wilson Centre, Collycroft
97C43	The Approach, Leamington Spa
64A43	The Arches, Kenilworth
11B32	The Aspens, Kingsbury
128C41	The Avenue, Bishopton, Stratford upon Avon
78A23	The Avenue, Rowington
156B12	The Bank, Bidford
149B12	The Bank, Lighthorne
156B24	The Bank, Marcliff, Bidford
65B41	The Bank, Stoneleigh
89C22	The Banks, Kilsby
64B14	The Beeches, Gibbet Hill, Coventry
117A44	The Beeches, Harbury
6A33	The Beeches, Polesworth
145A14	The Beeches, Stratford upon Avon
16B21	The Belfry Hotel, Wishaw
16B21	The Belfry, Wishaw
41A12	The Birches, Bulkington, Bedworth
30A22	The Bull Ring, Coten, Nuneaton
134B12	The Bull Ring, Harbury
101A32	The Bungalow, Long Itchington
191C33	The Bungalows, Long Compton
158B11	The Bungalows, Welford on Avon
147B12	The Bungalows, Wellesbourne
191C42	The Butts, Long Compton
120C33	The Butts, Napton on The Hill
96C33	The Butts, Warwick
97B24	The Cedars, Leamington Spa
97A21	The Chantry, Percy Estate, Warwick
176B12	The Chapel, Radway
39C21	The Chestnuts, Bedworth
22B34	The Chines, Weddington, Nuneaton
29C12	The Circle, Stockingford, Nuneaton
97C13	The Cloisters, Leamington Spa
138A43	The Cloisters, Priors Hardwick
119B23	The Cloisters, Southam
107B14	The Cloisters, Studley
92B32	The Close, Beaudesert
51A41	The Close, Brandon
162A42	The Close, Ettington
167B32	The Close, Farnborough
173A34	The Close, Halford
130C33	The Close, Hampton Lucy
64A41	The Close, Kenilworth
116A11	The Close, Leamington Spa
170A14	The Close, Lower Quinton, Quinton
188B32	The Close, Sutton Under Brailes
56A12	The Close, Swinford
127C24	The Close, Wilmcote, Aston Cantlow
22C41	The Clunes, Nuneaton

Map ref	Address	Map ref	Address
92B23	The Coach Houses, Henley in Arden	9A44	The Falcons, Sutton Coldfield
25A41	The Colesleys, Coleshill	104A32	The Farm, Sawbridge, Wolfhamcote
13C33	The Common, Baddesley Ensor, Baxterley	193A21	The Firs, Ascott
		193A21	The Firs, Ascott, Whichford
13B21	The Common, Grendon	39C21	The Firs, Bedworth Woodlands, Bedworth
64B41	The Common, Kenilworth		
15A41	The Coppice, Mancetter	11B34	The Firs, Kingsbury
22B33	The Coppice, Weddington, Nuneaton	170B13	The Firs, Lower Quinton, Quinton
87B14	The Copse House, Dunchurch	135C21	The Folly Road, Bishops Itchington
40A34	The Copse, Exhall, Bedworth	135C13	The Folly Road, Ladbroke
26A23	The Cottage Farm, Shustoke	13B32	The Folly, Merevale
84B33	The Cottage, Eathorpe	107C13	The Foredraught, Studley
81B13	The Courtyard, Kenilworth	34A44	The Foredrift, Chelmsley Wood
164B23	The Courtyard, Little Kineton, Kineton	41B34	The Furlongs Farm, Bedworth
19B11	The Crawshaws, Bentley	97C22	The Gables, Leamington Spa
13B13	The Crescent, Baddesley Ensor	6A21	The Gables, Polesworth
110C42	The Crescent, Bearley Cross, Wootton Wawen	6A21	The Gables, Polesworth
		98C43	The Gardens, Radford Semele
141B44	The Crescent, Bidford	86C14	The Gardens, Thurlaston
51C12	The Crescent, Brinklow	81A14	The Gardens, Windy Arbour, Kenilworth
53A14	The Crescent, Harborough Magna		
38C42	The Crescent, Keresley Newlands, Keresley	133C22	The Gated Road, Lighthorne
		38A34	The Glebe, Corley
69B41	The Crescent, Lawford Heath, Long Lawford	82C44	The Grange, Cubbington
		98A22	The Grange, Lillington, Leamington
120C42	The Crescent, Napton on The Hill	132C41	The Grange, Little Morrell, Moreton Morrell
98C21	The Crest, Lillington, Leamington Spa		
41A22	The Croft, Bulkington, Bedworth	97A34	The Grange, Myton, Leamington
72A31	The Croft, Hillmorton, Rugby	16A22	The Gravel, Overgreen, Wishaw
93C32	The Cumsey, Claverdon	135B23	The Greaves Way, Bishops Itchington
94B13	The Cumsey, Rowington	57B23	The Green Farm, Forshaw Heath, Tanworth in Arden
94B13	The Cumsley, Shrewley Common, Rowington		
		56A41	The Green Farm, Lilbourne
36A42	The Dairy Farm, Great Packington	34A42	The Green Way, Chelmsley Wood
36A41	The Dairy Farm, Little Packington	2A42	The Green, Amington, Tamworth
22B32	The Dairy Farm, Weddington, Nuneaton	132B31	The Green, Ashorne
110B13	The Dale, Wootton Wawen	30C21	The Green, Attleborough, Nuneaton
97C23	The Dell, Leamington Spa	4A24	The Green, Austrey
110B12	The Dell, Wootton Wawen	89B23	The Green, Barby
21C41	The Dingle, Camphill, Nuneaton	70B32	The Green, Bilton, Rugby
85A24	The Dingles, Frankton	105B23	The Green, Braunston
184C23	The Dingles, Upper Tysoe, Tysoe	102B31	The Green, Broadwell, Leamington Hastings
116B13	The Doglands, Whitnash, Leamington Spa		
		49A42	The Green, Churchover
181C32	The Driftway, Shipston on Stour	93C31	The Green, Claverdon
40B14	The Elizabeth Centre, Bedworth	87B13	The Green, Dunchurch
22B21	The Elms Farm, Caldecote	190B22	The Green, Great Wolford
32A12	The Elms Farm, Stretton Baskerville	95A13	The Green, Hatton Green, Hatton
55A43	The Elms Paddock, Clifton upon Dunsmore	177B33	The Green, Hornton
		11B41	The Green, Kingsbury
39C21	The Elms, Bedworth Woodlands, Bedworth	164B23	The Green, Little Kineton, Kineton
		191A13	The Green, Little Wolford
87B11	The Elms, Dunchurch, Rugby	101A33	The Green, Long Itchington
92B23	The Elms, Henley in Arden	70A11	The Green, Long Lawford
77B14	The Elms, Lapworth	158B43	The Green, Long Marston
80C42	The Elms, Leek Wootton	14C44	The Green, Mancetter
145A11	The Elms, Stratford upon Avon	175B44	The Green, Middle Tysoe, Tysoe
84C34	The Elms Farm, Eathorpe	165B44	The Green, Radway
97B22	The Fairways, Leamington Spa	107B23	The Green, Sambourne

...p ref	Address	Map ref	Address
33	The Green, Sheepy Parva, Sheepy	141C43	The Leys, Bidford
...22	The Green, Shustoke	173A33	The Leys, Little Wolford
...A21	The Green, Snitterfield	174B41	The Leys, Whatcote
41	The Green, Stoneleigh	57A32	The Limes Farm, Forshaw Heath, Tanworth In Arden
...44	The Green, Stretton on Dunsmore	39C21	The Limes, Bedworth Woodlands, Bedworth
...C23	The Green, Stretton on Fosse	101A33	The Limes, Long Itchington
B32	The Green, Sutton Under Brailes	39C21	The Lines, Bedworth Woodlands, Bedworth
...23	The Green, Tanworth in Arden		
1	The Green, Twycross	72A24	The Locks, Clifton upon Dunsmore
A23	The Green, Upper Quinton	72A24	The Locks, Lower Hillmorton, Rugby
C23	The Green, Wilmcote, Aston Cantlow	23B41	The Long Shoot, Nuneaton
14	The Greenways, Lillington, Leamington Spa	30B22	The Lynch, Attleborough, Nuneaton
42	The Greswoldes, Radford Semele	5C23	The Lynch, Polesworth
13	The Grove, Bedworth	186C11	The Maldens, Shipston on Stour
11	The Grove, Coleshill	97A41	The Malins, Myton, Leamington Spa
44	The Grove, Ebrington	97C21	The Maltings, Lillington, Leamington Spa
22	The Grove, Littlewood Green, Studley		
12	The Grove, Radway	22C43	The Maltings, Nuneaton
2	The Gullet, Polesworth	145A21	The Maltings, Stratford upon Avon
1	The Hall Close, Dunchurch	87A43	The Manor Farm, Kites Hardwick, Leamington Hastings
41	The Hall Farm, Wormleighton	164B23	The Mansion House, Little Kineton, Kineton
3	The Hamlet, Leek Wootton		
4	The Hawthorns, Kingsbury	144B12	The Mansley Centre, Stratford upon Avon
4	The Heath, Dunchurch		
3	The Heath, Wolvey Heath, Wolvey	39C21	The Maples, Bedworth Woodlands, Bedworth
12	The Hermitage, Radway		
4	The High Leys, Crick	73C44	The Marsh, Crick
12	The Hill Farm, Inkberrow	116B24	The Meadows Farm, Whitnash
4	The Hill Farm, Tanworth In Arden	156A12	The Meadows, Bidford
3	The Hill, Little Shrewley	81A33	The Meadows, Leek Wootton
44	The Hill, Stockton	14B32	The Mews, Atherstone
4	The Hobb, Bermuda, Nuneaton	80C13	The Mews, Kenilworth
11	The Hobbins, Shipston on Stour	110B11	The Mews, Wootton Wawen
2	The Hollies Farm, Lapworth	145A13	The Minories, Stratford upon Avon
2	The Holloway, Warwick	37B34	The Moor House Farm, Corley Moor
43	The Holmes, Radway	125A32	The Moors, Alcester
4	The Holt, Lillington, Leamington Spa	16A42	The Mount, Curdworth
4	The Horsepool, Lilbourne	144C44	The Nashes, Clifford Chambers
3	The Horseshoe, Bearley	107C21	The Newlands, Studley
	The Jawbones, Dordon	30C23	The Nook, Nuneaton
	The Jawbones, Grendon	39C21	The Oaks, Bedworth Woodlands, Bedworth
	The Jubilee Park, Bedworth		
	The Kent, Clifton upon Dunsmore	97B32	The Oaks, Leamington Spa
	The Kent, Lower Hillmorton, Rugby	120C33	The Old Bakery, Napton
	The Knibbs, Warwick	144B22	The Old Square, Shottery, Stratford upon Avon
4	The Knob, Snitterfield		
2	The Lane, Burmington	129B42	The Old Tollgate, Stratford upon Avon
3	The Langlands, Hampton Lucy	148B42	The Old Walled Garden, Compton Verney
	The Larches, Exhall, Bedworth		
	The Larches, Kingsbury	13B33	The Orchard, Baxterley
	The Laurels Farm, Kings Newnham	98A11	The Orchard, Leamington Spa
	The Laurels, Kingsbury	170A21	The Orchard, Lower Quinton, Quinton
4	The Lawns, Whitnash, Leamington Spa	84C41	The Orchard, Marton
	The Lawns, Wootton Wawen	170A22	The Orchard, Quinton
4	The Lawyers Farm, Upper Quinton, Quinton	174B41	The Orchard, Whatcote
	The Lees, Bishops Tachbrook	58B12	The Orchards, Cheswick Green
	The Leys Estate, Newton And Biggin		

Map ref	Address
54C24	The Orchards, Newton And Biggin
127C23	The Orchards, Wilmcote, Aston Cantlow
41A14	The Paddocks, Bulkington, Bedworth
64A44	The Paddocks, Kenilworth
178C13	The Paddocks, Mollington
68A43	The Paddocks, Stretton on Dunsmore
96C34	The Paddocks, Warwick
67C44	The Paddox, Stretton on Dunsmore
40B13	The Palace Bingo Club, Bedworth
30A14	The Parade, Coten, Nuneaton
97C24	The Parade, Leamington Spa
188C14	The Park, Brailes
188B14	The Park, Lower Brailes
121C42	The Pastures, Napton on The Hill
114A22	The Peacocks, Longbridge, Warwick
145C11	The Pinfold, Tiddington, Stratford upon Avon
156B13	The Pleck, Bidford
63C11	The Pools, Burton Green, Kenilworth
84B33	The Poplars Farm, Eathorpe
57B31	The Poplars Farm, Forshaw Heath, Tanworth in Arden
23A42	The Poplars Farm, Long Shoot, Nuneaton
8A41	The Poplars Farm, Sheepy Magna, Sheepy
120C33	The Poplars, Napton on The Hill
109B21	The Poplars, Shelfield, Aston Cantlow
29B22	The Poplars, Stockingford, Nuneaton
151B42	The Prebend, Northend, Burton Dassett
80C21	The Precinct, Kenilworth
71A13	The Precinct, Rugby
147B14	The Precinct, Wellesbourne Hasting, Wellesbourne
40B22	The Priors, Bedworth
29C14	The Raywoods, Heath End, Nuneaton
110B13	The Retreat, Wootton Wawen
13B24	The Riddings, Grendon
13B21	The Riddings, Grendon Common
127B34	The Ridgeway, Aston Cantlow
89B32	The Ridgeway, Barby
127B34	The Ridgeway, Drayton, Stratford upon Avon
89C24	The Ridgeway, Kilsby
97A23	The Ridgeway, Percy Estate, Warwick
121B22	The Rookery Farm, Lower Shuckburgh
125B33	The Rookery, Alcester
19B22	The Rookery, Birchley Heath, Ansley
20C43	The Rookery, Galley Common, Nuneaton
45B14	The Row, Anstey
65C22	The Row, Baginton
39C21	The Rowans, Bedworth
69B33	The Ryelands, Lawford Heath, Long Lawford
96B34	The Saltisford, Warwick
116B21	The Seekings, Whitnash, Leamington Spa
185C23	The Sharries, Stretton on Fosse
6A41	The Short Woods, Dordon
167A11	The Slade, Fenny Compton
107A14	The Slough, Sambourne
107A14	The Slough, Studley
68A42	The Small Holding Farm, Stretton o Dunsmore
29B42	The South Farm, Arbury, Nuneaton
135B23	The Spinney, Bishops Itchington
53A41	The Spinney, Long Lawford
15A41	The Spinney, Mancetter
97B23	The Spinney, Milverton, Leamingto Spa
29B11	The Spires, Stockingford, Nuneaton
30B22	The Square, Attleborough Green
30B22	The Square, Attleborough, Nuneatc
145A43	The Square, Clifford Chambers
87B14	The Square, Dunchurch
162A42	The Square, Ettington
80C12	The Square, Kenilworth
101A33	The Square, Long Itchington
175B42	The Square, Middle Tysoe, Tysoe
119C12	The Square, Stockton
42B12	The Square, Wolvey
92A44	The Square, Wootton Wawen
85C11	The Staight Mile, Oxley
5C43	The Straight Fields, Hall End, Pole
85C11	The Straight Mile, Carroway Head
145A21	The Swan Theatre, Stratford upon Avon
41C44	The Switchback, Withybrook
181C41	The Tannery, Shipston on Stour
184B14	The Tchure, Upper Tysoe, Tysoe
96C44	The Templars Bridge End, Warwi
153B31	The Ten Cottage, Wormleighton
129A21	The Terrace, Snitterfield
142C13	The Terrace, Temple Grafton
18C41	The Uplands, Over Whitacre
116C12	The Valley, Radford Semele
64B43	The Wardens, Kenilworth
95C34	The Warwicks, Hampton Magna, Budbrooke
127C24	The Wharf, Wilmcote, Aston Can
144C21	The Willows N, Stratford upon A
14C13	The Willows, Atherstone
39C21	The Willows, Bedworth
144C21	The Willows, Stratford upon Avc
21A31	The Woodlands, Hartshill
96B34	Theatre Street, Warwick
131B23	Thelsford Farm, Thelsford, Charl
81A14	Thickthorn Close, Kenilworth
81A24	Thickthorn Island, Leek Wootton
81A24	Thickthorn Island, Warwick by p
81A22	Thickthorn Orchards, Kenilwortt
81A24	Thickthorn To Gaveston, Warwic pass
81A24	Thickthorn To Stoneleigh, Warw pass
64B41	Thirlestane Close, Kenilworth

Map ref	Address	Map ref	Address
C42	Thirlmere Avenue, Saint Nicholas Park, Nuneaton	145C11	Tiddington Fields, Tiddington, Stratford upon Avon
A21	Thirlmere Road, Bedworth	145A22	Tiddington Road, Tiddington, Stratford upon Avon
B33	Thirlmere, Brownsover, Rugby	81A33	Tidmarsh Road, Leek Wootton
A13	Thomas Street, Bedworth	130B34	Tile Barn Farm, Hampton Lucy
A23	Thomas Street, Leamington Spa	85C14	Tile Farm, Bourton on Dunsmore
A44	Thomas Way, Long Lawford	85C14	Tile Farm, Oxley
B21	Thompson Close, Braunston	24A43	Tile Green, Kingshurst
41	Thompsons Farm, Keresley, Coventry	181C33	Tilemans Lane, Shipston on Stour
41	Thompsons Lane, Bramcote, Wolvey	2A44	Tilia Road, Amington, Tamworth
42	Thompsons Road, Keresley, Coventry	89B41	Tiltups Holt Farm, Braunston
34	Thorn Close, Brownsover, Rugby	144C13	Timothy Bridge Road, Stratford upon Avon
B22	Thorn Furlong Farm, Napton on The Hill	116C12	Tinkers Close, Radford Semele
31	Thorn Hill Farm, Whitestone, Nuneaton	76B24	Tinkers Farm, Lapworth
33	Thorn Stile Close, Cubbington	5A41	Tinkers Green Road, Tamworth
A33	Thorn Way, Long Itchington	76C23	Tinkers Lane, Lapworth
32	Thornbank, Leamington Spa	58B34	Tinkers Lane, Warings Green, Tanworth in Arden
14	Thornby Avenue, Windy Arbour, Kenilworth	81B11	Tintagel Grove, Windy Arbour, Kenilworth
32	Thorncliffe Way, Ansley Common	30C12	Tintager Way, Nuneaton
31	Thornhill Drive, Whitestone, Nuneaton	40B21	Tinterley, Bedworth
A42	Thornhill Farm, Arrow	27C41	Tippers Hill Farm, Fillongley
C12	Thornley Close, Radford Semele	27C42	Tippers Hill Lane, Fillongley
4	Thornton Close, Woodloes, Warwick	31A33	Tippett Close, Whitestone, Nuneaton
23	Thornton Farm, Ettington	64A44	Tisdale Rise, Kenilworth
41	Thorntons Lane, Chapel Green, Napton on Hill	95C32	Tithe Barn Close, Hampton Magna, Budbrooke
2	Thorntons Way, Stockingford, Nuneaton	58B32	Tithe Barn Lane, Warings Green, Tanworth in Arden
	Thorpe Lane, Thorpe Constantine	161A44	Tithe Barn, Alderminster
11	Thorpe Mews, Wellesbourne	161A44	Tithe Farm, Alderminster
14	Three Bridges Farm, Mountford, Wellesbourne	19C31	Tithe Farm, Birchley Heath, Ansley
1	Three Cornered Close, Cubbington	100C11	Tithe Farm, Marton
21	Three Gates, Lighthorne Rough, Moreton Morrell	48B32	Tithe Farm, Pailton Pastures, Pailton
1	Three Pots Farm, Hinckley	44B23	Tithe Platts Farm, Wibtoft
4	Throck Morton Road, Kinwarton	2A44	Tiua Road, Amington, Tamworth
2	Thurlaston Island To Blue Boar Island, Park Farm South	22C44	Tiverton Drive, Nuneaton
	Thurlaston Island, Aa45	190B22	Todenham Road, Great Wolford
	Thurlaston Island, Dunchurch	186B32	Todenham Road, Tidmington
	Thurlaston Island, M45	190B21	Todenham Road, Todenham
	Thurlaston Island, Park Farm South	87A32	Toft Cottage Farm, Toft, Dunchurch
	Thurlow Close, Atherstone	87B31	Toft Farm, Toft, Dunchurch
	Thurmaston Court, Leamington Spa	22A42	Toler Road, Nuneaton
	Thurnmill Road, Rugby	144A14	Toll Gate Close, Stratford on Avon
	Thursfield Road, Lillington, Leamington Spa	119A22	Toll Gate Road, Southam
	Tib Hill Farm, Kingsbury	87C32	Tollgate Farm, Grandborough
	Tibbets Close, Alcester	132B12	Tollgate Farm, Oakley Wood, Bishops Tachbrook
	Tibbits Farm, Nethercote, Wolfhamcote	71B11	Tom Brown Street, Rugby
	Tibbitts Court, Warwick	40A33	Tom Ellis Court, Exhall, Bedworth
	Tiber Way, Glebe Farm Estate, Rugby	75A22	Tom Hill, Tanworth in Arden
	Tiberius Close, Coleshill	29C14	Tomkinson Road, Stockingford, Nuneaton
	Tidbury Castle Farm, Corley Moor, Allesley	120B11	Tomlow Farm, Stockton
	Tiddington Court, Tiddington, Stratford upon Avon	120C23	Tomlow Road, Napton on The Hill
		188B14	Tommys Turn Lane, Grove End, Brailes

Map ref	Address
107B24	Toms Town, Studley
107C23	Toms Town Lane, Tomstown, Studley
119A22	Tomwell Close, Southam
106B32	Tookeys Farm, Astwood Bank
165B43	Top End, Radway
170C34	Top Farm, Admington
53C14	Top Farm, Cosford
101B32	Top Farm, Long Itchington
101A12	Top Farm, Marton
179A32	Top Farm, Mickleton
22C31	Top Farm, Weddington, Nuneaton
39B24	Top Heath, Goodyears End, Bedworth
103B43	Top House Farm, Grandborough
178B34	Top Lane, Shotteswell
21C11	Top Leather Mill Farm, Hartshill
120A13	Top New Zealand Farm, Stockton
41A34	Top Road, Barnacle, Shilton
151B34	Top Street, Northend, Burton Dassett
39B24	Topps Drive, Goodyears End, Bedworth
70C14	Torrance Road, Rugby
5A34	Torside, Stoneydelph, Tamworth
140B42	Tothall Farm, Salford Priors
140B34	Tothall Lane, Dunnington, Salford Priors
	Tower, The, Gatehouse Lane, Bedworth
129A43	Tower Close, Stratford upon Avon
141C44	Tower Croft, Bidford
34A12	Tower Croft, Chelmsley Wood
29A21	Tower Farm, Robinsons End, Nuneaton
71A32	Tower Farm, Saddlers, Rugby
141C43	Tower Hill, Bidford
26C34	Tower Lane, Shawbury, Fillongley
	Tower Lodge, Tower Road, Bedworth
40A22	Tower Road, Bedworth
71B23	Tower Road, Hillmorton, Rugby
98A41	Tower Street, Leamington Spa
29A14	Tower View Crescent, Stockingford, Nuneaton
80C22	Towers Close, Kenilworth
185C23	Town Farm, Stretton on Fosse
163C24	Town Ground, Butlers Marston
177A11	Town Hill, Ratley, Ratley And Upton
52B21	Town Thorns Farm, Easenhall
52A13	Town Thorns, Easenhall
51C14	Town Yard, Brinklow
143A23	Townsend Close, Binton
3C11	Townsend Close, Newton Regis
96C24	Townsend Close, Woodloes, Warwick
30C22	Townsend Drive, Attleborough, Nuneaton
165C42	Townsend Farm Bungalow, Radway
165C44	Townsend Farm, Radway
53A43	Townsend Lane, Long Lawford
70B11	Townsend Lane, Rugby
71C11	Townsend Road, Rugby
145C13	Townsend Road, Tiddington, Stratford upon Avon
32A24	Townsends Close, Burton Hastings
91A21	Tracy Farm, Oldberrow
156B12	Trafalgar Court, Bidford
14B14	Trafford Close, Atherstone
21B43	Trafford Drive, Whittleford, Nuneat
98A34	Trafford Lodge, Leamington Spa
64A41	Training School, Kenilworth
193B13	Traitors Ford Lane, Ascott, Whichfc
188B41	Traitorsford Road, Stourton
188B41	Traitorsford Road, Sutton Under Brailes
24C24	Trajan Hill, Coleshill
117A44	Treenshill, Harbury
2A44	Trefoil, Amington, Tamworth
40A34	Tregorrick Road, Exhall, Bedworth
40A34	Tregullan Road, Exhall, Bedworth
40A34	Trelawney Road, Exhall, Bedworth
28A33	Tremmelling Way, New Arley, Arl
40A34	Trenance Road, Exhall, Bedworth
40A34	Treneere Road, Exhall, Bedworth
41A21	Trent Road, Bulkington, Bedworth
22B44	Trent Road, Nuneaton
64B43	Trentham Gardens, Kenilworth
21A21	Trentham Road, Hartshill
40A34	Tresillian Road, Exhall, Bedworth
93C41	Trevelyan Close, Claverdon
144B12	Trevelyan Close, Stratford upon A
144B14	Trevelyan Crescent, Stratford upor Avon
40A33	Treviscoe Close, Exhall, Bedworth
71B23	Trevor White Drive, Rugby
40A34	Trevose Avenue, Exhall, Bedwortl
40A34	Trewint Close, Exhall, Bedworth
9C21	Trickley Coppice Farm, Middletor
145A31	Trinity Close, Stratford upon Avo
6C11	Trinity Close, Warton, Poleswortl
71A14	Trinity Court, Rugby
144C24	Trinity Place, Stratford upon Avo
11C33	Trinity Road, Kingsbury
11C33	Trinity Road, Piccadilly
97C23	Trinity Street, Leamington Spa
144C32	Trinity Street, Stratford upon Av
30B22	Trinity Walk, Attleborough, Nun
53C32	Tritan Park, Rugby
40C43	Trossacks, Barnacle, Shilton
70B21	Troubridge Walk, Bilton, Rugby
8A32	Trout Ponds Farm, Sheepy
97B21	Troutbeck Avenue, Leamington !
96C31	Trueman Close, Packmores, War
30C12	Truro Close, Nuneaton
34A23	Truro Walk, Chelmsley Wood
107A24	Trust Cottages, Sambourne
49C43	Trusteel Houses, Churchover
29C12	Tryan Road, Stockingford, Nune
53A21	Tuckeys Farm, Cathiron, Harbor Magna
119C11	Tuckwell Close, Stockton
39B34	Tudor Court, Goodyeson, Bedw
96B44	Tudor Court, Warwick
14C21	Tudor Crescent, Atherstone
119A32	Tudor Lane, Southam

Map ref	Address	Map ref	Address
334	Tudor Road, Camphill, Nuneaton	74C41	Ullenhall Lane, Ullenhall
C14	Tulip Court, Leamington Spa	97B21	Ullswater Avenue, Leamington Spa
A12	Tulip Tree Avenue, Windy Arbour, Kenilworth	22C42	Ullswater Avenue, Saint Nicholas Park, Nuneaton
A12	Tulip Tree Court, Windy Arbour, Kenilworth	40A21	Ullswater Road, Bedworth
A12	Tulliver Close, Bedworth	54C33	Ulverston, Brownsover, Rugby
23	Tulliver Road, Caldwell, Nuneaton	58A32	Umberslade Road, Earlswood, Tanworth in Arden
11	Tunnel Barn Farm, Shrewley Common, Rowington	75C24	Umberslade Road, Umberslade Park, Tanworth in Arden
11	Tunnel Road, Ansley, Nuneaton	184A43	Under Hill Farm, Winderton, Brailes
41	Turberville Drive, Leamington Spa	65B14	Underhill Close, Finham
13	Turkey Farm, Hatton	97B24	Union Road, Milverton, Leamington Spa
23	Turnberry Drive, Whitestone, Nuneaton	98A43	Union Row, Leamington Spa
4	Turnberry, Amington, Tamworth	71A21	Union Street, Rugby
11	Turner Close, Collycroft, Bedworth	145A13	Union Street, Stratford upon Avon
24	Turner Close, Lower Hillmorton, Rugby	98A41	Union Walk, Leamington Spa
31	Turners End Farm, Rowington	60B42	Uplands Farm, Chessetts Wood, Lapworth
21	Turnpike Drive, Water Orton	93B11	Uplands Farm, Lowsonford, Rowington
41	Turpin Court, Leamington Spa	176C24	Uplands Farm, Ratley And Upton
43	Turpin House, Rugby	96B24	Upper Cape, The Cape, Warwick
2	Turton Way, Kenilworth	183C34	Upper Chelmscote Farm, Upper Chelmscote, Brailes
11	Tusbrook Farm, Grove End, Brailes	142B41	Upper Common Farm, Temple Grafton
4	Tutbury Lane, Bretford	122B42	Upper Farm, Catesby
2	Tutbury Lane, Brinklow	159C42	Upper Farm, Radbrook, Preston on Stour
4	Tutehill, Stoneydelph, Tamworth		
44	Tutnells Hill Farm, Newnham, Aston Cantlow	174A44	Upper Farm, Whatcote
2	Tuttle Hill, Nuneaton	113B43	Upper Fulbrook Farm, Fulbrook
3	Tuttle Way, Nuneaton	161C21	Upper Goldicote Farm, Goldicote, Alderminster
4	Twenty one Oaks, Bentley	188B22	Upper Grove Farm, Grove End, Brailes
4	Twenty one Oaks, Merevale	97C23	Upper Grove Street, Leamington Spa
	Two Gates, Tamworth	98A23	Upper Hill Street, Leamington Spa
	Twychell Lane, Sheepy Magna, Sheepy	98A31	Upper Holly Walk, Leamington Spa
	Twycross Lane, Twycross	10A13	Upper House Farm, Middleton
	Twycross Road, Sheepy Magna, Sheepy	146C11	Upper Hunscote Farm, Hunscote, Charlecote
	Twycross Walk, Woodloes, Warwick	106B12	Upper Hunt End Farm, Hunt End
13	Tyler Street, Stratford upon Avon	64A33	Upper Ladyes Hills, Kenilworth
	Tyne Close, Chelmsley Wood	106C44	Upper Park Farm, Great Barr
	Tynley Close, Binley Woods	137A23	Upper Radbourne Farm, Upper Radbourne
	Tysoe Close, Hockley Heath, Cheswick Green	63C44	Upper Rosemary Hill, Kenilworth
1	Tysoe Fields Road, Tysoe	183A23	Upper Saint Dennis Farm, Honington
4	Tysoe Hill Farm, Upper Tysoe, Tysoe	90B11	Upper Skilts Farm, Gorcott, Studley
4	Tysoe Hill, Upper Tysoe, Tysoe	108C23	Upper Spernall Farm, Morgrove Coppice, Spernall
3	Tysoe Road, Butlers Marston		
4	Tysoe Road, Little Kineton, Kineton	108C23	Upper Spernall Hill, Spernall
2	Tysoe Road, Radway	135A43	Upper Spring Farm, Bishops Itchington
1	Tysoe Road, Tysoe	63C34	Upper Spring Lane, Kenilworth
4	Tysoe Vale Farm, Lower Tysoe, Tysoe	172B14	Upthorpe Farm, Ettington Park, Ettington
	Tything Road, Coughton		
	Tything Road, Kinwarton, Alcester	176B32	Upton House, Ratley And Upton, Edgehill
2	Ufton Crossroads, Ufton		
	Ufton Fields, Ufton	70B14	Upton Road, New Bilton, Rugby
	Ufton Hill, Ufton	72A33	Vale Close, Hillmorton, Rugby
	Ufton Lane, Ufton		
	Ugly Bridge, Budbrooke, Warwick		
	Ullenhall Lane, Beoley		
	Ullenhall Lane, Gorcott Hill, Oldberrow		

Map ref	Address
23A12	Vale Farm, Higham, Higham on The Hill
29C13	Vale View, Stockingford, Nuneaton
180B13	Valenders Road, Ilmington
144B24	Valentine Close, Stratford upon Avon
58C22	Valentines Farm, Illshaw Heath, Cheswick Green
147A24	Valetta Close, Mountford, Wellesbourne
147A24	Valetta Way, Mountford, Wellesbourne
125A24	Vallet Avenue, Alcester
86C44	Valley Farm, Kites Hardwick, Leamington Hastings
60C33	Valley Farm, Lapworth
116C11	Valley Farm, Radford Semele
165B34	Valley Farm, Radway
29A11	Valley Farm, Robinsons End, Nuneaton
178B24	Valley Farm, Shotteswell
93C23	Valley Farm, Yarningale, Claverdon
113A44	Valley Fields Farm, Fulbrook
60B34	Valley Lane, Lapworth
58A23	Valley Road, Cheswick Green
58A32	Valley Road, Earlswood, Tanworth in Arden
28C12	Valley Road, Galley Common, Nuneaton
86C44	Valley Road, Kites Hardwick, Leamington Hastings
98B13	Valley Road, Lillington, Leamington Spa
116C12	Valley Road, Radford Semele
165B34	Valley Road, Radway
71C11	Valley Sports Club, Rugby
116C12	Valley Street, Radford Semele
65B13	Vardon Drive, Finham
38C14	Vauls Farm, Astley
142A23	Vauxhall Farm, Ardens Grafton, Bidford
30C22	Veasley Close, Attleborough, Nuneaton
120C11	Ventnor Farm, Calcutt, Grandborough
22B42	Ventnor Street, Weddington, Nuneaton
114A12	Verden Avenue, Warwick
114B34	Verdon Place, Barford
116A24	Verdun Close, Whitnash
71C24	Vere Road, Hillmorton, Rugby
192C22	Vermon House Farm, Ascott
98C43	Vermont Grove, Sydenham Farm Estate, Leamington Spa
163C31	Verney Close, Butlers Marston
149B14	Verney Close, Lighthorne
129A41	Verney Drive, Stratford upon Avon
129A43	Verney Gardens, Stratford upon Avon
164B31	Verney Houses, Little Kineton, Kineton
134C43	Verney Road, Lighthorne Heath, Lighthorne
71C31	Vernon Avenue, The Paddox, Rugby
97C13	Vernon Close, Leamington Spa
102A21	Vernon Field House Farm, Leamington Hastings

Map ref	Address
193A22	Vernon House Farm, Ascott, Whichford
29C12	Vernons Court, Stockingford, Nunea
29C12	Vernons Lane, Stockingford, Nuneat
129A41	Verny Drive, Stratford upon Avon
114A12	Veroen Avenue
31A24	Verona Close, Whitestone, Nuneato
145A11	Verona, Stratford upon Avon
24A22	Vesey Close, Water Orton
5C44	Vicarage Close, Hall End, Dordon
14C33	Vicarage Close, Mancetter
120C34	Vicarage Close, Napton on The Hill
178C31	Vicarage Close, Shotteswell
51B42	Vicarage Farm, Bretford
74C14	Vicarage Farm, Tanworth in Arden
51B42	Vicarage Farm, Wolston
97A31	Vicarage Fields, All Saints, Warwic
81A21	Vicarage Gardens, Kenilworth
10A24	Vicarage Hill, Middleton
54C43	Vicarage Hill, Rugby
75A23	Vicarage Hill, Tanworth in Arden
39B41	Vicarage Lane, Ash Green, Bedwo
87B14	Vicarage Lane, Dunchurch
134C11	Vicarage Lane, Harbury
191C42	Vicarage Lane, Long Compton
138B34	Vicarage Lane, Priors Marston
114A23	Vicarage Lane, Sherbourne
178C31	Vicarage Lane, Shotteswell
24B22	Vicarage Lane, Water Orton
115B32	Vicarage Rise, Bishops Tachbrook
58B13	Vicarage Road, Cheswick Green
60A33	Vicarage Road, Darley Green
59C33	Vicarage Road, Dorridge
87B11	Vicarage Road, Dunchurch
122B11	Vicarage Road, Flecknoe, Wolfhar
98A14	Vicarage Road, Lillington, Leamin Spa
120C32	Vicarage Road, Napton on The H
59C33	Vicarage Road, Packwood
70C14	Vicarage Road, Rugby
65A42	Vicarage Road, Stoneleigh
174B43	Vicarage Road, Whatcote
30B11	Vicarage Street, Nuneaton
70C12	Victoria Avenue, Rugby
145A13	Victoria Close, Stratford upon A
97C34	Victoria Colonnade, Leamington
165C43	Victoria Cottage, Radway
145A22	Victoria Cottage, Stratford upon
96B34	Victoria Mews, Warwick
97C33	Victoria Park, Leamington Spa
141B41	Victoria Road, Bidford
21A34	Victoria Road, Chapel End, Nun
21A34	Victoria Road, Hartshill
97C33	Victoria Road, Leamington Spa
14C42	Victoria Road, Mancetter
97C33	Victoria Street, Leamington Spa
70C14	Victoria Street, New Bilton, Rug
30B11	Victoria Street, Nuneaton
96B34	Victoria Street, Warwick

Map ref	Address
?34	Victoria Terrace, Leamington Spa
?C12	Victoria Terrace, Stockton
?B11	Victoria Way, Bidford
?23	Villa Close, Bulkington, Bedworth
?23	Villa Crescent, Bulkington, Bedworth
?41	Villa Farm, Withybrook
?12	Village Farm, Ansley
?C23	Village Farm, Gaydon
?44	Village Farm, Hampton on The Hill, Budbrooke
?32	Vicarage Mews, Rugby
?33	Village Farm, Offchurch
?A13	Village Road, Little Wolford
?332	Village Road, Sutton Under Brailes
?A42	Village Street, Harvington
?42	Villiers Hill Farm, Kenilworth
?44	Villiers Road, Kenilworth
?23	Villiers Street, Leamington Spa
?14	Villiers Street, Nuneaton
?12	Vincent Avenue, Stratford upon Avon
?24	Vincent Street, Leamington Spa
?33	Vine House Farm, Whatcote
?1	Vine Lane, Packmores, Warwick
?4	Virginia Place, Nuneaton
?3	Viscount Close, Leamington Spa
?4	Vodena Court, Leamington Spa
?1	Wackrill Drive, Lillington, Leamington Spa
?14	Wadbury Hill, Dagtail End
?2	Waddington Wood Farm, Nuneaton
?34	Waddon Farm, Shipston on Stour
?3	Wade Grove, Woodloes, Warwick
?14	Wade Lane, Lighthorne Heath.lighthorne
?2	Wadebridge Drive, Nuneaton
?	Waggoners Close, Bubbenhall
?	Wagstaff Farm, Shawbury, Fillongley
?1	Wagstaffe Close, Harbury
?3	Wahut Thatch, Radway
?23	Wain Close, Kinwarton
?	Wainbody Wood Farm, Stoneleigh
	Wainrigg, Stoneydelph, Tamworth
?	Wakefield Close, Hurley, Kingsbury
	Wakefield Green, Water Orton
	Wakeford Close, Mancetter
	Wakeford Close, Ridge Lane, Atherstone
?3	Walcote Farm, Walcote, Haselor
?3	Waldron Court, Stratford upon Avon
	Walford Green, Woodloes, Warwick
	Walford Place, The Paddox, Rugby
	Walkers Orchard, Stoneleigh
?3	Walkers Road, Stratford upon Avon
	Walkers Terrace, Brinklow
	Walkers Way, Coleshill
	Wall Avenue, Coleshill
	Wall Hill Farm, Corley Moor, Corley
	Wall Hill Road, Allesley

Map ref	Address
37B34	Wall Hill Road, Chapel Green, Fillongley
37B43	Wall Hill Road, Corley Moor
80C33	Waller Close, Leek Wootton
98A21	Waller Street, Leamington Spa
23A33	Wallingford Avenue, Saint Nicholas Park, Nuneaton
96B42	Wallwin Court, Hampton Street, Warwick
21C41	Walnut Close, Camphill, Nuneaton
34B23	Walnut Close, Chelmsley Wood
184B22	Walnut Close, Upper Tysoe, Tysoe
13B31	Walnut Croft, Baddesley Ensor
98A14	Walnut Drive, Leamington Spa
91B22	Walnut Hill Farm, Ullenhall
184B13	Walnut Paddocks, Upper Tysoe, Tysoe
81A14	Walnut Tree Close, Windy Arbour, Kenilworth
70A22	Walnut Way, Long Lawford
45B42	Walsgrave Hill Farm, Coombe Fields
45A24	Walsgrave Road, Anstey
40B24	Walter Scot Road, Bedworth
21B43	Waltham Crescent, Whittleford, Nuneaton
31A33	Walton Close, Whitestone, Nuneaton
164C22	Walton Farm, Kineton
147C32	Walton Farm, Walton, Wellesbourne
147C42	Walton Hall Hotel, Walton, Wellesbourne
147C42	Walton Hall, Walton, Wellesbourne
148A43	Walton Hill Farm, Walton Park, Wellesbourne
174A11	Walton Lane, Pillerton Priors
162C31	Walton Road, Pillerton Hersey
162C21	Walton Road, Walton Park, Ettington
147C32	Walton Road, Wellesbourne
135A21	Walworth Farm, Harbury
24C23	Wantage Road, Coleshill
23B31	Wapping Farm, Nuneaton
95B43	Warboro Farm, Budbrooke
84C43	Ward Close, Marton
97A34	Ward Grove, Myton, Warwick
34B21	Wardour Drive, Chelmsley Wood
112C14	Wards Hill Farm, Norton Lindsey
112C13	Wards Hill, Norton Lindsey
112B13	Wards Hill, Wolverton
73C22	Wards Lane, Yelvertoft
89B21	Ware Orchard, Barby
89B22	Ware Road, Barby
87B12	Waring Way, Dunchurch
58B32	Warings Green Farm, Warings Green, Tanworth in Arden
58B32	Warings Green Road, Earlswood
58B32	Warings Green Road, Warings Green, Tanworth in Arden
96A32	Warmington Green, Warwick
96A32	Warmington Grove, Warwick
177C14	Warmington Hill, Warmington
167B33	Warmington Lane, Farnborough

Map ref	Address
98A41	Warneford Mews, Leamington Spa
98A41	Virginia Mews, Leamington Spa
96B24	Warner Close, Woodloes, Warwick
98A13	Warren Close, Leamington Spa
98A13	Warren Court, Leamington Spa
35A41	Warren Farm, Bickenhill
58A31	Warren Farm, Earlswood, Tanworth in Arden
67A31	Warren Farm, Ryton on Dunsmore
106C32	Warren Farm, Sambourne
61B41	Warren Farm, Wroxhall
67A24	Warren Field, Ryton on Dunsmore
71B24	Warren Road, Rugby
62C33	Warriors Lodge Farm, Burton Green, Kenilworth
81B13	Warton Close, Kenilworth
3C32	Warton Lane, Austrey
7A42	Warton Lane, Grendon
7B11	Warton Lane, Twycross
96C32	Warwick And General Hospital, Warwick
67A41	Warwick Avenue, Ryton on Dunsmore
114A22	Warwick by passage, Warwick
96C41	Warwick Castle, Warwick
96C43	Warwick Castle, Warwick
107B22	Warwick Close, Studley
97C32	Warwick Court, Leamington Spa
145A13	Warwick Court, Stratford upon Avon
145A13	Warwick Crescent, Stratford upon Avon
14B14	Warwick Drive, Atherstone
29C13	Warwick Gardens, Stockingford, Nuneaton
96C32	Warwick General Hospital, Warwick
90A21	Warwick Highway, Redditch
41B24	Warwick Green, Bulkington, Bedworth
96C32	Warwick Hospital, Warwick
96B31	Warwick Industrial Estate, Warwick
97B32	Warwick New Road, Leamington Spa
97B31	Warwick New Road, Warwick
97B24	Warwick Place, Milverton, Leamington Spa
181C41	Warwick Place, Shipston on Stour
119A32	Warwick Place, Southam
61A42	Warwick Road, Baddesley Clinton
129C24	Warwick Road, Blackhill, Hampton Lucy
60C22	Warwick Road, Chadwick End
93A34	Warwick Road, Claverdon
60B13	Warwick Road, Dorridge
162A33	Warwick Road, Ettington
129B34	Warwick Road, Hampton Lucy
178B44	Warwick Road, Hanwell
92B33	Warwick Road, Henley in Arden
81A13	Warwick Road, Kenilworth
164B13	Warwick Road, Kineton
80C42	Warwick Road, Leek Wootton
113B41	Warwick Road, Marraway Turn, Fulbrook
163A42	Warwick Road, Pillerton Hersey
113C31	Warwick Road, Sherbourne
178B33	Warwick Road, Shotteswell
119A31	Warwick Road, Southam
145A13	Warwick Road, Stratford upon Avon
131B23	Warwick Road, Thelsford, Charlecot
131B23	Warwick Road, Wasperton
131B24	Warwick Road, Wellesbourne
68A12	Warwick Road, Wolston
92A31	Warwick Road, Wootton Wawen
97C23	Warwick Street, Leamington Spa
71A13	Warwick Street, Rugby
119A32	Warwick Street, Southam
115A12	Warwick Technology Park, Heathcc Warwick
97C23	Warwick Terrace, Leamington Spa
64B13	Warwick University, Gibbet Hill, Coventry
148B12	Warwickshire Agricultural College, Moreton Morrell
148B13	Warwickshire College Of Agricultu Moreton Morrell
97B21	Wasdale Close, Leamington Spa
116A21	Washbourne Road, Whitnash
180B14	Washbrook Place, Ilmington
107C12	Washford Mill, Studley
131B11	Wasperton Farm, Wasperton
114B43	Wasperton Lane, Barford
132A11	Wasperton Lane, Wasperton
12B31	Waste Farm, Hurley Common, Kingsbury
79A42	Waste Green, Haseley
79B33	Waste Green, Waste Green, Hasel
14A21	Waste Lane, Merevale
24A13	Water Orton Court, Water Orton
24A11	Water Orton Lane, Barton
24A11	Water Orton Lane, Kingshurst
24A11	Water Orton Lane, Minworth
24A11	Water Orton Lane, Water Orton
63C42	Water Tower Lane, Kenilworth
191C33	Waterditch Farm, Long Compton
98B41	Waterfield Gardens, Sydenham F Estate, Leamington Spa
103B23	Watergall Farm, Grandborough
152B22	Watergall Farm, Watergall
34A12	Waterloo Avenue, Chelmsley Wc
147A32	Waterloo Close, Mountford, Wellesbourne
97C23	Waterloo Court, Leamington Spa
97A31	Waterloo Court, Warwick
141C41	Waterloo Crescent, Bidford
145B24	Waterloo Drive, Stratford upon
145B32	Waterloo Hill, Stratford upon Av
141C41	Waterloo Industrial Estate, Bidfo
97C23	Waterloo Place, Leamington Spa
141C43	Waterloo Road, Bidford
98B41	Waterloo Street, Leamington Sp
145A21	Waterside, Stratford upon Avon
30B23	Waterside Gardens, Nuneaton

Map ref	Address	Map ref	Address
C13	Waterson Crescent, Chelmsley Wood	30C33	Waverley Square, Nuneaton
A32	Waterworks Lane, All Saints, Warwick	83B13	Waverley Wood Farm, Waverley Woods, Bubbenhall
322	Waterworks Lane, Bentley		
342	Watery Lane, Allesley	6C11	Waverton Avenue, Warton, Polesworth
A24	Watery Lane, Baddesley Ensor	116B14	Waverton Mews, Sydenham Farm Estate, Leamington Spa
311	Watery Lane, Cheswick Green		
B11	Watery Lane, Combrook	96B33	Wavytree Close, Warwick
342	Watery Lane, Corley Moor, Corley	110B13	Wawensmere Road, Wootton Wawen
C13	Watery Lane, Dorridge	129A13	Wayfield Farm, Snitterfield
341	Watery Lane, Pillerton Hersey	152B34	Wayland Farm, Fenny Compton
A23	Watery Lane, Sherbourne	96C22	Weale Green, Woodloes, Warwick
C34	Watery Lane, Shipston on Stour	91A31	Weatheroak Farm, Morton Bagot
22	Watery Lane, Shustoke	125B31	Weatheroak Road, Alcester
13	Watery Lane, Ullenhall	53B43	Weaver Drive, Rugby
44	Watford Road, Crick	181C32	Weavers Close, Shipston on Stour
21	Wathen Road, Leamington Spa	106B12	Weavers Hill, Hunt End
31	Wathen Road, Packmores, Warwick	54C31	Webb Drive, Brownsover, Rugby
34	Watkins Farm, Rugby	70C22	Webb Ellis Road, Rugby
24	Watling Crescent, Newton And Biggin	29B14	Webb Street, Stockingford, Nuneaton
41	Watling Farm, Willey	64A44	Webster Avenue, Kenilworth
42	Watling Road, Kenilworth	135C32	Weddington Farm, Chapel Ascote
31	Watling Street Roman Road, Smockington, Hinckley	22A24	Weddington Lane, Caldecote
		22B44	Weddington Road, Weddington, Nuneaton
13	Watling Street, Caldecote		
34	Watling Street, Claybrook Parva	22B43	Weddington Terrace, Weddington, Nuneaton
43	Watling Street, Clifton upon Dunsmore		
42	Watling Street, Cross in Hand, Monks Kirby	96B32	Wedgenock Green, Packmores, Warwick
		96B21	Wedgenock Lane, Guys Cliffe
1	Watling Street, Grendon	96A14	Wedgenock Lane, Leek Wootton
	Watling Street, Hall End, Dordon	96B31	Wedgenock Lane, Packmores, Warwick
4	Watling Street, Hartshill	96A21	Wedgenock Park Farm, Budbrooke
4	Watling Street, Hinckley	140A11	Weethley Farm, Weethley
1	Watling Street, Lilbourne	24A22	Weland Close, Water Orton
1	Watling Street, Mancetter	32B12	Welbeck Avenue, Hinckley
4	Watling Street, Merevale, Atherstone	129B33	Welcombe Bank Farm, Ingon, Hampton Lucy
4	Watling Street, Newton And Biggin		
3	Watling Street, Nuneaton	145A14	Welcombe Road, Stratford upon Avon
1	Watling Street, Rugby	14C31	Welcome Street, Atherstone
	Watling Street, Stoneydelph, Tamworth	158A24	Welford Hill Farm, Rumer Hill, Welford on Avon
3	Watling Street, Yelvertoft		
3	Watson Close, Woodloes, Warwick	157B13	Welford Pastures Farm, Welford on Avon
3	Watt Pit Farm, Honiley		
4	Watters Drive, Atherstone	156C22	Welford Road, Barton, Bidford
	Watton Lane, Water Orton	158B33	Welford Road, Long Marston
23	Wattons Lane, Southam	71B11	Welford Road, Rugby
4	Watts Lane, Hillmorton, Rugby	157B13	Welford Road, Welford on Avon
3	Watts Road, Studley	52C11	Welkin Farm, Easenhall
4	Waugh Close, Chelmsley Wood	41B24	Well Green Farm, Bulkington, Bedworth
	Wavebeck Court, Rugby	73C44	Well Hill Close, Crick
	Wavere Court, Brownsover, Rugby	75A24	Well Lane, Tanworth in Arden
	Waverley Avenue, Attleborough, Nuneaton	14C32	Well Spring Close, Atherstone
		53B43	Welland Close, Rugby
	Waverley Edge, Waverley Woods, Bubbenhall	147A21	Wellesbourne Airfield, Loxley, Wellesbourne
	Waverley Farm, Stoneleigh	147A11	Wellesbourne by pass, Wellesbourne
	Waverley Road, Kenilworth	147B22	Wellesbourne Farm, Wellesbourne
	Waverley Road, Leamington Spa	144C22	Wellesbourne Grove, Stratford upon Avon
	Waverley Road, Lower Hillmorton, Rugby		

Map ref	Address
130A43	Wellesbourne Road, Alveston, Stratford upon Avon
114B43	Wellesbourne Road, Barford
146B11	Wellesbourne Road, Charlecote
148C22	Wellesbourne Road, Compton Verney
146C42	Wellesbourne Road, Loxley
148B21	Wellesbourne Road, Moreton Paddox, Moreton Morrell
146C12	Wellesbourne Road, Wellesbourne
147A32	Wellington Close, Mountford, Wellesbourne
98B24	Wellington Road, Lillington, Leamington Spa
29A11	Wells Close, Galley Common, Nuneaton
94A24	Wells Farm, Pinley Green, Rowington
71B11	Wells Street, Rugby
34A23	Wells Walk, Chelmsley Wood
8B33	Wellsborough Road, Sheepy Parva, Sheepy
96C13	Welsh Close, Woodloes, Warwick
137A14	Welsh Road E, Napton on The Hill
119B32	Welsh Road E, Southam
99C41	Welsh Road Farm, Offchurch
119A22	Welsh Road W, Southam
118C21	Welsh Road, Bascote Heath, Long Itchington
98C11	Welsh Road, Cubbington
118A12	Welsh Road, Long Itchington
137C23	Welsh Road, Marston Doles, Priors Hardwick
137C23	Welsh Road, Marston Doles, Priors Marston
99A24	Welsh Road, Offchurch
138A41	Welsh Road, Priors Hardwick
136C12	Welsh Road, Southam
137B21	Welsh Road, Upper Radbourne
184B12	Welshman Place, Middle Tysoe, Tysoe
71B32	Welton Place, Ashlawn Estate, Rugby
105C23	Welton Road, Little Braunston, Braunston
96B23	Welton Road, Wedgenock Industrial, Warwick
30B22	Wembrook Close, Attleborough, Nuneaton
29A12	Wenlock Way, Stockingford, Nuneaton
31A21	Wentworth Drive, Whitestone, Nuneaton
70C24	Wentworth Road, Overslade, Rugby
98B44	Wentworth Road, Sydenham Farm Estate, Leamington Spa
72A31	Wesley Road, Hillmorton, Rugby
5A34	Wessenden, Stoneydelph, Tamworth
40A11	Wessex Close, Bedworth
141C42	Wessons Farm, Bidford
141C42	Wessons Road, Bidford
40C21	West Avenue, Bedworth
110B12	West Drive, Wootton Wawen
177B33	West End, Hornton
165B43	West End, Radway
22B42	West Field Close, Weddington, Nuneaton
144B13	West Green Drive, Stratford upon Avon
97B31	West Grove Terrace, Milverton, Leamington Spa
71A13	West Leys, Rugby
78A33	West Of Saint Laurence, Rowington
96B34	West Rock, Warwick
97C42	West Street, Leamington Spa
53A43	West Street, Long Lawford
181C34	West Street, Shipston on Stour
144C24	West Street, Stratford upon Avon
96B42	West Street, Warwick
20C31	West View, Ainsley Common
158A14	West View Caravan Site, Welford Avon
82B43	West View Road, Cubbington
70C13	West View Road, New Bilton, Rugby
71A13	West Way, Rugby
123B11	Westall Hall Farm, Inkberrow
70C24	Westbourn Road, Overslade, Rugby
70C24	Westbourne Road, Overslade, Rugby
29C13	Westbury Road, Stockingford, Nuneaton
96C21	Westcliffe Drive, Woodloes, Warwick
176A12	Westcote Farm, Tysoe
176B21	Westcote Manor Farm, Tysoe
106B24	Western Hill Close, Astwood Bank
144C14	Western Road Industrial Estate, Stratford upon Avon
144C14	Western Road Trading Estate, Stratford upon Avon
144C12	Western Road, Stratford upon Avon
59C22	Westfield Close, Dorridge
128C44	Westfield Close, Stratford upon Avon
147A22	Westfield Crescent, Mountford, Wellesbourne
117A34	Westfield Farm, Harbury
146B31	Westfield Farm, Loxley
70C22	Westfield Road, Rugby
119A41	Westfield Road, Southam
149A14	Westfields Court, Lighthorne
96B42	Westgate Close, Warwick
71C23	Westgate Road, Rugby
114A44	Westham Lane, Barford
82A42	Westhill Farm, Cubbington
82A41	Westhill Road, Blackdown
82A42	Westhill Road, Cubbington
156B12	Westholme Court, Bidford
156B11	Westholme Road, Bidford
97C41	Westlea Road, Leamington Spa
107C21	Westmead Avenue, Studley
163C34	Westmead Cottage, Butlers Marston
46C11	Westmead Farm, Withybrook
21A42	Westminster Drive, Bucks Hill, Nuneaton
29C13	Westmorland Avenue, Stockingford, Nuneaton
87B12	Weston Close, Dunchurch

Map ref	Address	Map ref	Address
B44	Weston Close, Sydenham Farm Estate, Leamington	97B22	Wheathill Close, Leamington Spa
		110B41	Wheathills Farm, Aston Cantlow
C42	Weston Close, Warwick	24C42	Wheatley Grange, Coleshill
1C42	Weston Court, Long Compton	76B33	Wheatsheaf Farm, Tanworth in Arden
8B12	Weston Farm, Weston on Avon	76B32	Wheatsheaf Lane, Lapworth
B22	Weston Fields Farm, Weston Under Wetherley	94A41	Wheel Barrow Lane, Claverdon
		34C14	Wheeley Moor Farm, Coleshill
C23	Weston Hall Farm, Turners Green, Rowington	24A43	Wheeley Moor Road, Kingshurst
		39B43	Wheelwright Lane, Exhall, Bedworth
A42	Weston Hall Farm, Weston Under Wetherley	54B33	Whernside, Brownsover, Rugby
		54C32	Whestone Drive, Brownston, Rugby
A22	Weston Hall Hotel, Bulkington, Bedworth	193A34	Whichford Lodge Farm, Ascott, Whichford
C31	Weston Hayes Farm, Carroway Head, Bedworth	188C43	Whichford Mill, Whichford
		188A41	Whichford Road, Stourton
B13	Weston Hill Farm, Bulkington, Bedworth	192B14	Whichford Road, Whichford
		192C22	Whichford Sharps Hill Road, Whichford
43	Weston Hospital, Weston Under Wetherley	55A43	Whiley Close, Clifton upon Dunsmore
A22	Weston Lane, Bulkington, Bedworth	17B33	Whitacre Heath Farm, Whitacre Heath, Nether Whitacre
21	Weston Lane, Waverley Woods, Bubbenhall	30C11	Whitacre Industrial Estate, Nuneaton
32	Weston Lane, Weston Under Wetherley	98A21	Whitacre Road, Lillington, Leamington Spa
24	Weston Lawn Farm, Weston in Arden, Bedworth	30C11	Whitacre Road, Nuneaton
C23	Weston Park Road, Long Compton	39A22	Whitburn Road, Goodyears End, Bedworth
B14	Weston Road, Weston on Avon	160C43	Whitchurch Farm, Whitchurch
33	Weston Road, Weston Under Wetherley	176C21	White Bottom Farm, Edgehill, Ratley And Upton
C14	Weston Sands Farm, Weston Sands, Weston on Avon	15A23	White Gate Farm, Witherley
		92B14	White Hall Farm, Buckley Green, Beaudesert
43	Weston Wood Farm, Weston in Arden, Bedworth	100C33	White Hall Farm, Long Itchington
1	Westonbirt Close, Kenilworth	21A13	White Hall Farm, Mancetter
13	Westwood Court, Leamington Spa	117C24	White Hart Lane, Ufton
4	Westwood Crescent, Atherstone	129B14	White Horse Hill, Snitterfield
4	Westwood Road, Atherstone	166B12	White House Farm, Burton Dassett
4	Westwood Road, Rugby	27B23	White House Farm, Devitts Green, Arley
4	Wetherell Way, Brownsover, Rugby	67A44	White House Farm, Ryton on Dunsmore
1	Wfrs Headquarters, Leamington Spa		
22	Wharf And Lowkes Farm, Lower Shuckburgh	67A44	White House Farm, Stretton on Dunsmore
4	Wharf Farm, Hillmorton, Rugby	104C13	White House Farm, Willoughby
4	Wharf Lane, Lapworth	92B31	White House Flats, Henley in Arden
34	Wharf Road, Fenny Compton	110A44	White House Hill, Aston Cantlow
42	Wharf Road, Stratford upon Avon	65C31	White Lodge Farm, Baginton
3	Wharf Street, Warwick	34B24	Whitebeam Road, Chelmsley Wood
41	Wharrage Road, Alcester	172A42	Whitegates Farm, Armscote, Tredington
3	Whatcote Farm, Honiley		
3	Whatcote Road, Idlicote	134B13	Whitegates Farm, Harbury
3	Whatcote Road, Oxhill	21A21	Whitehall Close, Hartshill
3	Whatcote Road, Whatcote	125B31	Whitehall Farm, Alcester
	Whateley Lane Farm, Kingsbury	87B42	Whitehall Farm, Dunchurch
	Whateley Lane, Whately, Kingsbury	88C12	Whitehall Farm, onley
	Whateleys Drive, Kenilworth	71B13	Whitehall Road, Rugby
	Wheat Croft Drive, Chelmsley Wood	64B41	Whitehead Drive, Kenilworth
	Wheat Street, Nuneaton	97C32	Whiteheads Court, Leamington Spa
	Wheaten Close, Chelmsley Wood	98A22	Whiteholm Drive, Leamington Spa
	Wheatfied Road, Bilton, Rugby		
	Wheatfield Close, Kingshurst		

Map ref	Address
40A42	Whitehorse Close, Exhall, Bedworth
29B14	Whitehouse Crescent, Stockingford, Nuneaton
22C24	Whitehouse Farm Cottage, Nuneaton
11B32	Whitehouse Farm Estate, Kingsbury
57C33	Whitehouse Farm, Clowes Wood, Tanworth in Arden
10B33	Whitehouse Farm, Hunts Green, Middleton
173B43	Whitehouse Farm, Idlicote
18A42	Whitehouse Farm, Nether Whitacre
37B23	Whitehouse Farm, Newhall Green, Fillongley
110A44	Whitehouse Farm, Newnham, Aston Cantlow
1C41	Whitehouse Farm, No Mans Heath, Newton Regis
112C13	Whitehouse Farm, Norton Lindsey
176B11	Whitehouse Farm, Radway
22C32	Whitehouse Farm, Saint Nicholas Park, Nuneaton
5C34	Whitehouse Road, Polesworth
107A32	Whitemoor Farm, Coughton
107A32	Whitemoor Lane, Alcester
107A33	Whitemoor Lane, Hangingwell, Alcester
107B23	Whitemoor Lane, Sambourne
81A12	Whitemoor Road, Windy Arbour, Kenilworth
76A44	Whitepump Lane, Ullenhall
13A33	Whites Farm, Baxterley
81B13	Whites Row, Kenilworth
36B41	Whitestitch Farm, Great Packington
36A42	Whitestitch Lane, Great Packington
54C32	Whitestone Drive, Newton Biggin, Rugby
31B31	Whitestone Road, Whitestone, Nuneaton
145C11	Whitfield Close, Tiddington, Stratford upon Avon
162A21	Whitfield Farm, Ettington
169B24	Whithill Farm, Alderminster
92C31	Whitley Farm, Henley in Arden
14A14	Whitley Farm, Whittington, Grendon
92B32	Whitley Road, Beaudesert, Henley in Arden
116A21	Whitmore Road, Whitnash, Leamington Spa
116A11	Whitnash Road, Whitnash
97A32	Whittington Close, All Saints, Warwick
14A14	Whittington Farm, Whittington, Grendon
14A21	Whittington Lane, Merevale
14A14	Whittington Lane, Whittington, Grendon
70B34	Whittle Close, Woodlands, Rugby
98A32	Whittle Court, Leamington Spa
23C31	Whittle Road, Hinckley
29B12	Whittleford Road, Stockingford, Nuneaton
29B11	Whittleford Road, Whittleford
147A24	Whitworth Close, Mountford, Wellesbourne
98A14	Wickham Court, Leamington Spa
107C22	Wickham Road, Studley
13B42	Wickston Hill, Baxterley
29B13	Wiclif Way, Stockingford, Nuneaton
59C12	Widney Road, Dorridge
11B11	Wigford Road, Dosthill, Tamworth
132C12	Wiggerland Wood Farm, Bishops Tachbrook
24A42	Wight Croft, Kingshurst
72A31	Wigston Road, Hillmorton, Rugby
107B23	Wike Lane, Coughton
107B23	Wike Lane, Sambourne
135A34	Wilcox Close, Bishops Itchington
148C11	Wilcox Leys, Moreton Morrell
116C33	Wilderness Farm, Whitnash
110B12	Wilderness, Wootton Wawen
39B21	Wildey Road, Market End, Bedwor
143C12	Wildmoor Farm, Stratford upon A
173C23	Wilkes Farm, Fulready, Ettington
156B12	Wilkes Way, Bidford
114A42	Wilkins Close, Barford
14B14	Willday Drive, Atherstone
98A34	Willes Court, Leamington Spa
152B12	Willes Pasture Road, Wormleighto
98A31	Willes Road, Leamington Spa
98A34	Willes Terrace, Leamington Spa
147B11	Willett Gardens, Wellesbourne
147B11	Willett House, Wellesbourne
44B32	Willey Fields Farm, Willey
30C13	William Street, Attleborough, Nur
40B22	William Street, Bedworth
98A31	William Street, Leamington Spa
71A14	William Street, Rugby
97A33	William Tarver Close, Emscote, Warwick
116C11	Williams Road, Radford Semele
159B31	Willicote Farm, Clifford Chamber
187A32	Willington Road, Burmington
187A22	Willington Road, Willington, Barcheston
22A44	Willington Street, Nuneaton
187A14	Willington Village Road, Willingt Barcheston
40B14	Willis Green, Bedworth
40B14	Willis Grove, Bedworth
80C13	Willoughby Avenue, Kenilworth
125A21	Willoughby Close, Kings Cought Alcester
174C31	Willoghby Grounds, Oxhill
71B32	Willoughby Place, Ashlawn Esta Rugby
143A44	Willow Bank, Welford on Avon
118B43	Willow Break Farm, Deppers Br Harbury
135C23	Willow Brook Farm, Bishops Itc
125A42	Willow Close, Alcester

Map ref	Address
A33	Willow Close, Bucks Hill, Nuneaton
A43	Willow Close, Collycroft, Bedworth
B34	Willow Close, Kingsbury
5B24	Willow Close, Whitnash
7B24	Willow Dene, Wilmcote, Aston Cantlow
312	Willow Drive, Cheswick Green
7B13	Willow Drive, Mountford, Wellesbourne
A12	Willow Farm, Withybrook
A32	Willow Gardens, Southam
A32	Willow Grove, Long Itchington
21	Willow Lane, Rugby
A43	Willow Meer, Kenilworth
42	Willow Road, Camphill, Nuneaton
32	Willow Tree Gardens, Hillmorton, Rugby
41	Willow Sheets Meadow, Cubbington
23	Willow Tree Farm, Rumbush, Tidbury Green
23	Willow Walk, Arley
24	Willow Way, Chelmsley Wood
23	Willow Way, Studley
343	Willowbrook Farm, Pillerton Hersey
44	Willowbrook Road, Wolston
21	Willowfields Road, Whitestone, Nuneaton
A22	Willows Farm, Halford
21	Willows Road, Stratford upon Avon
23	Willows Way, Studley
11	Wilmcote Lane, Aston Cantlow
32	Wilmcote Manor Farm, Wilmcote, Drayton
2	Wilmot Avenue, Coleshill
11	Wilnecote Grove, Sydenham Farm Estate, Leamington Spa
1	Wilson Close, Bilton, Rugby
	Wilson Drive, Sutton Coldfield
4	Wilson Grove, Kenilworth
2	Wilsons Lane, Exhall, Bedworth
2	Wilsons Lane, Longford
3	Wiltshire Close, Bedworth
4	Wimborne Close, Whittleford, Nuneaton
1	Wimpstone Farm, Wimpstone, Whitchurch
3	Wimpstone Fields Farm, Whitchurch
2	Wimpstone Lane, Alderminster
1	Wimpstone Lane, Wimpstone, Whitchurch
2	Winchcomb Farm, Middle Tysoe, Tysoe
1	Winchcombe Road, Kinwarton
	Winchester Avenue, Weddington, Nuneaton
	Winchester Drive, Chelmsley Wood
3	Wincot Farm, Quinton
	Wincote Close, Windy Arbour, Kenilworth
	Wincote Farm, High Cross Claybrook
145B23	Wincott Close, Stratford upon Avon
22C42	Windermere Avenue, Saint Nicholas Park, Nuneaton
54B33	Windermere Close, Brownsover, Rugby
97B22	Windermere Drive, Leamington Spa
184A41	Winderton Farm, Winderton, Brailes
184A24	Winderton Road, Compton Wynyates
24C32	Windmill Avenue, Cole End, Coleshill
180B14	Windmill Close, Ilmington
64A41	Windmill Close, Kenilworth
6C14	Windmill Close, Little Warton, Polesworth
28B42	Windmill Farm, Astley, Nuneaton
37B42	Windmill Farm, Chapel Green, Fillongley
37B41	Windmill Farm, Corley Moor
60A33	Windmill Farm, Darley Green
60A33	Windmill Farm, Dorridge
87A11	Windmill Farm, Dunchurch
164A12	Windmill Farm, Kineton
175A14	Windmill Farm, Oxhill
195C31	Windmill Farm, Salford
28C41	Windmill Hill Farm, Astley, Nuneaton
133C13	Windmill Hill Farm, Chesterton
174A14	Windmill Hill Farm, Pillerton Priors
82B44	Windmill Hill, Cubbington
28C41	Windmill Lane, Astley
4A14	Windmill Lane, Austrey
62B14	Windmill Lane, Balsall Common
13C41	Windmill Lane, Baxterley
37B34	Windmill Lane, Chapel Green, Fillongley
37B41	Windmill Lane, Corley Moor
60A33	Windmill Lane, Darley Green
59C24	Windmill Lane, Dorridge
87A11	Windmill Lane, Dunchurch
167C23	Windmill Lane, Farnborough
136A14	Windmill Lane, Ladbroke
14C23	Windmill Road, Atherstone
21B34	Windmill Road, Camphill, Nuneaton
40A31	Windmill Road, Exhall, Bedworth
115C12	Windmill Road, Whitnash, Leamington Spa
119A21	Windmill Way, Southam
97C31	Windsor Chambers, Leamington Spa
97C31	Windsor Court, Leamington Spa
144C14	Windsor Court, Stratford upon Avon
29C11	Windsor Gardens, Nuneaton
97C31	Windsor Place, Leamington Spa
24A33	Windsor Road, Kingshurst
6A13	Windsor Road, Polesworth
97C31	Windsor Street, Leamington Spa
30A14	Windsor Street, Nuneaton
71B14	Windsor Street, Rugby
145A13	Windsor Street, Stratford upon Avon
24A33	Windward Way, Kingshurst
81A12	Windy Arbour, Windy Arbour, Kenilworth
71A22	Winfield Recreation Ground, Rugby

Map ref	Address
22A44	Winfield Road, Nuneaton
71B12	Winfield Street, Rugby
25A41	Wingfield Road, Coleshill
97B23	Winslow Close, Milverton, Leamington Spa
39A33	Winster Close, Keresley Newlands, Keresley
144B24	Winston Close, Stratford upon Avon
98B22	Winston Crescent, Lillington, Leamington Spa
58C13	Winterton Farm, Cheswick Green
41B22	Winterton Road, Bulkington, Bedworth
189A13	Winterton Road, Lower Brailles
87A24	Winton Hall, Toft, Dunchurch
70B31	Winwick Place, Bilton, Rugby
150A11	Winyates Road, Lighthorne Heath, Lighthorne
96C13	Wise Green, Woodloes, Warwick
71C22	Wise Grove, Rugby
97C42	Wise Street, Leamington Spa
97C42	Wise Terrace, Leamington Spa
16A34	Wishaw Lane, Curdworth
10A44	Wishaw Lane, Hunts Green, Middleton
16A12	Wishaw Lane, Wishaw
64B43	Wisley Grove, Kenilworth
70A22	Witchelm Close, Long Lawford
15A24	Witherley Fields Farm, Witherley
14C34	Witherley Road, Atherstone
9A34	Withy Hill Farm, Sutton Coldfield
9B31	Withy Hill Road, Middleton
9B31	Withy Hill Road, Sutton Coldfield
136B23	Withy Tree Farm, Ladbroke
46C12	Withybrook Hall Farm, Withybrook
42A23	Withybrook Road B4112, Bulkington, Bedworth
41B22	Withybrook Road, Bulkington, Bedworth
47A22	Withybrook Road, Monks Kirby
42B32	Withybrook Road, Withybrook
41C23	Withybrook Road, Wolvey
183C21	Withycombe Lane, Compton Wyngates
116C11	Woburn Close, Sydenham Farm Estate, Leamington
30A23	Woburn Drive, Heath End, Nuneaton
42C11	Wolds Lane, Wolvey
70B42	Wolsey Road, Woodlands, Rugby
68A11	Wolston Business Park, Wolston
67C13	Wolston Fields Farm, Wolston
67C22	Wolston Grounds Farm, Wolston
67B24	Wolston Lane, Ryton on Dunsmore
67C21	Wolston Lane, Wolston
67A33	Wolverhampton Road, Ryton on Dunsmore
112A32	Wolverton Grange Farm, Wolverton
112C13	Wolverton Road, Norton Lindsey
112B14	Wolverton Road, Norton Lindsey
112A34	Wolverton Road, Snitterfield
112A34	Wolverton Road, Wolverton
42C24	Wolvey Fields Farm, Wolvey
42C11	Wolvey House Farm, Wolvey
33A43	Wolvey Lodge Farm, Wolvey Heath, Wolvey
41C21	Wolvey Road, Bulkington
41C21	Wolvey Road, Ryton, Bedworth
41C22	Wolvey Road, Wolvey
42B22	Wolvey Villa Farm, Wolvey
20B41	Wood Barn Farm, Galley Common, Nuneaton
140A31	Wood Bevington Farm, Wood Bevington, Salford Priors
34A13	Wood Close Road, Chelmsley Wood
25A33	Wood Close, Coleshill
78B14	Wood Corner Farm, Baddesley Clin
36C21	Wood Corner Farm, Green End, Fillongley
38A12	Wood End Farm, Fillongley
36C44	Wood End Farm, Meriden
38A14	Wood End Farm, Wood End
74C12	Wood End Lane, Earlswood
38A14	Wood End Lane, Fillongley
74C12	Wood End Lane, Tanworth in Arde
28C42	Wood Farm, Astley
83C13	Wood Farm, Bubbenhall
62A32	Wood Farm, Frogmore
126B12	Wood Farm, Great Alne
44A33	Wood Farm, Monks Kirby
148B11	Wood Farm, Morton Morrell
118A13	Wood Farm, Ufton
19B43	Wood Lane, Ansley
126C24	Wood Lane, Aston Cantlow
187C44	Wood Lane, Cherington
58A23	Wood Lane, Cheswick Green
126C21	Wood Lane, Haselor
22B22	Wood Lane, Higham, Higham on Hill
123C14	Wood Lane, Inkberrow
41B43	Wood Lane, Shilton
30A44	Wood Street, Collycroft, Bedworth
98A31	Wood Street, Leamington Spa
54A43	Wood Street, Rugby
119A24	Wood Street, Southam
29C12	Wood Street, Stockingford, Nunea
145A21	Wood Street, Stratford upon Avo
12B23	Wood Street, Wood End, Kingsbu
107A24	Wood Terrace, Sambourne
59B44	Woodbine Cottage, Lapworth
97C31	Woodbine Cottage, Leamington S
103A32	Woodbine Farm, Grandborough
118C31	Woodbine Hill, Southam
97C31	Woodbine Street, Leamington Sp
59C13	Woodchester Road, Dorridge
74C13	Woodcock Close, Tanworth in A
63B42	Woodcote Avenue, Kenilworth
22C32	Woodcote Avenue, Saint Nichola Nuneaton
80C33	Woodcote Drive, Leek Wootton
80C31	Woodcote Lane, Leek Wootton
127B24	Woodcote Park Drive, Wilmcote Aston Cantlow

ap ref	Address	Map ref	Address
C13	Woodcote Road, Leamington Spa	3A42	Woodside Farm, Polesworth
C32	Woodcote Road, Packmores, Warwick	74C31	Woodside Farm, Tanworth in Arden
A21	Woodfield Farm, Cheswick Green	27B24	Woodside, Arley
A32	Woodfields Farm, Napton on The Hill	54A44	Woodsied Park, Newbold on Avon
343	Woodford Close, Ash Green, Bedworth	30C23	Woodstock Road, Nuneaton
312	Woodford Close, Stockingford, Nuneaton	14C41	Woodview Road, Mancetter, Atherstone
344	Woodford Lane, Mancetter, Hartshill	96C31	Woodville Road, Packmores, Warwick
14	Woodhill Farm, Coombe Fields	116A23	Woodward Close, Whitnash
A41	Woodhouse Farm, Great Alne	95C34	Woodway Avenue, Hampton Magna, Budbrooke
4	Woodhouse Farm, Polesworth	95B42	Woodway Farm, Hampton Magna, Budbrooke
43	Woodhouse Lane, Amington, Tamworth	189C42	Woodway Farm, Sibford Ferris
44	Woodhouse Street, Forbes Estate, Warwick	44B13	Woodway Lane, Claybrook Parva
33	Woodhurst Farm, Lea Marston	45A12	Woodway Lane, Shilton
3	Woodington Road, Sutton Coldfield	95B34	Woodway, Hampton on The Hill
3	Woodland Close, Dordon	42B32	Woodyard Farm, Withybrook
31	Woodland Grange, Overslade, Rugby	14C31	Woolpack Way, Atherstone
324	Woodland House Farm, Ladbroke	103C12	Woolscott Farm, Woolscott, Grandborough
3	Woodland Road, Amington Ind.est., Tamworth	104B12	Woolscott Road, Willoughby
34	Woodland Road, Crackley, Kenilworth	104A12	Woolscott Road, Woolscott, Grandborough
3	Woodland Terrace, Dordon	87C23	Woolscott, Dunchurch
1	Woodland Way, Birchman, Polesworth	40B22	Wooton Street, Bedworth
23	Woodlands Avenue, Water Orton	145B22	Wootton Close, Stratford upon Avon
2	Woodlands Court, Binley Woods	80C44	Wootton Court Farm, Leek Wootton
42	Woodlands Farm, Bearley	97C22	Wootton Court, Leamington Spa
4	Woodlands Farm, Bedworth	80C41	Wootton Court, Leek Wootton
	Woodlands, Bedworth	81A23	Wootton Grange Farm, Leek Wootton
23	Woodlands Farm, Grendon	110B13	Wootton Hall, Wootton Wawen
	Woodlands Farm, Middleton	110A11	Wootton Hill Farm, Wootton Wawen
33	Woodlands Farm, Mountford, Wellesbourne	110A14	Wootton Rise, Wootton Wawen
3	Woodlands Farm, Tanworth in Arden	181C41	Worcester Place, Shipston on Stour
2	Woodlands House Farm, Bedworth	124B21	Worcester Road, Arrow
3	Woodlands Lane, Bedworth	81A14	Worcester Road, Windy Arbour, Kenilworth
4	Woodlands Road Farm, Bedworth	71A11	Worcester Street, Rugby
4	Woodlands Road, Bedworth	34A31	Worcester Walk, Chelmsley Wood
2	Woodlands Road, Binley Woods	96B43	Wordsworth Avenue, Forbes Estate, Warwick
44	Woodlands Road, Stratford upon Avon	81B13	Wordsworth Drive, Kenilworth
	Woodlands Way, Chelmsley Wood	40B32	Wordsworth Road, Bedworth
3	Woodlane Farm, Bearley	70C34	Wordsworth Road, Shakespeare Gardens, Rugby
	Woodloes Avenue N, Woodloes, Warwick	135B23	Works Lane, Bishops Itchington
	Woodloes Avenue S, Woodloes, Warwick	42B23	Workshops Farm, Withybrook
	Woodloes Avenue, Woodloes, Warwick	152C21	Wormleighton Grange Farm, Wormleighton
	Woodloes Farm, Guys Cliffe	20C12	Worthington Farm, Mancetter
2	Woodman Court, Stratford upon Avon	85C41	Wren Court, Birdingbury
4	Woodmeadow Farm, Nebsworth, Ilmington	11B44	Wright Close, Kingsbury
	Woodpecker Close, Kingshurst	78C21	Wroxhall Abbey School, Wroxhall, Warwick
	Woodrow Crescent, Dorridge	101A42	Wulfstan Drive, Long Itchington
	Woods Farm, Tanworth in Arden	9A42	Wyatt Road, Sutton Coldfield
	Woodside, Arley	40B13	Wyatts Court, Bedworth
	Woodside Cherry Tree Farm, Gorcott, Studley	58B41	Wychpitts Farm, Tanworth in Arden
	Woodside Farm, Bishops Tachbrook	115C31	Wychwood Close, Bishops Tachbrook
	Woodside Farm, Middleton		

Map ref	Address	Map ref	Address
30B11	Wycliff Way, Nuneaton	58B22	Yew Tree Farm, Cheswick Green
41A22	Wye Close, Bulkington, Bedworth	77A31	Yew Tree Farm, Copt Green, Lapwo
98B14	Wye Close, Lillington, Leamington Spa	38A14	Yew Tree Farm, Corley
54B33	Wykenham House, Rugby	6C44	Yew Tree Farm, Dordon
25A42	Wyndshiels, Coleshill	38A14	Yew Tree Farm, Fillongley
70B14	Wynter Road, New Bilton, Rugby	57B33	Yew Tree Farm, Forshaw Heath,
158B41	Wyre Lane, Long Marston		Tanworth in Arden
54C31	Wythburn Way, Brownsover, Rugby	30C42	Yew Tree Farm, Marston Jabbett,
54C33	Wythurn Way, Brownsover, Rugby		Nuneaton
65B13	Wythwood Avenue, Finham	26A22	Yew Tree Farm, Shustoke
147A24	Wyvern Close, Mountford,	91B11	Yew Tree Farm, Ullenhall
	Wellesbourne	110B14	Yew Tree Farm, Wootton Wawen
65B23	Yardley Chase Road, Edgehill Site,	92A32	Yew Tree Gardens, Henley in Arde
	Kineton	51C13	Yew Tree Hill, Brinklow
93C23	Yarningale Common, Yarningale,	77A32	Yew Tree Lane, Bushwood
	Claverdon	77A31	Yew Tree Lane, Copt Green, Lapwc
93C31	Yarningale Cottage Farm, Lye Green,	34B21	Yew Walk, Chelmsley Wood
	Claverdon	39B21	Yews, The, Marlet, Bedworth
93B24	Yarningale Lane, Yarningale, Claverdon	48A31	Yews Farm, Pailton
128B44	Yarranton Close, Stratford upon Avon	111C13	Yewtree Farm, Langley
54C23	Yarrow Close, Brownsover, Rugby	159B12	Ynot Farm, Clifford Chambers
53C42	Yates Avenue, Newbold on Avon,	14C21	York Avenue, Atherstone
	Rugby	40B22	York Avenue, Bedworth
26B11	Ye Old Farm, Furnace End, Over	107B14	York Close, Studley Common, Stu
	Whitacre	171A42	York Farm, Ilmington
73C23	Yelvertoft Road, Crick	97C23	York House, Leamington Spa
56A41	Yelvertoft Road, Lilbourne	97C33	York Road, Leamington Spa
73C42	Yelverton Road, Crick	70C12	York Street, New Bilton, Rugby
96C34	Yeomanry Close, Warwick	30A11	York Street, Nuneaton
191C42	Yerdley Farm, Long Compton	34B21	Yorkminster Drive, Chelmsley Wo
77B14	Yew Tree Close, Kingswood, Lapworth	150A13	Young Drive, Lighthorne Heath,
166C31	Yew Tree Farm, Avon Dassett		Lighthorne
60C34	Yew Tree Farm, Chadwick End	21A44	Zorina Close, Whittleford, Nuneat

THE
PEUGEOT 306.

TAKE YOUR IMAGINATION
FOR A TEST DRIVE

Call 0500 306 306 and set the wheels in motion.

PEUGEOT

THE PEUGEOT 306. DRIVES THE IMAGINATION

WARWICKSHIRE
FIRE & RESCUE SERVICE

The Warwickshire Fire and Rescue Service recognises the need to provide a training service which satisfies the specialised requirements of the businesss community, and can provide these services, either at our own Training Centre at Leamington Spa or at a location to suit your selves. Professional specialist staff offer expert tuition in the many aspects of fire fighting techniques and fire safety to enable your Company to deal with an emergency in its early stages which may save lives and money for you. We can also offer driver tuition to whatever standards you require.

Each year fire exacts a heavy toll on domestic, commercial and industrial premises. Disruption to business may include delayed orders and contracts, lost research data and the dislocation of other companies connected with the affected organisation.

The cost in human life and injury is equally high — approximately 1000 people die per year from burns or from the highly toxic chemicals contained within the smoke.

The range and variety of training courses available can be readily tailored to meet your individual requirements. Whatever the size of your business, large or small, one of our Officers would be pleased to discuss your specific training needs and advise on how to achieve the best response from your staff.

Challenge us to meet your specific training needs

For our brochure and further details,
contact the
Officer in Charge (Industrial/Commercial Training)
Warwickshire Fire and Rescue Service,
Warwick Street, Leamington Spa,
Telephone 01926 423231

The maps in this atlas are copies of those used by Warwickshire Fire and Rescue Service in their daily work of protecting people and property. We strive to ensure that they are as detailed and accurate as possible.

The originals, used by the Fire and Rescue Crews, are constantly updated.

If you know of any inaccuracies, please send a drawing or photocopy of the area to:

Warwickshire Fire and Rescue Service,
Warwick Street,
Leamington Spa,
Warwickshire.

and enclose this form.

Chief Fire Officer
W W A REDFORD

Name .... Title ....

Address ....

....

....

Tel: ....

Warwickshire Street Maps III 3.95